DOING BUSINESS

DOING BUSINESS

THE ANTHROPOLOGY OF

STRIVING,

THRIVING,

AND

BEATING OUT

THE

COMPETITION

OLIVIA VLAHOS

Franklin Watts
1985
New York Toronto

Library of Congress Cataloging in Publication Data

Vlahos, Olivia.
Doing business.

Bibliography: p.
Includes index.
1 Business—History.   I. Title.
HF5341.V57   1985   650'.09   85-13792
ISBN 0-531-09700-5

Printed in the United States of America
6 5 4 3 2 1

TO THE MEMORY OF

*B. A. Riesner, Robert Lockart,
Louis Vlahos*

*Grandfather, Father,
Father-in-Law*

*They were men of business who
strove, throve, and made it big
in America*

CONTENTS

CONTENTS

CONTENTS

AUTHOR'S NOTE

The anthropology of *business?''* friends and colleagues have queried, looking puzzled and more than a little dubious. Like oil and water, the two propositions seem an unlikely mix. And seemed so once to me.

Then sometime toward the end of the 1970s, the students populating my anthropology classes began, unaccountably, to dwindle in number. What had been a flood during the Counterculture years slowed to a trickle. Who had turned off the spigot? Where were they going?

Into business. Into courses about business. They now had no time for the ancient, the exotic, the primitive.

But surely, I thought, there is always much to be learned from the past and from the ways of other human beings, much that explains present circumstances and gathering trends. Why, for example, had business—the generator of prosperity—been so consistently dishonored through time and place? Why had trade—often the creator of writing and the focus of cities—been so discounted as a stimulus to civilization? I would set out to learn.

But first there was much to learn *about* business. To this task I brought the supreme ignorance that any practitioner of anthropology brings to the study of a previously undiscovered people. Many men and women of business have graciously provided insights and instruction. Among them were Eric Berg, Technicomp, Inc.; Holmes Brown, The Institute for Applied Economics; Eugenie Cody, Norden Systems of United Technologies; Dr. Bern Dibner, Burndy Corporation and the Burndy Library; Kevin G. Gilmartin, Norwalk Savings Society and Project Business; Julianne Grace, The Perkin-Elmer Corporation; Ronald Hummel, Maxwell House Division of General Foods Corporation; Henry Klein, Klein's of Westport; Connie Mitchell, Junior Achievement, Inc.; Robert D. Ready, Hewitt Associates; Eleanor Rudolph, Junior Achievement medalist; Eugene F. Scarangella, Gene's Variety Store; Sally Scudo, Pitney Bowes, Inc.; Nancy Stamas, Technicomp, Inc.

To my own teachers of long ago—my academic line of descent—I owe a debt of gratitude for curiosity kindled and method instilled. Thank you, Gilbert McAllister, Irving Goldman, Joseph Campbell. To teachers I have never met but whose works have inspired this effort, I am also grateful. Thank you, Robert McC. Adams, Leo Pospisil, and Peter F. Drucker. Your elegant prose has charmed while teaching.

In my own place of business, Norwalk Community College, many friends and colleagues deserve warm thanks: President William Schwab for his encouragement and for recommending the sabbatical leave which permitted completion of the manuscript; Dean Robert Verna, chief fiscal officer, for patient instruction. Empathy, enthusiasm, and much practical assistance were provided by Carmen Bayles and Thomas Gallagher in the college library; James Catrambone of the Business Administration Department; Don Paulson, my computer expert; Karen Shiarella, Department

AUTHOR'S NOTE

of Social and Behavioral Sciences; Ann Ireland of the college staff.

Students and former students have generously offered assistance. Among them, Laura Allen, Anne Hummel, Joan Willcox. Eugenie Cody's help in assembling the manuscript deserves three loud cheers and much else besides.

It was my friend Maryanne Colas who first believed that what I hoped to do could be done—and made it happen. Bless her.

Dr. Michael Vlahos, my-son-the-historian, has gone far beyond filial duty in aid and interest. Bless him. Any errors in history should be laid at my door, however, not his.

For John Vlahos, the dramatist and my life partner, there are simply no thanks adequate to his many contributions. As in all else in life, this book is as much his as mine. But then, ours has always been a family sort of business.

PROLOGUE

NOT A DIRTY WORD

In proportion as rich men are honored in the state, virtue and the virtuous are dishonored and so at last, instead of craving contention and glory, men become lovers of trade and money.

PLATO[1]

PROLOGUE

With the possible exception of the military profession, no human activity has been more subject to public praise or blame than that of business. (The balance in recent years has tipped decidedly toward the negative.) Although the businessman is, from time to time, given recognition as the source of prosperity, his image also evokes more than a suggestion of menace. "Bloated Capitalist" is the descriptive term as familiar at home as abroad. And business itself (particularly when prefaced by "Big") often functions as a useful symbol for avarice or careless disregard of human values or both at once.

The student of human foibles and follies (which constitute much of the anthropologist's stock in trade) has to wonder why this is so. After all, business makes jobs, and that's good, isn't it? How can something good be bad as well? How can the very engine of national economy be regarded in some quarters as a sort of necessary evil? And if not evil altogether, then certainly grubby, gray, and greedy—which may be worse. "Do business if you must, but don't enjoy it. Above all, discuss it only in the office." So we have been admonished by society's style setters, pacemakers, and leaders of opinion.

Was it always thus? A sortie through the past turns up more of the same. Not everywhere, it is true. Not among all peoples. There are, in fact, some curious contradictions to be found. Consider the two books of the Bible. Old Testament Proverbs speak favorably of the man "in trade" and of his proper attributes:

> "Seest thou a man diligent in his business? He shall stand before kings."
>
> (22:29)

> "Wealth gotten by vanity shall be diminished: but he that gathereth by labor shall increase."
>
> (13:11)

And there are others that admonish:

"Rob not the poor, because he is poor: neither oppress the afflicted in the gate."

(22:22)

"Divers weights are an abomination unto the Lord; and a false balance is not good."

(20:23)

Concern about weights appears in several verses. Clearly the anticipated sins of the biblical merchant were an abomination unto the Lord, but the occupation itself carried no stigma. Business was not a dirty word.

Nor was it a dirty word in Phoenicia when the Prophet Isaiah (23:8) described Tyre as "the crowning city whose merchants are princes, whose traffickers are the honorable of the earth." He thundered against the high living of those honorables. Not against their profession.

The Old Testament is a true reflection of values and attitudes common to the Middle East from earliest times. Two thousand years before Isaiah's fulminations, the chief god of the ancient Sumerian pantheon was described in hymns of praise as "Merchant of the Wide Earth."[2] Commerce retains in the region a certain aura of magic to this day as Sam Pickering, Jr., reports. A Fulbright Scholar teaching English in a Syrian university, he was given by his students their formula for success: "Go to America and shine shoes. Return to Syria a *merchant!*"[3] Not a dirty word.

That other holy book of the Middle East, the Koran, also speaks of merchants. The same Old Testament admonitions regarding sharp dealing are there, to be sure, the same exhortations to practice charity, but business itself is not characterized as dishonorable. Why should it have been? The sacred Black Stone of Mecca was from earliest times in the care of merchant tribes, and the Prophet himself was a member of that profession.

But in the New Testament, though itself emergent from the same Middle Eastern culture sphere, has only bad things to say of the merchants of Jerusalem, of the men who at that time constituted the Establishment. The Savior is seen throwing money changers out of the Temple. He is heard declaring it more difficult for a rich man to enter Heaven than for a camel to pass through the eye of a needle. The philanthropies of Joseph of Arimathea to the contrary notwithstanding, it was not his sort who might expect to inherit the early Christian kingdom, but the poor and the meek whose wholly understandable views of the businessman as oppressor were shared by Jesus.

Elsewhere in the ancient world the businessman was apt to be regarded not as oppressor, but as a figure of shame, the butt of a thousand dirty jokes. Herodotus of Halicarnassus, often called the Father of History, a man who traveled through much of the fifth century B.C. world, observed that the man "in trade" was despised by many peoples, among them the Persians, the Scyths, and the Egyptians. He thought his fellow Greeks might have learned disdain from that ancient civilization along the Nile.[4] Not so. The attitude was homegrown and cultivated originally by that half-barbarous people as they struggled through their dark age half a millennium before Herodotus wrote. It was then a time when the warrior ethos prevailed, and might made right. The man of low birth might just make good by way of a strong sword arm. The man who depended on his wits, particularly if applied to trade, could never be acceptable. Piracy was honorable; commerce was not. Kings went to war to replenish their treasuries; they did not balance trade accounts.

The epic verse of Homer well describes this attitude through the adventures of Odysseus wending his roundabout way homeward. Often he was insulted by slurs cast on his bona fides. Said one doubter:

"He boasts no claim
Among the great, unlike the sons of Fame.
A wandering merchant, he frequents the main:
Some mean seafarer in pursuit of gain,
Studious of freight."[5]

The translation by Alexander Pope uses a word unknown in Homer's Greek which had no synonym for merchant and made do with various descriptions, as of the Phoenicians, "famed for ships, greedy men."

By classical times, a number of terms had become available; none of them especially flattering. To be an *emporus*, a traveler therefore a trader, was not something to which the honorable citizen aspired or was allowed to aspire. In Athens it was an occupation reserved for noncitizens, freedmen and foreigners, excluded from every civic right and responsibility save that of paying taxes. Every theater-going Greek recognized as a cue for derision the mask of the rich man "in trade," presuming beyond his station.

Even philosophers—ever molded by their native traditions while pluming their objectivity the while—found *emporus* a dirty word. There are, said Aristotle, two kinds of economies:

> "One is a part of household management; the other is retail trade: the former is necessary and honorable, while that which consists in exchange is justly censured, for it is unnatural and a mode by which men gain from one another."[6]

He went on later to advise:

> "Citizens must not lead the life of mechanics and tradesmen, for such a life is ignoble and inimical to virtue."[7]

Proper Romans, farmers, and warriors settled inland from the sea, inherited Greek disdain for commerce:

> "Happy the man,' sang the poet Horace, 'who far from schemes of business . . . ploughs again his ancestral land . . . with no yoke of usury on his neck!"[8]

Cicero voiced the common view that retail trade was "mean" because men engaged in it could "make no profit without much lying." He added a modification. Commerce on a small scale was mean but if it involved much travel and widespread distribution "without misrepresentation," then it was not "greatly to be censured." [9]

It was an assessment not limited to the West. In the China of Han Dynasty times (which coincided neatly with the rise and fall of Rome), Ssu-ma Chi'en, the Grand Historian of the Court, described the unavailing efforts of emperor and officialdom to curb men of business and restrict their profits. The merchants, for their part, presented a united front with respect to taxes and regulations. Yes, they were willing to assume any burden the court wished to impose *provided* it cease forthwith to brand commerce as an ignominious profession. They must have succeeded in pressing their case, for Ssu-ma Chi'en laments the fact that, quite soon after, anybody with money could be anything he chose, never mind his birth or breeding. [10]

This is one of the very few protests lodged anywhere by men of business disinclined to see themselves as they were seen. Elsewhere they have smarted in silence under their denigration, accepted traditional standards of worth, and schemed to achieve them. Forbidden to farm, the man of business farmed his money and made it multiply. Forbidden to lend at interest, he found ways around the strictures. In short, he learned to strive and thrive by beating out the competition, whether it be of his own kind or royal monopoly. Given only the smallest opportunity to rise in rank, he made the most of it. Tirelessly he sought a pedigree for his offspring knowing well they would be shamed by his efforts and disavow their ancestry. Tirelessly he sought the right to citizenship through public-spirited efforts which often served to enrich a city or a monarch while ruining him in the process. Sometimes those efforts enticed citizens into his own value system. So it was in Greece and Rome where every honorable gentleman in time sought privately to turn a profit, however much and however loudly such activities might be condemned in public.

Nearly everywhere on earth, sovereigns or established churches or both have issued decrees forbidding merchants to dress well with what were considered ill-gotten gains. Severe penalties, in various times and places, have been attached to the display of furs or jewels or to the assumption of airs and graces inappropriate to lowly station. Men of business have nevertheless found ways to enjoy creature comforts and even luxury. Forbidden bright colors, they have substituted richness of fabric. Forbidden silken outer garments, they have worn them underneath. Forbidden even this, merchants of eighteenth-century Japan turned ingenuity and fortune to the elaborate decoration of their skins. Among themselves, gorgeous, full-body tattoos came into vogue.[11]

Merchants of Aztec Mexico, the *pochteca,* took care to enter and leave the city of Tenochtitlan dressed in rags. Thus they hoped to blunt the all-too-dangerous envy of the great warriors. Since these worthies would hardly bring themselves to grace a *pochteca* hovel, they could be kept ignorant of the treasures beautifully displayed therein.[12]

Aztec wealth, much enhanced by *pochteca* efforts, was despoiled by Spanish conquistadores who certainly did not view the New World as a source of trade but rather one of plunder. Doubtless they would have sympathized with the Aztec warriors' low opinion of merchants, had an exchange of views been made at all possible.

But times were changing even then in the European homeland. New World booty sent back to Spain was transferred—almost before it could be unloaded—to the royal creditors. These were the despised bankers of Italy and southern Germany who had learned to strive and thrive while Spain, with the fewest skilled businessmen in Europe, hewed to aristocratic tenets and twice went bankrupt as a result. This Most Catholic Country hewed also to the teachings of the early Christian faith which held that commerce was certainly evil and to be avoided at all costs by him who would save his soul. *Homo mercator vix aut nunquam potest Deo placere,* was the holy precept. "The man of business is but seldom acceptable to God."[13] And this was reinforced whenever possible by a denial of the sacraments and even Christian burial. Impossible to determine the number of medieval merchants who went unshriven to an antibusiness hereafter.

Only with the Protestant Reformation did the Western man of business come briefly into his own, achieving a modicum of honor along with wealth, and a certain odor of sanctity besides. This was because the Reformation, with special emphasis on its Calvinist branch, interpreted material success as a sign of Heavenly grace. More specifically, it represented the reward of diligence in a calling, of service to the God who gave talent, mind, and skill. For the proper Calvinist—the Puritan, as he came to be called in England and America—work was almost its own reward. Gain was certainly good but effort was better. And the fruits of effort were not to be squandered or even enjoyed unduly; they were to be tended. No outside authority need impose sumptuary laws; the Puritan merchant imposed them on himself, together with the rules of honesty, frugality, and right conduct that made him fair in the sight of God.

Much attenuated and secularized, this spirit was to fuel the Industrial Revolution and to be transferred to America where it took root so firmly as to affect the idiom. "Business" came to denote the personal concerns, the secrets of each individual ("That's *my* business"); stern admonition ("You have no business doing that"); a characteristic of the voyeur ("She sticks her nose in everybody's business"); a guide to proper conduct ("Let's handle this divorce in a businesslike fashion"); and the ultimate put-down ("Mind your own business"). In an extrapolation from the individual to the nation, one American president was prompted to declare, "The business of America is business!" Clearly, it was not a dirty word.

But that was before the Great Depression, which began as Milton and Rose Friedman hold,[14] in the United States and spread worldwide. Soon the old opprobrium was again heaped on business. Two national leaders—very different in their values, character, and aspirations—found a common cause for the calamity and a common remedy.

"The money-changers have fled the high seats in the temple of our civilization," said Franklin D. Roosevelt in his first inaugural address, invoking thus the Savior's right-eous wrath together with just a hint that, without these villains, happy days might come again.

In Germany, Adolph Hitler promised to "break interest slavery" and to "bring the money barons to heel." He then proceeded to serve up the Jews of Germany in earnest of his intentions while leaving "Aryan" moneymen un-touched.[15]

Marxian views of good and evil had long sounded a similar note. For adherents of this ideology, the effective dirty word was *capitalism*. Writing in the late 1920s, the anarchist Alexander Berkman described capitalism as a monstrous international conspiracy bent on dominating workers and beating them into submission. And all the in-stitutions of society, including the unions, functioned to serve the capitalist masters in their cruel purpose.[16] (The conspir-acy view of capitalism is still popular in some quarters. Not long ago a bishop of the United Methodist church echoed Berkman in declaring: "We are hostages to a vast system of cruelty structures that are preordaining that the rich get richer and the poor get poorer.")[17]

All such condemnations were muted with the coming of World War II. American industry and industrialists per-formed so effectively in achieving victory that one of their number, a secretary of defense in the Eisenhower cabinet, could get away with saying, "What's good for General Mo-tors is good for America." That is how he was quoted. What he actually said was, "What's good for the *country* is good, etc." Nobody much minded the transposition. Business re-habilitated. But not for long.[18]

With the 1960s and a change of generation came a new concern for the environment and its fragility and a new social consciousness. It was then not only socially im-proper—but indeed unthinkable—to apply old stereotypes to any number of categories: gender, color, religion, age, sexual orientation. Each individual, so popular morality held, must be given the benefit of his or her special and unique qualities. This splendid intolerance of the stereotype did not apply, however, to occupation, particularly when that had to do with commerce. For commerce had come to constitute the snake in a new environmental Eden. The operative dirty word was *corporation,* that fictitious "person" more visible than Divine Providence but human enough to shoulder blame. In *The Greening of America,* Charles Reich describes what he calls "Corporate America":

> "This apparatus of power has become a mindless juggernaut, destroying the environment, obliterating human values, and assuming domination over the minds and lives of its subjects."[19]

Today the paradoxes are at work again. With the appearance of recession, suddenly everybody wanted to do business while continuing to feel vaguely guilty about it. In colleges and universities, liberal arts curricula go begging while courses in accounting and data processing are oversubscribed. Everybody disavows dirty business and then proceeds to climb the corporate ladder as fast as ever he (or she) can. "Big business may be bad," is the disclaimer, "but don't blame me. I'm just doing my best to survive and thrive, and if I have to beat out competition along the way, well, that's *my* business!"

Not a dirty word. Not necessarily a clean one either. Just a word to denote occupations and activities which figure in the economic scheme of things. Whether the man who does business is to be honored for his pains, proscribed for his pains, or tolerated as a necessary evil depends very much on changing times and traditions deeply rooted in the past. In each social pattern the needs of the group are continually weighed against the desires of the individual; the need for cooperation against the latitude allowed for competition. In each culture, there is a tilt toward one—or toward the other.

Make no mistake about it, the man of enterprise is an

individual. Like those other individuals, the warrior, the nascent scientist, the poet, he has often been something of an outsider. It was guaranteed from the beginning by travel. Human beings can and have lived off the land, hunting its animals and gathering its bounty. Still, they need implements for the job, and good weapon-stone is not everywhere to be found. Someone must travel for it. And someone did. The evidence is there to prove it.

Human beings have lived and can live in isolated villages, tied to field and harvest. Deprived of animal flesh, their bodies will then require salt. They will have to dig for it or evaporate brine for it. Or someone will have to travel to places where these things are done and bring goods to trade for the salt. And someone did.

Through all times and places and ways of life, religion has required for its expression certain precious artifacts. And someone has had to travel to obtain them. In some times and places, chiefs have demanded the trappings of prestige and authority, and someone has undertaken to search them out. The treasures of ancient shrines, the grave offerings for chiefs bear witness.

We can see such journeys reenacted to this day by living folk whose societies can be located all along the scale of organization from simple to complex. Whether in quest of religion or prestige or commodities, men willing so to venture, or chosen for the effort, are now and have always been of a somewhat different sort from those who remain at home. And on their quests they become more different still. Abroad, new things are seen, new ideas are learned, ideas which can then be compared with what is known. When such ideas return with the traveler, some kind of change becomes inevitable, and society takes another tack, overturning the old verities. Perhaps this is one reason why traders have acquired an unsavory reputation and are so carefully excluded from every philosopher's utopia.

The process by which states were created from tribal beginnings took place long before there were means of recording the seminal events as they occurred, long before there was anyone trained to ring the changes from one way of life to another. A few things about those changes, however, can be surmised: the merchant was there. Whether as tribal adventurer or sober professional, he was there, trafficking in new things, things that were needed, and things for which need could be created along the way. The earliest cities of the world appear along known trade routes and were surely constructed as much to accommodate the traveling salesman as the priest. Here at the heart of urban beginnings are representatives of the world's oldest professions. (That often-mentioned other one, though a facet of city life, cannot be cited as a point of origin.)

Some specialists call writing the hallmark of civilization. Doubtless they have in mind the king lists, the god lists, and the works of liturgy by which events and processes can be traced, through which mind communicates to mind, whatever the years between. Instead, new findings now suggest that earliest writing appeared as an adjunct to business and continued to be so for millennia before it ever was turned to the service of literature.

Now there is a thought to redeem the image. Might one say: "The business of civilization is business"? It is, at least, a possibility worth considering.

PART ONE

BUSINESS
AND
BEGINNINGS

THE ENTREPRENEUR

HOW TO SUCCEED BY TRYING

When you are on your own, you get paid what you are worth, not what your job is worth.

MARY KAY ASH, FOUNDER
OF MARY KAY COSMETICS.[1]

It is really very simple. You need Pluck and Luck. A little Talent doesn't hurt (but is not absolutely essential). You need Optimism (never say die!). A willingness to Work Hard (nose to the grindstone!). Say it again. WORK. Also Save. Clean Living and Self-Denial always help. So does Honesty.

Let Ragged Dick show you his way.

A street kid, he was, bootblack by trade, self-supporting since the age of seven. In New York of the 1870s there were as yet no governmental agencies to undertake Dick's care. Did he repine? No, indeed. He put a big smile on his face, merriment on his tongue, and his heart in his work. So good a bootblack was he that money was never lacking for a theatre ticket, a good dinner, or an occasional bed in the Newsboys' Lodging House. He was even able to treat younger boys and those of a nature less go-getting than his own. No prig was our bootblack, however. He smoked, he swore like a top, he loved to gamble. But he never, never stole, for that was *mean*.

His cheerful self-reliance, his sturdy honesty won for him the admiration of many well-placed businessmen. At their urging, he began to save his money rather than gamble it away, to study books rather than theatre bills. He hired as tutor another boy, one with a good education but little gift for blacking boots.

After a series of splendid Good Deeds and Lucky Breaks, Dick's Effort and Optimism were rewarded by a Fine Job. Respectability and Success were assured. He would climb the ladder to Fame and Fortune, marry the boss's daughter, and live happily ever after.[2]

Is this a true story? Yes and no. Certainly Dick's times abounded in real life successes. John Jacob Astor, once a German shop clerk, had by then cornered the fur market and become the richest man in America. Andrew Carnegie, the Scottish immigrant and former bobbin boy in a textile mill, was well on his way to achieving fame as a steel magnate and philanthropist.

Dick's story amounted to something more than truth. It was a million American dreams put in print for young and old to read. It captured a growing nation's ideals and raised them to a new and higher level of Truth. It was, in short, a myth.

Like all myths, it was continually retold. Ragged Dick lived his story under hundreds of names and in books of many titles. For he was the one and only hero of his creator, the Reverend Horatio Alger, Jr., a gentleman as far different from the mythic Dick as it is possible to be. Born in 1832, Horatio was intended by his stern and clerical father for the ministry. Alas, he was as much a failure at that as he had been in an earlier flirtation with journalism. Even the Union Army, hard up as it was for volunteers to fight the Confederacy, rejected his effort to enlist.

No wonder Horatio Alger wrote about success. No wonder he glorified poor boys who, all unconstrained by Harvard educations, genteel circumstances, and dominating parents, made it on their own and made it big. And no wonder that Americans took his stories (meant, really, for the juvenile market) to their bosoms and made him the most popular author of his time. Some say he was the most influential of his generation.

But tastes as well as times have changed. The memory of Ragged Dick and his avatars has not lingered on. The name of their creator remains. Indeed, people still speak of Horatio Alger as though he were, himself, the mythic hero and not the failed author of same (he'd probably like that!).

The rags-to-riches myth remains as well. It is retold in every generation with all the quirks and warts peculiar to the time. The novel *What Makes Sammy Run* was about a Ragged Dick of the motion picture industry. Its accent fell on ambition and hard work. The less said about virtue, the better. The book and later musical comedy, *How to Succeed in Business Without Really Trying* emphasized luck and pluck, the go-getting style without the substance, and as little effort as humanly possible.[3]

The myth lives because it reflects values and promises that Americans still respect (even though many think they ought not). It lives in the hopes of every immigrant kid to reach these shores. While other Western nations may offer the promise of upward mobility by way of the work ethic, none has yet produced a mythology to spur success in business.

Perhaps the closest is the medieval English legend of Dick Whittington whose cat charmed a Barbary prince and earned him a rich reward. He then rose to be lord mayor of London more by luck and fortunate connections, it must be said, than by work and push. Once there, he could rise no further. The highest and the best rewards were, in his day and time (and, indeed, down to the Reform Act of 1832), reserved for those of proper birth, endowed with land and impeccable antecedents. Napoleon may have called England "a nation of shopkeepers," but no well-born Englishman aspired to a career "in trade." There was certainly no appreciable literature to honor this endeavor. The rich merchant or manufacturer strove, therefore, to acquire land for his offspring and the means to permit of more agreeable, more genteel pursuits. Who remembers now that the scientific labors of Charles Darwin were underwritten by the pluck, luck, and pottery of his ancestor, old Josiah Wedgewood?

Only in America, the Alger myth suggests, can the rugged individual, however poor and uneducated, rise to riches and position through his own efforts and in his own lifetime. Only in America, it would seem, has the myth remained a national tenet of faith, to be refreshed and reenshrined by each succeeding wave of immigration.

A CROSS-CULTURAL ALGER

But is the uniqueness of the story itself part of the myth? Can we find a Ragged Dick in the mythology of other people, non-Western people, simpler, closer to the land?

Highly unlikely, current wisdom would insist. The honest-to-goodness entrepreneur is usually thought to be an invention of recent times and complex societies. Foragers and farmers, the experts tell us, people living as our earliest ancestors once did, exalt the needs of the group, never those of the individual. They forbid competition and therefore ambition.

Well, yes. Many do. Perhaps most do—or did; there are few genuine primitives left in the world. But not all. Consider the following tale:

> There was a boy, Toàn by name, who grew up on the wrong side of the river. His address by rights should have been high on the hill overlooking shanty town. Indeed, he could see his grandfather's great house up there, elegant, imposing, its doors forever closed to him because his mother had loved not wisely but too well a shanty town youth with neither the wealth nor the breeding to sue for her hand.
>
> Her own father had disinherited her and, being a very powerful personage indeed, had seen to it that the unfortunate suitor was disposed of permanently. In those times and that place, one just did not aspire beyond one's station and expect to emerge in one piece.
>
> And so it was that the daughter of a great house bore her bastard son in the ramshackle hut of her dead lover's mother. There they were cherished and pitied, for the neighbors were too poor to follow the scruples of their betters. The young mother's former friends pitied her, too, and so did her grandfather in the hilltop mansion. In secret he offered help. Between them they taught the boy to be industrious, ambitious, and genteel. In time, he became so wealthy—and yet withal so generous, so gracious of demeanor, so elegant of bearing— that his uncles invited him to lead the family and live in the great house on the hill.[4]

Toàn had Pluck. In addition to grandfather, Luck brought him a magic whale who had been washed up the Klamath River one day when the earth tilted (as it was wont to do regularly in that time and place) and became trapped in a certain inland lake. There Toàn had the good fortune to walk on her back, thinking her a submerged log. Herself a bastard like the boy, she pitied him and endowed him with the potential to succeed. As in our world, celestial beings of that time and place (be they whales or otherwise) were inclined to help those who helped themselves. Toàn did, and Toàn made it big.

Where? In northern California. When? Any time before 1850, before the white man came. It was the Yurok tribe of that region which created Toàn's Horatio Alger story to reflect Yurok dreams of success. It has been retold by Theodora Kroeber who also wrote the famous *Ishi in Two Worlds*.

Now the Yurok in their heyday had no stores, no markets, no business. There were no farms, either, for they were hunters and gatherers. There was no government. There were no public leaders elected, appointed, or by inheritance. Order was maintained, for the most part, by way of the respect accorded all men of renown. Otherwise, disputes between families were settled through negotiations and an elaborate system of fines and fees. For if the Yurok were without business as we know it, they were not without money. Shell money.

And how did the enterprising individual acquire money? By first acquiring valuables—red woodpecker scalps, white deerskins, exotic flints beautifully worked, and the carved wooden boxes in which these might be kept. Acquisition required Industry, Pluck, and Luck. One hunted for the skins and scalps unremittingly and in preference to good square meals.

One traveled and explored for flints. And one carried on judicious swapping and exchange. One also minded one's manners the while. One did without the comforts of the connubial couch. For the Heavenly Powers favored only those who practiced clean living and self-denial. No wonder the hopeful hunter nightly and with tears streaming down his face besought an anonymous pantheon, "Make me successful! Make me rich!"

Ditto here and now. Ditto you and me. Except maybe the denial part. Current values extol the reverse behavior. Even so, the true climber takes his work to bed and never mind the snickers.

Riches in Yurok terms did not, alas, translate well into

the modern American idiom. And Yurok pluck and luck did not make the transition to American business acumen. The swamping effect of a dominant people, however similar their values, did not permit continuity within change.

FROM NO STREET TO WALL STREET

But not all such people are swamped. We can see a successful transition from Stone Age patterns to modern times going on today in New Guinea. There, under many a nose plug and coat of body paint, you will find Ragged Dick climbing the ladder of business success. In pidgin English, which is the lingua franca of the island, his worldly success is marked by the title, Big Fella Man Bilong Bisnis—or what we might call the Tycoon.

Thirty years ago Big Fella Men were warriors who now and then took enemy heads for trophies and ate what remained for dinner. They were tough and mean and macho. They were also wealthy.

For wealth, read pigs and lots of them. Read shell and feather treasures and women. The name of the game was to give away one to get the other. And, of course, the more one gave, the more one got Giving and getting, always on a supergrand scale, were very much admired. The best givers and getters were also obeyed. For entrepreneurial skills were thought to mark those favored by the Powers. What is more, the strength and glory of the Powers were expressed through the man of renown.

How did a man get started along the road to renown? (The Powers helped those who helped themselves.) With a boost from clansmen and friends willing to invest in his personal success. They contributed pigs and valuables for his feasts and ceremonial exchanges, knowing well they would be repaid by this "comer" when he attained success. Perhaps, too, the Powers would rub off by association.

During its trusteeship in eastern New Guinea, the Australian government managed to suppress tribal warfare. (It has returned since 1975 and the achievement of independence.) Adventures with incoming Europeans then took the place of war in establishing a man's reputation for initiative and strength. After all, it takes initiative for a boy of fifteen voluntarily to leave his own isolated village and join a survey party of Europeans, knowing neither their language nor those of their New Guinea retinue. This act of eager and confident reaching out for something new has been witnessed by countless European visitors.

As for the rest of the success equation, manipulation of pigs was quickly replaced by manipulation of capital assets. Australian dollars replaced shell and were squirreled away with a passion. In western New Guinea, ditto with Dutch guilders and later with Indonesian rupees. All in all, the New Guinea people, particularly those of the highlands, east and west, took to business as a duck takes to water. In the Goroka District, then under Australian control, they learned first to plant coffee as a cash crop. They then invested the profits in cattle, trucks, trade stores, and restaurants. These generated their own return. They also made possible that conspicuous display so necessary to the Big Fella Man Bilong Bisnis.

How does one get to be a Big Fella Man Bilong Bisnis? Simple. By applying the same Horatio Alger formula that took a man to the top in nineteenth-century America. Consider the story of Mr. Z. We'll call him that because he is a composite of the many Big Men studied by anthropologist Ben R. Finney:

Because Mr. Z was an orphan, adopted by someone of another clan, he had no inherent rights in land. Unlike other "comers," he had not worked for Europeans. Neither did he have any schooling. Was he then downhearted? Not on your life. He invented a business idea new in New Guinea. He would *rent* land.

He did just that with the small amount of money he had earned selling melons and passion fruit. And *saved,* don't forget that. On rented land, he planted his first coffee trees and tended them carefully.

When these brought in cash, he conceived another idea. He would buy coffee from all the farmers in his remote and isolated mountain village and transport the entire crop to the coast. How? By truck. How to get the truck? From his clients-to-be.

Did the locals snoot the idea? Indeed they did not. Why walk each crop to market, they reasoned, if the market can be brought to us? At once they began to take an interest in the family-poor Mr. Z. Enough of an interest to kick in funds for his first truck—as once they might have supported his maiden pig feast.

As of 1968, Mr. Z. was not quite the richest Big Fella Man around. He did not have the largest coffee plantation. But he did own the most trucks and the most cattle. Like his fellow Big Men, he has also stood for elective office in the House of Assembly (now, with Independence, the Papua New Guinea Parliament). His expectations of eventual election are solidly founded. The PGN voters do not favor Western-educated intellectuals opposed (as Finney says) to private commerce. They put their faith in the traditional Big Fella Man who had made his reputation by doing business.[5]

Do we hear echoes of Horatio? "Certainly not," the skeptic will demur. "Maybe there are superficial resemblances to Ragged Dick in the drive, the striving, the single-minded ambition of the Big Fella Man. Ditto for the rugged individualism, though goodness knows why *that* is such a grand thing after all. Don't forget, however, that we're still dealing with a primitive society here, or one only recently so. After all, there were no cities in traditional New Guinea, no markets, no cash. Pigs and women, I grant you, may constitute a kind of status currency, but can they honestly be thought of as the real thing? No," the skeptic will add, "Ragged Dick is a by-product of the Industrial Revolution and purely Western capitalism. So is your Mr. Z. Kindly take your analogies elsewhere."

Agreed. Elsewhere. Also else-when.

HEREWITH: A CITY

Not a Western city. Not of recent times. It is nevertheless, a very considerable city, well enclosed. Like most of its sister cities of Sumer—that southern part of Mesopotamia—it is a river port, drawing trade and also tourists. They come to see the temple, largest in the entire region. So resplendent is this stepped edifice, this *ziggurat,* that it will later be immortalized in the Old Testament as the Tower of Babel. The city is Ur at the time of its Third Dynasty, about 2100 B.C. In time the sand will cover all. But that is yet to come.

During this period Ur's balance of trade was mainly in the hands of seafaring merchants, members of a select brotherhood whose livelihood depended on copper commerce with Telmun (Dilmun), now the island of Bahrain. The group was small because the risks were great: pirates, highwaymen, the sea itself, for the navigation of which special skills were needed. Diplomatic niceties were crucial to the trade. One had to know the customs and preferences of the Telmun people in order to obtain special permission to land on Telmun's shores and do business there. (All in all, not so very different from the skills needed by modern oil entrepreneurs when doing business with the present Arab occupants.)

So great were the hazards of the trade that merchants and sailors continually solicited the aid of their patron goddess, Ningal. They bribed her with lavish offerings. They also recorded on clay tablets the details of each religious transaction together with details of the commercial arrangements which had made offerings possible. Contracts, agreements, even business letters were deposited with Ningal. One collection of tablets, described by A. Leo Oppenheim, was that of Ea-nasir, greatest of the seafaring merchants. Only fragments remain, and from these we piece together something of his story:

> Ea-nasir's agreements with the investors who underwrote his
> voyages specified that they were to receive interest on their

loans but would share neither profits nor losses of the ventures. (Businessmen of Ur were then beginning to develop a real maritime insurance that would spread the risk.)

On the particular voyage described, Ea-nasir was able to dispose quickly of his fifty woolen garments, for such were in great demand among the Telmun folk. He took in trade copper, fish-eyes (probably pearls), ivory, and gem-stone beads. Very rich profits.

Back in home port, he had first to satisfy the customs agent and pay taxes on his haul. (Excessive, he noted.) After that, he sent a servant with the copper to repay the loan from one of his investors.

The investor complained that the copper was of poor quality. The servant, ever pert and off-hand, invited the merchant to "take it or leave it." Enraged by Ea-nasir's rudeness, this worthy promptly shot off a letter of recrimination.[6]

This is as far as the tablets go. We do not learn how, bad manners or no, Ea-nasir managed to climb to the top of his profession. There is, however, one line in the creditor's letter which offers a clue. "That this should happen between gentlemen!" the investor complains. Complains? The line could be read as a slur on Ea-nasir's breeding. Thus: "If you were a gentleman, you would not have behaved so or allowed your underlings to behave so!"

Ea-nasir's boorishness, as reflected by a poorly trained staff, suggests a quick rise from humble beginnings. To learn how he *could* have risen, from what background and experiences, it is necessary to consult tablets from other sources.

One of the best is an essay of frustration addressed by a rich man to the playboy son who would not apply himself in scribal school:

". . . Never in all my life did I make you carry reeds to the canebrake. The reed rushes which the young or the little carry, you, never in your life did you carry them. . . . I never sent you to work, to plow my field. . . . I never sent you to work as a laborer. . . . Others like you support their parents by working. . . . They are the sons of fathers who make their sons labor, but me. . . . I didn't make you work like them. . . . Night and day you waste in pleasure. . . .

"You who wander about in the public square, would you achieve success? Then . . . go to school. It will benefit you . . ."[7]

It is unlikely that Ea-nasir had the chances squandered by the rich man's son. *His* learning would have been won in the school of hard knocks while apprenticed to a merchant. (Countless Sumerian tablets record contracts of apprenticeship.)

In this service he would have learned to sail the unwieldly ships of the time. He would certainly have learned to reckon and keep accounts, to negotiate contracts with other merchants, to pick up the Telmun lingo. And all this while swabbing decks, carrying bundles, running interminable errands—and being beaten for his pains. He also would have garnered tips from the master's clients. Thriftily saved and cannily invested, tips might well have become a ship. Or at least the down payment on one.

That is one way of explaining Ea-nasir's rise from rags to riches. But we are forgetting something else. Sumerian society itself provided a push. Ur and her sister cities honored the man of business, the man of enterprise, and had done so for a long time.

Case in point: Foreign-trade expeditions of Egypt and other nations of the time were normally undertaken at the behest and with the support of king or temple or both. It is true that temples probably served as banks and warehouses, especially in the beginning of Sumeria's rise to prominence. They did not, however, set the tone of trade, though specialists in the field have always supposed that this was the case.

As Sumerologist Marvin Powell points out, temple hierarchies as far back as 2800 B.C. had learned that the loan of a herd of cattle at a fixed percentage of the herd's increase was far more profitable, far less trouble than the maintenance of that same herd at temple expense. And the cattle would be healthier and more fertile to boot, for the herdsman had an extra incentive to careful husbandry. He could hope to develop a herd of his own with the animals remaining after the temple's interest had been paid. If priests had learned the value of this sort of transaction, why should they then have maintained shipmasters on their payrolls and dabbled in foreign trade?[8]

Clearly, free-market capitalism is no new thing in the world. The very gods worshipped in Mesopotamian temples were fiercely competitive, seeking continually to advance their own interests—just as the Mesopotamian trader was wont to do. And we must remember that the chief god of the pantheon was Enlil, "Merchant of the Wide Earth."[9] Such celestial role models made success for the Mesopotamian man of business a kind of moral imperative. Like cleanliness in our world, it was an achievement next to godliness. And the Lord was sure to help those who helped themselves.

Like Ragged Dick, like Toàn of the Yurok or the enterprising New Guinea highlander, Ea-nasir was not only free to work hard and to profit from his labors, he was encouraged to do so. His society provided models, both mythological and actual, against which he could pattern his own destiny, toward which he could aim his aspirations.

PROFIT WITHOUT HONOR

But what if the society lauds other heroes and relegates the activities of buying and selling, trading, lending, profiting—the entire constellation of commerce—to the dust bin of official values? Clearly, those that can will exercise their talents in other, more rewarding occupations. Those that cannot will have to do business in spite of the odds and let profit substitute for honor.

There is the story of Pasion, a resident of Athens in the fourth century B.C. Were it not for the speeches of Demosthenes, who functioned as an attorney when he was not denouncing Macedonian Philip, we should not know of Pasion at all. Nor would Demosthenes have taken much notice of him, either, for Pasion was a slave. Pasion was also the richest banker in Athens. *That* made a difference.

How could such a contradiction come to be? To understand that we shall need a brief reexposure to the values of classical times.

All Greek cities—even democratic Athens—shared rather rigid notions of class. The citizen must be a landowner, first and foremost, the descendant of citizens as far back as records could be traced. The citizen was expected to bear arms and participate in city government. Were he a gentleman as well, he must cultivate mind and body. That was his proper occupation. Manual labor of any kind was demeaning. There were slaves for that. Equally demeaning was any aspect of commerce—buying and selling, changing money or lending it, embarking on trade ventures. One might invest in such enterprises but only as a very silent partner.

There was really something dirty about money (had not the great philosophers said it?). Not about *having* it, of course. Not about *spending* it (who, after all, did not *love* spending?). It was just the working with money, the handling of it, the accounting for it that was so onerous and unclean.

There were slaves for that, too. Or freedmen. Or "metics," foreign-born businessmen who chose to settle in Athens. Though taxed like citizens, drafted like citizens, expected to make voluntary contributions to the public purse, metics could not own land, marry into citizen families, vote, or plead in court. Their businesses were nevertheless protected, for these were necessary to the state, however low. Indeed, metics were encouraged from time to time by the city's gift of theatre tickets and reserved seats for the plays. And yet, debarred as they were from public honor or recognition, members of the underclass strove somehow to rise. In the words of the old cliché, they dreamed the impossible dream.

Pasion was one of these and, given the inimical environment, his success surely outshines that of any Horatio hero.

History (which concentrates exclusively on religion and politics) does not record how or whence he was enslaved. Probably as a child taken by slavers from some barbarian shore. Then again, he might well have been sold into slavery as part of a job-lot: the entire population of a city defeated in war.

In any case, his masters were members of a metic banking firm. His quick head for figures, his sterling character we must infer from the reputation he acquired in later life. At that time, Pasion's word and his precise ledgers were accepted in countless courts of law as incontrovertible evidence. And this in a culture in which metics, let alone slaves, had no right of judicial appeal.

Perhaps he managed to buy his freedom, for it was as a freedman that he assumed command of the bank. Later still, after having poured his private resources into the Athenian navy and performed countless other works of civic virtue, he was enrolled as an Athenian citizen.[10]

For some that was the world turned upside down. Imagine, a freedman hobnobbing with citizens! And a moneyman, at that! They had not marked how their world had changed. It was now a world in which Pasion and his fellow bankers had gained for Athens (defeated first by Sparta and then by the Macedonians) a new lease on glory as a financial center. A century before, Pasion's elevation could not have been even remotely possible.

The personal story of this self-made man ends on a familiar note. His spoiled and pampered gentleman-son squandered practically all the father had acquired by hard work, honesty, and self-denial.

FAMILY INCENTIVE

Not so the sons of Meyer Amchel Rothschild of Jew Street, Frankfort. They would uphold the work ethic and the founder's edict of family solidarity down through the generations—long after they managed to establish the world's greatest family enterprise.

> Seeing little orphan Meyer, who would have thought it possible? He was as ragged, as cringing as any other Jew. With his brothers he eked out a living in old clothes, buying them and selling them. There were not a great many occupations permitted Jews at the time and always those which decent, Gentile folk found despicable.
>
> Jews in the German states of the eighteenth century could not own land or farm. They certainly had no voice in government (and would not, even in Victorian England, until a Rothschild was elected to parliament and permitted to take his seat there). The ghetto was barred at night by chains. Out of the ghetto, Jews were required to wear on their clothing certain identifying signs. They bowed and scraped to the Gentiles even when these were hateful urchins who delighted in shrieking, "Jew do your duty!" And Meyer Amchel did, without protest, for he had a dream.
>
> Along with the rags, he bought old coins about the history of which he soon acquired expert knowledge. And, in spite of all his ghetto crudities, he learned a courtier's charm.
>
> Very rare coins he sold cheaply to men of distinction and soon gained admittance to the grandest of them all, the Landgrave of Hesse (whose father provided mercenary soldiers to defend the British cause in America). Little by little, Meyer's business acumen and eventually his growing purse became indispensable to the Great One.
>
> The five Rothschild sons, as brilliant as their father and with even greater drive, eventually established commercial houses in all the great cities of Europe. Five fingers of a single hand, they were. Later came the honors, painfully sought and often bought. Later. After success had been won by running harder than anyone else down the only avenue left open to Jews.[11]

And yet, even in the worst times, during pogroms and extermination, despised as they were by Christians, the Jews were not without their own models of success. Nobody knows whether freedmen and metics of classical times cultivated fellow feeling and a sense of identity. History records how the Jews established a community wherever their wanderings took them. Their values encouraged individual achievement in whatever way the individual *could* achieve. For the success of one favored individual meant protection for many. No one was quite alone.

Who *can* live altogether alone—without esteem, without approval, without the sympathy of his fellows? What is more to the point, who can succeed without success? If the enterprising soul cannot hope even for the grudging acceptance accorded the necessary evil, why should he do business at all?

The Marxist philosopher would reply, "Why, indeed?" Therein lies yet another story. And another reality.

INITIATIVE CAN BE HARMFUL TO YOUR HEALTH

Nowhere in societies ancient or modern, pagan or Christian, is the suspicion of native business enterprise more profound than in the Soviet Union. It is more than suspicion. Individual enterprise is a crime punishable by long prison sentences, if not death. Thieves, rapists, even garden-variety murderers are regarded with more tolerance than the economic criminal. Never mind that he wishes to supply what people want and can't otherwise obtain. It is for the State to supply all wants, not the individual.

Crimes of theft and violence do not go unpunished, of course. But their origin prompts compassion. Such acts are considered abberations, unfortunate vestiges of the capitalist society which created such behavior. When the perfect Socialist Order is achieved, crime will of itself wither away, as the State will wither away. (At present writing, both appear to be in full vigor.) Attainment of the Perfect Order is perpetually being thwarted by the rugged individualist and his desire to traffic and haggle, thwarted by nascent capitalism which ever rears its ugly head. Capitalism is the real crime. More than that, it is mortal sin. As such, it must be extirpated, root and branch.

There is even Soviet honor among Soviet thieves who head the underworld pecking order. According to Yuri Brokhin, an émigré filmmaker, the Thieves' Guild will expel any member caught dabbling in underground business ventures, such as factories. Stealing is, after all, honorable; business is not. Thus, the entrepreneur is cut adrift, even from the underworld society which might otherwise applaud his criminal achievements and spur him on.[12]

This is not to say that all individual ability is allowed to languish. Talent is admired in the Soviet Union and generously rewarded, especially talent in the sciences and the arts. Individual effort on behalf of the Communist party is also appreciated and admired. But talent must not strike out in directions unauthorized by the State, must not innovate without permission. For it is the State from which all blessings flow. Can flow. Must flow. It is the State which defines success and decides who shall have it (along with all the perks that success guarantees). And Heaven help the individual who decides to help himself.

Heaven must, because people *do* strive in illicit occupations. Some even thrive. But not for long.

One of these was Yelizaveta Tyntareva, whose exploits were described in *Time Magazine*, June, 1980. An attorney stationed in Lithuania, Yelizaveta was a member of the minor elite. As a privileged person, she was able to obtain a Russian-made car. She then sold it (presumably at a profit; cars are hard for unauthorized persons to come by) and used the money to buy items for which there was a big demand and no supply in sight. Sunglasses, for example, salon-styled wigs, blue jeans, watches, cameras. She sold these by mail order to customers far away from Western borders over which such items are smuggled.

Now it is axiomatic among observers of the human scene that one must attend, rather, to what people do than to what they say they do. Russian people condemn capitalism. They nevertheless put their money where their mouths are not. For Yelizaveta's wares they gladly paid top ruble.

So successful, in fact, did her genteel black market enterprise become that she had to hire a staff to handle the volume of business.

Next stop the gulag, for a twelve-year stay.[13]

At least she avoided the firing squad. Other underground entrepreneurs have not been so lucky. Yuri Brokhin has written about one of the greatest tycoons in Russia of the 1960s:

This rags to riches individual began his career as a laborer in a small rural factory producing nylon sleeping bags for mountain climbers. Quite soon he was promoted to manager. Then his entrepreneurial career began.

While quotas of sleeping bags were faithfully met, the workers managed to moonlight another product. They made string shopping bags which required very little nylon, were always in short supply, and could be marketed at a handsome profit. In no time at all, the factory workers had made a bundle out of bags. So did the manager.

He next dabbled in high fashion clothing. For this venture new underground factories were established, bright young designers were employed (to moonlight, of course), and newer merchandising techniques were brought into play. His new lines sold like the proverbial hotcakes. With the profits, our tycoon was able to diversify into many areas, including sports.

In the United States, with venture capital ready at hand, our illicit tycoon could have made it big by following the straight and narrow. And his native enterprise would doubtless have attracted the notice of reporters from the *Wall Street Journal* and *Business Week*.

In Russia it was a different story. However sought-after his products were by the buying public, he was officially equated with the American gangster. In order to survive (and thrive), he maintained a low profile and was always just one jump ahead of the law. Fortunately he was able to grease enough bureaucratic palms to assure protection for a good long time. Illicit success caught up with him at last, however, and he was shot for economic crimes.[14]

Can gains ever be worth such terrible risks? Can it be just for a taste of Western-style affluence that underground businessmen of Russia keep trying to make their mark? It would seem not. The degree of invested effort, the persistence, the enthusiasm, the relish for a job well done—these would argue for another motivation. Or, at least, an augmented one.

Yuri Brokhin tells of a petty criminal who once shared a cell with Moscow's arch speculator in gold. There he was privy to the life story, the exploits of a financial wizard so talented he could easily have followed the official paths to success. He did not and was doomed to die. Why had he made such a choice? Was it for the money? No, he said. His burning desire was never for money but, rather, to be *known*—known to the whole world. He had risen from rags to riches. He had done it *his* way. Never mind the rest.[15]

Yes, Horatio, your ultimate protagonist—or misfit—is alive and well and striving in (would you believe?) the Soviet Union. He finds there no myths and models to encourage effort in business and everything to discourage it. Still, the real live Alger article survives.

He can be found in countless other places as well. In some, he is a culture hero. In others, he is a villain. In this nation, today, he is a little of both, with the balance now beginning to swing in his favor as young entrepreneurs of the Baby Boom generation take center stage.

His saga is not and has never been peculiar to nineteenth century America, as many specialists have held. Quite simply, it recounts in economic terms that hero journey which Joseph Campbell, the great mythologist, has called the "one, shape-shifting yet marvelously constant story (told) throughout the inhabited world, in all times and under every circumstance."[16]

As in all mythic journeys, the would-be hero of enterprise receives the "summons to adventure," the challenge to win a more rewarding life. Initially he rejects the summons, fearing the trials that lie ahead. He is given aid in some form or another (for Toàn, the magic whale; for Ragged Dick, the friendly businessman). He is tempted by women, easy money, bad companions. He suffers setbacks and despair. But he surmounts all obstacles through valor and vision. He achieves the conquest of self and rebirth into a newer, larger world.

The hero of Joseph Campbell's journey wears, as he says, a thousand faces. One of them surely belongs to the Alger prototype, the prodigy who succeeds in business against all odds. But let Horatio the yea-sayer describe the hero journey in his own words:

> "Strive and Succeed, the world's
> Temptations flee
> Be Brave and Bold, and Strong
> and Steady be.
> Go Slow and Sure, and prosper
> then you must
> With Fame and Fortune, while
> you Try and Trust."[17]

Or as today's young entrepreneur might well advise, "Go for it!"

2

TRADE

THAT'S HOW CITIES WERE BORN

The commerce and manufactures of cities, instead of being the effect, have been the cause and occasion of the improvement and cultivation of the country.

ADAM SMITH[1]

Where does the entrepreneur, the merchant, the man of business hang his hat? In the city. It is stamping ground and habitat, haven and lure. The old World War I song told it all:

> "How're ya gonna keep 'em
> Down on the farm
> After they've seen Paree?"

Substitute Babylon for Paris; the lure remains. Substitute Ur or Ebla or cities even older, cities so ancient as to be without names, the lure remains. For the village world is a small world, infinitely small and circumscribed. Too small to hold the restless and rootless, the curious and adventurous, the misfits and malcontents. Then as now these managed to escape (or were forcibly ejected) and soon thereafter made tracks for the city. There they found the docks and wharves, the markets and manufactories and shops, and always the crossroads of trade.

As Adam Smith has said: "There are two means of generating wealth: that of agriculture or that of commerce."[2] The talented and obstreperous, given half a chance, are likely to choose the latter. And commerce is always the wealth of cities.

Yet the *image* of City rarely includes the freight yard or warehouse, the commercial underpinning of life, and it is curiously divorced from vulgar striving. Instead, the image is architectural and color coordinated.

> "Thine alabaster cities gleam,
> Undimmed by human tears,"

was Katherine Lee Bates's nineteenth-century vision of America the beautiful. In other poesy, cities are "rose red" or "white walled" or "golden." They are "topless towered" and "pinnacled." They are places of refuge:

> ". . . I saw a city invincible to the attacks of the whole of the rest of the earth . . ."[3]

sang Walt Whitman, calling his image The New City of Friends. For City is always holy, too, the beginning place, the locus of utopia.

> "Let there be one man who has a city obedient to his will, and he might well bring into existence the ideal polity about which the world is so incredulous . . ."[4]

said Plato, confidently, in his *Republic*. (Hard to imagine the obstreperous and talented conforming to anyone's will!)

St. Augustine wrote about the City of God, which may have been Heaven or, perhaps, the New Jerusalem invoked in the Book of Revelations.

City is also apostrophized as Heroic, Proud, and Rich. Literary convention, of course, requires that the *source* of riches be tactfully overlooked. (Carl Sandburg's ode to Chicago, "hog butcher of the world," is an exception.)

There is a counterimage, equally mythic and outsized. City is Dirty, Sinful, and Corrupting. Thomas Jefferson thought the American republic needed cities the way a human body needs running sores. Writing of the deplorable effects of the Industrial Revolution, John and Barbara Hammond inveighed against "treadmill cities where the daylight never broke upon the beauty and wisdom of the world."[5] Even Karl Marx, that lifelong urbanite, advocated "a more equable distribution of the population over the country."[6] Cambodian Communists in recent years took the words of the master to heart—with what results the world now knows. Whatever image of City you prefer, we have cities in plenty and getting more all the time.

Lewis Mumford, who in the 1960s wrote much about city life, located its beginnings in the village, in a central meeting place for people with "many other reasons for assembly than merely doing business." For him the city is the "chief container of culture." Indeed, a new kind of life was brought into being with cities and now, he says, the world itself has become a giant city. Ideally, then,

> "We must conceive of the city not primarily as a place of

business or government, but as the essential organ for expressing and actualizing the new human personality. . . . Not industry but education will be the center of their [city dwellers]activities . . . while the city itself provides a vivid theatre for the spontaneous encounters and challenges and embraces of daily life. . . . The best economy of cities is the care and nurture of men."[7]

And yet, in his view, Amsterdam is the most beautiful and humane of all cities. It was, alas, planned for business and by businessmen. ("The commercial spirit at its best," Mumford concedes.) Another glorious city by worldwide consensus is Venice, also built by and for commerce.

ARCHITECTURAL UTOPIAS

Not all cities are planned. Most, in fact, grow by haphazard accretion unless catastrophe or urban renewal make possible a revision on the foundations of what has been. Yet, cities planned from scratch constitute the architect's utopia.

No one has planned with greater enthusiasm than Paolo Soleri.[8] From his Arizona atelier come designs for cities which thrust up rather than *out*. He envisions cities built to hold a million souls in a setting so "miniaturized" and "complex" (to use his favored terms) that the cultural center is within equal walking distance for each citizen. His is always a *bounded* city, without suburbs, so that citizens may enjoy a wild and unsullied countryside. It is a city without specified location or reason for being other than that of life enhancement—or, perhaps, "personality actualization," to use Lewis Mumford's phrase. There are, to be sure, provisions for "automated factories" consigned to deep, subterranean lairs. Even the design for a huge artificial cave, intended as intellectual refuge for a community of scholars, makes room for industry—underground and well separated from the cerebral denizens above stairs. It is a sort of commercial afterthought. One thing is forgotten. Automated or not, factories do require human attention and human care.

Somebody will have to spend waking hours underground. And who wants to be a troglodyte?

Let us suppose, just for the sake of argument, that managers of these anonymous factories are able to attract the necessary personnel, and suppose these same workers, after toiling all day underground, want to commute to homes in the countryside. How then does the architect prevent the formation of unwanted suburbs? How can he make people do what is presumably good for them? And just what is good, anyway? Who says?

In recent years, many large corporations have moved their headquarters out of large cities and into suburbia—or even into exurbia. Among the advantages projected for such relocations are the lower tax structures, diminished stress, and the beauty of the surroundings. Union Carbide left New York to build its mammoth quarter-mile-long industrial castle on 674 acres of country land near the small Connecticut city of Danbury. Offices for the 3,000-member work force were decorated to suit individual or group tastes. A cafeteria complex now includes six dining rooms, each with its unique ambiance. There is a bank and a sophisticated general store on the premises. And yet, says architecture critic Paul Goldberger, despite all the comfort, convenience, and beauty, "this remains a compound cut off not only from the life of New York, but even from the life of Danbury."[9] Do some workers yearn for the bustle of city life? It would seem so. Can worker happiness be ensured through architecture, low taxes, and scenery? How to make people want what, presumably, they ought to want?

One of Soleri's "arcologies" can be seen on an Arizona plateau near Scottsdale where it has been in the building process for over fifteen years. As a model for humane urban living, one which does not encroach on the environment, it attracts quantities of idealistic student labor and an occasional cultural event. There are, alas, few permanent residents occupying its complex and miniaturized apartments. For while dreams are by-products of city life, dreams do not a city make. Art does not a city make. Commerce does. Only afterward can art enrich what commerce has established. First things first.

BUT HOW?

To put first things first, we must begin at the beginning. We start with the question: What is a city? Is it a city when a thousand or more people decide to settle cheek by jowl? Not necessarily. Not if they are farmers who choose to live close and work afar. That is a village. Ditto people who commute to distant offices. Their community is a suburb, an exurb, or a bedroom town. A city is something more than an exercise in numbers. It always was. Some years ago, Vere Gordon Childe, the then dean of British archaeology, compiled a list of urban attributes. He had in mind the task of the archaeologist who needs to label the ancient settlement sites he unearths.[10]

Monumental architecture, according to Childe, should be the first sign of urban evolution to appear. A ceremonial center, perhaps. Whatever the purpose of construction, the results should be *big*. (From the archaeologist's point of view, monumental building has the unparalleled advantage of being perfectly obvious.) Next, said Childe, there should be in evidence a great art style created by full-time artists, together with craft specialists of all sorts. A city economy cannot be based on hand-to-mouth subsistence but must enjoy a food surplus—its capital, so to speak. He does not mention markets but does plump for foreign trade. As to size, he stipulates at least 5,000 residents. There should be available for their use numerical notation and/or writing, together with predictive science.

Needless to say, not all urban complexes of the distant past fill Professor Childe's bill in every particular. There are, however, two of his criteria which appear to be essential and universal. The first is a class-structured society and the second is a state form of government. Archaeological evidence for the first can be rather easily read in the range of offerings found in graves and in the varying size and richness of dwelling remains. These bespeak a population of haves and have-nots, of highborn and low, of ins and outs, of demands which stimulate supply.

If evidence of rank can be tied to evidence of craft specialists (with all the sense of exclusiveness specialization fosters), of religious specialists with their own clerical axes to grind, of foreign folk along with foreign goods, then there must be on hand leaders responsible for keeping all these diverse interests and factions and moralities in reasonable balance, reasonable harmony. A simple tribal chief and council of elders will not be able to control or motivate this volatile mix. Chiefs and councilors (whether wholly religious or wholly political or some mixture of both) must be transformed into officeholders who report to superior officeholders. And there you have the chain of command, the bureaucracy in full cry. "You can't fight city hall!" must surely have been the first urban plaint.

The appearance of a city hall marks the beginning of the state—that ultimate in political complexity—for cities were the first states. And they are at the heart of civilization.

GETTING FROM THERE TO HERE

Difference, variety, diversity. These are key words. Cities are essentially havens for people who, unlike village folk, are not all alike. They may live on the food produced by village labor but they themselves are emancipated from the fields.

How is difference created? What turns a village into a city? Many explanations have been proposed, each one meant to be a "prime mover" in the transition to civilized society. Consider these:

Irrigation farming. Guaranteed, say proponents, to produce a food surplus and social classes as well. In any given piece of real estate, after all, there is only so much fertile land with easy access to water. Those who have it are richer than those who do not. Simple.

(Maybe not so simple. The archaeological record reveals that big hydraulic systems seem to follow *the creating of cities, not the other way around. And the newly uncovered site of Tell Leilan in northern Mesopotamia reveals civilized beginnings fully as ancient as those in the south and based on rain-watered rather than irrigation farming.)*[11]

War. Conquerors certainly outrank the conquered and can lay down the law to them as well.

(In some instances, yes. It must be said, however, that walls—those tip-off defensive structures—more often than not come after *the development of the city.)*

New technology. Professor Childe considered the invention of metallurgy, with its specialists and created wants, a sort of economic prime mover in the Middle East.

The tribal chief. Lewis Mumford saw in this personage a political prime mover, particularly if he happened to be bolstered by religious charisma.

Religion. Never underestimate the power of the sacred to draw people to a central place, to motivate different sorts of individuals and make them all one in the bosom of the deity.

Trade. It has, say proponents, the advantage of introducing new ideas along with new goods slowly, painlessly. It constitutes a kind of contact with foreign folk while keeping them at arm's length.[12]

As the old saying goes, "You pays your money, and you takes your choice." Some choices are, nevertheless, more popular than others. In academic circles there has been considerable resistance to the notion of trade as prime mover on the road to civilization. Trade smacks altogether too much of vulgar material motivations and present-day concerns for personal profit. Never mind that trade—especially when the world was young—required courage of the trader, a quick and questing mind, and eagerness to reach out to the new. Such attributes better please modern tastes when coupled to science, religion, or art.

Besides, any mention of "trader" conjures up images of individual human beings. Dare we credit far-reaching social change to personal intervention? Dare we link great events to great men? Especially when this connection cannot be conclusively demonstrated in the archaeological record. Therefore, some specialists admonish, let us think process and not event. Let us think networks, not men. Certainly not the entrepreneur.

A GIANT STEP BACKWARD

And yet, what shall we do about those troubling artifacts in the cities and even in the villages of prehistory? Those objects made from materials not to be found on the local scene. How can we explain their presence?

Somebody brought them, the experts will concede. But not in any way reminiscent of modern trading practices. We must never imagine that ancient peoples exchanged goods in the manner customary today or for the same reasons. Neither do traditional people whose lifeways today reflect older patterns.

Case in point:

> It is known that until early in this century pueblo folk of New Mexico and Arizona had diets based mostly on corn and therefore lacking in salt. Village volunteers went on pilgrimages to obtain the precious mineral. While en route, pilgrims were enjoined to chastity, abstinence, and the pious performance of ritual so essential to this sacred task.[13]
>
> Was the quest for salt an economic act? Only partly.

Here is another case in point:

The famous Kula "trade" among people of coastal New Guinea and its outlying islands is really not trade at all. It is a kind of religious and political event involving the exchange of shell "trophies." Great seaborne expeditions are organized to carry shell arm bands from one point on a huge compass to another. Shell necklaces travel in the opposite direction, always from one Kula partner to another, describing great circles over time.

It is true that, in the wake of these dramas, a good deal of ordinary barter takes place, but that is beside the point. Barter is only incidental. Kula is wealth enhancing, but more importantly, it is *worth* enhancing, and it is at the service of the *group*.[14]

In primitive societies, according to this view, trade—indeed the entire economy—is deeply "embedded" in more important institutional contexts, in family, religion, rule. It took modern times to jolt economies free of such constraints and make the profit motivation transcendent.

Some archaeologists believe they can demonstrate such "embeddedness" in the record of prehistory. By plotting the distribution of exotic goods in a given area, they believe they can demonstrate whether those goods were obtained by pilgrimage or through successive exchanges along boundary lines, village to village, each group keeping some of the commodity and passing the rest down the line until the surplus was exhausted.[15] Such a process is thought to approximate the Kula model.

Better forget trade as a prime mover—so goes this line of thinking—when, in its earliest appearances, it has nothing whatever to do with the economy.

Another group of experts is not so sure. Its members hold that at least some motivations for trade were in the beginning exactly what they are today: you have something I need; I have something you need, so let's swap. Man to man. Need to need. They do not deny the reality of pilgrimage or Kula. They do not question the complexity of motivations. They merely insist on offering another dimension. So what if the entrepreneur covers his archaeological tracks? This seeming lack of evidence does not serve to rule out his existence. Not, at least, in their view.

And there is something more. If we are not to see the past through the lens of the present, they say, we should also be careful about using the lens of the primitive. For the patterns of *some* preliterate cultures do not and cannot represent them all.

There are many patterns which do not fit the mold. Consider that of the capitalistic Yurok whose culture hero, the lucky and plucky Toàn, we met earlier. And then there are the Bigfella Men of New Guinea.

THE NEW GUINEA ENTREPRENEUR REVISITED

Like the Bigfella Men observed by Ben Finney in the eastern highlands, the Kapauku of the west are now and have always been devoted to business. Indeed, says Leo Pospisil, who has studied them on and off for twenty years, they were traditionally primitive capitalists to whom the concept of the gift was unknown and everything had its price in shell money.[16] Since there were no shells in the highlands, enterprising Kapauku traders, usually alone, journeyed to the coast for them. There they dealt with people who were, like themselves, keen traders but also (and unlike themselves) headhunters and cannibals. The unlucky Kapauku trader, says Pospisil, "might be taken as a commodity for which no price was paid." Even so, hope of gain outweighed fear. For gain could be considerable. There were to be obtained on the coast certain large bailer shells especially prized in the highlands. A man could hide these shells in the limestone cliffs, awaiting the day when supplies were low and prices rose accordingly. The canny speculator might well reap a profit of 200 percent.

While not exactly a pacific folk, the Kapauku would always rather trade than fight. And they did so constantly not only among themselves (for pigs, raw materials, manufactured articles), but with neighboring tribes (for wild game, wholly missing from their part of the Kamu Valley.) A chain of individual transactions regularly brought red ochre, palm wood, and crafted implements of serpentine and jadeite from the northeast. From yet another direction came salt. From the coast came shells, iron axes, and machetes. To the coast went dogs, net bags, and tobacco. All these goods were carried by individual traders for short distances and then exchanged with neighbors for other commodities. If this is down-the-line trade, it is certainly disembedded from contexts familial, religious, or political. "I need this," says the Kapauku trader or fabricator of raw material. "I want to do it for my own benefit." No mention of the group.[17]

So versed in the lexicon of trade are the Kapauku that when the Dutch moved into their valley in 1954 they were able to exploit the event to their advantage. A few of the boldest entrepreneurs, says Dr. Pospisil, chartered their own airplanes for trading expeditions—they who not too many years before had fled in panic at the sound of engines. By 1962, when Indonesia supplanted the Dutch as colonial administrators, the Kapauku had spread all over western New Guinea and were negotiating every twentieth-century currency with ease and aplomb.

Never mind the nose plugs and penis sheaths (which constituted proper attire until the advent of Western shorts), the Kapauku seem to us to exhibit attitudes and outlooks characteristic of modern times. It is not just the profit orientation, it is the unvarnished secularity, the pragmatic approach to life and change that have a familiar ring. Clearly, their economy is a "disembedded" one.

Of course, there were no cities prior to the arrival of Europeans. And it must be admitted that—however dominant a place in life trade held in highland New Guinea—it did not there constitute the stepping-stone to civilization. It was not *the* prime mover.

Perhaps there never was *a* prime mover except in our imaginations. And, indeed, why should a single cause bear the entire responsibility for an effect, especially one so important and consequential for life on earth? Instead of a prime mover, why not multiple movers? Better yet, why not a *recipe* for civilization? We merely stipulate ingredients and then expect the proportions to vary over time and place. For the sake of brevity (and also levity), we might follow the formula for the bride's dress—with some adjustments. Thus:

> Something old,
> Something new,
> Something borrowed,
> And some glue.

The "glue" represents, of course, the binding force of style common to a given people—of a common purpose or soul or ethos. (Oshkosh is not Atlanta, after all. New York and Los Angeles are not the same. It is as much a matter of outlook as of location.) Whatever the proportion of the ingredients, whatever the vessel of meaning in which they are mixed, the "something new" clearly must include trade.

To demonstrate we shall have to return to the Middle East where the record of city beginnings can be seen. Call in the archaeologists.

PREMIER PERFORMANCES

> "Joshua fit the battle of Jericho,
>   Jericho, Jericho,
> Joshua fit the battle of Jericho,
> And the walls came tumblin'
> down."

So goes the old spiritual in praise of a Biblical event which occurred around 1250 B.C. The walls said to have fallen at the blast of Joshua's trumpets were not the first ones built at Jericho although they were erected on the foundations of the first walls. Those may well be the oldest in the world, for they were constructed some ten thousand years ago. And constructed solidly of stone nearly six feet thick and at least thirteen feet high (that is all that survives today). The walls surmounted a very considerable man-made ditch and included a stone watchtower more than thirty feet high with an internal flight of stone steps. There were associated water tanks and grain "bins." And all this for ten acres of round, mud-brick huts whose inhabitants were not far beyond the nomadic, hunting life of their forebears.[18]

Never mind that. If Jericho was not a city, it was certainly no overgrown village, either, but a town, perhaps the world's oldest. The very existence of the walls says "town." Their construction had to be planned. The labor of building them had to be directed. The workers had to be fed. That took considerable organization. It was monumentality for fair.

Why a wall? What needed protection? The location speaks to that. Jericho is an oasis, made so by three powerful never-failing springs. The land around them spreads in an alluvial fan down into the Jordan Valley. It is rich land. Harvests of barley and wheat must have been plentiful. Were there wanderers in the area—shepherd folk perhaps—to cast covetous eyes on Jericho's bounty? Was it against them the walls were built?

There is more. In Jericho itself have been found quantities of salt, sulfur, and bitumen (good for waterproofing baskets; Jericho's early occupants made no pottery). The source for these minerals is not to be found anywhere near the town. They came from the Dead Sea. Jericho held goods brought from even greater distances: shells from the Red Sea, turquoise from the Sinai, and from Anatolia, five hundred miles distant, greenstone and obsidian. It is in layers dating to 8300 B.C. that the first obsidian is found. In those days no material was more precious than this volcanic glass. Nothing makes better weapon stone. "What steel is to us," says anthropologist Robert Colbean "obsidian was to the ancients."[19]

TRADE

The fertile Middle East has no sources of obsidian. There is none to be found in the Levant, in Egypt, in Syria, or in Mesopotamia. The big obsidian centers are located in Ethiopia, Armenia, in the Zagros Mountains, and in Anatolia, now modern Turkey. Obsidian has the virtue of easy identification by way of its trace elements.[20] These pinpoint the Anatolian source for the weapon stone in Jericho. How was it brought? By down-the-line trade? Possibly. There is another alternative. Perhaps the shepherds, those hovering nomads, alternated trade with raids and, between hostilities, transported many goods in exchange for Jericho grain. The pattern is still followed by Bedouins of the desert and in many other parts of the Middle East.[21]

Anthropologist Frank Hole has written of nomadic folk in Iran today, marginal people of little importance in the tribal scheme of things. Lacking land, lacking large herds, they take to business—to buying and selling and the carrying trade—in order to survive among more affluent and traditional neighbors. As it is now, perhaps it may always have been.[22]

Some two hundred or so miles north in Syria stood another Neolithic town, larger and even better fixed than Jericho, though unwalled. The "tell," or earth mound that covered it and gave it a name, Abu Hureyra, has recently been excavated by Andrew M.T. Moore and his colleagues in hopes of retrieving the past before its obliteration under the rising waters of a nearby dam.[23]

As old as Jericho, with the same sequence of occupation—from those of mainly hunting people to those of mainly farming folk—Abu Hureyra housed thousands of people in its heyday (c. 6500 B.C.). They made use of the same sorts of trade goods found in Jericho—with two interesting additions. One was soapstone from the Zagros Mountains. This would be essential in years to come for the manufacture of cylinder seals. Another was green malachite. This mineral was found powdered and stored in shells. (Eye shadow for elegant ladies, perhaps?)

If we envision Jericho as an oasis stronghold, a caravan

stop, we can imagine Abu Hureyra as a market town. To find a city we must travel north again, this time to the Konya Plain in Turkey.

THE FIRST CITY

"Hüyük" is Turkish for earth mound, or "tell," and the mound of Çatal is a huge one, covering thirty-two acres and rising fifty feet in height. City upon city accumulated here over a period of about a thousand years, from 6500 B.C. to 5650 B.C. It is certain to be older still; excavations have not yet plumbed beginnings.[24]

The architecture of Çatal Hüyük more closely resembles that of Pueblo Indians of the American Southwest than of its Neolithic contemporaries. Rooms were entered by way of a ladder from the roof, and the whole was built up— apartment level by apartment level—rather like the typical modern condominium.

Professor James Mellaart was able to excavate only one portion of the site. He believes it to have been the religious quarter of the city, with priestly residences and shrines. On shrine walls were modeled the heads of bulls and rams and figures of the mother goddess. There were many murals, including one remarkable view of the city itself with erupting volcanoes in the background.

From these volcanoes were obtained the marvelous stones—marbles and alabasters, obsidian and green-stones—which workers of Çatal Hüyük fashioned into ceremonial weapons, exquisite vessels, and the highly polished mirrors used by the women of Çatal Hüyük in applying their cosmetics. Not only malachite eyeshadow, but "rouge" made of ocher mixed with fats has been found.

All of these artifacts come from priestly burials. The workshops and weaving rooms and factories must lie elsewhere in the unexcavated portions of the mound. That some citizens could specialize in ritual activity, emancipated from the labor of field or loom, that they could use and adorn themselves with beautiful things made by others goes far to explain why James Mellaart calls this a city. It was (so he believes) not only control of the obsidian trade but also the export of manufactured articles which served to make Çatal wealthy and sophisticated.

Export. That sounds suspiciously modern. Were there merchants in Çatal Hüyük? We might not recognize their countinghouses and workshops if we were to see them. Was Çatal visited by contingents of farmers from outlying villages sent to procure goods for home consumption? Was merchandise consigned to caravans of nomads? There is no record of either possibility. We know only that the raw materials were brought to Çatal, transformed at Çatal, exported by Çatal in operations complex enough to make it the center of the Neolithic world and perhaps a prototype for cities yet to come.

IF NOT BEGINNINGS, THEN ENDINGS

The appearance of trade goods in earliest cities is no longer an occasion for surprise. They are everywhere, even in ancient village settings. We do not know who carried the goods. Nor do we know just how ideas, traveling with goods, figured in the formation of cities. There is one thing that can be traced, however, and that is the demise of cities which occurs with the end of trade.

For a glimpse of this, we must move to periods more recent in time, to the long-drawn-out end of Rome and its empire in Europe. Readjust focus, if you please.

Assaults by barbarians, the slowing of tribute, economic mismanagement, rampant inflation; all these served to account for Rome's steady decline. Crime and chronic shortages in the mother city and in many other cities of the empire sent aristocrats scurrying to their country seats or villas. Bit by bit, these estates became agricultural islands turned inward, and laborers in the villas (the original villains) were tied to the soil. By the fifth century Europe could no longer claim great cities. Most formerly urban centers had shrunk into citadels, walled enclosures protecting the great homes of local rulers, the clergy, and the servants of both. Nothing resembling a middle class remained.

Because of barbarian peoples surging across a by now wholly agricultural landscape, trade ground to a halt. Who, after all, would chance taking a vessel up one or another of the great rivers or around the coast? Who would venture overland in a caravan when such rash behavior courted capture or worse? (Think of old-time movie westerns and wagon trains across the prairie.) The Germanic hordes, of course, coveted the *things* and the *life* of the cities—and thought they could simply take all they wanted and settle in. What they very nearly achieved was the destruction of that way of life. All trade north of the Rhine was abandoned in the sixth century. The resulting dearth of luxury imports then prompted Scandinavian rovers—the dreaded Vikings—to go in search of them. With a further depression of trade.

In the seventh century, the rise of Islam cut off all contacts with Byzantium and the Middle East and strangled trade in the southern parts of Europe. But because of high demand, two sorts of commodities continued to trickle along the old trade routes. These were salt and slaves. It was a trade conducted largely by "guest" people: foreigners, Jews, and Moslem converts. By maintaining connections with Spanish Moslems, they also had access to a few luxury goods, such as incense, which they procured for European churchmen. When the Vikings muscled in on the slave trade, it increased appreciably. (They had, after all, the whole Slavic hinterland on which to draw.) During one five-year period of the ninth century, they displayed more than ten thousand slaves in the great market of Cordoba.[25]

Goods necessary for prestige were often sought by agents in the service of local chieftains and petty kings who, when luxuries grew increasingly short, did try to stabilize currency, did try to protect whatever merchants could be found in ports and along the routes of travel. They also required these same merchants to pay many tolls, taxes, and tributes, thus effectively discouraging the very trade they wished to promote (a contradictory message often relayed to the modern businessman).

The church had its own means of discouraging trade. In the clerical view, one lived this life in hope of life to come, and God preferred those who did without. Therefore, what good was there in seeking to better one's lot, to acquire worldly goods, or to rise above one's station? Anybody who did so disturbed the ordained plan and so merited penalty and condemnation. Double ditto for those who encouraged and catered to frivolous wants. Beware the salesman, so to speak.

STAGING A COMEBACK

Trade was at its lowest ebb in the late 800s. Only one trading center, one real city existed at that time in Europe, and that was Venice, a republic when republics had long since gone out of style. Driven onto marshy islands by successive barbarian invaders, deprived of farms on the mainland, the people of Venice turned their faces to the sea and made trade their livelihood, their politics, and (it was said by envious or disgruntled contemporaries) their religion as well.

Yet, by the end of the next century, a score of trading and also manufacturing cities had appeared, among them Genoa, Pisa, Bruges, Florence, Ypres, Ghent. How did it happen?

Because of the revival of trade.

Throughout these dark times there were in the countryside, along with the "foreign" people (all merchants were considered foreign), vagabonds of various ilk: dispossessed freeholders, disinherited younger sons of minor nobility, runaway serfs. They learned to live by their wits. By brigandage, suggests historian Henri Pirenne, but also by supplying local needs, by carrying wheat to a starving village, for example. Without feudal obligations or homes, they were outside the laws of the land and those of the Church as well. (Their role was rather similar to that of the nomads whose presence we have already imagined around Jericho and along the great travel lanes of the Middle East.)

Eventually, says Pirenne, these vagabonds clubbed together in great cart caravans and traveled regular circuits. Fairs and markets were developed around their visits and fairgrounds were set aside for them. Eventually each group of merchants chose to make its home base outside the walls of one fortified citadel or another and eventually walled its own quarters there. Along the circuits of trade true cities began to blossom. Some were even pioneered in the hinterland by merchant consortia.

So began the beautiful medieval city which Lewis Mumford hails as the ideal model of cities anywhere. However empty his belly, the citizen could feast his eyes on beauty everywhere.

There was beauty because prosperous merchants paid the artists for it. Indeed, they planned in every way for the health, safety and sustenance of their cities. For, in spite of the opposition of landed dukes and princes, they came at last to manage and govern their own in a way and with a purpose quite different from the familiar feudal style. "The air of the city makes free."[26] So ran a German proverb of the time. It echoes the sentiments expressed in another city, thousands of years earlier. "Even a dog is free when he enters the city of Babylon."[27]

In spite of the condemnation of the Church, medieval merchants maintained an ardent piety focused on their special municipal saints, shrines, and cathedrals; and they lavished them with rich gifts. So they glorified the city, their city, in which business could again be done.

AMERICAN BEGINNINGS

In the annals of American mythology, no symbol is more cherished than that of the Pilgrim Father in search of religious liberty. We have quite forgotten the consortia of English businessmen, who were willing to establish these dissidents in settings of their choice, more or less, and to maintain them there, all in hopes of turning an eventual profit. Most European countries were busy doing the same.

The original hope lay, not only in the resources of the new land (mostly grain, it was assumed at first, or dried fish) which settlers would produce in abundance, but also in the nature of their needs. They would constitute a market for the mother country's manufactured products: a mercantilist tit for tat.

This worked very well for the Virginia colony—especially after tobacco became the major crop. It worked less well for the colonies in New England. The land was not bountifully fertile, the climate was harsh, and the crops were few. There was a brief boomlet in furs (a sort of mini-gold rush) until the animals fled or were hunted to extinction.

In 1641 the civil war in England cut off the mother country's support, and New Englanders resolved to trade elsewhere. They had to in order to survive. In short order, the shipmasters of Boston became indispensable to the planters of the West Indies. They brought food of all kinds so planters could concentrate on sugarcane, which Boston ships then carried home for distillation into rum. They ran the slave trade and even a flourishing carrying trade, transporting passengers and goods from New England to the southern colonies and back again. They pinned their profit to low costs, ever better ships, faster (and therefore cheaper) runs, and a willingness to "trye all ports to force a trade."[28]

Boston became the queen city of Colonial America. Its broad avenues teemed with foreigners, including merchants whose cases were tried in special maritime courts. It was, after all, a merchant's town. The Puritan Fathers, ever concerned that trade might be dangerous to the soul, were forced at last to come to terms with the new order of things— with businessmen on their way to becoming merchant princes. It could not be otherwise, holds the geographer, James Vance:

"Wholesaling and cities came to America on the Mayflower and were as much tools of pioneering as axe and hoe . . . Trade did not grow out of American economic development, but rather it induced that development."[29]

Colonial sea towns supplied by inland market centers multiplied: Salem, Charleston, later Philadelphia and New York. Inland cities followed, always at the unraveling points of trade. The merchants—and the peddlers (America's original traveling salesman)—made their way outward into the wilderness. Wherever a mining settlement opened, wherever a riverboat landing received pioneers, there were the commercial scouts with a surprisingly rich array of goods to offer.

Already, before the colonies were scarcely thirty years old, some hopeful cities had diminished into sleepy towns. Such a city was New Haven founded by Puritan merchants, both as a refuge for God-fearing men and a prospective port for the fur trade. It was one of the first casualties of commerce. Merchants of the town were able to scrape together just one rich cargo of furs. Alas, the ship was lost and with it many hopes. One Samuel Maverick, a considerable man of business, would later say, "The merchants are either dead or gone away. The rest have gotten to their farms."[30] There would be, in times to come, many such civic casualties.

They are occurring still as the pathways of commerce change their course. Many cities today, once busy and populous, are waning in size while others see only growth ahead. One of these "cities of the future" is Tampa, Florida, whose Mayor Bob Martinez exulted on television, "We are no longer just a tourist attraction. We are a banking center. We are a port city for ships, rail lines, airplanes. We are the commercial hub of the area. Now all we need is a baseball team!"[31]

Instead of a ziggurat for merchants to adorn, instead of a gothic cathedral, Tampa will build a great sports stadium paid for by private funds and because of civic pride. Who knows? She may one day join the ranks of the mighty, all those ancient and not-so-ancient queen cities of trade: Ur, Ebla, Byblos, Alexandria, Rhodes, Samarkand, Venice, Bruges, London, Boston, New York, Hong Kong.

It is to catapult their own cities into that illustrious roster—or, more practically, to keep them alive—that mayors of U.S. cities have now taken to the international hustings. They are currently hopping around the world more energetically than your average ambassador, trying to drum up foreign business. They know what officials at the higher, more abstract levels of government often seem not to know: that without commerce there are no jobs. Without jobs, there is no city.[32]

A PREVIEW OF COMING ATTRACTIONS

What next? And where? Business today is poised to participate in the conquest of space. Some groups of investors have even launched their first hopeful rockets. Others are helping to finance the voyages of the NASA space shuttles. McDonald Douglass and Ortho Pharmaceuticals sent their own commercial traveler aloft on the August 1984 flight of Discovery. He supervised the production of certain drugs best synthesized in a weightless environment. Flights to test products of 3M Corporation, Space, Ltd., Dupont, and many others are scheduled. A cargo-booking service awaits the chance to go into operation. Fairchild Industries plans one day to construct an "industrial park in space" and lease facilities there. Corporations have been formed to develop remote-sensing devices, earth-survey satellites, space services in contexts and under conditions now only imaginable and in some unimaginable as yet.[33]

When enough commercial uses of space are developed, when enough jobs are waiting to be filled, then there will be built a new city in space. It *will* be a planned city, not with a utopian goal in view, not directed by somebody's vision of how men *should* live, but by practical considerations of how they *can* live in an environment hostile to life. And above all, how they can work to make their city thrive.

Several plans are now on the drawing boards. One of these describes an enormous wheel whose eternal spin will provide a comfortable gravitational pull for residents living and working around the rim. In this tubular ring will be houses and parks; lakes and playing fields; schools and hospitals; shopping centers, theaters, restaurants, amusement parks; offices and industries; warehouses and docks.

Jump the decades and see it in your mind's eye, spinning out there against the backdrop of night—a bright, manmade pebble holding life where life was never meant to be. An oasis city. A city walled against nothingness. A refuge city. And something more. A symbol of human valor and human vision.

But it is—it will be—a working city, as well, and it is there because it is a paying proposition. It is there because industry is there. It is there to send forth merchant ships to "trye all ports" in search of trade, in search of new goods and new ideas that will turn a profit and, only incidentally, may enlarge civilization itself and the quality of life on earth.

For some, reality may tarnish image. Like it or not, that's how civilization began—and begins. Over and over again.

3

RECORDS

BOOKKEEPING BEFORE POETRY: THAT'S HOW WRITING WAS BORN

> Though business accounts may seem a derogatory criterion of civilization, they make quite a good one.
>
> D.H. TRUMP[1]

When the boss says, "Take a letter, Miss Smith," he does not expect to dictate undying prose. His secretary does not expect to transcribe undying prose. And the letter's recipient could be more than a little put off by undue felicity of expression, subtle nuance, or extensive vocabulary. Leave all that to the literati, they would agree. It is quite enough to see that quantities, times, numbers are nailed down. Thus:

October 5, 1985

Dear Sir or Madam:

Thank you for your interest in our firm. We are prepared to ship your order of 89 high-gauge steel widgets at a price of $500 per widget. Shipment will be made on our receipt of your check.

Yours truly,

John Blank
Vice President, Sales

The protocols of business communication forbid flights of personal feeling or the employment of airy phrases. Such was the tradition 250 years ago when Daniel Defoe wrote the first how-to of modern business, *The Complete English Tradesman*. That the soul of a novelist could share houseroom with the spirit of business enterprise may come as something of a surprise to those who associate the name with *Robinson Crusoe, Moll Flanders,* or *A Diary of the Plague Years*. Nevertheless, such was the case with Daniel, son of James Foe, a tallow chandler of London. He neither forgot nor relinquished his early enthusiasms even after styling himself more elegantly as *De*foe.

In his comprehensive manual of trade, he advises the young businessman as follows:

"A tradesman's letters should be plain, concise, and to the

purpose. . . . He that affects a rumbling and bombast style and fills his letter with compliments and flourishes makes a very ridiculous figure in trade."[2]

And he offers clear examples. Never thus, he says:

"Sir . . . the destinies having so appointed it, and my dark stars concurring, that I, who by nature was framed for better things, was put out to trade . . . [but] . . . I am [now] entered upon my business and hereby let you know that I shall have occasion for the goods hereafter mentioned."[3]

But rather thus:

"Sir, Being obliged by my master's decease to enter immediately upon business, and consequently open my shop without coming up to London. . . . I have sent you a small order as underwritten. . . . I have enclosed a bill of exchange, payable to your order, at one-and-twenty days sight.

Your humble servant,"[4]

Guess which order the wholesaler would be likely to fill, and the same day, too.

EARLIER CORRESPONDENCE

Four thousand or so years ago in the Middle East, men and women of business were following similar principles in their business writing: Get the facts straight, get the numbers straight, and never mind the flourishes. Here is a sample:

"A message from Silla-Labbum and Elani. Tell Puzur-Assur, Amua, and Assur-samsi:
Thirty years ago you left the city of Assur. You have never made a deposit since, and we have not recovered one shekel of silver from you, but we have never made you feel bad about this. Our tablets have been going to you with caravan after caravan, but no report from you has ever come here.

We have addressed claims to your father, but we have not
been claiming one shekel of your private silver. . . . Please
do come back right away or deposit the silver for us. If not,
we will send you a notice from the local ruler and the police,
and thus put you to shame in the assembly of merchants.
You will also cease to be one of us."[5]

The modern debt collector would be hard put to better that
communication. Written on a clay tablet (sealed in its own
clay envelope) the letter was sent by caravan from the city
of Assur on the Tigris River to one of the princely cities in
Anatolia (now modern Turkey) where Mesopotamian merchants had long ago established trading colonies. For the
fine textiles and finished clothing of their various homelands, they received copper, silver, and gold in which the
Anatolians were rich.

We have not yet reached the beginnings of business
correspondence. Four hundred years before the above dun-
ning letter was written, Mesopotamian missives are even
more to the point:

> "Thus says Ur-Utu:
> Say to Ses-Ses,
> Agade-Lugal-Am,
> A man of Agade,
> Must not make purchases!
> Let him return to Irgigi."[6]

Doubtless the salesman had got himself in trouble and was
ordered home lest he squander company funds.

Businessmen and women of the time (c. 2400 B.C.) were
as careful as they are today to "put it in writing." And with
words bearing a truly modern ring. "Fund," "price,"
"equivalent," "capital," "asset." These are just a few of the
terms available in the Mesopotamian lexicon of business.
They pepper, not only business letters, but contracts, tax
receipts, sales and purchase memoranda, inventories, and
instructions to brokers or agents. The instructions of Amae,
a businesswoman of the city of Umma are typical:

"20 minas of wool: Ama-e said to Barag-nita: 'buy.'
15 minas of wool: Ama-e sold it to Barag-nita.
18 minas of wool: Ama-e sold it to Barag-nita
                     when he went to Zabala.
 8 minas of wool: Ama-e has on deposit with
                     Barag-nita from that time."[7]

Zabala was the main port and commercial center of Umma, and minas and talents indicate quantities with equivalents in silver. So we are told by Benjamin Foster, a specialist in Mesopotamian studies.

When Ama-e, businesswoman of Umma, inscribed those instructions to her broker (or had her secretary do the job), she was using the written word in the only way thought appropriate at the time: for the business of business or for the business of government. This had been so for a thousand years, ever since the appearance of the first true tablets bearing inscribed signs. Only recently in her world—since shortly before 2500 B.C. or so by our reckoning—had scribes begun to produce tablets devoted to other sorts of information. One of the earliest yet deciphered (according to Samuel Noah Kramer) is the myth about Father Enlil and his sister, Ninhursag.

Archaeologists can verify this seeming anomaly. In every ancient city site yet uncovered in the Middle East the tablets of business far outnumber those that could be considered literary in nature—myths and legends, prayers, king lists, even personal missives. Indeed, these appear long after the instruments of business are in widespread use and as a sort of afterthought, a new use of an old invention.

Now, one of the markers of civilization has always been (at least in the view of some specialists) the existence of writing, that pinnacle of human creativity. How sad to find the muse "in trade," as it were. What a disappointment for the literati. Archaeologist D.H. Trump, in his excellent survey of Mediterranean prehistory, makes the point:

"Though business accounts may seem a derogatory criterion of civilization, they make quite a good one."[8]

NOW YOU SEE IT, NOW YOU DON'T

Unlike the famous wheel which, once invented, stays in use, writing appears to be a sometime skill, quickly forgotten when times change drastically or civilization-as-we-know-it goes by the board. Case in point: the Dark Ages.

After the power of Rome had finally declined, literacy in medieval Europe became the monopoly of two sorts of beings: men of the cloth and men of business. Very nearly everyone else got along without writing—peasants because they had to, the aristocracy because they wanted to. Upper-class males (who valued their skill in battle) took pride in ignorance. Your average petty baron considered himself too mighty for priestly pursuits and too wellborn for trade. He might not forbid learning to wife or daughter. The woman who could keep manorial accounts, or, at least, read well enough to check up on the clerics who did the job, was an exceedingly useful creature. But this was a feminine ornament. Not for him the taint of cloister or countinghouse.

Not surprisingly, the first medieval schools not strictly intended for the education of priests were those organized by merchants. And it was they who, in the interest of business, began to write in their native Italian, German, French, or English rather than the clerical Latin of the time. Little did they know they were paving the way for literati of the Renaissance. Certainly they were not then given the credit for so doing. Nor very often afterward.

Nor were the mercantile Phoenicians of the ninth century B.C. given much credit by classical Greeks for introducing the subtle alphabet in which the glories of their *Iliad* and *Odyssey*—not to mention the poetry of Hesiod, Pindar, or Simonides—were at last to be preserved. There had once been writing in Aegean lands, two successive forms of it. One (now called Linear B) was found to represent the spoken syllables of an early Greek language. Clerks attached to Mycenaean warlords (around 1400 B.C.) had cobbled the script from a still earlier form of writing invented by the Minoan masters of Crete. Both were lost after savage marauders destroyed one after another of the Mycenaean towns and plunged the Aegean people into a Dark Age of their own.

Unlike the medieval Dark Age, this one was without monastic refuges for learning. And even if there had been such hiding places, what was there to be saved? The inscribed clay "leaves" of Linear B, baked hard in the many conflagrations of the time (1200 B.C.) do little to illuminate the nature of the catastrophe or of the culture that was destroyed. They merely record inventories of food, clothing, slaves, and the bronze gear of war. (The contents of a hundred accountants' waste baskets, says John Chadwick, who has labored at the tablets' decipherment.) No hint of history, much less of song.[9]

TO JOG THE MEMORY, LET ME COUNT THE WAYS

Then, as in classical Greece, the literary muse may have been kept deliberately on the wing. The Homeric Odes (folk memories of vanished times) describe bards who chanted the deeds of gods and heroes, composing on the spot from a wealth of remembered lore. And conservative poets even into the Golden Age cherished the belief that poetry memorized and repeated—worse yet, written down and read— was poetry bastardized and demeaned. The tones, the life, the nuances, the *magic*—all that was killed by the written word. Something written became at once anybody's property, not something uniquely one's own. Besides, writing was the province of lowly bookkeepers and their vulgar accounts.

In some ways, perhaps, they were right. At least in terms of poetry remembered. There is quite a lot that can be retained in the human brain—especially if each line rhymes at the end. That is why nursery doggerel lives for centuries and free verse that is all the rage today will be quite forgotten week after next.

The Inca of Peru were said to have maintained a university of "talking books"—learned professors, each of whom had committed to memory a body of inherited wisdom which he would pass on to a chosen successor. It was merely the numbers which wanted recording. And for the Incas, recording was accomplished by a system of strings and knots called *quipus*. Color indicated *what* was to be recorded: tribute, treasure, numbers of soldiers, goods of various kinds in the government warehouses. A decimal system of knots along the string, all carrying place value, provided documentation for calculations performed earlier by means of pebbles.[10]

Like the Inca, rulers of Dahomey (a West African kingdom, now the modern state of Benin) maintained a retinue of remembering bards. And each governmental agreement or transaction took place in the presence of royal wives assigned as witnesses for correct remembering. Things which could not be trusted to memory—numbers of taxpayers, potential draftees, births, deaths—were recorded by pebbles stored in boxes and bags, color coded or labeled with fabric pictures to signify content. There was little danger of tampering or falsification. The "house of the census" was sacred with entry forbidden to all but the king, a few elderly priests, and the successors to whom they bequeathed numerical lore.[11] (One is reminded that in Rome—and in Medieval Europe until 1500 or so—business calculations were performed with pebbles on a counting board. The results were then recorded by way of unwieldy Roman numerals. Arabic number symbols took nearly five hundred years more to catch on.)

Daniel Defoe speaks of a tradesman of his acquaintance who had never learned to read or write and yet had found so efficient a means of keeping accounts that he and his family enjoyed very considerable success. Indeed, he was elected mayor of his town.

This is how he managed. For each of his customers there was a separate drawer in a large chest. Each of these contained sticks of various sizes, shapes, and color—such differences signifying commodities sold. Each stick bore chalk marks and notches, the chalk for sums under a pound sterling, the notches on one side of the stick for single pounds, the other for tens. When a customer came in to settle his account, the tradesman calculated the amount owed by using six spoons. With these he could count as high as thirty-six. Above that number, he was driven to multiply in his head, always by sixes, never higher. Alas, says Defoe, with that ingenuity, the man could easily have become literate and saved the bother. With or without writing, our clever tradesman nonetheless managed to live up to Defoe's highest maxim:

> "A tradesman's books, like a Christian's conscience, should always be kept clean and neat; and he that is not careful of both, will give but a sad account of himself either to God or man."[12]

In the end, it is numbers that cannot be remembered, that must somehow be recorded. What number? Why, whatever one is interested in counting. The Incas counted tribute. The Dahomeans counted heads. Our illiterate tradesman counted sales. People of the ancient Middle East, long before cities appeared, counted their sheep. They counted the measures of seed needed to plant a field in the spring. They counted what they carried in trade and what they brought back home in payment. And they were doing so at least five millennia before their numerical signs developed into written symbols.

BACK TO BEGINNINGS

The understanding of this singular evolution is the work of Denise Schmandt-Besserat of the Center for Middle Eastern Studies, University of Texas. Before publication of her findings, students of ancient history had been puzzled by the business records of Mesopotamia. The marvel always was their sophistication, their completeness. The little pictures incised in clay around 3500 B.C. were crudely made but, in terms of vocabulary, respectably complete. Even the earliest tablets bore signs which were already ideographic, no longer representative merely of things but of ideas as well. Among all the shards and fragments, beginnings were not to be found. Writing seemed to appear at a stroke, full blown and finished. An invention of a single genius? Perhaps diffusion from an unknown source? Or had earliest attempts at writing been made on perishable materials—wood, skin, on the ground itself?

The young Denise Schmandt-Besserat knew all the questions about early Mesopotamian writing but had no intention of supplying answers when, in 1969, she began her doctoral research. It was the many uses of clay in the ancient Middle East which had always intrigued her, and she set out to visit the various museums where there were archaeological collections taken from Neolithic sites, from early villages where men were learning to domesticate plants and animals and settle down beside their fields. (A beginning date around 8000 B.C. is now assigned to this process.) Among all the little clay figures of fat females and crude animals there appeared other constant forms: little "tokens" finger-pinched into shape and then fired. There were spheres, cones, cylinders, round disks, little pyramids, ovoids—about twenty shapes in all.

Artifacts rather like these tokens had been earlier described by Professor A. Leo Oppenheim. His tokens had been associated with the remains of Nuzi, a three-thousand-year-old site in northern Iraq. There they seem to have figured out a full-blown accounting system, a sort of double-entry system, including both tokens and written records of each transaction.

Imagine the shock of finding the tokens and accounting system of 1500 B.C. in simple Neolithic contexts where they had no business being at all! No one had ever made much of them before. In report after archaeological report, the tokens had been dismissed as children's toys, phallic symbols, counters used in gambling (antediluvian poker chips, so to speak). One expert had likened them to suppositories.

Struck by the tokens' universality of appearance as well as their surprising antiquity, Dr. Schmandt-Besserat began to plot distribution. They had been found as far west as Khartoum, at the confluence of the Blue and White Nile, and as far east as the Iranian Plateau; and from what is now southern Turkey to the Indus River in what is now Pakistan. Dates of appearance ranged from 8500 B.C. to 1500 B.C. She consulted the site reports to learn more about the contexts in which the tokens had been found. Often they had been uncovered in heaps as if originally enclosed in containers long since decayed. Often they were located in rooms away from other household artifacts.

MAKING CONNECTIONS

She quickly noted the resemblances between some of the token shapes and certain symbols impressed into earliest Mesopotamian written tablets, perhaps as old as 3500 B.C. The small cone shapes, she thought, could be equated with the Mesopotamian written symbol for number one, the large cone with that for number sixty. The small spherical token seemed to resemble the Mesopotamian sign for number ten and the larger sphere that for number 100 or number 3600.

But what was being counted? Incan *quipus* had been color coded. Dahomean pebble accounts identified by picture appliqué. Perhaps shape would yield a clue.

Building on the work of specialists in early Mesopotamian written symbols, Dr. Schmandt-Besserat eventually deduced that the cones and spherical shapes were units of barley measurement. The cone, she thought, represented a deep bowl and was equatable with the written sign for *ban,* a standard measure for six liters (about one and one-half gallons) of grain. Flat triangular tokens should then represent a fraction of a *ban.* The sphere—perhaps representing a bag full of barley—was the equivalent of the *barriga*—a measure six times larger than the *ban*.

These same tokens—modified by lines or punched holes—would equate with the *iku* and *bur*, units of land measurement. Why? Because area was, in those times, calculated in terms of the amount of seed necessary for its sowing.[13]

Cylinders and disks—the two other shapes most frequently represented in collections—figured in animal tallies, she thought, particularly those for sheep, the most common of the Middle Eastern barnyard roster. Various simple markings on the disks themselves should then indicate sex and age. More complex markings perhaps permitted the reckoning of products derived from sheep: wool, fabric, finished clothing.

Among the twenty or so original tokens were incised ovoids—looking rather like elongated acorns with their caps on. This shape, Dr. Schmandt-Besserat equates with the Mesopotamian ideogram for oil. The shape may represent the watertight skin bags which held perishable or liquid commodities. Oil, certainly, and possibly butter and dates as well. Another of the token shapes—the little pyramid—has been discovered in remains of the Babylonian city of Sippar (dated to about 1900 B.C.) Certain inscriptions describe such tokens as wage dockets, probably meant to identify part-time workers not well known to the boss. That these token shapes are found, as well, in simple agricultural sites as old as ten thousand years says much about the values of a society in which labor is a commodity which need not be given but can be exchanged for grain.

By the time large cities appeared in the Middle East, the ancient accounting system had taken on added intricacy— rather like the move in the Western world from abacus to cash register. Tokens were being made in many new shapes, and the old ones carried many more markings. All to designate newer and better merchandise. Customer demand was not only high but, it appears, ever more sophisticated.

RECORDS

Merchants needed improved ways of keeping track of sales. Such ways were invented.

Tokens, which had been previously strung together loosely or collected in special containers, were now being enclosed in hollow balls of clay. To discourage tampering, each was sealed shut with the impression of a carved cylinder rolled all around the container. (A signature? A notary's stamp? Approval by a government functionary?). Pierre Amiet, the French archaeologist who found such fist-shaped envelopes in early Susa, called them "bills of lading," and their appearance in the Middle East is nearly as widespread as that of the earlier separate tokens. Envelopes—or "bullae"—have been found in temple sites, in administrative centers, and in fine private homes (the merchant's countinghouse?). Dr. Schmandt-Besserat thinks that the bullae may indicate contracts, sales, notes for borrowed funds, as well as mercantile shipments.

There was just one drawback. How could one check the contents of the sealed envelope without breaking it? How recall the exact nature of the debt or quantity of goods transported? Easy. One could affix an extra set of tokens to the *outside* of the sealed envelope. Someone did just that; the evidence has been found.

But why waste tokens? The question must have been asked at once and answered at once because few attached-token envelopes have ever been found. The answer? Simply *impress* the tokens for a given transaction into the damp clay exterior of the envelope before sealing them within. At Nuzi, the 1500 B.C. site mentioned earlier, archaeologists found such an envelope bearing forty-eight impressions exactly matching the forty-eight tokens inside. The entire collection was redundantly described in writing. Clearly, the old-fashioned accountants of Nuzi preferred the methods of yesteryear even though the rest of the civilized world had adopted better means of record keeping. (One thinks of the hold-out businessmen of today, still resisting the inexorable march of the computer.)

Everywhere but Nuzi the envelope of clay had been collapsed into a tablet (its convex shape the one remaining echo of origins). On the damp clay of the tablet, tokens could be impressed. Nobody needed to see the real thing. Eventually scribes took to drawing the token shapes with a stylus.

This was the beginning of writing in the Middle East. The first written symbol was the pictograph of a token. Only afterward came the recognition that pictures might represent other things, other ideas, indeed, the very sounds of the spoken word.

BEGINNINGS ELSEWHERE

Might other ancient systems of writing have followed a similar path of development—from counting to writing, from records to literature? Evolutionary paths have yet to be revealed. Specialists have yet to apply Dr. Schmandt-Besserat's insights to archaeological troves collected in other areas of the world.

Mesopotamian tokens have been found along the Nile, and some forty round clay envelopes have been reported at the 3500 B.C. site of Abydos. We cannot tell whether these artifacts figured importantly in Egyptian commerce or, indeed, had any impact at all on Egyptian thinking; for the earliest recognizable writing in Egypt (dated to about 3100 B.C.) is not a record of business transactions but rather of conquest. On a large stone slab the king of Upper Egypt is shown conquering his rival of the delta region and uniting the two lands. The only things the Egyptians of the time found worth counting were the headless bodies of enemies and the captives of the king's mace.

At the other end of the Middle Eastern world was the Indus River along which flowered the great Harappan civilization. There, too, are found in ancient sites the pinched clay tokens characteristic of Mesopotamian accounting. The writing of the Harappans (what there is of it) turns up as graffiti on pots and in elegant symbols on carved soapstone seals. The connections with business are tenuous at best, for the figures appear to designate titles, proper names, family names.[14]

It is not altogether impossible that the developmental sequence in Mesopotamia might well have sufficed for all adjacent areas, linked as we now know by the ubiquitous token. It is not altogether impossible that the thing-picture, turned in Mesopotamia to business uses, could have prompted others to portray in this manner their own things, ideas, and language sounds.

Some scholars have long suggested that the idea of writing might well have crossed wide steppes to China. Not so, claim the sinologists, preferring to trace earliest written symbols to markings impressed by potters in their wares as long ago as 4500 B.C. Among these signs are some (a rake-like figure, for example) that appear in other ancient writings. And there are many thought to represent number. Dr. K.C. Chang, one of the great American sinologists, nevertheless believes the markings have to do with family identification rather than economic transactions.[15]

When next we see Chinese pictographs (about 1800 B.C.) they are in a city setting, of Shang Dynasty times, a royal setting where they have become part of a complete system of writing turned to the service of divination. For time out of mind Siberian hunting folk and, later, Neolithic farmers of northern China had tried to foresee the future in the shoulder blades of animals. Touched with a hot stone or burning stick, these would pop and crack in ways thought to give answers to questions carefully phrased. Early Chinese writing immortalized the questions which were inscribed directly onto the oracle bone:

> "On the twenty-seventh day Diviner Pin inquires: Should the king conduct a military campaign against the Yi barbarians?"

> "On the twenty-seventh day Diviner Pin inquires: Should the king NOT conduct a military campaign against the Yi barbarians?"[16]

According to Dr. Hung-hsiang Chou some few bones, (also the carapaces and plastrons of turtles) were used exclusively for calendrical records and tables of tribute (the Shang dynasts were conquerors). No evidence has been found so far (as in Mesopotamia) of private accounts, of trade, or of the contracts associated with trade. But trade was certainly being carried on. Among all the celebrations of gods, ancestors, and kings, one finds emblems that depict human figures dangling strings of cowrie shells which in those times served as currency. Just so, Dr. Chang tells us, was the trading profession represented and the kin-groups of merchant-venturers. No doubt leading figures of these lineages carried some importance during Shang Dynasty times. This must be true because, even today, the Chinese word for merchant is *shang jen,* the very word for the people of Shang.

We hear nothing more of merchants—those purveyors and consumers of number—until 219 B.C. when they had become successful enough, and visible enough, for the Emperor Huang-ti to restrict commerce and physically deport shopkeepers. Yet shopkeepers and merchants had long since invented the subtle abacus. And one of the Chinese classics, said to have been compiled by Confucius himself, holds that, before writing, computations were preserved by variously knotted cords—rather like the Peruvian quipus. Certainly shell currency long remained in use. Marco Polo, during his thirteenth century journeys in the Far East, reported the schedule of equivalence: eighty shells equaled one *saggi* of good silver which, in his terms, equaled two Venetian groats or one groat of gold. He also discovered the source of the cowries (the Malay Peninsula) and later traveled there to see it for himself.[17]

NUMERACY AND BUSINESS

Does a cultural preoccupation with trade incline the child of that culture to a love of number? In spite of every obstacle, overseas Chinese of recent times have achieved outstanding success in business and trade. This is a well-known phenomenon in Southeast Asia, and economist Thomas Sowell has described it for us.[18] Less well known, there as here, is the capacity of the Chinese schoolchild to outperform in mathematics the scions of other races and cultures, whatever the affluence of their families.

Such a talent can be observed among simpler people, elsewhere. Anthropologist Leopold Pospisil lived among the New Guinea Kapauku in 1954–1955 before civilization had begun to encroach on their valley. He noted then their passion for numbers and counting. As he said, "They count their wives, children, days, visitors at feasts, and, of course, their shell and bead money."[19] Their numerical system is decimal to number sixty, with 600 and 3600 as higher units. (This combination of decimal and sexagesimal systems reminds us of the sophisticated Mesopotamians.) Of all the pictures of America he showed them, the most popular were those filled with things to count: spectators watching a football game, a skyscraper with many windows, a navy carrier with countable airplanes. The picture of a pretty girl was appreciated only if the subject had a wide smile and the teeth could then be counted.

Years later on one of his return visits, Dr. Pospisil found Kapauku turning this passion for numbers to another use: education. He watched as forty elementary school children were given a stiff test in mathematics. Virtually all made perfect scores. It goes without saying that many go on to university educations and professional life. All do well in business.

CLOSER TO HOME

In 1842 Charles Dickens called America

> "That vast counting house that lies beyond the Atlantic. . . . where everybody is a merchant [and for whom there is a] national love of trade."[20]

Perhaps that accounts for our being a calculating people. Patricia Cline Cohen in her recent book says we became so, that we achieved numeracy only after arithmetic "began to lose its commercial taint." In other words when it attracted a higher-minded clientele. But she adds, "because commerce was no longer restricted to a small segment of the American population." By 1840 "better" people were doing math. Also more of them.[21]

Whatever the reason then—more business or extended uses of numbers—many Americans today base a good part of their lives on number facts. Many of us do read columns of figures every day in the *Wall Street Journal,* and some of us even enjoy them. No one more than J. Peter Grace, chairman and chief executive officer of W.R. Grace and Company, Inc., a firm with many product lines and plants the world over. Edward Meadows, who has written most recently about him, quotes a Grace lieutenant as follows:

> "He [Grace] likes to play with them [numbers], try new relationships, look at them in different ways. We find some surprising things by taking publicly available numbers, pulling them apart, and adding them to other numbers."[22]

It was to Peter Grace that President Reagan turned for an analysis of the U.S. budget and ways in which the government could economize. The blue-ribbon commission Grace headed found 2,478 ways to trim the budget and cut the deficit by some $454 billion dollars.

The announcement of his recommendations was greeted in some quarters by amused smiles and references to the familiar hymn "Amazing Grace." Not only can't we economize, was the general tone of the criticism, but who cares anyway? Aren't petty frugalities somehow demeaning in the face of genuine human want? Isn't a grim concern with numbers just a little vulgar after all? For, truly, can people and numbers ever really mix? Can literature, the humanities, the great ideas, the splendid visions be constrained by calculations? Of course one will concede the importance of numbers in higher mathematics, physics, and medical discoveries; and polls and statistics do serve conveniently to buttress one's argument of the moment. But businessmen? Can they ever do humanity any real, any glorious service?

We have come a long way from Dickens's observation. If some of us enjoy business and numeracy, a great many others emphatically do not. In intellectual America, a seam has opened between its two worlds of the mind. One recalls the "two cultures" theme sounded years ago by C.P. Snow, the British philosopher and novelist. In his view, the gap then lay between science and everything else. Today it appears to divide business from everything else. So it is that members of the intellectual elite approach the nation's balance sheets and their keepers with something of the disdain expressed by Thomas Hamilton, an English traveler, who in 1833 pronounced Americans "a guessing, reckoning, expecting, and calculating people" to whom arithmetic seemed to come "by instinct."[23]

TO COMPUTE OR NOT TO COMPUTE

And yet, the selfsame arbiters of intellectual elegance approach the computer with hushed reverence, quite oblivious to the fact that in America it evolved mainly in the service of business and still finds its chief employment there. Businessmen know that. Professionals in other fields often do not. For them, it is not so much tool as magic, an instant panacea for everything, even chronic dullness. Teachers of social sciences and humanities (where quantification plays a minor role) are regularly urged to pep up their classes with computer magic. "You'd better get with it and achieve computer literacy," goes the exhortation. "The world is changing. You'll be left behind."

The world is changing, to be sure. It is slowly returning by way of the computer to number, to the literal, to what can be quantified. (The literati seem oblivious to the trend.) Information must be tailored to suit the computer and may not be returned without the proper password.

Think for a moment about the public library. One day soon all the books will be put on microfiche, storable in several medium-sized chests of little drawers. Better yet, relegate them to the library computer whence they can be served up on demand and read by way of the client's own handy home computer. Bibliographical data will also be computerized, obtainable only by the "On-Line" search and various other indices. No more can the hopeful researcher, flipping randomly through old-fashioned catalog cards, find unexpected treasure. No longer can he browse happily in the library stacks, dipping into book after book like a butterfly on the wing. The researcher's place, henceforth, will be before his computer, ordering it to gather information, record information, and sort it out in proper form.

But what if the aforesaid antiquated dodo, addicted to the stacks, also thinks by means of the written word, the thoughts shaping slowly on the end of pencil or pen? He'd better keep quiet about it lest he be pegged as hopelessly outdated, rather like the Nuzi accountant still wedded to his old-fashioned tokens.

One may well question the revolution all the same. For there is no change without its unanticipated consequences. Will the achievement of universal computer literacy impair literacy of the other kind?

A great many of us have already moved away from traditional literacy, with or without electronic intervention. Children, so the polls tell us, read ever fewer books even though their ability to take scholastic aptitude tests may be marginally improved. What's the good of reading after all? Television, that tireless storyteller, keeps us entertained and passably well informed. And now we can play with the computer which will serve up games and even illicit adventure as it strives, on our command, to plumb the secrets of other computers. Never mind where.

Why write? The telephone provides instant communication. If for some reason it is not available, if we find ourselves in a foreign country or on a ship at sea, we can always confide our thoughts to a handy recorder and send the tape to our loved ones through the mail. For even those few remaining events requiring the use of a pen—the graceful note of appreciation, condolence, congratulations, regret— a ready solution can be found in any handy variety shop. Commercial cards. Not only do they bear appropriate sentiments, they even simulate human penmanship. With a difference. Unlike the real thing, the printed script is always decipherable.

Let's face it. We have come to prefer the spoken word. Wills and other contracts are now and then put on tape and considered just as legal as the written document. Voiceprints, we are told, are as uniquely ours as thumbprints and more readily obtainable. Any college teacher receives at least one request annually to permit the recording of a term paper. At the end of a difficult grading session, he often thinks more kindly of the request. For, sad to say, each generation of college students writes (and spells) less ably than the one before it. Why not? One in seven American adults is functionally illiterate, so U.S. Department of Education statistics tells us, and that one will soon be two. The National Survey of Educational Progress, in a recent poll of seventeen-year-old high school students found that only 15 percent were able to write a simple business letter requesting the correction of a billing error. When dropouts were added, the level of functional illiteracy was even higher.[24] Do such statistics worry the young? Especially the young who *should* worry? Not much, it would appear. They have found heroes and heroines who have made it plenty big, thank you, without the help of the three R's. As an eight-year-old girl told Linda Stevens of the *New York Post:*

> "I seen *Flashdance.* I ain't no dummy. That girl didn't know nothin' and look at her, she made a million dollars in that movie."[25]

We hear. We watch. Read seldom. Write never. We have almost ceased to believe in the existence of a writer unless his name is on a book (which, of course, we do not crack unless it is our professional obligation to do so). Teleplays and screenplays are surely something else. Does someone really *write* a motion picture? Don't the director and actors make it all up as they go along (with a big assist from Special Effects)?

OTHER SCENARIOS

Let us extrapolate. One day the computer will be voice activated, and we shall not need to learn even the alphabetically marked keys by which information can be received on command. Banish, therefore, all pens, pencils, paper. If the computer talks back to you, relates the necessary information in ever so pleasant a voice, the need to read will go as completely by the board as the need to write. Literary arts will be on the wing once again. Compositions will be declaimed to huge audiences, for electronic nets are flung worldwide.

Now then, let us imagine a disaster of some magnitude, something like that which brought on the Greek Dark Age. It can be atomic, of course, but there is no need to invoke the standard horror. An exceedingly large volcanic explosion would serve to blanket and darken the atmosphere with a circulating cloud of ash, perhaps for years on end; the collision of a very large meteor with earth would do an even more effective job. (The extinction of the dinosaurs is now being attributed to just such an event.) If, by the time of the catastrophe, we had achieved total solar power—no more coal, oil, wood, or gas, and certainly nothing nuclear—then the flow of electricity would be shut down.

And what then? The computers would grind to a halt. All the careful contingency plans developed by banks, corporations, and government agencies would be useless. For the sky would be darkened for years on end. There would be no information flow (the telephone company is the world's largest computer system). Gridlock would occur in all major cities (traffic lights are computerized.) There would be no records, compactly filed and ready for voice retrieval. The libraries full of books would long since have been eliminated. (Remember that it has been several hundred years since anyone has *wanted* to hold a book in hand.) Some few private libraries might still be owned by eccentrics able to give them houseroom. Not enough, however, to stem a tidal wave of ignorance.

Billings to customers would be lost. Banking records would be lost. The records of births, deaths, and taxes—lost. The ownership of property could be disputed; how trace the deed? Wills, agreements, contracts, all lost. Not to mention the results of scientific experiments, legislation, treaties, accords. Not to mention what had passed for literature and scholarship and art.

Eventually the sky clears. Eventually people settle on the land, far away from the abandoned cities, and learn once again to grow their own food. Eventually, this farmer and that one will have more grain than his family needs in the coming year. But how can he be sure? He makes careful calculations: so many scoops of grain must be reserved for planting next spring, so many scoops to feed us. Must he repeat this task next year? How can he remember?

The farmer takes his surplus grain to where people meet, just on the edge of a deserted town. How many scoops does he have in his bag? What should he ask in return for each scoop? What is each measure worth? How can he *remember?*

Perhaps he ties knots in a string. Breaks sticks into a basket. Collects pebbles in a bowl. And records the tally on a wax-covered board. Perhaps with a stick of charcoal applied to a bit of fabric, a pottery shard, a sheet of bark. Little by little there would be discovered again the means of reckoning time and happenings, the means of binding yesterday to tomorrow. Little by little ways would be found to capture words that sing and stir the blood and summon tears.

And all from the numbers and markings through which men do business.

THE CUSTOMER

SALESMANSHIP AS ANTHROPOLOGY

Are you, Sir, calling America's salesmen liars?

MARVIN LEFFLER, CHAIRMAN,
NATIONAL COUNCIL OF SALESMAN'S ORGANIZATIONS.
TO THE EDITOR OF
THE *NEW YORK TIMES.*[1]

Fast-talking and a little slimy," said the attractive woman on the television screen, "that was my image of the typical salesman. I thought sales was the last thing I'd ever want to go into. I was a college graduate, for goodness' sake, an educated person!"[2]

But Jody Peters did go into sales, as she admitted to her interviewer on the television program, "Fast Track for Women." Indeed, she became the sales manager for a high-tech concern. In the process, she learned two important things: that not a single salesman she encountered quite fitted the popular (and negative) image, and that women are extraordinarily good at selling.

Is it because of their great skill in applying the "personal touch"? Jody Peters thought that might be relevant. After all, the salesman's basic task is not only to know his business but the customer's business as well. More importantly, he needs to know the customer. How many in the family? Likes and dislikes? Habits and beliefs? What is needed in the way of product?

And yet, before the personal touch can be applied, one must first get the customer's attention. There's the rub; there image comes into play. A pretty face will surely help—a natural plus for the saleswoman. A warm smile helps. So does an outgoing, cheerful manner. Ditto an air of jaunty confidence. Ditto a snappy suit, shined shoes, neat haircut. Altogether, the indispensable Good Front. Today it is called "dressing for success."

In *Tales of the Road*, written eighty years ago, Charles Newman Crewdson makes much of the Glad Hand and the Good Front. For him this includes an air of impervious optimism. The novice is advised never to show disappointment when he fails to score. "The salesman who drops a crippled wing weakens himself," warns Crewdson. You must be square, he adds, but never weak. ("Square" in those times meant "fair," not "dull" as it does today.) And there is no place in selling for drones. Still, it is a great life, full of adventure and camaraderie among "knights of the grip"; full of challenge and surprise. (Does anyone today know what a "grip" is?) And it is an important life, he wants the novice to know, first among the professions. Don't forget, he says,

> "Salesmanship is the business of the world: it is about all there is to the world of business."[3] •

There must be something in what he said, since most of the chief executive officers (CEOs) of major companies are drawn from Sales—from the men and women who know the customers, know their territories, know the nature of need. In order to stay attuned to its customers, IBM not only closely monitors its sales force, but insists that its corporate officers make regular sales calls.

"Salesman," however, is seldom the current preferred title, especially when prefaced by "traveling." There are more delicate ways to convey the nature of occupation. Case in point: the television commercial for a credit card firm.

> Two young professionals, dressed for success, are seen unlocking mail boxes in their apartment building. He notices her. She notices him. Instant attraction.
>
> He: I haven't seen you around before.
>
> She: I travel a lot—on business.
>
> Neither mentions selling. If pressed for a title, each might admit, "I'm an account executive," or "I'm a company representative," or "I'm a consultant." If pressed further then, "I'm in marketing." NEVER: "I'm a traveling salesman/woman." There are, or used to be, too many jokes about that.

In 1874, however, W.H. Baldwin was not burdened by negative connotations. Indeed, he did not even neglect the now odious "drummer," then the British term for a commercial traveler. For his listeners at the Young Men's Christian Union, he extolled the life. "It is a grand way to see the country," he said, adding, "but the calling is one which either makes or breaks the young man who engages in it."[4]

"Are you determined to make your mark as a traveling salesman?" he asked his audience. Doubtless bolstered by general assent he proceeded to detail the necessary qualities of mind and character: fidelity, truth, and the keenest sense of honor to your employer and to your buyers. He advised the cultivation of perseverance, patience, attention to duty. For, he added,

> "Such a man has the opportunity to form valuable acquaintances, of securing a list of buyers to whom he can look as real business friends and who sooner or later will be as capital to him, and thereby the means to command a position of importance with his employers to whom he has thus been faithful and proved himself of great value, and almost indispensable, to them."[5]

But beware of temptations, he cautions,

> "These [the young salesman] must early determine to meet manfully and with the voice of unwavering decision say NO . . . the customer will think better of you for it."[6]

In 1874, traveling salesmen at the edges of the remaining western frontier were still called "peddler-men." They probably hated it as much as the latter-day "drummer." Never mind the name. The same rules prevailed then as now: find your customer, discover his wants and needs, make the sale.

AMERICA'S FIRST TRAVELING SALESMEN

No matter how far a frontier family had traveled beyond the outposts of civilization, no matter how lonely their cabin, soon there would appear at the edge of the clearing a peddler halooing the house and asking to show his wares. Out of the tin boxes carried on his shoulders came needles and pins; buttons and combs; knives, spoons, and other utensils of tin; bits of bright ribbon and delicate lace; swatches of fancy cloth and the thread to sew them with; and, best of all, spices, coffee, and tea—comfortable reminders of a world left behind, all the little "things" with which that world could be created anew. The peddler had still more to offer. He carried news and stories of life back home. He was the essential link between the center of a growing nation and its far-flung outposts.[7] It goes without saying that the peddler was as welcome in that frontier cabin for himself as for his goods. Only in our time would town fathers see fit (as they did some years ago in South Carolina) to post signs reading: "We shoot every third salesman. The second just left."[8]

The frontiersman need suffer no discomfiture through inability to pay cash. The obliging peddler would take in trade whatever might be produced from the land. Furs, of course, were preferable. Lacking these, the householder might offer honey, woodenware he had worked by firelight, grain from his field. All these the peddler could turn into cash to finance yet another tour of duty. Because of him, goods flowed as continually *from* the frontier as toward it.

From earliest times, peddlers circulated like blood through the young America. Like blood, they were as urgently needed. The retail store, after all, did not come into existence until 1800 or so and then only in a few places. Not surprisingly, the founders of these establishments had been themselves peddlers or the sons of peddlers. Some early firms, so founded, have continued into our own time. The Brooks brothers, whose firm now purveys the ultimate in conservative men's wear, began their business life as suppliers of cloth to peddlers. The great Atlantic and Pacific Tea Company started off with George H. Hartford on the road. Ditto Sears and Roebuck, as well as a host of others.

The Plymouth and Massachusetts Bay colonies had hardly been planted, says J.R. Dolan, a student of commercial life in early America, when peddlers began to ply the trails between them. Who were these peddlers and how did they get their act together? Given the implacably religious character of early Massachusetts, one wonders how any young man would want or even dare to enter an occupation so morally suspect. There was no lack of candidates. In any contest between moral rectitude and the hope of adventure, the latter is bound to win. There was, as well, another powerful incentive at work. The youth of humble family and little property could look forward to no voice in community or religious life. For him, then, the wilderness and its Indian trails beckoned. There would be hardships and dangers. One risked death by exposure to the elements or at the hands of wild Indians. But how small was the investment necessary to enter business, and how great might be the rewards! Great enough, perhaps, to permit one to settle in one's native place with property and preference, with the right to doff the second-rate title "Goodman" (reserved for the impecunious) and say to the world at large: "Call me *Mister!*"

So was born the Yankee Peddler, and a familiar figure he was, slogging through dust and mire with his fifty-pound tin boxes, one for each shoulder. Then with his packhorses. Then on a raft, poling up coastal rivers, or in a keel boat, assiduously plying the large, inland waterways. Finally, in a huge wagon, the Conestoga, especially designed for the transport of trade goods. These wagons with their thick rimmed wheels helped widen trails and consolidate the roads these trails eventually became.

To serve the traveling salesmen—as well as ordinary travelers—came the innkeepers and stablemen. Their taverns and hostelries fringed some popular turnpikes with the density of modern motels along a superhighway. Since peddlers were their most frequent patrons—in the rainy season, virtually their only patrons—accommodations were planned with the peddlers' needs in mind. (Today's innkeepers must provide special amenities—such as hair dryers in every room—for the newest peddlers on the road, the supersaleswomen.)

In the old days most peddlers hailed from Connecticut or Massachusetts—home of tin shops, button and comb manufactories, and even printers for the reading, spelling, and arithmetic primers which sold like hotcakes on the frontier. As many peddlers as sailors were the main support of some small Connecticut communities. In the early 1800s, the village of Burlington counted eight traveling salesmen among its residents, while the town of Hartford boasted sixty.

No wonder salesmen were called "Yankee Peddlers." Still more often, "Connecticut Yankee Peddlers." In the south the favored term was "Damned Connecticut Yankee Peddler." The traveling salesman and the farmer's daughter jokes had not yet appeared. But it was here, apparently, that the "slimy" and "fast-talking" image was created. Everywhere welcomed. But also, everywhere despised. Everywhere suspected of sharp dealing and of craftiness (the sale of wooden nutmegs was the scam most frequently mentioned). The peddler suffered from an image problem; it went with the territory.

Was the image deserved? Yes and no. With so many peddlers on the road (over ten thousand were noted in the census of 1850), there were bound to be cheats aplenty. And yet, the hope of profit must needs have constrained even those whom conscience could not. For these men traveled regular circuits. They could not afford a blackened reputation any more than the modern salesman or woman whose continued business existence depends on offering a service and generating good will. Many peddlers were, moreover, looking for likely places along the road in which to start small general stores, to settle down and leave off their footloose ways.

THE SALESMAN AS EXPLORER

The Yankee Peddler did not think of himself as an explorer, though in many ways he deserved the title. He was certainly an advance scout, bringing back to home base news of farthest marches on the distant frontier, encouraging prospective settlers, and describing for them the lay of the land.

Neither did his professional ancestors, the traveling merchants of Medieval Europe, think of themselves as pioneers. Although their business travels might range from Viking settlements along the great rivers of Russia to faraway England, they thought nothing of that. The greater the distance, they said, the greater the profit. Nor were the vagabond salesmen of western Europe overawed by distance. The tradition-bound, stay-at-home villagers called them *pedes pulverosi*, "men with dusty feet," which in England was eventually rendered as "piepowder men."[9]

However many languages at his command, however conversant he might be with local custom, the piepowder man was always an outsider and a suspicious one at that. By the piepowder man's own lights, familiarity with the local lingo was, then as now, an unwritten rule of the road, essential to good business. He did not aspire to intellectual eminence. That was for the clergy. He certainly did not consider himself an explorer, for he made no conscious effort to explore.

But some salesmen, some merchant venturers have attained scientific and literary recognition, and the greatest of these was Marco Polo. Son and nephew of the Messrs. Niccolo and Maffeo Polo of Venice, he was at age seventeen to travel with them into unknown Asia and come back with them twenty-four years later to tell the tale—which was not at the time believed anyhow.

The senior Polos had in the year 1260 initiated this odyssey with an attempt to sell jewels to the chief of the western Tatars, a personage known only vaguely in Constantinople. After a series of mishaps they tumbled into the court of the Tatar emperor, Kublai Khan. So charmed was this worthy by his guests and so inspired by their descriptions of the Christian West that he sent them home to collect young Marco, a supply of holy oil, and clerical representatives of the pope. They returned with the first two but not the third, the holy men having lost interest in a journey whose present dangers loomed more urgently than the need of souls to be saved.

Naturally, the Polos lost no time in learning the Tatar tongue. Young Marco himself commanded four languages—just which he does not say—and business skills so outstanding that the emperor not only had him undertake an assortment of diplomatic commissions, but made him governor of the Province of Yangchow. Marco's dictated manuscript specifically mentions this expertise and Kublai Khan's appreciation of it. What is more, his descriptions of each city he visited reflect his keen professional interests. Each begins, typically, with such phrases as:

"Where commerce and manufactures flourish . . ."

"They subsist by trade and manufacturing . . ."

"They are places of great commerce . . ."

"Large consignments of merchandise are forwarded to this city in order that the goods may be transported by means of the river to various other places . . ."[10]

Yet in the index of the John Day Edition of Marco Polo's adventures, the topics of trade, commerce, and manufacture are not thought worthy of note. The editor's introduction points out Marco's interest in odd sexual habits and in pressing the cause of Christianity. No mention is made of his equally enthusiastic interest in commerce. In Pearl Buck's foreword, Marco is characterized as "First Citizen of the World." One would think him and his relatives wide-eyed hippies with a wanderlust rather than enterprising businessmen out to open a new trade route and make a buck doing it. In sober fact, the adventure was only incidental and the practiced Polo ease of bearing and address in a wholly exotic situation part of the salesman's natural equipment. Only once is the Polo profession mentioned in the explanatory material where the three are identified as "noblemen and merchants of Venice." Of course. Up through the ranks of trade. That was the only ennoblement possible in mercantile Venice. How else?

His to-and-froing on business, official or otherwise, took Marco from Byzantium to the China Seas (both South and East), through Central Asia to India, and from Southeast Asia to the Siberian wastes. There he was impressed by the wealth of furbearing animals—white bear, black foxes, and sables, prized by Tatars as the queen of furs. A perfect pelt, Marco noted, was valued at two thousand besants of gold. He had more to say about the fur trade:

> "For the purpose . . . of enabling the merchants to frequent their country, and purchase their furs, in which all their trade consists, these people have exerted themselves to render the marshy desert passable for travelers, by erecting at each day's stage a wooden house, raised some height above the ground, where persons are stationed, whose business it is to receive and accommodate the merchants, and on the following day to conduct them to the next station of this kind . . . [by way of] a sledge . . . drawn by . . . certain animals resembling dogs. Six of them, in couples, are harnessed to each carriage, which contains only the driver who manages the dogs, and one merchant, with his package of goods." [11]

No one in Venice believed his story of the dogsled. Years later, however, Prince Rupert of the Palatinate was moved by Marco's descriptions to found the Hudson Bay Company. He apparently hoped to discover a new route to the Siberian fur bonanza and found, instead, an even better source of supply.

THE FUR RUSH

It is hard for us today to imagine a world in which the desire for furs led all other wants. To do so we should have to imagine houses without central heating. That prospect evokes, not a yearning for furs, but the dreary possibility of petroleum cut off at the Middle Eastern spigot. It is an appropriate parallel. For the fur trade was, in many ways, rather like the oil trade. Both have caused widespread political consequences. Both were and are based on nonrenewable resources. When animal populations were depleted, when oil wells run dry, the hunt is—and was—on for virgin sources of supply. Because of furs, czarist Russia explored, colonized, and conquered Siberia. Because of furs, she pressed eastward into Alaska and the northern Pacific Coast of America. And it was largely because the fur ran out that she sold her interests in this continent to the United States.

Beginning in the 1600s the lure of peltries had stimulated a push westward from the English and French colonies on the continent's opposite coast. The untouched wilderness of North America became the world's newest "gusher," a place where an enterprising trader could get rich quick—and often did. (John Jacob Astor is a case in point.)

That the excellent woolen cloth of England and northern Europe was adequately proof against cold diminished the demand not one whit. Fashion took up where need left off, and male fashion in particular set the tone. The dashing tricorn hat, a feature of the early 1700s, was made of felted beaver fur. And when this gave way to the towering top hat requiring even more fur for its manufacture, the days of the beaver were numbered.

Everybody was seized by fur fever. Even the staid Pilgrims of Massachusetts. So enthusiastic were their efforts that by 1637 pelt plenty had become pelt dearth. Hopeful explorers then trekked up the coastal rivers in search of the peltry El Dorado, as mythical as the Spaniard's long-sought source of gold. Alas, wherever the Pilgrims went, trading companies of other nations had preceded them and cut off the source of supply. And so they took to other business ventures, as we have seen.

LOCATING THE GOODS

Unlike the peddler who carried merchandise to his customers, the fur salesman had to travel for the merchandise he sought, bringing along whatever might tickle the supplier's fancy and induce him to part with more peltries. This was the pattern in Marco Polo's time. The only exception to the rule, the only instance in which fur suppliers acted to cut out the middleman, occurred in the Baltic Sea region and among those fierce yet enterprising folk, the Vikings.

A Swedish group, circa A.D. 800 discovered that, by negotiating coastal rivers and easy portages, the traveler could get to the Volga River, thence to the Caspian Sea, thence to Arab outposts ashore. Later they learned to navigate the Dnieper River to the Black Sea and to Constantinople. Along the way they established strongholds at Novgorod and Kiev where they were called *Rus* by the locals. These same locals they cheerfully took captive (as we have seen) and sold in the south in great numbers (originating thereby the word "Slave" from the tribal "Slav"). They also carried the furs of their northern homelands and took in exchange gold jewelry, brocades, gold and silver coins, and various other luxuries by addiction to which they were gradually drawn into the civilized orbit of Byzantium.

An emissary of the caliph of Bagdadh had occasion in A.D. 922 to view these commercial *Rus* in one of their Volga communities. He wrote of them as follows:

> "Everyone carries an axe, sword, and knife at all times . . . [and is] tatooed from the tip of the fingernails to the neck. . . . They are the filthiest people God ever created. They do not . . . wash themselves . . . any more than if they were wild asses."[12]

He went on to describe their long houses in which every natural act to which flesh is heir was carried on in full view of all, the men lining up to enjoy their slave merchandise. Prospective Arab buyers simply had to wait. Among the

Vikings, the customer was definitely *not* always right. They had not heard about the salesman's Good Front and Glad Hand. And who cared about *knowing* the customer? They had mastered the laws of supply and demand. What else remained?

And yet, observed Ibn Fadlan, as soon as their ships landed, each man went ashore and prostrated himself before wooden staves, each bearing the likeness of a human face, and implored:

> "Oh, my lord, I am come from a far country, bringing with me so and so many girls, and so and so many pelts of sable. . . . I desire thee to bestow upon me a purchaser who has gold and silver coins and who will buy from me to my heart's content, and who will refuse none of my demands."[13]

With which he deposited an offering, to be incrementally increased if the trading went unexpectedly awry.

While on the Volga, Ibn Fadlan witnessed a Viking Funeral and was horrified, not so much by the cremation of the Very Important Person on his boat, but by what was done beforehand to the slave girl who elected to accompany him. It was one of the earliest recorded cases of culture shock.

THE SALESMAN AS OBSERVER

Much the same sort of culture shock was experienced by American fur traders as they dealt with those lords of the wilderness, the Indians. But because they went to the source of supply, because, in order to strike a deal, they had to know their customers as individuals, shock was often tempered by understanding, by tolerance if not by acceptance.

The men of the fur trade, by and large, have enjoyed no better press than the Yankee Peddlers. Unfairly so, in the view of some experts. It is true that free-lance traders and trappers may have been (so it is suggested) more savage than the locals. And shipmasters visiting the northern Pacific Coast were often predatory and cruel, for they planned never to return to the scene. Licensed traders, however, and those connected with commercial concerns had to stay where they were, visible and often vulnerable. They had to know their territories and the people in them, had to identify wants and interests so as to attract furs. Did the customers want beads of various colors, beads much like the shell wampum so highly prized? Then get beads. Did they want practical objects of metal or fad items such as iron necklaces (for the Indian was not immune to fashion)? Get them. Were guns or liquor desired? Those too. If you don't supply the customer's wants, someone else surely will.

Often these traders were educated men, curious and thoughtful, keen observers of everything about the Indian. So we are told by Lewis Saum in his book *The Fur Trader and the Indian,* a synthesis of documents written by the traders themselves.[14]

At a time when public fancy back home identified Indians with the Lost Tribes of Israel, veterans of the fur trade insisted on Asiatic origins, noting that the Eskimo appeared to be of somewhat different stock. (Anthropologists now know they arrived much more recently than most Indians.) The typical back-easterner might ask the trader, home for a visit, "Do you speak Indian?" Doubtless the trader shrugged in mild dismay at the gaffe, being himself aware of the rich variety of languages spoken on the frontier. Indeed, depending on his travels, he might have been able to locate the language of the eastern Canadian Naskapi in the same Algonquian group as those of the western Arapaho, Cheyenne, and Blackfoot. Several could do so with fine anthropological discrimination. And as for differences in custom, subsistence, religion—all these had been duly described for the home office on forms rather reminiscent of an ethnographic questionnaire. One observant trader noted that the Chinook, a people of the Northwest Coast, seemed to him more like Pacific Islanders than the proper tribesmen of the interior. The observation has been echoed in anthropological circles as well.

In spite of tribal differences, traders were also aware of common themes of the Indian "personality." Many of their observations coincide with the findings of anthropologists George and Louise Spindler who published their studies in 1957.[15] Traders remarked on the Indian ability to withstand cold, hunger, pain; their patience under suffering; the emphasis on the dignity of the individual. Traders recognized that Indians were capable of emotion but expressed it differently from the white man. They recognized a common tendency to observe etiquette and therefore to give misleading answers, to tell the trader what they thought he wanted to hear. They recognized a common dislike of revealing personal names or personal history.

At a time when the literati back home spoke glowingly of "the noble savage" and frontier farmers of "bloodthirsty savages," the fur trader saw something in between these images, saw a figure sometimes appealing, sometimes appalling. If the trader recognized common "personality" themes, he also knew something about culture and found differences among the tribes. He hated the Blackfoot, despised the village Arikara, admired the Crow. Even within these boundaries, however, he saw differences among individuals. And however exasperated the trader might become, however insurmountable the cultural barriers, always there was the chance of personal chemistry, the old camaraderie of the sale. "I took his skins at hazard," said one, "He was an old friend."[16] Another noted that

"there is no want of individual character, and almost every character in civilized society can be traced among them, from the gravity of a judge to a merry jester, and from open hearted generosity to the avaricious miser."[17]

There is personal dislike as well. Consider the experience of Alexander Ross who agreed to pay a Columbia River native a set of coat buttons if he would carry the trader's pack over a difficult portage. Once in possession of the pack, the would-be porter flung it over the nearest precipice, then howled with glee as Ross scrambled after it. Next, he coolly demanded, not only his buttons, but a coat to go with them. And Ross paid up. The customer is always right. Besides, the customer might well send the salesman after his pack.

LOOKING OUT FOR NUMBER ONE

"Trust to their honor and you [and your goods] are safe; trust to their honesty, and they will steal the hair off your head."[18]

That comment by the upper Missouri trader, Robert Campbell, represented no idle fear. Between 1820 and 1831, more than one hundred fifty traders lost their lives in the line of duty. Only the Crow could be depended on never to kill. "If we did that," they told trader William Gordon, "the traders would not come back to us, and we would lose the chance to steal from them." In one way or another, most Indian groups were willing and able to look out for number one.[19]

It was the extreme of practicality, of self-interest "disembedded," the specialist would say, from considerations of religion or prestige or the honor of the formally struck bargain that most disturbed traders about their Indian customers. Though traders often tried to explain or excuse many customs different from those followed back home, there was a lessened degree of tolerance for behavior that flouted the business ethic. One wonders whether it was the apparent cynicism, the contradictions to the Indian's own expressed values that were found jarring.

Students of the fur trade for the past twenty years or so have tended to chalk up such behavior to moral infection by the traders' own Yankee capitalism. And if the trader got the short end of the stick, why, so much the better.

Missing from this point of view is a recognition of the past. Trade with neighbors, even long-distance trade, had been familiar to Native Americans for thousands of years, and their trading skills were well honed. Indeed, several forms of communication were developed to facilitate trade, among them the famous sign language of the Plains Indians.

Another Indian behavior that disturbed trader-observers was an apparent willingness to slaughter the game without qualm. Said Alexander Ross, "They look at animals with more a butcher's than a herdsman's eye."[20] Others related instances of deer killed by the score for their tongues alone. The otherwise intact corpses were later allowed to wash out to sea on the next tide.

Was conspicuous waste a by-product of new technology and a latent spirit of commercialism, or was it imposed by traders and their demands for ever more pelts?

There is no simple answer, so we are told by anthropologist Calvin Martin who has studied the Ojibwa, the Micmac, and the eastern fur trade. To be able to wreak wholesale destruction on the animals, however, Indians of the Northeast would have had to undergo a profound spiritual about-face.[21]

Long ago, Native Americans believed the animals to be more powerful than men. Out of kindness and generosity, so the myths hold, animals gave themselves and their flesh to sustain human life. Such a gift required of the recipient certain marks of respect and proper atonement in ceremony. And then, at some time in the past, the Indian lost both fear and reverence and was thus freed to make war on the animals.

The erosion began, thinks Dr. Martin, long before the New World had been properly "discovered." It may have begun by 1480 when fishermen from England, northern France, and the Basque country accidentally found their way into North Atlantic coastal waters and encountered the people who lived on the shore—probably people like the Micmac or the Naskapi. From them the fishermen took furs to sell back home and, in return, gave metal fittings from their ship and anything else bright and novel. They also transmitted several decimating diseases which the natives were ill equipped to withstand. Those who survived had already begun to lose their faith in the animals long before the first proper colonists arrived, and disaffection spread more slowly but just as surely as disease.

Not necessarily the fur trader's fault, then. Not directly.

THE SALESMAN AND CHANGE

Other sorts of change in North American life were stimulated by contact and by trade in ways as complex and often as indirect. Some, holds anthropologist Harold E. Driver, permitted Native Americans to hold on to their cultures longer than they might otherwise have done.[22]

In order to attract bright goods and have the prestige of a trader resident in their midst, tribes took to slandering one another. They went still further. The five fierce tribes of the Iroquois mounted military campaigns to drive out their enemies from the Great Lakes region and so dominate the fur trade in what is now upper New York State. For the same reasons, the Cree pushed the Chipewyans of west central Canada, and the Ojibwa (or Chippewa) pushed the Sioux. To no avail. With the dearth of animals in the woods, the Ojibwa had neither furs nor food and had to revamp their patterns of residence. Once they had lived year-round in large, congenial village groups. Now they fell back on the nuclear family unit which did the best it could to survive the winter on its isolated preserve.

Among the Blackfoot of Montana, Oscar Lewis noted still more striking changes.[23] Only mildly infected by beaver-fever, the Blackfoot were mainly suppliers of buffalo robes. A brave's wife processed the skins, but with the best will in the world she could only do so much. How to stimulate production? By changing the marriage pattern, by making polygyny (always an available option) the preferred norm. The energetic entrepreneur now set out to woo or capture as many wives as possible, and the richer his wives made him, the more eligible he became as a suitor for yet more brides. With a staff of twenty or so and piles of stored skins, he needed a larger tipi. That took a lot more skins but he had plenty to spare. When moving day rolled around, however, yet another problem surfaced. More transport was needed. How to acquire additional horses? Step up the raiding and trading operations. That meant increased intertribal contacts and the exposure to different customs. From the village Mandan, for example, the Blackfoot borrowed an age-grade system—something rather like the Masonic Order in organization.

All changes triggered by the fur trade. There were still others.

Since 1788 and in spite of Russian efforts to interdict the area, Boston merchant ships—and those of England as well—had traded with Indians of the Northwest Coast, not for beaver, but for sea otter pelts. These could be exchanged in China—where demand and prices were high—for silks, spices, and tea. When the otters had been hunted virtually to extinction, coastal people, a highly sophisticated lot who lived in redwood plank houses and accounted high social rank the ultimate good in life, turned inland for a new source of supply.

Among these hopeful middlemen were venturers of the Tlingit tribe who scraped up a connection with the inland Tagish and Teslin. Cousins in language, they nevertheless had nothing to compare with Tlingit airs, graces, and trade goods, and they gladly provided furs in abundance. In short order, however, the simple Tagish and Teslin began to absorb Tlingit customs as well as payment. They instituted strict rank order and acquired slaves (who knows whence?). Families found they could not hold up their heads in society unless they could count themselves part of a clan which—Tlingit fashion—reckoned descent along the mother's line. Language, myths, costume, bearing—all reflected Tlingit patterns and were grafted into the uncomplicated, foraging way of life the Tagish and Teslin had always practiced.[24]

Change by trade. Home grown. No outsiders.

THE SALESMAN AND CHANGE: AN ARCHAEOLOGICAL HYPOTHESIS

Perhaps, suggests archaeologist Kent Flannery, some of the changes we see in the record of prehistory happened in just this way. Scouts from a center of relative sophistication scour the countryside for goods needed back home. Never mind what trinkets they use to impress the natives or to exchange with them, inevitably their own style of life will have a profound impact. Inevitably they will set change into motion.

He uses the Tlingit–Teslin analogy to explain an interesting archaeological phenomenon in Mexico. Between 1200–900 B.C. in the Valley of Oaxaca, early farmers were consolidating their villages and constructing ceremonial architecture. In the remains of these structures, archaeologists today find religious forms and figurines characteristic of an Olmec center on the Caribbean coast. The Olmec site was already at that time much more complex and elegant than anything the Oaxaca people could boast. The Olmec had a taste for luxury goods, among them mirrors of polished magnetite. Where was the source of magnetite? Oaxaca.[25]

Olmec venturers traveled everywhere in Mesoamerica as they prospected for weapon-stone, carving-stone, and jade. Everywhere they left behind Olmec style and the imprint of Olmec culture. And different people became, in time, more and more like one another in outlook if not in speech.

Commenting on Dr. Flannery's views, Dr. Michael D. Coe, Olmec specialist par excellence, observed that:

"When you look at the Mesoamerican pattern of migration, it is not really something out of the Bible. It is more reminiscent of contemporary American Coca-Cola salesmanship—

small groups of commercial people with plenty of fire-power, moving into a region and taking it over commercially."[26]

SAME GEOGRAPHY, DIFFERENT TIME

Intimidation of the customer is not the preferred technique of salesmanship; and if Olmec merchant venturers practiced it, their commercial descendants in Mesoamerica probably did not.

They were indeed professionals. The thousand-year-old site of Casas Grandes in northern Mexico was home to one such group. Its salesmen carried imported shells to their pueblo customers in what are now the states of Arizona and New Mexico. They also peddled live parrots bred at Casas Grandes and copper bells manufactured there. Payment was made in turquoise for which the area was famous, then as now.[27]

The Aztec, who apparently put Casas Grandes out of business, called their salesmen *pochteca* (as we've noted earlier). The *pochteca* had their own patron god, the long-nosed *Yacatecuhtli*. His Mayan counterpart was *Ek Chuah*, protector of overland traders (who traveled in much the same way as Yankee Peddlers). Whether Mayan seafaring merchants were under similar protection we do not know. These same merchants, however, were not slow to help themselves, a fact confirmed by Spanish seamen on the first ships to visit Cozumel Island off the east coast of Yucatan.

As the archaeological work of Jeremy Sabloff and William Rathje demonstrates, Cozumel had become by A.D. 800 a commercial center for certain Maya merchants dealing in salt, cacao beans, quetzal plumes, copper, jade, and obsidian. To obtain these commodities, they traveled all around the periphery of Yucatan. The remains of their sturdy warehouse platforms at Cozumel, their causeways, their less elegant, false-fronted homes testify that good business was valued over pretentious housing.[28]

Columbus spotted one of their cargo-laden vessels—a

large dugout with twenty paddlers—off the coast of Honduras in 1502 and promptly abducted its old captain to serve as an interpreter. Between 1517 and 1519, other Spanish vessels appeared off Yucatan, and landing parties were dispatched. The mainland Maya attacked; the people of Cozumel retreated in silence. Later, with the appearance of Cortes, "they went among us as if they had been friendly with us all their lives." So reports Bernal Diaz del Castillo who was an eyewitness. Indeed when Cortes took his leave of Cozumel, the merchants there asked him for a letter recommending them to other Spanish gentlemen who might pay a later visit.[29]

Whatever their apprehension, the businessmen of Cozumel were quite prepared to jump whichever way the winds of change blew. After all, these strange creatures might well be the customers of the future. Nothing ventured, nothing gained. How quickly they reset their sights.

GETTING TO KNOW YOU

Salesman Crewdson in 1901 observed, "Those we meet are to a great extent but reflections of ourselves."[30]

Not always, it must be admitted. Not quite. Not when the customer belongs to a world based on premises radically different from one's own. Not when the most ordinary act of courtesy, taken for granted at home, can give bitter offense and queer a deal (as agents of the fur trade were learning right up to the time of its demise). Even when business is conducted in countries with economies geared, seemingly, to the demands of the twentieth century, the traveling salesman cannot be truly at home abroad.

There are, first of all, the questions concerning the nature of courtesy:

> To shake hands or not to shake? Will his customer be standoffish or go for the Latin double embrace? (This will undoubtedly make the salesman uncomfortable.) Can he be pally

and drape an arm casually over the shoulder of his business acquaintance? In Southeast Asia, never! It is an unpardonable affront. Worse yet is to sit in such a way as to reveal the sole of the shoe. Outrageous!

To wait or not to wait? Should he plan to cool his heels for a half-hour after appointment time, or should he expect to be ushered in on the dot?

To speak up or to tone down? If he goes for modulated tones in the Middle East, he'll likely be considered a wimp.

To move in or maintain distance? The Latins not only converse man to man, but virtually head to head. The Chinese require a larger bubble of space.[31]

These are aspects of communication—detailed for us by William Foote Whyte and Edward Hall—that are beyond language. Knowing the language is, of course, a must for the salesman as for the anthropologist. It will not, in and of itself, guarantee total understanding. In addition to the spoken language, one must command both the silent language and the language of idiom. It is a formidable task. Consider some blunders of idiom committed by businessmen and gathered for us by David Ricks:

An airline advertised the "rendezvous lounges" on its 707 flights in Brazil and lost customers. "Rendezvous" in Portuguese is a place to have sex.

The Chevrolet Nova, popular in this country, would not sell in Latin American markets. Nobody noticed that, in Spanish, *no va* means "does not go."

Pepsi's "come alive" campaign was translated across Asia as "bring your ancestors back from the dead." The reviews were definitely mixed.[32]

So much for the big marketing campaigns. In private, in the traditional selling scenario, the salesman can work to offset the blunders inevitable in intercultural exchanges, and many have. If he (or she) is at all sensitive, he will pick up behavioral cues as they are telegraphed by the eyes, the tilt of the head, the gestures of the customer. In a real quandary, the salesman, like the anthropologist, might say to his customer, "Forgive my clumsiness. I am here to learn your ways as well as to show you my wares." So much candor, however, takes not only nerve, but very real confidence as well.

THE EXOTIC AMERICAN

We forget that our business customs are foreign to everybody else in the world and must be studied and mastered by them. Consider the following scene:

> We are in Olean, New York. Though a small, upstate town, it boasts diversified industry and some very important plants. The Hysol Division of Dexter Corporation is one. They supply compounds for the epoxy adhesives. Another is AVX, the world's largest manufacturer of ceramic dielectric capacitors.
>
> The time is early morning. We visit the breakfast room of a leading motel. It is crowded with salesmen and two saleswomen, dressed for success and sitting alone. Conversations are laced with references to commissions and sales quotas.
>
> "Boy, did that make me laugh," says one man. "He thought he had the inside track with the purchasing agent. He thought she really went for him. Him and everybody else!"
>
> Two Japanese enter the room. Their clothing approximates in cost, cut, and degree of informality, that of every other salesman present. They walk from the shoulders, Americanlike. They order large plates of bacon and eggs, sunny-side up. They greet their fellow knights of the road with hearty handshakes. The older of the two manages the look-'em-in-the-eye component of the ritual better than the younger, who is obviously learning the ropes. Learning how to sell in America, American style.

SELLING SCENARIOS OF THE FUTURE
ARE THOSE OF THE PAST. . . .

The wonders of electronics have revolutionized selling—or so we are told by the purveyors of telecommunications. One need not be physically present to clinch a deal. There is the handy telephone with added visual components tricked up for conference calls, repeat calls, and goodness knows what else besides.

But the telephone cannot reveal the telltale facial expression, the twitches, the tics, the eyebrow raised, the mouth downturned—all the little cues that let the salesman know whether or not he is getting through. And even if there is a video component, the screen is not sufficiently sensitive to reveal eye changes—the unintended "sparkle," the dilated pupil that, better than anything else, signals a sale. Ring it up![33]

So it's still peddling time, out there on the hustings. Few other than the intrepid Avon Lady or Fuller Brush Man ring random doorbells in a residential area. In small town after small town, however, salesmen still knock on business doors up one street and down the other. They peddle some surprising merchandise. One of these—described by Carrie Dolan in the *Wall Street Journal*—is G. Neil Anderson. He sells Apple microcomputers from the back of his car:

> His territory is Idaho in small towns the likes of Blackfoot, Chubbuck, and Soda Springs. He is not welcomed with open arms by store owners just panting to join the computer revolution. He must convince each proprietor of a hardware store, each meat-packer, each farmer, each brake-shop manager that the Apple will really help business. He must be able to demonstrate exactly how and be willing to woo the customer over a period of months until the sale is made.
>
> And that is just the beginning of the relationship. Afterward comes the follow-up, the handholding, the servicing, the sales of additional hard and software. "A computer is just like a car," he tells customers who grumble at the added costs.

"After you buy a car, you have to pay for repairs and keep putting gas into it, don't you?"

Whatever Neil Anderson is doing, it must be right. Apple plans not to renew contracts with its distributors and will, in future, deal directly with retailers and salesmen like Neil Anderson—a latter-day Yankee Peddler of the computer revolution.[34]

THE SALESMAN IN A GLASS, DARKLY

The American theater has never lacked plays about business. They often focus on the fast talking, somewhat slimy salesman, willing to do *anything*—to tout a house built on marsh land, a defective car, a dangerous drug—just to keep on top. The most successful of these plays, certainly the most acclaimed, is *Death of a Salesman* by Arthur Miller. It has been variously interpreted as an indictment of the spurious American Dream, as the personal failure of a self-deluded incompetent, and as a picture of the American Everyman, chasing the bubble of success. At the end of the play, Willy Loman, no longer able to cut the mustard, is heartlessly dropped by his company and commits suicide. Miller has one of his characters say of the hero:

> "Willy was a salesman. And for a salesman, there is no rock bottom to the life. . . . He's a man way out there in the blue, riding on a smile and a shoeshine. And when they start not smiling back—that's an earthquake. . . . A salesman is got to dream, boy. It comes with the territory."[35]

That is Miller's epitaph for a man all flash and no substance. For what was Willy selling? The playwright does not tell us. We are not meant to know or care.

But the real salesman has to know and has to care. Otherwise he is in the wrong line of work. As Willy Loman obviously was. Real salesmen die, too, and people write epitaphs for them. Here is one:

> "Robert Lockart was a part first of Kirby Lumber Company and later Kirby Lumber Corporation for sixty-eight years; his sales activities from 1903 until his death on March 16, 1971, contributed much to the welfare of this company. His integrity, intelligence, and warm personality made him the valued friend and counsel both of numerous customers and of the company's personnel with and for whom he worked. BE IT RESOLVED that Kirby Lumber Corporation, through its directors, expresses its appreciation of the character and life of Robert Lockart and its deep sorrow and sense of loss at his passing."[36]

He was a salesman. He traveled. He helped to build a business. He enjoyed his work, and he was good at it. Even when felled by serious illness and deprived of his salesman's voice, he continued to sell. That was his life. Who should know better than his daughter who remembers him in these pages?

Said Bill Woods, yet another traveling salesman as he tooled his car around the back roads of South Carolina, "I wonder where America would be without us?"[37]

Where indeed?

THE
MARKET

SOMETHING MORE THAN
A PLACE OF EXCHANGE

*The market can be distorted.
But it cannot be thwarted. The
moment the consumer has any
choice, the market, rather than
the planner, is back in control.*

PETER F. DRUCKER[1]

The doors slide open noiselessly, and we enter the world of the Food Bazaar. Just inside are masses of cut flowers, suitably arranged to grace an elegant dinner table or be presented as a party gift. There are tubs of philodendron and ficus—very green, very chic, very "in"—also very easy to maintain in small, dark apartments or corporate offices.

Just beyond are tempting racks of fruit, including a full range of exotic, imported fare. Vegetables are fresh and moist and crisp, a treat for the eye. Among the produce, the shopper finds tempting ingredients for a salad, to be made up and eaten on the spot or while wandering.

There are displays of heat-and-eat dishes, a rotisserie with chickens at all degrees of doneness. There are confectionery counters with hand-decorated sweets (no vulgar prepackaged items anywhere). There is a shop in which one can find both wine and cheese arranged for maximal ease of choice. And, right in the middle of it all, there is a small, chic restaurant, palm-fronded and ivy-twined, where the weary shopper can abandon all thought of dinner preparation and be pampered by the management. Indeed, since each of the small tables is set intimately for two, dinner shared with another weary shopper is encouraged—introductions by courtesy of the house.

No run-of-the-mill supermarket, this. Doubtless disposable diapers cluster somewhere along with bathroom tissue, waiting to be squeezed. These do not cross one's line of sight. Announcements of sales and specials do not mar the decor. Shoppers here do not flash coupons or food stamps. Here one sees few children but many men and women, all alone and with the lean and hungry look that bespeaks life at the corporate top or a reasonable facsimile thereof. The Food Bazaar is dedicated to the enhancement of that image. "You truly are what you eat," might well be the motto of this establishment.

It is a market—a place of exchange. It is a market devoted to special commodities, things for which there is a demand—also known as "market." The nature of demand has been identified by "market research" and then supplied with goods appropriately produced, promoted, and packaged by means of approved "marketing techniques." The tastes of the modern consumer cannot be served by local suppliers alone, and so the Food Bazaar participates—through its wholesalers—in another kind of "market," one that is worldwide in scope.

In that market and in all the lesser ones, a seller is free to set prices that will cover his costs, his time, his labor, his risk and give him a profit into the bargain. It is up to the buyer to decide whether the price is right and how much is too much. The seller must compete with his opposite numbers to attract buyers for his wares and to keep those buyers coming back for more. His prices will have to reflect this reality as well. Buying, selling, competition, profit—these represent the "market principle" of exchange. It is not the only means by which goods change hands (as we have noted earlier). Its use throughout the whole of society, however, reveals something about ideas and ideals, about attitudes and beliefs as well as about habits of provisioning.

The Food Bazaar is, thus, a place of exchange. And a great deal more besides.

THE MARKET THAT'S A SOMETIME THING

"Don't forever be running to markets!" So the mighty Charlemagne admonished his serfs.[2] Not that there were many to run to in the early ninth century. Whatever markets convened in fortified burghs or in abbeys or on cathedral squares were poor local affairs, displaying the small surpluses of peasant farms. Only when the piepowder men of the road arrived in their caravans was anything like a real market to be found.

What spectacles! Why, a body could see wonderful fabrics woven on looms a hundred miles away. (Might as well be the moon for someone bound to his master's land.) There were jars of wine from southern vineyards. There were furs and fanciful pottery. There were trinkets and foreign coins of silver and bright gold—something the peasant could never hope to jungle in his purse.

And what things to do! One could see plays performed and jugglers and acrobats in their bright costumes. One could hear strange music and smell the scent of rare and costly oils and spices. Even if nothing could be purchased, it was a treat just be caught up in the excitement. For this market was a fair, the medieval prototype of all the fairs to come—from county fairs to oyster festivals; from automobile shows to book marts to fashion extravaganzas. Everything right up to and including the great world's fairs.

By A.D. 1000, local barons all over Europe had learned that, however much churchmen might thunder, fairs could be extremely useful events. They tended, for one thing, to line noble purses, always short of cash. For there were entrance fees to be charged and tolls to be levied on the merchants themselves plus all manner of small fines and taxes to be extracted from those who attended. Fairs offered, moreover, a wonderful means of communicating information to one's subjects. Who would stay away from a fair? Especially if it went on for six weeks and attracted merchants from every Western kingdom known to the clergy, and some that were not.

No wonder that the astute baron saw to it that peace was maintained within the fair grounds. Often he did more than that, managing to persuade local priests to lift temporarily the ban on gambling and even on usury. The fair became in time a kind of sanctuary—as was the cathedral, as was the city for a runaway serf. Special courts—piepowder courts—were developed to adjudicate business disputes at the fair. After all, what good to the businessman were trials by ordeal, trials by battle, or appeals to divine intervention? Practical problems of weights and measures, money changing, and quality control necessitated impartial judges with a practical turn of mind and some knowledge of business. Business law—which was outside the law of church and state—moved like an unseen current in a theological sea, to emerge at last as the law of cities, administered by city folk.

THE PREDICTABLE MARKETPLACE

Wherever markets appear, there, too, is market peace and market law. Judging by available ethnographic evidence, that coexistence bids fair to be a universal given. Anthropologist Paul Bohannon describes markets of the Tiv as they were in the 1960s. A Nigerian tribe of farmers without chiefs or towns, the Tiv had little need of the market as a source of supply.[3] Nevertheless, they flocked to area markets, each of which was in operation once every five days. They appeared betimes with their loads of produce, their hand-crafted baskets and woodwork, their palm wine and maize beer and cooked food. They bought and sold, exchanging and haggling and having fun. They sang, danced, and talked. More fun. Everywhere were watchful elders from the family compound on whose land the market was held. Always they were ready to settle disputes and grievances and give any self-confessed culprit the safety of the market.

In the cities and towns of West Africa, especially those of Nigeria, we see the same principles at work in a more formal and commercial setting. In 1857 the Reverend T.J. Bowen, an American missionary, wrote about a traditional city market:

> ". . . a large area, shaded with trees, and surrounded and sometimes sprinkled over with little open sheds. . . . At half an hour before sunset, all sorts of people . . . are pouring in from all directions to buy and sell and talk . . . their united voices roar like the waves of the sea . . . Every fifth day there is a "large market," when the few thousand people who attend daily are increased to a multitude."[4]

Who did the selling? "Here the women sit and chat all day from early morning till 9 o'clock at night, to sell their various merchandise." What was true in 1857 remains so today. Men do the farming. Selling is women's work. For many parts of West Africa this is the essential division of labor. So much so that the new baby is not considered properly settled in this life until it is introduced to the market, and little girls play with merchandise and practice haggling as American girls play with dolls and sing lullabies. (Or did. Newer divisions of labor may require different toys and play before the decade is out.)

Typically, a woman goes to work when she marries. Her husband's wedding gift provides the capital for her trading ventures. If she lives in a small town, she might buy a head-load of yams from a local farmer. (Not usually from her husband; men worry that their own wives will cheat them.) She can then retail her purchase in the local small-town market or sell it to a city trader looking to buy cheap and sell dear. The city woman might, in her turn, choose to sell the load of yams to a city wholesaler and expend her own efforts in other directions.

Some women make cooked foods to sell alongside others offering exactly the same dishes. This arrangement is decreed by the town's "Mother at the Market" who settles disputes and also represents the women in any negotiations with male suppliers of goods and services: the palm wine tappers, the grinders of grain, the wood-carvers, the smiths, the weavers. If she can't prevail or at least effect a compromise, she might well call some or all of the market women out on strike.[5] No imitation of Western labor tactics, this, but a method of protest homegrown in ancient markets long since forgotten.

Some women are hired as agents by local artisans. Say a weaver gives a saleswoman several bolts of cloth on consignment. He fixes the price and offers a commission for her efforts. If she sells at a price greater than that quoted, she keeps the difference *and* the fee. With such incentives for salesmanship, no wonder that there is here a division of enterpise as well as labor.

Whatever the woman's line of work, pregnancy permits

greater concentration, for she can relinquish wifely duties and return to her parents' compound until after the child is weaned. Other wives take up the slack, and, if her husband lacks the wherewithal to obtain a substitute, she will gladly float a loan. For, however much prestige attaches to the ownership of land, the market woman knows—as did Daniel Defoe in 1737—that

> ". . . an estate's a pond, but trade's a spring: [it is] an inexhausted current, which not only fills the pond, and keeps it full, but is continually running over, and fills all the lower ponds and places about it."[6]

For the market woman, trade could be a veritable river, permitting her the luxury of sending her children to a university abroad or buying a fleet of trucks for long-distance trading or, indeed, of resigning from marriage altogether. She may serve her husband's dinner on bended knee (they never eat together), speak only when addressed and then in a low, respectful tone. She knows, nevertheless, who can buy and sell whom. And he knows it, too.

MARKETS AND THE BATTLE OF THE SEXES

It comes as no surprise, then, that West African men harbor considerable resentment. Some regions support a thriving literature of protest. That is new. Older expressions of pique tend to be rooted in the supernatural.

The mercantile Nupe of central Nigeria take it for granted that the daytime market women are nighttime witches, led by the woman chief of the market and one male renegade, thought necessary to make the evil stick. When too many bodies of youths are seen floating in the Niger River, the men of the city form themselves into a society of sorcerers. Their banner is a cloth mask with which an ancient Nupe king is said to have smothered his domineering mother. The Nupe seem to be the only people outside the continental United States who insist that boys are regularly bewitched by their moms.[7]

Among the Yoruba of southern Nigeria, whose women are the most forceful and independent in Africa, men are not so much resentful as emasculated and envious. I am using the words of anthropologist Robert LeVine who has studied Yoruba city-states. Local doctors—both Western trained and traditional healers—are besieged with pleas to cure impotence. Nowhere in Africa is the incidence of transvestitism higher. Male priests wear woman's garb for countless rites and male religious groups parade in drag. So do musicians who tour the countryside with songs (ancient and modern) celebrating heroes magically empowered to bear children.[8]

Is there a message here for our own times, a message of economic role change and the battle of the sexes? Possibly. Half the American work force is female. In the 1950s one in every four married women worked outside the home; today it is one in two. Of those, some six million already outperform their husbands in the paycheck department. How does that alter relationships? Divison of labor has already been redefined but we have not yet developed the rules and amenities, the mandate of tradition that will make new roles comfortable to play. We are, so to speak, writing the script as we go along. That means we are in for a period of uncertainty and tension.

So are the Yoruba, but in a different way. In the 1960s when Dr. LeVine was in southern Nigeria, men had already begun to muscle into the market, and women were deeply affronted by the invasion. Men have persisted, nonetheless. Those grown rich on their own account or with mother's backing, those with university educations have made marriages in the Western style of the 1950s: monogamous, based on confidence and companionship, and with labor divided in terms of house and office rather than field and market. Already, fashionable women were taking their positions in society according to their husband's achievements, not their own. In this part of the world, after all, women's lib is old hat.

If the habits of the trendy become general, then Western glamour will have succeeded better than Islam in redefining the traditional female role in West Africa—at least where occupation is concerned. In the fourteenth century, Islam arrived with African converts and Arab merchants among the Hausa of northern Nigeria, since remote times a long-distance trading people. Following religious dicta, they slowly pushed their women into purdah, into seclusion within mud-brick walls. This will seem to the American reader—particularly the American female reader—that Islam succeeded all too well in role redefinition. It certainly kept women within doors. It did not, however, hamper their pursuit of trade or alter their desire to do business. Prevented from taking their places in the market, they put their children to work there. For children, girls as well as boys, could go anywhere, and they very quickly learned everything there was to know about business.

To this day, anthropologist Enid Schildkrout tells us, children do the buying and selling for their mothers. Let us say a woman prepares several kinds of cooked foods to retail, among them *tuwo,* a stiff porridge of sorghum grain. Her children, starting about age six, will purchase the raw material, have it pounded into flour, and then peddle her *tuwo* in the marketplace. Over the years they will have built up a carefully cultivated string of regular customers whose needs are supplied early every morning. Whatever *tuwo* remains must be disposed of on the open market, and the children cry out the superior virtues of their mother's cooking loudly and agressively.

In between jobs for mother, they are free to run errands for other adults who, unless related, will be glad to tip for services rendered. These add up in time to a small amount of capital which the children will use to finance businesses of their own. Boys make toys for sale to other children or rent bicycles. Girls make pancakes and other snacks on little charcoal grills placed outside their own front door. These entrepreneurial children even lend money to one another.[9]

EARLIER MARKETPLACES

Farther west, over the great bend of the Niger River, at the ancient Malian trading town of Jenne, women participate openly in the market. Depending on clan affiliation, many practice the potter's art. There is really not much choice in terms of occupation. One does what one's parents did, and if mother was a potter, then her daughter will be a potter, too. Son is destined to be a smith because potters marry smiths. No option. Both are snubbed by the master masons, who are snubbed by merchants, clergy, and nobles. Potters and smiths, in their turn, can snub the leather workers and the storytellers (the equivalent, in our world, to actors and other entertainers who were not, themselves, welcome guests in anybody's country club until recent times). It is a sort of caste system, an occupational layer cake that dates back to the appearance of iron in the area, and that is as old as Jenne itself.

Or rather, it is as old as the ancestral city, Jenne-jeno, not quite two miles away, its "tells" and rubble perfectly visible in aerial photographs. Old Jenne has been a ghost town since A.D. 1300 or thereabouts. Converts to Islam, in search of proper religious surroundings, founded new Jenne and tried to forget the pagan gods, the "bad" old ways.

Those old ways are only now being uncovered by Susan and Roderick McIntosh, professors of archaeology at Rice University, Houston. Many surprises have been forthcoming. Jenne-jeno began as a village[10] sometime around 250 B.C., began as a home for people escaping the Sahara's increasing aridity. That journey the McIntoshes read in Jenne-jeno's ancient pottery, so very like that found in the desert that once was green and inviting. And also so very like pottery being made today by the women of Jenne.

Perhaps the villagers brought with them the knowledge of iron smelting. In any case, iron is present in Jenne-jeno from the beginning. Somebody had to bring the ore; there is none in their marshy inland delta. Nor is stone to be found there. Somebody brought that, too. Almost certainly in exchange for the grain in which the land here abounds.

Jenne-jeno grew apace. Other villagers settled nearby— villagers with the kinds of special skills we see today in the occupational hierarchy of Jenne. The villages merged. (The urban recipe at work again.) Copper was added to the balance of trade, copper from more than a thousand miles into the Sahara. The ancient smelters have been located in the desert hills of Äir. With Saharan copper must have come Saharan salt. The McIntoshes infer this from the dietary needs of farming folk and from historical records.

Sometime after A.D. 400, after the copper, came gold, brought from mines located far to the south. And after that, walls were built to enclose what was by now a very considerable city. All of this occurred long before cities were supposed to have been built in Africa, long before the arrival of Arabs who have been credited with the beginnings of trade.

Did the trade come first and the market after? It seems likely. But market there was in time, a market teeming with merchants and their donkey caravans. This must be so because Jenne, the daughter city, has itself long been home to a famous market. Arab travelers have written of it. So have native scholars who, armed with Arabic writing, manned the universities which blossomed at Jenne and its sister city, Timbuctu. One Ahdarrahman as-Sadi, writing in the early 1600s, described Jenne as one of the principal markets of Africa where gathered merchants from the north bartering Sahara salt for gold. "It is," he said, "because of this blessed town that caravans come to Timbuctu from all points of the horizon."[11] No wonder he called Jenne "blessed." Timbuctu is said to have bought all its food there.

A century earlier a Moorish traveler, later to become

the Christian slave Leo Africanus, commented on the great market at Jenne, rich in barley, rice, cattle, fish, and cotton, which

> ". . . they sell unto the merchants of Barbarie, for cloth of Europe, for brazen vessels, for armour, and other such commodities. Their coin is of gold without any stamp or inscription at all." [12]

So, too, was the coin of Timbuctu. But, he pointed out, "In matters of small value, they use certain shells, brought out of the Kingdom of Persia." [13] He was referring to the cowries which have been used as currency in West Africa for time out of mind.

Even today, we learn from the McIntoshes, the Monday Market at Jenne draws people from far-distant places. They pack themselves into a plaza the size of a football field where they can buy many of the items sold long ago, and doubtless in the same way, in the market at Old Jenne.

A PRINCIPLE OF EXCHANGE

From all the foregoing, we may be reasonably sure that ancient salt merchants, as modern ones, disposed of their goods for the highest return the market would bear. Price hinged, they realized, on how much salt was available on any given day, how many people needed it, and how many people had it for sale. Ancient salt merchants apparently did much better than gold dealers who often went home again with half their stock unsold. This is supply and demand, modified by profit and competition. If allowed to operate more or less freely, the factors add up to the market principle.

Not all places of exchange operate according to the market principle. Prices can be arbitrarily set. Participation in the market can be limited according to some exclusionary rule. Supply can be artificially limited through discouragement of production or monopoly of product. Demand can be limited by reserving consumption of certain commodities to favored groups or individuals. Traditionally, the possession of leopard skins in Africa has been limited to royalty.

Restriction, to some degree or another, constitutes the principle of command. And it was not unknown in African marketplaces. In Dahomey, the king took an active role in determining prices. In the Yoruba city of Ife, wholesaling— particularly long-distance wholesaling—was once controlled by a guild of importers, most of them men. All foreign merchandise would enter the city only under their auspices, and woe betide the woman who tried to import her own or to conduct business with a foreign merchant. (Anyone from another Yoruba city was "foreign.") It was proper for such a one to present himself immediately to the head of the guild who purchased all or the desired part of the merchandise at *his* price. What remained must be carted elsewhere. No ifs, ands, or buts. The chief of the guild then distributed the stock among guild members for resale at *their* prices, half of which had to be remitted to—guess who! [14]

Command of the market is nothing new, anywhere or at any time. Whether introduced by kings or merchants themselves, seeking to corner the goodies, everyone has tried somehow to tether the goose that lays golden eggs and maybe squeeze her just a little without killing her outright. Since medieval times, English merchants had labored under a host of restrictive laws meant to protect English farmers and the products of English workers from foreign competition. During the time of Elizabeth I, any farmer who sold good English sheep for breeding outside the country was liable to confiscation of all his property forever, a year's imprisonment, and the loss of his left hand, to be severed on the public block and nailed up for all to see. A second offense would cost his life. [15]

Just before 1776, when the American colonists declared

their independence from Great Britain, a few scholars had begun to wonder just how productive these restrictions were. The Scotsman Adam Smith was bold enough to address the Royal Society in Edinburgh on behalf of free trade. Mr. Smith was a liberal, and liberal thinking was then coming into vogue. It must be noted, however, that the liberalism of Smith's time favored a loosening of government control over private lives and business; not, as today, the tightening thereof.[16]

Most of Smith's free spirited colleagues nevertheless found free trade a bit too radical to suit their tastes. And so his views were not widely heralded even after publication of *An Inquiry into the Nature and Causes of the Wealth of Nations,* a book that continues to attract adherents as it adds on years. Of the advantages of an open market he said:

> "Were all nations to follow the liberal system of free exportation and free importation, the different states into which a great continent was divided would so far resemble the different provinces of a great empire."[17]

For in his view, the free market merely reflects aspirations common to human beings everywhere:

> "The natural effort of every individual to better his own condition, when suffered to exert itself with freedom and security, is so powerful a principle, that it is alone and without any assistance, not only capable of carrying on the society to wealth and prosperity, but of surmounting a hundred impertinent obstructions with which the folly of human laws too often incumbers its operations."[18]

What is good for the individual, then is also good for the society at large:

> "It is his own advantage, indeed, and not that of society, which he has in view. But the study of his own advantage naturally, or rather necessarily, leads him to prefer that employment which is most advantageous to society."[19]

THE COMMAND ECONOMY

That a philosophy of the free market, which is to say free trade, translates in some minds today as license to exploit, as a glorification of greed owes mainly to what happened in England and on the continent after Adam Smith.

The French Revolution happened after Adam Smith, and though it failed in achieving all the utopian changes envisioned by its leaders, it inspired generations of French—and later German intellectuals—with a new view of human nature and the natural order to things.

The Industrial Revolution—or rather, its second phase— happened after Adam Smith. With it came a succession of very real though much less prominent events. There was a baby boom, not only homegrown, but swelled in 1815 by a flood of Irish immigrants. Widespread unemployment followed. There were poor harvests and high prices because of heavy tariffs on foreign grain. In any time of change and dislocation there is ample blame to go around. In industrial England, blame happened to settle on machines and on the men who owned them.[20]

Earlier, in 1737, Daniel Defoe could sing the praises of English trade and its happy consequences:

> ". . . the working manufacturing people of England eat the fat, drink the sweet, live better, and fare better, than the working poor of any other nation in Europe; they make better wages of their work, and spend more of the money on their backs and bellies than in any other country."[21]

A hundred years later, Karl Marx and his collaborator, Friedrich Engels, son of an English manufacturer, were to call the workingman in Britain and everywhere else the "proletariat," those who must sell their labor power in order to live. Unlike Defoe, Marx and Engels portrayed workers

> ". . . crowded into the factory . . . organized like soldiers.

As privates of the industrial army they are placed under the command of a perfect hierarchy of officers and sergeants. Not only are they slaves of the bourgeois class and of the bourgeois state, they are daily and hourly enslaved by the machine." [22]

The remedy for this unconscionable state of affairs was revolution as prescribed in *The Communist Manifesto*. (The tract was originally to be titled *The Socialist Manifesto*, for that properly characterized the economic program. Because of its bourgeois connotations, however, Marx and Engels ditched "socialist" in favor of "communist," a term dear to the workingman.) It was a call to arms:

". . . communists everywhere support every revolutionary movement against the existing social and political order of things . . . They openly declare that their ends can be attained only by the forcible overthrow of all existing social conditions. Let the ruling classes tremble at a communistic revolution. The proletarians have nothing to lose but their chains. They have a world to win." [23]

In bourgeois society, said Marx and Engels, replying with scorn to their detractors, freedom merely means free *buying* and *selling*, and

"all the other 'brave words' . . . have no meaning when opposed to the communistic abolition of buying and selling, of the bourgeois conditions of production, and of the bourgeoisie itself. . . . You reproach us with intending to do away with your property. Precisely so; that is just what we intend." [24]

The manifesto included many other prescriptions. Among them were a heavy progressive or graduated income tax; all communication and transportation to be centrally controlled; all factories and farm production to be centrally controlled; all credit to be centrally controlled. Wherever communism prevailed henceforth, the market pinciple was to be abolished. Society was to be provisioned according to strict plan. None of your "invisible hand of the market" here; that smacked altogether too much of magic. Planning, on the other hand, is *rational*. Above all, it is *scientific* (a halo word in those times as in ours).

THE MARKET AND HUMAN NATURE

Adam Smith had seen human beings as naturally inclined to "truck, barter, and exchange one thing for another." It was, he said,

> ". . . this disposition which forms that difference of talents, so remarkable among men of different professions . . . so it is this same disposition which renders that difference useful."[25]

Human beings were born to make choices favorable to themselves, and—providing no undue compulsion was applied—this seeming selfishness would achieve the common good. More than that, it would achieve prosperity. It was the source of national wealth.

Marx and his followers were deeply distrustful of human nature with its foibles and caprices. For them self-interest was not a force to be liberated, not a force for good. It was a force for disorder, a force which deflected individual effort from a search for the *common* good, and it was therefore to be restricted and controlled. People should not be allowed to buy with their wages what they *wanted* to buy. In time they would learn to want only what *should* be wanted. They would learn always to ask, "What does society need?" before saying, "This is what I want." The proper reward for labor should be the joy of working for the common good. Wages should merely serve to keep body and soul together.

Too bad about America, Marx grumbled in a letter written in 1852:

> "How far bourgeois society in the United States still is from being mature enough to make the class struggle obvious and comprehensible . . ."[26]

The exploiters were not yet exploiting according to plan. Never mind, his disciples have been wont to murmur, as did Lewis Feuer in 1959, ". . . as freedom is reborn in Eastern Europe and Asia, it will speak in the Marxist idiom."[27]

And that has come to pass, not only in the East, but in the new nations of Africa as they achieved independence after 1960. Many espoused the economy of command and, with it, the Marxian view of human nature.

What may have fed the spirit, however, has starved the body. And so, one by one, Marxist states have begun to look, not for what *should* be, but for what *is*. More than that, for what actually brings prosperity. For what *works*.

They need look no further than the Manifesto which pays grudging tribute to the prescriptions of Adam Smith:

> "The bourgeoisie [say Marx and Engels] during its rule of scarce one hundred years, has created more massive and more colossal productive forces than have all preceding generations together. Subjection of nature's forces to man, machinery, application of chemistry to industry and agriculture, steam navigation, railways, electric telegraphs, clearing of whole continents for cultivation, canalization of rivers, whole populations conjured out of the ground—what earlier century had even a presentiment that such productive forces slumbered in the lap of social labor?"[28]

"But never mind *that*," respond dedicated Marxists. "It is not, after all, *what* was done; it was the *way* it was done. And that was *bad*."

"Bad or not," mutter the converts, "we'll have some, please. Better full bellies and uneasy consciences than the other way around." As the director of Senegal's National School of Applied Economics told Journalist Art Pine:

"I used to believe in socialist theories, but failure has changed my mind. Instead of freeing people, socialism has reduced their capacity to produce. People are ready to reject it."[29]

Senegal, of course, has at hand the example of the Ivory Coast with its booming market in a becalmed sea of command economies. Perhaps that has sparked imitation. In any case, Senegal has sold off some of its government-operated factories to private owners (how they got the cash is not divulged). And it has opened the only free-trade zone in its part of Africa.

China's tentative experiments with the market principle have been noted by the American media since the return to power of the tough and pragmatic Deng Xiaoping. Journalist James Sterba, who visited Shanghai in 1981, reported that this ancient home of enterprise had been getting its act together even before the government's decision to let the entrepreneurial genie out of its Communist bottle. He spoke with an elderly florist, once popular with Chinese and foreigners alike. The Cultural Revolution had put him out of business for the sin of selling "symbols of bourgeois decadence" and for being a "capitalist tail." Now that restrictions had been relaxed, his customers had returned and business at his stall was brisk.[30]

There have been other changes. Farms have been decollectivized. That spelled the end of food shortages. Special economic zones have been established on the continent across from Taipei, Macao, and Hong Kong, that premier boom city of the Orient. In these enterprise areas, foreign investment is permitted and a limited form of native capitalism as well. In July of 1984, journalist Victor Fung reported that the government was flirting with a homegrown stock market. When corporate shares went on sale recently in a Bank of China branch, would-be investors traveled for miles around to buy. Once stock issues were scorned as "capitalist devices of evil speculators and profiteers." No longer. What *should* be is taking a back seat to what *works*.[31]

By 1983, even Soviet officialdom was reading a confidential memo advocating relaxation of government controls in order to achieve higher levels of productivity. Whenever rules and regulations about private plots, fishing limits, etc. were established, the memo noted that

> "[people] look for ways to circumvent the constraints and satisfy their requirements. Then the state introduces still harsher measures to block undesirable forms of activity, in response to which the population comes up with more refined methods that make it possible to meet their interests under the new conditions."[32]

Not only was illicit business on the increase, but the ordinary worker wanted to be paid regardless of how well he worked:

> "The type of worker that such a system cultivates [has an] indifferent attitude to work, a shoddy quality of work, social inactivity, a well-pronounced consumer mentality, and low code of ethics."[33]

Factories may not be humming, but Soviet farmers are working. They are working, in any case, on their private plots. Indeed, according to journalist David Brand, private farmers working only 3 percent of the cultivated land provide 25 percent of the nation's food. They sell in big-city farmers' markets called *rinki* at the highest prices the market will bear. (This is in quiet violation of prices dictated from on high). Soviet officialdom threatens from time to time to punish profiteers, and now and again it does. (A "profiteer" in fruit juice was shot not long ago.) But the *rinki* just keep rolling along—on the market principle.[34]

There is even a special class of entrepreneur catering to the Russian lonely-hearts market. According to *Literaturnaya Gazeta*, these "wheeler-dealers with a keen sense of the market have defied laws against private enterprise and have set up dating services with charges as high as 200 rubles ($275) for introductions and surcharges of 500 rubles ($685) if an initial encounter leads to marriage." Shocking, the *Gazeta* editor scolds, that there can be loneliness in a society where there are "no class or economic barriers obstructing personal contacts."[35]

What *ought* to be and what *is* rarely coincide. Enterprise merely recognizes the reality. How, after all, is some sixty-year-old planner in the Politburo to know how hard it is for boy to meet girl in a world bereft of matchmakers in babushkas, nosey aunts, church choirs, and graduation balls? And if he did, what could he do about it? Enter the "Meet Market."

MARKET IS ALSO A VERB

HOW TO MEET REMARKABLE PEOPLE
AND HAVE THE TIME OF YOUR LIFE DOING IT!

That is the banner caption of a recent full-page ad in the *New York Times* (asking price $5,000 and up). The specialty club being promoted aims at success in the Meet Market, and the size and placement of the ad suggests a certain success already achieved. The words "romance" and "practicality" are featured but there is no mention of price. "Remarkable" gets the biggest play. It is reinforced by testimonials from "an attractive female radiologist, an advertising executive, the president of a large corporation." Members are said to include a world-class tennis player, a best-selling author, a Pulitzer Prize winner, a Salesperson of the Year, and judges, lawyers, doctors, playwrights, and so on down the list of prestige occupations.[36]

Clearly, the club plans to supply, not the Meet Market in general, but a particular segment thereof—that of the well-heeled professional, fed up with the singles-bar marketplaces. To accomplish this, its staff has carefully re-

searched the needs, interests, and tastes of its chosen con-
stituency, and how much they will be willing to pay for the
services to be rendered. (Quite a lot, the layout and copy
suggest.) The very polls, questionnaires, and interviews that
revealed the nature of special need have been used to draft
the advertising—the words to be used, the placement of
copy and in what magazines and newspapers. (Upscale, we
know, because they are listed). Staff appearances on prestige TV talk shows are listed. Entry into the international
market is announced. Even the People's Republic of China,
we are told, has expressed an interest. (As well they might.
Their large cities are stuffed with singles between the ages
of thirty and forty—127,000 in Shanghai alone.) [37] Everything is designed to eliminate the sleaze factor and to convey an impression of respectability, taste, and trust.

That's marketing. The club has been presented in a way
best calculated to attract a large share of the targeted market segment and beat out whatever competition happens to
be gathering steam. It is the act of "putting one's best foot
forward" carried to its ultimate expression.

There is nothing new about that. At least one variety of
pottery in the ancient world was developed for the marketing of wine. And nobody produced more elegant packaging
than the people of the Aegean Islands. No wonder. Wine
and olive oil were virtually their only exports. Each island
had its own vintage, and its merchants no doubt tried every
trick in the book to secure a market share. Small markets.
Good word-of-mouth promotion. Big demand.

In the market that is continent wide, alas, it is not enough
to build a better mousetrap. The world will not automatically beat a path to your door, never mind what the old
proverb says. Not if people don't hear about your invention
or, worse yet, if they have superior cats. Only within the
last hundred years or so have manufacturers and their
salesmen attempted to make systematic studies of need according to region, culture, occupations, ages, and a score of
other variables. These studies have blossomed into a science. Today's marketing experts work with more than

demographics. They have tried to plumb as well the nature of human association, memory, and the images that modify need.[38]

Why are rice and tea perceived in America as feminine foods? Why are potatoes and beef masculine fare? Why does soup connote home and milk security? And how should a knowledge of these perceptions affect marketing? Cigarettes may not be so hot for your health, but if they carry overtones of "cool," the image of the macho man and femme fatale, how do we use *that* to promote the product?

Women constitute some 50 percent of the work force. What new demand is created by that fact? What products and services will be needed? And, what's more, how does it alter the image of the consumer? Tell people what they want to hear along with providing what they want to buy. Show people what they want to see. Never mind what they *should* see.

What does the automobile mean to the American public, specifically to the male contingent? Romance, prestige, power. The automobile is the love object that replaced the horse.

"Years ago when I was with the Ford Motor Company," said Holmes Brown, now president of the Institute for Applied Economics,

> "we decided to emphasize new safety features in our marketing. In short order, the big guns from General Motors paid us a visit and said, 'You can't do this. You can't tell people their love object might kill them. It's a breach of trust. It's bad for all of us.' Guess what. The marketing campaign was changed. Not until after Ralph Nader's attacks did you hear anything about safety in cars."[39]

Marketing is a combination of national pulse taking and psychoanalysis conducted on a grand scale, on a body of patients so volatile and unpredictable that experts have formed corporations to do nothing but practice marketing for other corporations. It is the ultimate in division of labor.

"Why hire more marketing employees when times are booming?" ask these new entrepreneurs. "Why expand your permanent work force? Call us instead. We can devise a training program for your sales personnel, stage a big-bucks contest to stimulate your customers, find ways to propel you into a new market altogether." It seems, all in all, like a combination of Office Temporaries and Mandrake the Magician.

The specialization of marketing can be carried still farther. Professor Peter F. Drucker—who practically invented modern concepts of management—forsees the transnational corporation of tomorrow organized on that principle. He predicts federations of related business enterprises orchestrated by a separate marketing-management concern.[40] To use a biological metaphor, think of the human body with all its processes and components integrated by a central nervous system. Now think of a marketing nervous system for the business body.

Division of labor is always cost effective, in marketing as in all else. How *effective* marketing will be is something else again. Which is to ask, How magical is it really? Can marketing experts truly predict what will be demanded? Better still, can they so manipulate the many variables as to *create* demand? Can they *coerce* the consumer? Outside business circles, a lot of people would probably answer yes. Intimidation through marketing, corporation control of the consumer's purse—these are widely held beliefs.

Marketing managers of the fashion industry heard just this belief expressed at a recent conference meant to explore the psychological dimensions of fashion:

"It's all your fault," thundered a prominent professor of psychology. "You fashion leaders can blame yourselves for all the young women suffering from anorexia and bulimia today. You told them that only THIN could be fashionable and that, if they wanted to be in the swim, they had better be able to wear tight jeans. They're starving themselves to do it!"

Marketing managers in the auditorium looked at one another sheepishly or rolled eyes heavenward. Each no doubt recalled in vivid detail the maxi skirts, the sack dresses, the Cretan décolletages that, at one time or another, had made fashion news on the Paris runways and bombed in Peoria, marketing expertise to the contrary notwithstanding. Nobody present had the temerity (or energy) to point out, "Hey, don't blame us. Blame the movie business. Blame *Urban Cowboys.* We don't start trends. We follow them. Too bad about THIN."

BEYOND EXCHANGE

There are other trends, deeper, longer lasting, more profound. Changes in a people's belief system that have consequences in the real world:

> "It is only our Western societies that quite recently turned man into an economic animal. . . . For a long time, man was something quite different; and it is not so long now since he became a machine—a calculating machine."[41]

Those are the words of Marcel Mauss, the great French anthropologist. For him, the humane and admirable primitive with his acts of provisioning deeply embedded in a world of other meanings is contrasted with *Homo oeconomicus,* that rational being who knows exactly what he wants and exactly how to get it in an economic world geared to cold efficiency. It is the very model of the modern Western capitalist, maximizing his creature comforts in an economy disembedded by the market principle from tradition and from all considerations save that of gain.

Marketing managers know better. For it is their business to deal with the overtones and undertones of any exchange transaction. And they rarely meet *Homo oeconomicus* undiluted, unvarnished, and pristine. Wall Street analysts know better, too. With all the best will and research in the world, nobody can quite explain why the value of stock in certain corporations rises and falls or why investors buy and sell their shares in seemingly blind panic or wild euphoria. John Maynard Keynes, the British economist, said of the stock market,

> ". . . It is a game of Snap, of Old Maid, of Musical Chairs . . . a pastime in which he is the victor who says "Snap" neither too soon nor too late, who passes the Old Maid to his neighbor before the game is over, who secures a chair for himself when the music stops."[42]

In 1982, social psychologists Stanley Schacter and Donald Hood advised perplexed investors to consult with a *bubba*, the quintessential Jewish grandmother who knows "without benefit of graduate training" that market prices are unpredictable and that people are not coldly rational.[43] Neither is the stock market. Models of prophecy are regularly confounded by what really happens. What *should* be at odds with what *is*.

Markets are not new, says anthropologist Manning Nash, and they are not peculiar to the West. What *is* peculiar to the West is the elaborate theoretical models developed to explain the market's behavior and the attachment to it of the notions of good and evil.[44]

So what happened to *Homo oeconomicus?* And whose market is disembedded anyway?[45]

If we are *not* to cast primitive economics in a modern market mold, if we *are* to think of primitive folk and the ancients as beings fundamentally and profoundly different from ourselves, then why do we seem to be so much like them? Especially in the meaning department.

Contemporary consumers may prate about price and value, profit and loss. Even so, each homely purchase trails its cloud of personal, peripheral implications. And market operations, while not exactly encumbered by those claims of religion, family, and chiefliness familiar to students of primitive economics, nevertheless take place within a firm context of belief concerning what it means to be human. And more than that, what it means to be the *right* kind of human being.

For at least half the world's people, being right means upholding an economy without a market, an economy in which supply and demand are harnessed to a vision of human perfectability. And they would rather be right than be prosperous.

If that's not an embedded economy, what is?

For most Americans—though certainly not all—the market economy is a similar tenet of faith. It is a faith that echoes personal attitudes and political process. It is rooted in freedom of choice for every individual so long as he restricts the choice of no other individual. And anybody can choose, whatever his intention, motivation, or state of grace. For free choice brings prosperity. And prosperity is *good*.

If that's not an embedded economy, what is?

It also delivers the goods—most of the time.

MONEY

SOMETHING MORE THAN
A MEDIUM OF EXCHANGE

*There are few ways in which a
man can be more innocently employed than in getting money.*

SAMUEL JOHNSON[1]

Money may not make the world go around, but it certainly fuels the market. So who got the idea and how? To hear many people tell it, money is a gift of God. Now it is true, of course, that you and I may speak of the Almighty Dollar and of "worshipping Mammon," without having in mind either the Creator or religious celebration. In other languages, however, the connection between currency and deity is explicit and precise. The words say what they mean and mean what they say: pennies *are* from Heaven.

The cowrie shell money of West African Dahomey was said to have had just such a beginning. True, it appeared at the command of a king. But then Dahomean monarchs were themselves considered sacred, their divinity proclaimed by the shells which dangled in fringes from the royal crown, hiding the royal face from public view.

Eventually, Dahomey was conquered by the French. Eventually, as anthropologist Melville Herskovits tells us, cowrie shells gave way to francs in the African money market and finally lost their celestial backing altogether.[2]

Also of divine origin was the currency of Choiseul, an island in the South Pacific. It was the creation of a water god who said, "I must make something that can be the mark of the Big Man here." And, diving to the bottom of the sea, he fashioned *kesa,* large white rings bound together with palm fronds, nine to a set.

Predictably, his people fought most impolitely to see who could grab the most *kesa,* smashing quantities of it in the process. "Never mind," said the water god, "I'll get more." But he never did because, soon after, he was cooked in the earth oven of a rival god. His untimely end left *kesa* in such short supply that Big Men competed to acquire it. They still do even though today the largest and most valuable *kesa* is buried by its owners and seldom exposed to view, seldom allowed to "work." Some men are thereby emboldened to cultivate an image of affluence they really could not sustain in a monetary showdown.

More money could be made, suggests Harold Scheffler

who has lived with the Choiseulese. *Kesa,* after all, is only shell. But the Big Men claim not to know that and would not, in any case, dream of infringing on the prerogatives of a god. Therefore *kesa,* almost alone among the world's currencies, is proof against inflation. By divine default. Doubtless the Choiseulese could wish the same for the Australian dollars which are rapidly replacing *kesa* but are not similarly stable in value.[3]

In the Yurok belief, Five Brothers created the sky. Then they created human beings. Then they created dentalia, those long, white shells that look rather like walrus tusks and which, ever after, would constitute treasure. "If humans own money," reasoned the Five Brothers, "they will not be vindictive nor kill readily, for they will not wish to pay away in fines what they have and what they prize."[4]

Alfred Kroeber, who knew the Yurok best, tells this legend of a people at home in northern California long before the gold rush and who live there still. But with a difference. The Yurok have transferred their faith from the "long white" to the "long green." Just like the rest of us.

SHELLING OUT

In the old days it was a different story altogether. Then the Yurok turned, not only main thoughts, but very nearly every thought on dentalium shells. Men not only prayed for money, they dreamed of it, assuring their friends next morning, "A big dentalium was looking at me."

Women schemed for money. "If I can become a shaman," a talented girl child might muse, "people will give much dentalia to be cured." The Yurok preferred female practitioners and paid accordingly. The sex-linked difference in fees was great enough, indeed, to prompt some male shamans to don female dress.

The Yurok were not the only tribe to reckon worth by shell. It had been a regional custom for time out of mind. Nor was the tooth-shaped dentalium the only currency.

Many varieties of bivalve provided the calcareous medium of exchange. All forms derived value from scarcity, from labor of processing, or from travel distance to the source of supply. The Yurok imported dentalia from Vancouver Island in the southwestern part of Canada, never realizing that the precious animals burrowed in their own sand just offshore.[5]

The same attitudes prevailed on the other side of the continent. Inland tribes there valued shell far more than the coastal folk who lived closer to the source of supply, the clam and marine snail beds off the Long Island shore. It was from the shells of these mollusks that Native Americans fashioned those tubular beads, purple or white, known as wampum. (The scientific name of the quahog clam is, appropriately enough, *Mercenaria mercenaria*.) Nobody knows just when these replaced the porcupine quills which had earlier provided the visible indices of wealth and prestige. Incoming Europeans were quick to learn that plenty of wampum could buy American furs which could, in turn, be exchanged back home for "real money." And they soon outdid the natives in the manufacture of shell currency.[6]

DEFINITIONS AND POINTS OF VIEW

Dare we think of shells—wampum or dentalia or olivella—as "real money"? Did they truly figure in commercial exchange transactions? Could they be used to pay debts? Were they reliable standards of value? Yes and no, depending on the particular people. (Kapauku shells are about as "real" as money can be. Ditto the shells in Marco Polo's China.) Yes and no again, depending on the authority consulted at a given time.[7]

"Never," some of them would insist. "True money must be shorn of every subjective connection, personal or sacred; must be entirely anonymous and objective, entirely without sentiment. It must carry no connotation except in the economic sense. It must be a 'disembedded' instrument of exchange."

"Nevertheless," others would contest, "money *is* what money *does,* and what money does is entirely bound up in meaning. Always different meaning. But always meaning."

Certainly shell money in North America could do a number of things. It could procure a bride, pay a blood debt, celebrate a great event, cement a tribal alliance, call a truce, shore up prestige. All of these, it is true, are transactions which strike us as highly personal, ceremonial, special. All require for their fulfillment an appreciative audience and a grand occasion. None of them relates to what we know in the practical grind of daily disbursement: the expeditions to supermarket and bank; the tolls paid for highway travel; the coins dropped in vending machines.

Even our money idioms invoke practical realities. When we speak of "laundering" ill-gotten gains, we do not have in mind banknotes visibly sullied by crime. We simply refer to transactions that must be obscured, made untraceable by the watchdogs of the U.S. Treasury Department. The Yurok did not play such word games with their money. Dentalium shells were actually thought to be tainted by the manner of their acquisition. Had a prospective suitor garnered his wealth by murder, perhaps by wishing a relative dead? His dentalia stood no chance of inclining the fatherly heart toward his suit. Only money earned through clean living and self-denial, through abstinence from food and the calls of the flesh, through hard work and much sweat (literally, in the communal sweat-house) had true purchasing power.

The young husband behind in his installments of bridewealth sweated without benefit of steam and heated stones under the burden of his guilt. Private debts in our world cause similar strain, anxiety, and self-condemnation. Our collective debts, national debts, do not, or did not until quite recently. In other years, the government and its policies of high finance have been rather like the Five Brothers Who Live in the Sky, remote and incomprehensible, the magical source from which all dentalium flows. And so it was, when a national leader proposed to "bust the budget," he was considered benevolent by some folk, quixotic by others, reprehensible by none.

However magical the workings of government high finance, we do not apply its terms at the baptismal font. One would be hard put to find parents willing to name a son Dollars Smith or a daughter Liquid Assets instead of Mary Ann. About the closest we come to connecting currency with persons is via nicknames ("Old Money Bags," "Tightwad"), and these are seldom complimentary. People with less secular currencies value such associations. The Choiseulese *Tanakesa*, "He Who Seeks Kesa," was entirely honorable. So was *Hiawatha*, an Iroquois name said to enshrine the pursuit of wampum. Among members of this famous Native American confederacy, whose present-day descendants still live in New York State, the search for wampum was a search for truth as well as purchasing power. For wampum was thought to have spiritual connections both to the powers of the Underworld and to the Sun, source of light and life. Iroquois wampum sewed to a belt and presented to an assembled throng gave sure guarantee of the visitor's veracity and good intentions.[8]

In our world, guarantees of truth and trust are somewhat harder to come by. That is why, perhaps, we find the carefully drawn contract, clairvoyant with respect to every eventuality, so necessary to business life. Yet contracts can be breached. The ceaseless round of litigation demonstrates as much. And even in court our symbolic guarantee of truth—the hand on the Bible—is ultimately less effective than the penalty for perjury.

MONEY AT WORK

Perhaps the Native American troves of dentalium, whelk, and related shells should be called simply "limited purpose money." And yet, it may not be so much the purposes that are limited as the opportunities for use. The tribal world is short in that respect. Even so, the Yurok found surprisingly many transactions for dentalia. A man could, for example, buy a house with three strings of dentalium shells. A boat might sell for two twelve-strings or ten large woodpecker scalps. The going rate for a tract of land was one set of five-strings. The oak trees growing there were more valuable than the land itself, for the Yurok, like other Californians, had learned to process acorns so that they could serve as the starchy staple of their diet.

The cost of land was cheap compared to the cost of a wife. Given the fact that neither land nor available wives existed in short supply, given the importance of subsistence (which looms so large in standard economic interpretations), one might well think that the disparity in price ought to be turned the other way around. Until one remembers that the acquisition of a wife was not a commodity transaction. The larger the bridewealth given, why then, the greater the reputation gained by the prospective groom. The greater her price, the greater the honor accorded the prospective bride, the higher the rank assigned her offspring to come.[9]

We make a similar bid for social recognition in showy weddings. It is the father of the bride, however, who gains in reputation while depleting his bank account.

A Yurok suitor gladly "shelled out" ten strings of different sorts of dentalium, fifty red woodpecker scalps, a boat, and a quantity of obsidian blades—all representing negotiable assets. This was a rock-bottom figure for a girl of good family. The asking price for a poor girl of few social pretensions was considerably lower, perhaps eight strings of shell and a boat. For seducing this same girl out of wedlock, the fine was five strings, a difference that might well have inclined the financially embarrassed suitor to think less highly of matrimonial bliss. In our world, the higher taxes levied on married couples tend to have a similarly dampening effect.

Yurok penalties for every sort of offense fluctuated according to the relative rank of victim and perpetrator. For uttering the name of a wealthy man gone to his Heavenly reward, the ordinary villager had to pay a much higher fine than his social superior in similar circumstances. And for a moment's rage resulting in violence—worse yet, man-slaughter—he might have had to sell himself, perhaps even his children, into slavery. The Yurok rate for a slave was a four-string of dentalium. On Vancouver Island, where money was more plentiful, the price was a five-string set.

All in all, the Yurok were class-conscious to a fault. This seems all the more surprising when one remembers that there were among them no courts to levy fines and no po-lice to enforce collection. There was no state nor even a tribal chief. There were no markets and not much to sell in any case. For, as we have seen, the Yurok lived by hunting, fishing, and the gathering of wild foods. We can send them, therefore, to the bottom of that social scale ranging from "primitive" to "advanced." They can be labeled "foragers," at least in terms of subsistence pattern.

At once a favored image begins to blur. We feel much more comfortable picturing foragers in what we are pleased to call "a state of nature," wandering about here and there, grubbing up roots and killing a stray antelope or two. We see these in our mind's eye unceremoniously dumped at a communal campfire somewhere in the bush with a general invitation to "dig in." The reality never was and still is not that simple.

ENTER THE GIFT

Among people who fit the standard image to some degree, meat is never shared; it is given. Even today, the last free hunters of the Bushman bands, the *San* (as they call them-selves) of the Kalahari Desert, bring home, each one, his share of game to be given first to parents-in-law, then to own wife and children, then to individuals who have loaned or presented arrows to the hunter.[10] Recipients, in turn, repay their own prior obligations with portions of the gift meat until every one has been fed. Distribution, it could be said, has been accomplished in waves of giving.

Meanwhile, the spirit has also been nourished. For the giver has lived up to the highest values of his society. He has been unselfish, he has been generous. Next time, he will be on the receiving end. Thus the gift binds individuals, one to the other, establishing a state of equivalence between them. Thus does the gift, in binding each to each, bind each to all.

Whatever the evolutionary tides that swept us into complex economic seas, something of humanity's earliest habits remains with us still. Men who hunt and fish for the sport of it nevertheless feel constrained to share among friends and neighbors the fruit of their efforts. Everywhere, in all our private dramas and encounters, the gift network has remained intact, however many money markets have risen and collapsed. Money may not buy love, as the saying goes, but it can buy gifts. Chosen with effort and care, with the maximum possible generosity, and (ideally) with utter unselfishness, the gift can initiate a relationship or speed one along the way. ("One perfect rose. How utterly romantic of you!")

Only reciprocation establishes equivalence, however. And the return must be in kind. Favors for favors. ("I got your friend a job, pal. You owe me one.") Dinner parties for dinner parties. ("If we don't entertain the Greens soon, I shan't be able to look them in the face.") Christmas cards for Christmas cards. ("Nothing from your cousin again this year. He's off my list.") Even visiting heads of state strive to establish equivalence in their ceremonial gifts to one another.

Here is an exchange bearing the sanction of time. It came into being among tribal chieftains and was already institutionalized with the appearance of the first states and civilizations. Diplomatic tit-for-tat served to move a lot of luxury goods if not downright necessities. And monarchs were not above communicating wishes to their opposite numbers.

Pharaohs of Egypt during New Kingdom times (c. 1400 B.C.) felt free to ask kings of the Hittites for more of their "star metal," by which they meant iron.[11] The Hittites, alone among ancient empire builders, had developed the smelting process and, possessing ore ready to hand, made excellent military use of the knowledge. The Egyptians, for their part, had little in the way of metals except for gold which came from mines in Nubia and the eastern deserts. Though gold was not used as internal currency (the Egyptians, with their rigidly controlled economy, made do, for the most part, with payments in goods and had little use for metal currency until after the Macedonian Ptolemies came to rule). However, they did use gold externally. It was their link with the outside world.

Some kings of ancient times demanded of Egypt ever more gold to sweeten diplomatic exchanges. Others complained of too much, for they made use of silver in internal currency, not gold.

Gold as a link among great nations continues in our world but no longer figures in the gift. It represents purchasing power on a high level. You and I can no longer convert dollars into gold, but great nations can, and Uncle Sam has to pay up on demand. The relationship, in this case, involves those corporate personages known as central banks. Heads of state, however, must honor one another, not with gold, but with white stallions and hunting rifles, sets of porcelain and carved ivory—each gift as carefully chosen to woo the good will of the opposite number as the ardent suitor with his one perfect rose.

In a more homely sphere of life, though no less hedged around with protocol, are the obligatory birthday gifts that establish among girls of a certain age group the status of "best friend." Each gift must be in price and tastefulness fully equivalent to a prior gift, or the relationship soon goes sour. For to give more, to be able to give more than one can reasonably expect to receive, implies that one is somehow better and wants to make a point of the fact. The really small, close human group—whether in the bush or in someone's backyard—will take care to ridicule this kind of excess. But in societies with somewhat larger scope, the truly big spender may be elevated to chiefliness—provided he is willing to carry largesse as far as it will go.

The Cheyenne brave, horse thief par excellence, saw to it that most of his gains were given away without expectation of return, without a thought to the size of his own holdings. And people would nod and approve. "You can tell he's a chief," so the comments flew. "Generosity has made him poor."[12]

Our grudging appreciation of the big spender is apt to be: "He may be rich, but he's not cheap." Society, it seems, can forgive any amount of success so long as there is appropriate atonement in generosity. Every religious faith (certainly from the time its priestly admonitions could be recorded and doubtless long before that) has urged generosity on its devotees. "Give to the poor," the clergy exhorts. "Better still, give to Mother Church who alone can make sure that your celestial credit is good."

Not to be outdone by religion, the U.S. Internal Revenue Service rewards generosity with an abatement of taxes— but only if one gives to recipients on the approved list. On second thought, this sort of generosity might come under the heading of Tribute, or even of the Hostile Gift.

IT'S THE THOUGHT THAT COUNTS

No one has ever perfected the art of hostile giving to the degree attained by the Kwakiutl of British Columbia and Vancouver Island. These are the people popularly associated with "totem poles" which were not totemic at all, not in the sense of identifying a given family with a given animal, vegetable, or mineral. Rather, they were heraldic devices which trumpeted the pedigree of families renowned for conspicuous waste. In Kwakiutl hands, the gift ceased to be the glue of social solidarity and became a ladder for social climbing. And more besides.

For the Kwakiutl, every social promotion, every marriage, every birth, death, joy, even embarrassment was marked, validated, assuaged by a giveaway—sometimes right down to the planks that held up one's house. Everybody gave things away. And the chiefs of large bands of relatives gave most of all. First among treasure was the "shield" fashioned of cold-beaten copper, but it was the blanket woven of bark strings and wild-sheep wool that served as a standard of value, albeit a fluctuating one. The name of the game, after all, was inflation. One aimed to spend more, ever more, never less. And inflation worked because, for one thing, the land was rich, the people industrious, and the goals shared. For another, property (except that which was deliberately thrown away, killed, destroyed) tended to circulate. Whatever a chief gave away came back with interest and then went out again at the next feast. Friendly chiefs kept inflation at manageable levels. Rivals slugged it out with property. Ruth Benedict describes a chiefly skirmish during which one of the antagonists immolated his two daughters (or seemed to); his rival, lacking the fortitude to top that with his own offspring, committed suicide. Shortly thereafter, the supposedly sacrificed maidens were miraculously resurrected. But not the two slave girls who had served as substitutes in the burning.[13]

DEMONSTRATING WORTH

We know all about hostile gifts and even more about hostile display. ("If my friends could see me now!" So the advertising jingle invites one to stimulate envy through the trappings of class.) Among all the world's peoples, birth and couth needs must dignify a display of wealth. One or the other; preferably both. For us, what's up front seems to prevail. Display first. Only in America can one buy a slightly-used mink coat. Only in America can so many Cadillacs be found in seedy neighborhoods. Only in America is there cultivated a craze for "collectibles"—the dubious works of art, the commercial plates and plaques and medals guaranteed to appreciate in value ("Only fifty struck!") and which, meanwhile, give one the delicious illusion of hoarding treasure in the house. What, no Picasso? Never mind. You can display with pride your genuine Bicentennial Platter from Traditions Unlimited.

It is bad form to display the bankbook. That says, in any case, nothing about one's *worthiness* to possess wealth (and therefore rank), says nothing about the taste, discernment, discrimination that should validate the ability to buy. (Perhaps we do recognize the intangibles of class after all.)

A number of peoples the world over have found in the display of wives a very satisfactory way of demonstrating worth. The relative prestige of great men among Australian Aborigines was frequently reckoned in wives—those in residence and those promised but yet to mature. The more wives a man had, the more he could entertain. (For wives did the gathering of wild food and their sons brought home the bacon.) The more a man entertained, the more wives he was likely to be promised. Everybody loves a winner, and Aboriginal fathers could certainly recognize a political "comer" when they saw one.[14]

For members of the Liberian Kpelle, wives constitute an index of class. A man is definitely upper if he is a wife lender; at rock bottom if he is forced to borrow a wife; in between if he possesses only a couple of wives and children he can call his own. "Upright" men are rich, for wealth derives from the rice farms, their own and those inherited by their wives—all of them cultivated by a female labor force. A potentially more lucrative source of income (depending on the size of the wife pool) is the adultery fine (paid by men). The larger the establishment, the more certain the incidence of hanky-panky. And wives always confess. They must, otherwise the rice crop will be magically damaged.

The upper-class man may lend wives to poor men but

retains the right to any children that ensue (potential income through bridewealth) as well as the adultery fines that will be paid when the party of the second part is cuckolded. Wife borrowers are also obligated to applaud the political speeches of their benefactors, an important consideration since chiefs are elected from lists of candidates chosen by the elders from upper-class wife lenders.[15]

For the Venezuelan Yąnomamö, who call themselves "Fierce People," women constitute a visible demonstration of power. These jungle farmers live in villages, each one of which is a continuous circle of thatch surrounding an open plaza. Each is autonomous. Each is at war. Each needs alliances. To win friends, a village might have to give up some of its stock of females. But not too many lest it be perceived as dangerously weak. If it is ever forced to beg for succor, more women will be extorted than the suppliant village can afford to lose. Of course, its men can steal women from other villages if strays can be found far from home. And these will not only be interest-bearing but will often come with a bonus: the suckling child always carried on foraging expeditions in the expectation of just such a seizure.

There is never a sufficient supply of women to meet demand, for the Yąnomamö practice commodity regulation: female infanticide, sometimes to avert a husband's displeasure, always when a girl is the firstborn. Neither is the grown-up article highly prized, for all the currency transactions possible with her person. Men shore up their reputation for ferocity by beating their wives, sometimes fatally, with sticks and machetes. Beatings are moderated only when women can remain in their natal villages under the protection of their brothers. It is in their interests, therefore, to help strengthen the village reputation for ferocity, to egg on their menfolk to avenge every slight, test out every enemy weakness, maintain the balance of ferocity with every means at hand. Else they may find themselves borrowed, stolen, extorted, or defaced in a Yąnomamö quasi-currency transaction.[16]

A LEXICON OF CURRENCIES

Displays of worth become standardized units of value when wealth is on the hoof and in the open. A certain amount of risk is necessarily involved. Cattle, sheep, camels, horses can be rustled and, unlike shell currency, they are subject to disease and death. Nevertheless (and again unlike shell), they do multiply. What is more, their growing numbers offer visible testament to the herdsman's industry, canniness, and care. Also, perhaps, to the favor of Powers on High. The healthy herd may thus serve both as bank account and demonstration of grace.

Even when the herd is not healthy, when there are too many animals for available graze, the herdsman who sees cattle in the light of sacredness and sentiment as well as fiscal advantage is loath to reduce their numbers. Pastoralists of East Africa are apt to know each of their animals by name, and, while they may bleed their beasts or milk them for food, would not dream of killing one save under the most fearful religious compunction. Animals, like currency, may be lost in the payment of bridewealth or blood wealth, but never to satisfy the owner's appetite.

Though little in the way of sacredness seems to have accompanied domestication in the Western heritage, it is true that most of our words dealing with the medium of exchange are rooted in transactions, hoary with age, conducted by means of herd and flock. "Pecuniary," from the Latin *pecus* (livestock, or, as it later came to imply, cattle) is one of those money words. (The first Roman coins, indeed, made of copper and stamped with the image of an ox or sheep, were known as *pecus*.) And, since cattle were counted head by head *(capita)*, one's net worth eventually became "capital."

One of our favorite money terms is "buck." ("I wouldn't trade you, baby, for a million bucks.") It comes from the American frontier where deerskins or other furs constituted currency. Another favorite is "clam." ("Thirty clams is all you'll get from me, buster.") Here the echo of that seaside source of wampum which served Americans, native and transplant alike, in the early years of uneasy mingling. Only "dollar" and "bits" derive from familiar species of currency—dollar from the Austrian silver *thaler* and bits ("Shave and a haircut, two bits.") from the broken pieces (bits) of a Spanish *piaster*.

"Money" itself originates in a goddess—or rather, in the attribute by which she was known. In the fourth century B.C., so the story goes, the Gauls besieged Rome. Being unable to starve out the defenders strongly entrenched on one of the city's hills and unable to provoke a battle, the Gauls decided to sneak inside the Roman perimeter. On their way they chanced to startle the flock of sacred geese quartered in the temple of Juno. The frenzied cackling aroused the Roman garrison and saved the city. The divine lady became known thereafter as The Warner, Juno Moneta, she who would later protect in her precincts the Roman treasury and the Roman mint, which came into being long after most of the civilized world (except for conservative Egypt) had already adopted metal currencies.[17]

Products of field and vineyard have never been overlooked in the efforts to standardize value and facilitate exchange. Some time around 1800 B.C., the code of the Babylonian king, Hammurabi, specified that loans repaid in silver would carry 20 percent interest. Some loans could also be repaid in barley at an interest of 33⅓ percent. Who in his right mind would choose the latter method over the former? Only those who, according to law and social condition, could not do otherwise. Peasants, surely, those at the bottom of the social ladder. And, since barley is not indefinitely storable and during bad times must be consumed by the farmer's family, debt slavery must have been the frequent result of hunger appeased.[18]

Many other perishable or semiperishable commodities have served through human history as currency. During their feudal period, the Japanese were on a rice standard. Mongols of the last century substituted brick tea for livestock in exchange. Ancient Mesoamericans favored the cacao bean and even made shift to counterfeit the real article. Diaz del Castillo, the Spanish conquistador, found some in the great Aztec market at Tenochtitlan. Tobacco, a native American plant, was smoked, eaten, and, steeped in water, drunk or even inhaled by Native Americans. It figured as currency only for the new Americans, particularly those who founded the state of Virginia. And so prized did the Aztec-invented cigarette become in time that it provided a short-lived standard of value in Europe after World War II.[19]

COIN OF THE REALM:
ITS UPS AND DOWNS

For storage, hoarding, and display as treasure, for standardizing value, for portability in exchange, nothing beats metal. Relative rarity confers even greater charm. So does intrinsic value in terms of beauty or utility. Meteoric iron gradually fell out of market use after the knowledge of proper smelting was disseminated around 1200 B.C. Somehow tin (scarce enough, surely, during the Bronze Age) never saw much use as currency. Neither did lead. Copper, silver, gold—in order of discovery and use, though not in order of esteem— have retained their preeminence as standards of value.

Herodotus, the Greek historian who had seen everything there was to be seen in his world, tells us confidently that the first coins were minted by the Lydians around 750 B.C. Standardized as to weight, they were later stamped with the guarantee of King Croesus (whose name itself remains a standard of wealth).[20]

By 500 B.C. the Athenian heavy drachma, bearing Athena's owl of wisdom, was the international "dollar" of its time. The name derives from the "handful" of iron spikes that long before had served Greeks as currency. The ancient world had faith that the drachma would be unadulterated and full weight. The Athenians enjoyed a certain reputation for probity, and besides they had a silver mine to back the drachma. Eventually, when Athens was importing most of its food (the big farms having been entirely given over to olive and grape, whence came the highly exportable oil and wine) the silver mines plugged the balance-of-payments gap. As the land itself began to fail and rural unemployed mobbed the city, the mines could still pay them to attend political functions, feed them, and provide free theater tickets. After the ruinous Peloponnesian War (during which Sparta sank the ships which had kept Athens supplied with grain), land, mines, and dole declined together, and the population of Athens was cut in half. Not until Macedonian armies liquidated the gold and silver treasures of Persian kings did money flow freely in the Mediterranean world. A bit too freely, it would appear, for a galloping Hellenistic inflation was the result. (One remembers the several gold rushes which, during our own last century and a half, produced similar results.)

Roman money went through much the same cycle. The silver denarius eventually replaced the drachma as international coin of choice, and minting rights were reserved for the mother city of the expanding empire. The empire grew with conquest and on conquest it fed. Conquest brought tribute in silver and gold. Conquest brought slaves to work the great Roman estates which swelled in size as small farmers were bought out. As in Greece, the land was turned to the profitable cultivation of olive and grape.

Since the price of wheat bound for Rome was kept artificially low, farmers without land or employment hied themselves to Rome. There the city fathers fed them with subsidized wheat from Egypt and amused them with gladiatorial spectacles. As the land declined in fertility, the wines of Gaul and other Roman provinces cornered the markets. Roman magistrates countered by ordering Gallic vines destroyed. Even so, Italian vineyards could not compete. Slaves of the great estates could no longer be fed and were released. These in their turn descended on the capital, there to swell the ranks of the hard-core unemployed.[21]

In time, provincial tribute slowed to a silver trickle, and expenditure outran revenue. All sorts of fiscal remedies were tried. Taxes were raised (and sometimes paid in goods, not money). Prices were fixed. Workmen were tied to their jobs, peasants to the land, and their sons after them. Money was debased. At last the great absentee landlords, finding the capital an uncomfortable home, retired to their rural estates. These in time became the small-subsistence economies that marked the Middle Ages. Each estate was self-contained, closed in on itself, unmindful of the world and what lay beyond its own fields and forests. Until trade revived with piepowder caravans. Until cities bloomed once again. Until discovery of the New World revitalized the old and turned faces outward toward the promise of gold, gold with which Native Americans were still celebrating their gods and could not imagine as wealth.

MONEY AND METAPHOR

In the long run, as history has demonstrated over and over again, the real wealth of a people lies in its will to produce, to use, to strive for something better in life. Money simply represents this reality and, in that respect, is a special kind of language. Like language, money is a system of symbols ordered by its own "grammar," or rules of use. Like language, its meanings are quite arbitrarily imposed. The money metals are rare and therefore valuable. But they are by no means the only precious things of life, many of which do not and cannot serve as units of value—water, for example, clean air, love. By only minimal adjustments of "grammar," the precious aspect of money could be abandoned altogether. Tokens with no intrinsic value would serve as well; indeed, they have served so in the past and do so now while we pursue the glittering illusion of treasure.

No one knows where in Mesopotamia the custom arose of substituting clay tablets—marked with a promise to pay—

for the silver itself. Out of this grew, in millennial fits and starts, the institution of payment by check or through the elaborate green bills we call dollars; the French call francs; the Germans, marks; the British, pounds sterling. They all promise guaranteed redemption in gold or silver. They did once, that is, but do so no longer, merely proclaiming in one language or another that: "this bill is legal tender for all debts public or private." Even our coins are mostly copper now with only a little nickel to silver them up a bit and carry scarcely more in actual value than subway or bus tokens, when all is said and done. Yet nobody grumbles about debased coinage as they did in ancient times. Internal values today have little to do with the precious metals but everything to do with the government decision to mint or print.

With the high cost and complexity of money transactions, alternate currencies have begun to appear. Food stamps now function in any number of exchange situations which have nothing to do with food. And a number of small towns have inaugurated more or less complicated systems of barter. These range from the simple one-to-one transaction ("You fix my car, and I'll paint your house.") to the central clearinghouse which assigns quite arbitrary "credits" to certain products and services (from backyard chickens to baby-sitting) and then "banks" these for participants in the system.

As renewed barter takes us one step backward in the process of complete identification with money, the widespread use and misuse of credit cards takes us one step further along the road to money abstraction. Eventually, so the experts tell us, we can abandon our wallets—those overloaded collections of currency, credit cards, and sometimes coins, so heavy as to have induced known cases of trauma to hip or shoulder. Eventually our debits and credits will be handled by computers, and we shall have to identify ourselves only via thumbprint or voiceprint to activate the process. No more nickles and dimes.

Although the phenomenon of money has been well known in many cultures, nowhere have the operations of money become so separated from the comprehension of the ordinary mortal. The value of money, in all its transactions and permutations, seems to have an existence on a plane other than that of its creators, seems to function under its own immutable and inscrutable laws, and commands the reverence and dedication of countless experts. One might rather call them priests, for the analogies to religion are inescapable.

Money has temples (banks and stock exchanges). It has an arcane theological language used by an international clergy (GNP, Supply Side, the Prime Rate, the Mighty Fed). It has its own totemic beings: the Bull and the Bear. Its high-level operations are more or less separated from the mass of the uninitiated, the great ignorant populace (including you and me). There are even competing money churches, each with its holy writ, its deity figures, its elaborate dogma designed to bring utopia to the polity that accepts conversion.

No wonder British anthropologist Mary Douglas calls money "an extreme and specialized type of ritual."[22] Just as celebrations of the sacred make orderly the confusing experiences of self, so money brings order to many social and economic transactions. For like ritual, money standardizes worth and helps to evaluate experience. Like ritual, money forges a link between what has been and what will be. Like ritual, money depends for its effectiveness on faith.

SERMONS IN STONE

Consider Yap, a Micronesian island in the Pacific. It is dotted with stone disks ranging in size from a man's hand to a yard or more in diameter and weighing several tons. Each was pierced long ago to facilitate transport. For the largest, thirty men on each end of a palm tree would not be too many to achieve lift. Once in place, however, this treasure was seldom moved even when ownership changed. It was, rather, credited to a new owner's account in much the way that our gold "outflow" actually travels nowhere except in the ledgers of the Federal Reserve Bank.

In other times, payment for Yap goods and services could be made in shell money processed at home. Stone money was *best* money, the money of renown, the money of blood debt and loan debt, interest for which was payable in labor. Forever that money stands as a memorial to value and valor, for each stone was quarried on the distant island of Palau. The people there were perfectly willing to part with their stone since they used a different prestige currency, one said to have come from yet another island, mysterious and lost. After quarrying, each precious stone was towed home on frail rafts, towed home against the winds and tides which sent many a man and his money to the bottom of the sea.[23]

Over a century ago explorers and observers asked why. Why money in Paradise? Why debts and struggle where the living is easy, where food abounds, where every good thing is near to hand? But consider. If all is easy, how does one measure value? How understand one's own worth? How gauge one's potential? Quite simply by creating tests. "No gains without pains," the old proverb tells us. If there are no pains, they must be invented, for only thus can gains have meaning.

OTHER SERMONS

In that sense, our own money is not so different from the stones or shells we call "primitive." Neither is it so impersonal as we would like to suppose, so disembedded from its web of individual worth, its matrix of social values.

In our calculations, net worth has always indicated as much about personal competence as about potential purchasing power. Poets, scholars, inventors, artists are barely tolerated among us until their works receive the mandate of money. Quality, for us, is affirmed by the paying public or by affluent patrons willing to back their preferences with large amounts of ready cash. The reputations of physicians, attorneys, professors are enhanced by the trappings of wealth (the Cadillac, the Mercedes, the condominium, the country club). Not only does this bespeak superior professional skills but business acumen as well. Our society does not honor the poor manager, whatever his other accomplishments in life.

Like the Kwakiutl, we value what we pay for, and the more we pay, the greater our willingness to accentuate the positive. The incompetence of an executive commanding a large salary is much more likely to be excused than that of the poorly paid clerk. Time may well uncover the inadequacies of the one and the sterling qualities of the other. But time for us is often in shorter supply than money, and money meanwhile offers a quick index of worth.

Like the Kwakiutl, we insist that every achievement, every promotion be validated by money—money awarded, displayed, or at work in the bank. However moving the academic rites in which he is "hooded," the Ph.D. recipient remains in social limbo until he can translate his academic recognition into high-powered employment, for money is the ultimate validation of rank. By increasing purchasing power for great segments of individuals, trade-union negotiators over the years have done more to elevate the worker's sense of worth and social position than any leveling mechanism enacted into law. No wonder that women who once ran homes, reared children, managed charitable enterprises as unpaid volunteers, now demand monetary recognition even for activities hard to monetize or to sustain on that basis.

Ask an American college class to identify the nature of ultimate national value and at least one young cynic will confidently sing out, "The almighty dollar!" And have in mind simply greed. The image of the grasping American is, after all, one fondly cherished both in and outside our continental borders. And yet, even if that were the whole truth of the matter, one might well prefer greed to other currently available indices of personal worth: membership in caste or class; religious affiliation and ideological purity;

political affiliation and ideological purity. All the foregoing depend on the accidents of birth or the exigencies of group and leave little room for individual effort and individual hope.

Ultimately, it is effort and hope—for the nation as for the individual—that are symbolized for us in money. Indeed, the message has appeared and appears still on the currency itself.[24] Early American coins were stamped with thirteen interlocking rings to signify the uneasy union of the time, meanwhile adding these hopeful words, "We are one!" The reverse side carried a sundial. Over it in Latin was the word *fugio*, "I fly." Time flies? An emblem, then, of Heavenly grace through labor. The Puritan work ethic made manifest. As the good old hymn exhorts:

> "Work, for the night is coming,
> Work for the setting sun.
> Work, for the night is coming,
> When man's work is done."

The dollar today bears all the metaphors of the American political creed. The figure of the eagle, our totemic bird, is shown bearing an olive branch of peace with thirteen leaves. His other talons grasp a sheaf of thirteen arrows signifying readiness to defend the nation. Around and above the eagle's head are thirteen stars and the motto, *E pluribus unum*, "One out of many" (in thirteen letters). There is also a pyramid. It is thirteen-layered and yet unfinished to show that much labor remains if we would complete our undertaking. On the pyramid shines the all-seeing eye of Him who has favored that undertaking.

No, God did not create our money, but (the meaning is loud and clear) He has surely blessed the work that earned it.

PART TWO

BUSINESS

AND

SOCIETY

7

FAMILY
AND BUSINESS

THE IMPORTANCE OF FEELING
RELATED

*The ties that matter are the ties to
each other.*

S. I. NEWHOUSE, FOUNDER,
S. I. NEWHOUSE AND SONS.[1]

"Institution" is a heavy word, burdened with semantic freight and no little confusion. "Our institutions are at risk," we intone solemnly in vague reference to "The American Way of Life."

When we say, "That poor child will have to be institutionalized," we have in mind a building in which custodial care is provided.

When we say, "This curriculum change will be good for the institution," we are speaking of a particular organization, a school, a college.

Sometimes we use the word to describe people. "No, Miss Brown, Professor Castairs is *not* an institution even though he seems to have been here since the earth cooled."

For the social scientist, "institution" is shorthand for a fairly durable set of rules, forms, and procedures collected over time around a particular human task. It constitutes a guide for behavior, if you will, the ultimate "how to." We cannot see Economy, the institution, in action any more than we can see the Freudian Id (though sometimes we think we *ought* to, so vivid has the image become). What we *do* see is the corner grocery store which came into being by way of institutional models and functions according to institutional rules.

The economic institution, in short, has to do with keeping body and soul together. The striving and thriving part attended the business spinoffs—the creation of manufacturing, banking, and trading as separate institutions. (Marketing is now in process of institutionalizing on its own.)

The spinoff process is what the specialist might well call "disembedding." But it is by no means peculiar to business. Every modern "how-to" had its beginning in another institutional preserve. Education and medicine are offspring of religion (as almost what is not?). Even when societies are complex and support an array of rules and procedures for many separable tasks, some directives invariably command the rest. Every culture, every age has its dominant institutions, is given color and purpose by institutional metaphors. Religion and rule have each, in their turn, held sway over the minds of men. But first of all came family.

THE MASTER INSTITUTION

It was in small groups of relatives that our ancestors of a million and more years ago found their humanity. They doubtless celebrated the sacred in these groups with the eldest males (and sometimes eldest females) presiding over the mysteries—as hunting-and-gathering people do to this day. They brought up their young in the bosom of the family, and all that was to be known of the world and its ways was taught there. Family members sustained life by dividing the work among men and women, young and old. It should come as no surprise that "economy" itself derives from the Greek words *oikos*, "a household," and *nem*, "regulate, organize." In other words, survival was in the beginning, and has been for most of human time afterward, a family business.

Even today, when household norms locate mother in one job, father in another, children in school, and nary a common task unless it be play, some family businesses remain. You can see them in the bigger cities of America: the Korean grocery stores; the Chinese, Vietnamese, and Greek restaurants where Father cooks, Mother minds the cash register, and the children wait table before and after school.

Many of America's biggest enterprises had such humble beginnings and, instead of going public, have succeeded in keeping everything in the family. Indeed, as Dan Rottenberg reports in a recent article, they account for about 45 percent of all sales in the United States. Many could qualify for the Fortune 500 list but do not appear there because they are privately owned. One of these is Cargill, Inc., begun in the late 1800s by the operator of a country grain elevator. Though now a commodity conglomerate with sales that outstrip those of U.S. Steel or Gulf Oil, it is still a family business.[2] There are many others, some so small as to go unnoticed, even by their local Chambers of Commerce. One of these is Gene's Variety Store of Norwalk, Connecticut:

"We're a family kind of business," said Gene Scarangella. By that he had in mind not just the fact that his wife and children work with him. He was thinking as well of all the teenagers who, at one time or another, had also become 'family' in his store.

"I've had several kids work for me all through high school, some through college until they went to grad school," said Gene. "We've had some older women, too, recently widowed or divorced. They were scared at first to meet the public, scared to work the cash register. But because we've a family sort of store, because we're flexible, we could let them come in a few hours at a time until they felt comfortable and confident. Some of them have moved on to really important positions elsewhere.

"That's the beauty part about being what we are. We can make time. Some big chains can pay kids more, but they can't let them off for a football game, to take a driver's test, to study for a big exam. They can't even let the kids go to a prom. That's a big thing, a prom. I remember. But *we* can do that. We can make time."

What about his own children? "My daughter wanted to work here from the time she was in second grade. Eight years old and she was running the cash register and making the customers feel at home. My son is a little more shy with the public. I pay them regular salaries. But they think of the store as *theirs*. If we have a really sensational day, they are thrilled.

"I don't care if they follow me in the business. I want them to do something they enjoy doing as much as I love what I'm doing."[3]

The joy in a family business is the working *with* as much as the working *for*. "I believe in work," said Gene, "so that I can make a life with my family."

OLDER MODELS

In other places, other times, land was the family business
or the animals that graze the land. The proper herding family balked at consuming capital assets and gave up livestock
willingly only when acquiring wives for sons of the family.
In tribes where judicial procedures can be found, the most
common disputes still brought before the elders (and ran-
corous they are, too) are those over nonpayment of
bridewealth, delayed payment of bridewealth, defective animals given for bridewealth. A lively sense of profit and loss
is not unknown even in societies where family and inter-
family reciprocity is supposed to rule the economic roost.

Herding people (and I am thinking especially of East
African Nilotes) cannot subsist by milk alone or by blood
drawn from the necks of their cattle. They need grain, and
when their wives' meager fields are bare, they must trade
for it with farming tribes on the plains' periphery. In each
of these a man usually has a bond friend, a trading partner
who might well be the son of his own father's partner in
an inherited relationship that is not quite kin, but certainly
a close approximation. Some East Africans were wont to
solidify the metaphor, becoming brother in blood with the
trading partner. Thus they came to share, not only an interest in exchange but all the same avoidances and kinship
obligations as well. An excellent way to be at home abroad,
even while doing business.[4]

Since the Neolithic Revolution, there have always been
more farmers than herders to be found, more who tilled the
soil and called it Mother. No wonder that to this day, land
is called *real property,* for it was once the source of life and
all there was of wealth besides. Among most rural folk, the
connection between land and its holders is as much a spiritual as a legal reality. Even today's businessman-farmer
would understand how, in many places and times, land was
reckoned another kind of kin, inseparable from its "family." It could not be sold but could be "married into" an-

other family with bridewealth given in exchange. Many smiles and tears; many promises to visit soon and often. No owner, no buyer. Just a wedding.

In prerevolutionary China, the same procedures, the same attitudes prevailed. When land changed hands, the event was celebrated as a wedding by the receiving family, a funeral by those bereft. Indeed, before a piece of land could change ownership, every related male—close or distant—had to give assent. One suspects the ancestors themselves were consulted. For it was a man's duty to those who went before and to those as yet unborn to keep the patrimony intact, even to enlarge it if at all possible.

In the old China (and again today in newly constituted family farms) the land came first. Every member of the lineal family—three generations, usually—lived on it, worked it, or worked *for* it. Whatever a young man earned away from home was sent to father, who managed the collective finances. Even if the young man became a well-to-do merchant, the greatest part of his earnings would always be used to line the family purse and buy family land.[5]

In the course of time, however, and as the older generation passed on, merchants were likely to establish their own lines, which also owned but did not necessarily farm a family plot. The trading profession, as we have seen, was family-fixed from Shang Dynasty times, as were many other crafts and arts. Now, children often tend to do what their parents have done before them. The world dominated by family images comes in time, not merely to expect, but to insist on occupational inheritance. We have seen it in Africa across the Sudan. The Indian caste system enshrined such a principle. Roman emperors tried to impose it by fiat. Why? Because to connect land with blood; occupation with blood; skills, demeanor, inclinations, all with blood, is to invoke the most ancient and persuasive sanctions. Persuasive because rooted in an institution that has proved to give order, stability, and meaning in an all too disorderly world.

BEYOND BLOOD

But the commercial hazards of city life seemed to preserve neither family lines nor the businesses originated by family founders. Matsuyo Takaziwa, writing in 1927 of the disintegration of the Family System in feudal Japan, quotes an ancient source:

> "It is rare for a merchant family to last for many generations, but there are many families in the villages that are several hundred years old."[6]

Fritz Rorig, writing of medieval merchants in Europe, echoes those sentiments:

> "The grandchildren of economically outstanding fathers grew weak in business sense, preferring to live on fixed investments and died without leaving an heir. One can see just as frequently a branch of an old merchant family living an aristocratic-lord-of-the-manor life in the country and blossoming for generations, long after the original family in the town had died out."[7]

If, in the confusion of city life, family lines died out, *familylike* associations, conceived in the interests of trade, seemed to go on forever. Or as close to forever as human frailty permits. Before the Chinese Revolution suspended "forever," the Bankers' Guild at Ningpo maintained records which traced its beginnings back to the Chou Dynasty (1122–255 B.C.). The Druggist Guild at Wenchow merely alleged in their secret documents an existence "from the days of yore to the present."

"Brother," said the opium dealer to his colleague in the *t'ang,* or hall of the opium dealers' guild. "We are brothers." And so they were; so were all guild members brothers, united in opposition to a government that might practice extortion beyond its due, harass members, or meddle

in matters of business that were none of its business. Behind a solid wall of resistance, members policed one another, and woe betide the colleague who undercut prices, who kept too many apprentices, or lured a talented journeyman away from a brother and into his own employ. He could be boycotted, given the shunning treatment, put out of business. For every occupation or pursuit was organized into a guild—the chambermaids, the rickshaw coolies, the sweepers—everyone. And they could be enjoined, through their own guild leaders, to enforce a boycott.[8]

Even foreign merchants had their guilds which, among other things, would arrange to return deceased members to their natal cities. Only the wholesalers—who transported goods across China—were free-lance entrepreneurs; in such dangerous work, guild protection was of little help. This sort of merchant had to travel with his shipment from point to point. He had to have the talent and the courage to negotiate safe passage with bandits and warlords as well as government officials and somehow manage to keep the shipment intact.

> It is, perhaps, in keeping with the Chinese sense of tradition that the first private corporation to reappear at the behest of the People's Republic is a shipping company which once had a fleet of 150 vessels and was named Misheng. Its founder committed suicide when the firm was nationalized.
>
> Today, his son has been named to head the revived firm. Already, reports *Wall Street Journal* correspondent Victor Fung, surviving employees have surfaced. They will be part of an enterprise answerable only to its stockholders. The central government will be content to collect corporation taxes.
>
> So fully restored to grace is the long-gone capitalist that the government has authorized publication of a book honoring his memory. And everything is still in the family, with or without that fictive family, the guild.[9]

In ancient Mesopotamia, merchant venturers as well as those in foreign cities were organized into guilds, as much to evade the long arm of the law as to stave off unwanted intrusion into their affairs. *"Brother,"* they addressed one another in letters, such as this one from Anatolia: "Do not make me act on my own responsibility. The police stations are very strict at the moment."[10]

Those merchants who failed to meet their obligations were faced with "shame in the assembly of merchants" and the threat, "you will also cease to be one of us."[11]

"Brother," says the Portland longshoreman in his union's hiring hall. It may well be a matter of kin as well as kind. Until recently, union membership was extended only to sons, brothers, or brothers-in-law of members in good standing. Friends, maybe, but they had to be *close* friends. For it was "us against all employers everywhere." Indeed, the oath taken by all men joining the union includes the reference to fraternity:

> "I will strive to create a brotherly feeling between our Union and organizers who mean to uphold the dignity of labor and to affirm the nobility of all who earn their bread by the sweat of their brow, and I will not deal in any manner with any person who is an enemy of labor."[12]

"Brother," said the medieval merchant to his colleague in the *gildhalle,* for they were bound to one another by a similar oath of fidelity as well as by common peril. For in their trading forays they had to defend one another against bandits and robber barons swooping down from hilltop castles to pluck the loathsome mercantile geese and appropriate their golden eggs. These trading caravans were called *Hanse.* So were the merchants' Baltic ships. So was the alliance of merchants. And it was under the name of the Hanse that European trading cities all around the Baltic and North seas confederated in order to do business.

So powerful was the sense of brotherhood that these cities never warred on one another as did merchant cities of the southland. So powerful was the sense of brotherhood that "family values" in business were upheld by all. The fact is enshrined today in the British pound sterling which derives from "easterling," or the reliable man of the eastern Hanse with his reliable money.[13]

NATURE, NURTURE, AND THE BURGH

While the family image lent unity and staying power to medieval business associations, the real families of business men, safe behind the walls of their burghs, were developing new notions of family function. In the households of merchant men and craftsmen, artisans, butchers, bakers, clothiers, small manufacturers of every sort, there were slowly emerging attitudes and values quite different from anything known among the aristocracy in their country manors or by peasants tied to the soil.

In the aristocrat's world, rule was a function of blood; position was a function of blood. High or low, all was decreed by descent. The family metaphor again, at work in the feudal ordering of society. Since this was so, why fuss overmuch with the education of one's children? The essential attributes, after all—bearing, courage, grace—were theirs by birthright.

The peasant went along with his lord's view of reality, perhaps even with that saying common among the nobility, "The peasant is best when he is weeping." He believed it was his destiny to labor on the land, struggling to wring from it the necessities of life. He believed that, in return for protection and order, he owed the lord his grain, his service, and his deference. The new male baby in a peasant household was welcomed for the extra pair of hands he would eventually provide; meanwhile, his was another mouth to feed and a hindrance to his mother's labor. Why strive to better one's position when God had willed it so? Why strive at all when God had set limits to the good things on earth, when the success of one peasant could come only at the expense of another? Better and safer to accept one's lot and stay exactly the same as everybody else.[14]

The medieval man of business put his faith in nurture

and left nature for the men of the land, be they high or low. Had he not made himself? Had he not wrung from local grandees the right to give his own daughter in marriage, the right to bequeath his own property? Very well. He would guarantee his children's futures. He would teach his sons to build on his success, to make their own way in the world. His was a busy, bustling household, one in which everyone worked hard to prosper the family business. The apprentices and journeymen who were part of the household looked forward to being master tradesmen themselves one day. It was a heady prospect.

GETTING BUSINESS OUT OF THE FAMILY

In later medieval times, family life for the thriving businessman came to be increasingly separated from the workplace, and the notion of a woman's role underwent redesign. Mother was to be freed from business cares in order to focus undivided attention on her children; and children were freed from business to study, to play, to experience childhood—a concept (some specialists hold) that was created by the medieval business family. In the city there were no extended-family compounds of the sort we find among the West African Yoruba. The typical medieval family in trade consisted of father, mother, children, and assorted dependent relatives and servants. It was a unit small enough to nurture the individuality of its members but large enough, stable enough to provide the essential core of security without which no child can reach his full potential. This is the observation of Brigitte Berger and Peter L. Berger in their incisive book, *The War Over the Family*.[15]

While it is true that the wealthiest burghers often sought to ape their betters, mothers in most medieval business families were loath to abdicate their role to nurse or nanny, as was the habit of the aristocrats. Mother was a constant presence. And after the Protestant Reformation, her presence was apt to be an admonishing one, always insistent on piety, industry, personal responsibility, personal achievement, and refined behavior. She ruled the home as father ruled the business and spent her extra energy in charity, good works, and uplifting cultural programs. She proselytized among the urban poor for the family style and family values that, by the eighteenth century, were becoming dominant in the West. Hear Daniel Defoe on the subject:

> "The tradesman that does not delight in his family will never long delight in his business; for as one great end of an honest tradesman's diligence is the support of his family, so the very sight of an affectionate wife and children is the spur of his diligence; this puts an edge upon his mind, and makes a good parent or husband hunt the world for business, as eager as hounds hunt the woods for their game."[16]

Such a vision still seemed at that time utterly utopian to laboring men and women. Imagine the bliss of being free for the kiddies! Impossible when labor yielded such small return. And yet, as the decades brought increasing prosperity, the ideal became ever more attainable. Until the 1960s, as Peter Drucker points out, a workingman's self-respect was rooted in his ability to provide for the family so well that his wife need never work for wages away from home. It was her pride, too, though we tend to forget that amid the distractions of change.[17]

Whether or not getting business out of the family was a good thing will be a judgment of history. It must be admitted, however, that the straitlaced middle-class family tended to produce children strong on individualism, self-disciplined and self-starting. The Bergers suggest that these particular values are essential both to democracy and to entrepreneurial capitalism.

Karl Marx thought so, too, which explains why he inveighed so bitterly against what was called the *bourgeois family model*. "It creates," he said, "a world after its own image." That word "bourgeois," deriving from the various spellings of "town" (burgh, bourg) and meaning, essentially "middle class," had long been in use. Marx and his followers gave it a new aura of meaning, one that evoked images of everything selfish, petty, narrow, greedy, and stodgy. It is a usage that still prevails in some intellectual circles.

What to do about the bourgeois family? Abolish it, Marx recommends in the *Communist Manifesto:*

> "On what foundation is the present family, the bourgeois family based? On capital, on private gain. . . . Do you charge us with wanting to stop the exploitation of children by their parents? To this crime we plead guilty . . . [we will] rescue education from the influence of this ruling class. . . . The bourgeois sees in his wife a mere instrument of production . . . the real point aimed at [by communism] is to do away with the status of women as mere instruments of production. Bourgeois marriage is in reality a system of wives in common and thus, at the most, what the communists might be reproached with is what they desire to introduce, in substitution for a hypocritically concealed, an openly legalized community of women."[18]

Marx knew well the noneconomic nature of the bourgeois woman's role. We must therefore assume that when he says, "The bourgeois sees in his wife a mere instrument of production," he has in mind her function as childbearer, as provider of sexual satisfaction and domestic comfort to her lord and master.

Bourgeois society, led by its clergy, was naturally horrified by the call for "an openly legalized community of women." The American minister, Rev. Adolphus J.F. Behrends, writing in 1886, declared,

> We have a right to expect and to demand the clearest and most abundant proof for the revolutionary doctrine that communal marriage was the primary form of domestic life, in which the women were the wives of all the men . . . and the children possessed only a communal parentage."[19]

Marx and Engels found in the writings of Lewis Henry Morgan—an American attorney turned anthropologist—all the scientific validity they needed, and Engels popularized his treatise, *Ancient Society*.[20] Morgan postulated an evolutionary ladder of culture which all the world's peoples were presumed to have climbed or to be climbing still. Each rung, each stage and way of life, was marked by an appropriate technology, an appropriate mode of production, and appropriate rules for reproduction. Marx and Engels thought that something like the innocent early ages of human society—it came to be called primitive communism—would reappear with the withering away of the state, private property, and the bourgeois family. As Engels observed,

> "The first class opposition that appears in history coincides with the development of the antagonism between men and women in monogamous marriage, and the first class oppression coincides with that of the female sex by the male."[21]

No modern anthropologist puts much stock in Morgan's scheme. It has not stood the test of time or observation. (Hunting-and-gathering folk, for example, in a presumed stage of primitive communism, remain the world's most determinedly monogamous and nuclear in family orientation.) Nevertheless, Lewis Henry Morgan—or rather, his famous ladder—is alive and well and living in the Soviet Union where the archaeologist who knows what is good for him finds evidence for it in every dig.

ON THE ROAD TO PERFECTION

Marx and Engels were not alone in their vision of the perfect society. Nearly every utopia, late or soon, has included group marriage and the communal family among its list of imperatives along with common property and the abolition of money. Sometimes the dreams have been put into practice. Case in point: the Oneida Community of upper New York State.

Founded in 1847 by John Humphrey Noyes, a sometime minister, its members dispensed with private property up to and including sexual property. There were some exceptions, as described by William Kephart in his book, *Extraordinary Groups*. Noyes reserved the right to be "first husband" to every young girl reaching puberty. His every utterance was received as the Word from On High. "If Mr. Noyes takes a pinch of snuff, the whole community sneezes," was a favorite saying. Once, when a visitor commented on the interesting aroma that pervaded the mansion in which they all lived, he was told, "It must be the smell of crushed selfishness." Members signed formal documents which declared,[22]

> "We do not belong to ourselves in any respect, but first to God and second to Mr. Noyes as God's true representative."[23]

That the community did not at first abound with children owed to Noyes's system of *coitus reservatus*, or male continence. When members were permitted to reproduce, it was according to Noyes's strict concept of eugenics. (He himself had fathered ten different children with different mothers.) The children were brought up communally with no "special love" for parents permitted to develop.

This idyllic "family" experiment persisted for about forty years and then broke up in a welter of recrimination and hastily formalized marriages to avoid prosecution. It survives today as a corporation based on the silverware concern initiated during the communal days. Oneida, Ltd, is run by a descendant of Dr. Noyes, and so it remains, in some sense, a "family" business.

Another experiment in utopia had its beginnings in San Francisco. One day in 1970 a motley array of hippies, led by Steven Gaskin, a sometime teacher and full-time religious *guru*, boarded a collection of run-down school buses and headed east. They dreamed of finding safe haven for their unconventional life-style, a place where they could take dope, love freely, and do their own uninhibited thing.

They found such a place near Nashville, Tennessee, and called it, almost facetiously, "The Farm." Nobody then knew very much about farming or cared to learn.

Fifteen years later The Farm is still communal in terms of property. Everything is shared, and if a member manages to procure anything—like a camera, for example—he or she takes care to hide it under the bed. In all other respects the group has executed a 180 degree turn. They now live in strictly monogamous family units which produce lots of children. (Birth control and abortion are forbidden. So is extracurricular love of any sort.) The use of marijuana is reserved for ritual occasions as a kind of sacrament. Indeed, The Farm has developed its own religion based on dietary restrictions and "crushed selfishness."

Most surprising, the former hippies have embraced the work ethic. They have become highly efficient farmers, generating enough prosperity to permit the formation of ten satellite colonies and business ventures into publishing and repair of Citizens Band radios. Prosperity is abetted by personal donations, and members who work on the outside turn their wages over to the group. Women do traditional "women's work" and claim they could not imagine any other arrangement.

Lotus Land has been banished from The Farm. So has "doing your own thing." The Farm's will is Steven's will. As Kate Wenner reports, "Farm members are relieved of the burden of their ambitions by being offered, in its place, ambition on behalf of the group." As one member told her, "You've got to work it out with Steven, or you wouldn't want to be here."[24]

A similar dedication to work characterizes the famous Israeli kibbutzim, many of which constitute the world's only realized utopias based on Marxian principles. In the early days, just before and just after the creation of the Israeli state, the kibbutz was considered not only as the hope of Israeli society, but of the entire world. Anthropologist Melford Spiro, who lived for a year in a Marxist kibbutz and later revisited it, quotes one of its leaders when he called the kibbutz

> "the foundation cell of the future society that is already in process of realization today. . . . The property system, method of production, division of labor, foundation of the family, the character of human relations, the status of women, the foundation of education—all have changed in their fundamentals and are in the process of permanent change."[25]

The kibbutz was designed to be a child-centered society, a society in which "the child is emancipated from the rule of the father of the family"; a society in which a woman would be (in the words of a Kibbutz Federation document)

> "emancipated from the burden of the raising of children, emancipated from the feeling of 'belonging' to her husband, the provider and the one who commands. . . . We broke the shackles that chained her."[26]

In this large extended "family," all children were thought of as "our" children. They were tended and taught, therefore, by "our" surrogates, nurses, and teachers who lived with the children in their own special quarters.

Dr. Spiro was moved to ask in a 1954 article, "Is the Family Universal?"[27] Only later did he realize that he had missed something. True, the kibbutz in general frowned on marriage, and sexual relations were legalized only at the behest of the government. Still and all, kibbutz sensibilities forbade promiscuity and expected that the couple petitioning to be roommates would remain so until death parted them. And the children of such a couple—who saw their parents only briefly after each work day—still somehow thought of the couple's room as "home," finding in it a sense of belonging. The conjugal family lives after all, Dr. Spiro conceded.

Paradise was not without strains, however. Women found themselves doing "women's work" despite the ringing rhetoric. That being the case, some women murmured, why not do it for one's own family, not four hundred other people? Moreover, they *wanted* their children with them. They *wanted* to put them to bed at night and greet them in the morning. They'd also like to own a few possessions.

At a meeting of federated kibbutzim, the following statement was included in a resolution:

> "We believe in the individual but not for his own sake. The individuality of the new man is only valuable to the degree that it helps to build the new society."[28]

Education geared to this task is difficult to assess for results. Dr. Spiro noted that kibbutz *sabras*, native-born Israelis, displayed a strong sense of responsibility to others but had a tendency to remain closed emotionally, to be reserved, to form few attachments, to be hesitant of defying the group. As one girl told Dr. Spiro:

> "The general result of collective education over the years is that it restricts initiative. If I had to live in the outside world, I could not adjust to it."[29]

Even at the beginning, the kibbutz movement, though praised and respected throughout the country, constituted but a small portion of the economy. It is still smaller today, estimated at 5 percent of the population and shrinking as many sabras are lured to city life, to the pursuit of careers (frowned on in the kibbutz), or to find a little privacy. They leave behind communal farms that have begun to industralize as well. Indeed, kibbutz factories—producing everything from furniture to pipes—are so successful, earn so much money that some older kibbutzniks worry about capitalist contamination.

CHANGING VIEWS

"We are a socialist island in the midst of a capitalist sea."[30] That was the attitude of kibbutzniks among whom Melford

Spiro lived. Perhaps it is only in islands, physically separate from the dominant way of life that utopian beliefs concerning family and property can be fully realized. For attractions of the dominant mode are hard to resist. No wonder hopes of changing the dominant mode, the larger society, spring eternal in certain fervent hearts. The Marxian image of utopia has always carried greater appeal for intellectual members of society than for working men and women. Most of all, in recent years, for intellectuals of the feminist movement.

Jean Bethke Elshtain, associate professor of political science at the University of Massachusetts, said in a recent issue of *The Nation,*

"The insistence that the family must be destroyed or smashed (rather than reformed or reconstructed) is a theme running through much radical feminist literature."[31]

To feminists who denounce capitalism for encouraging dependence on the family, she replies that

" . . . one could make precisely the opposite case—that capitalists have historically had an interest in breaking up family units and eroding family ties. The capitalist ideal is a society of social atoms . . . who could be shunted about according to market imperatives alone."[32]

Interestingly enough, the Marxist feminists, of whom Professor Elshtain approves (as opposed to the radical feminists of whom she does not) have taken to extolling the monogamous nuclear family as a haven from "the soul destroying values of the market place."[33] Not standard Marxist fare, surely.

Whether you view the bourgeois family as haven or prison nearly everyone agrees that it has problems, or to put it another way, is in transition. Manifestations include a high divorce rate; every other marriage currently terminates in this manner. There are others. The rate of out-of-wedlock births has risen astronomically since 1960. The number of single-parent households has risen. Most of these are headed by women; most are living below the poverty line. The number of teenage suicides has risen; some have involved children as young as twelve. The rate of infanticide is up. Child abuse is up. Drug abuse among the young is higher than in any other Western nation. The urban schoolroom is frequently a battleground. More than 45 percent of the nation's mothers work outside the home; whether this constitutes a "problem" depends on the specialist queried. All the foregoing are being experienced to some degree in every developed nation, even in family-centered Japan.

Who's at fault? "Business," some experts are quick to respond. "Change the way business is done." Why? "Because modern business separates wives from their husbands and both from the children. Because there is too much emphasis on cost-effectiveness in business and not enough on family effectiveness."

It is hard to imagine what business can do to cement marriages and mind the children. Some corporations are making an effort, nevertheless. General Mills (ever a purveyor of family images) runs seminars and study groups about family problems. The Leo Burnett advertising agency and several other concerns help make new families possible by giving employees who want to adopt children up to $3,000 in aid. Generous as they are, these are efforts that can have little impact on society at large. Changes in values, after all, come from the grass-roots level of society and percolate upward.[34]

Sociologist Urie Bronfenbrenner finds wider causes for family disarray. Some of them have to do with urban layout and construction. Business and residential zones are separate; they should be merged. Because of the separation, no child sees Daddy—or Mother, for that matter—at work. And if he does, he's just a visitor, a hindrance. He has no reason to be there, no connection. Gone are neighborhood businesses. Supermarkets have replaced the small grocery shops whose owners knew and liked the children in the neighborhood.[35]

Who is minding the store? the sociologist wants to know. Who is watching out for the child? In the absence of parents, he is cared for by a succession of schoolteachers, baby-sitters, and the ever-present television set to which he gains access by a latchkey hung around his neck. There are few ways, says Dr. Bronfenbrenner, in which a youngster can relate *meaningfully* with adults, not as a custodial charge but as an assistant. And it is not just parents who are absent. All the significant, permanent adults have vanished from the child's life and he is thrown back for support on his peers, on a peer culture with values all its own. Bronfenbrenner and many others now regard with some nostalgia habits and practices discarded long ago as pernicious enemies of children: child labor, for example, and the apprentice system. Something of what that system meant for the young in 1737 we learn from Daniel Defoe:

"To leave a youth without government is indeed unworthy of any honest master; he cannot discharge himself as a master; for instead of taking care of him, he indeed casts him off, abandons him; and to put it into scripture words, he *leads him into temptation;* nay, he goes further, to use another scripture expression, he delivers him over to Satan."[36]

"I knew one very considerable tradesman in this city, and who always had five or six servants in his business, apprentices and journeymen, who lodged in his house, and he took this method with them; when he took an apprentice he told them beforehand the orders of his family and which he should oblige them to; particularly, that they should none of them be absent from his business without leave, nor out of the house after nine o'clock at night . . . [and] that if they had been out, he should ask them where they had been and in what company."[37]

Tyranny or concern? Take your pick.

The apprentice system operated in Harlem during the

1940s and 1950s to train young boys in the business of crime. Claude Brown, who wrote so poignantly about those days *(Manchild in the Promised Land)*, returned recently to find a very different place.

> "The neighborhood Fagins, so characteristic of the Harlem of my youth, are mostly absent. Contrary to what any sane observer might assume, these Dickensian scoundrels inadvertently exerted a restraining influence on the junior hoodlums.
> "They were not merely crime tutors who carefully selected pupils; they gave patient instruction in the commission of rational crimes. . . . They frowned on unnecessary violence." [38]

Today, says Claude Brown, the mugger who kills his victim is very much in style.

ADDRESSING THE PROBLEMS

"The family that *works* together stays together," specialists now seem to be saying. Demands to get-nasty-business-out-of-the-business-of-living are being replaced with recollections of how-sweet-it-was. Since not all children will have the opportunities of Gene Scarangella's children to make essential contributions to the family's welfare, since not all young people can be given employment by someone like Gene, the question seems to be: How can family members work together in meaningful ways?

Whatever the answer, there must first be time. How can large business concerns emulate the mom-and-pop store in flexibility? How arrange to give workers time away from business to pursue the business of family? Some corporations are experimenting with various forms of "flex-time." Plant employees of Mary Kay Cosmetics put in ten-hour days in a four-day week. Three days off. Hewlett-Packard allows an employee to work any eight-hour shift beginning at 6:00 A.M. For Rolm, another computer enterprise, your time is their time. Midnight, if you'd prefer.

Job sharing is another experiment being tried, mostly in professional settings. Say it's a university professorship. The teaching couple might share the same job. Ditto two female lawyers. Part-time work has long been an option for women who want to be at home when the children arrive from school. Long maternity (and, increasingly, paternity) leaves are being granted, and these include paid benefits and job guarantees. Some corporations are trying day-care allowances as part of their array of fringe benefits. Still others have organized day-care centers on company premises. It is too early yet to judge whether such efforts will have an impact on family life in America. They do, however, tend to mitigate the inhuman, uncaring image of Business.[39]

Some writers have wondered how many of these experiments would have taken place or how widespread they would be without the Japanese model, particularly since that model seemed at least partly responsible for a roaring economic boom. Though Japanese practice has been to provide generously for workers' families, however, its main emphasis has been on the corporation *as* family:

> The Japanese had always been family oriented, group oriented, with the individual subordinate to the head of his family and, finally, to the emperor, the father of the state. The effect of American occupation and the writing of a new constitution was to redirect the all powerful hold of the state into other institutions, also made dynamic by the family metaphor.
>
> Business was one of these and, perhaps, the most successful. Historian Paul Johnson describes the Kubata Iron and Machinery Works, which encouraged workers to think of their machines as "mothers and fathers," the products as "children," and factory visitors as "friends of the family."
>
> The facet of Japanese industry best known in the West is lifetime employment. That is not, as Peter Drucker points out,

typical of all business enterprises, but certainly of the larger ones. Once hired, the worker is guaranteed a job until he reaches age 55. (It has now been extended to 60.) Unless the man in question is to be one of the top leaders of the firm, he will then be terminated with two or three years' salary. He can afterward come back to his old job or move to a different plant, but at a very much reduced income.

Each young man in middle management is assigned a "big brother," a tutor and confidant who does not himself expect to reach the top. So, in a structure by no means as free and easy as its American counterpart, he has a friend and guide.

All workers are expected to learn most of the operations at their level. Management learns more. An accountant will be expected to learn, not only marketing, but perhaps welding as well. Lifetime learning is as important as lifetime earning to the Japanese. Productivity is the name of the game. And workers agree. Most turn up at the shop on Saturdays on their own time and stay late at work to discuss improvements in the product or in manufacturing processes.

They travel together, play together, drink together. They contribute enthusiastically to company news letters and literary journals. Everyone wears a company uniform, does group calisthenics before work, participates in company sports, and sings the company's song. The up-and-coming employee will certainly present his fiancee to the boss (and await approval before setting the wedding date). When in trouble, he is likely to turn to his boss rather than to a member of his natal family.[40]

The system has yielded spectacular results. The Japanese have captured world radio and television markets and seriously challenged American leadership in the automotive industry. They hope to steal a march in all high technology.

But there is a slight problem. The education which discourages individuality in favor of the group, the work life spent in the bosom of the family—these do not, somehow, foster innovation. "What the Japanese have generally been unable to achieve," says journalist Steve Lohr, "are the break-throughs, the scientific and technological leaps that can . . . create new industries and transform whole economies."

Japanese scientist Leo Esaki, who migrated to America and works for IBM, told Lohr, "If you are innovative, you like to challenge the unknown. Unfortunately, the group nature of Japanese society makes that very difficult." But innovation is what Japan seeks and its leaders are rethinking both education and the nature of their business institutions in order to achieve it.[41]

BENEVOLENCE, HOMEGROWN

Marxian images to the contrary notwithstanding, American industry has never lacked benevolent capitalists. One of the earliest water-powered factories in America was founded by a proper Bostonian, Francis Cabot Lowell, as the result of industrial espionage. While visiting a prominent English cotton manufacturer in 1810, Lowell memorized the machinery's design and "re-invented" it in Massachusetts. His corporation determined to create, as Benita Eisler tells us, "a labor force that would be a shining example of those ultimate Yankee ideals: profit and virtue, doing good and doing well."[42]

Help was drawn from the impoverished farms of New England—sturdy young women who came to earn the highest wages available to female employees anywhere at any type of work. For the proper care of its work force, the corporation established subsidized boardinghouses near the mills. These were managed by cheerful, God-fearing housemothers, widows with children to support. All in all, the experience was rather like finishing school, after which most girls would graduate into marriage (the average stint of employment was four years). The girls wrote home about their experiences:

> ". . . These mills are not such dreadful places as you imagine them to be. You think them dark, damp holes; as close

and black as—as the Black Hole. No, dear M., it is no such thing. They are high spacious well-built edifices, with neat paths around them, and beautiful plots of greensward. . . . One of the overseers . . . gave me a beautiful boquet [sic] the other morning. . . ."[43]

"You ask me how the girls behave in the mill and what are the punishments. . . . I have never heard of punishments or scoldings or anything of that sort. Sometimes an overseer . . . offends a girl by refusing to let her stay out of the mill, or some deprivation like that; and then . . . there are tears and pouts on her part."[44]

"When the [overseers] are fatherly sort of men, the girls frequently resort to them for advice and assistance about other affairs than their work. Very seldom is this confidence abused."[45]

"Let no one suppose that the "factory girls" are without guardian. We are placed in the care of overseers who feel under moral obligations to look out after our interests; and, if we are sick, to acquaint themselves with our situation and wants; and if need be, to remove us to the Hospital, where we are sure to have the best attendance. . ."[46]

"In Lowell, we enjoy abundant means of information, expecially in the way of public lectures. The time of lecturing is appointed to suit the confenience [sic] of the operatives; and sad indeed would be the picture of our Lyceums, Institutes, and scientific lecture rooms, if all the operatives should absent themselves."[47]

"Homework" assigned in these night schools often appeared in the official plant magazine, *The Lowell Offering*, published, edited, and written by the factory girls themselves.

There were similar "family-school" enterprises elsewhere. In addition to classes and reading rooms, H.J. Heinz provided dinners in a company dining room (the walls emblazoned with Algerlike epigrams), carriage rides, and weekly manicures. Hands that bottle pickles must, in Mr. Heinz's view, remain lovely to touch.[48]

Some scholars of Marxian persuasion have interpreted these experiments as "capitalistic ploys to break the family's control over work and workers." After a generation had been trained in proper work habits, presumably, cold efficiency and cost-effectiveness could then be allowed to take over.[49] It is not easy, however, to read worker exploitation into the policies of Thomas Watson, founder of International Business Machines Corporation some seventy years ago. In his company every worker could expect lifetime employment (and he held to this policy even during the Great Depression). He pioneered company country clubs, company dining rooms, company day-care centers, schools, libraries, and hotels. And it must be said that his care for company employees' welfare paid off handsomely in loyalty and productivity.[50]

Watson seemed to know instinctively what managers at General Motors learned in 1945. Employees there were invited to participate in a contest to choose the best among essays titled, "My Job and Why I Like It." What the essays revealed was the great importance workers placed on intangible things: a sense of fulfillment and pride of achievement; close and good relations with fellow workers and supervisors. All in all, an atmosphere approximating the good life in a real community.[51]

Today many companies aim to achieve that atmosphere, not necessarily in the spirit of the Yankee reformer, but because doing good makes doing well possible. Happy workers are productive workers; and educated workers are happy workers. What is more, educated workers are good candidates for promotion and that, too, makes for happiness all around. Modern industry probably underwrites the education of as many people as the U.S. Army Reserve. Indeed, it has become standard operating procedure in many companies, both large and small.

Policies differ, of course, and so does the amount of support offered. Some companies permit only job-related courses and reimburse the employee-student according to the grade earned. Some companies will see the employee through college and graduate school and provide time off besides. Colleges and universities, with their own tradition of faculty sabbaticals, have led the way in this department.

Typical of many educational benefit programs is that offered by the Norden Systems division of United Technologies Corporation. The company will support an employee in two courses per semester, reimbursing 100 percent of the tuition and fees for graduate-level courses and 75 percent for undergraduate courses and study in nondegree programs. There are no restrictions regarding topics of study. Norden encourages assistance to schools and cultural programs by offering to match any employee donation. Norden even helps—through offering merit scholarships—to finance the college educations of its employees' children.

As for in-house instruction, many companies offer that, too. Most popular are exercise and weight-loss programs conducted in company gyms. There are company magazines, special interest clubs, preretirement counseling. Champion Corporation, a leader in forestry and wood products, provides industrial craft centers in which its retirees can remain productively part of the company community. Company doctors and nurses are found on the premises of many plants, and social workers are being added.[52] Their task is to help employees through personal troubles, whether it be a loss in the family or a problem with alcohol. Company managers reason that it is better to offer help than to lose a productive worker. It is what a caring family does, all the same.

THE IMPORTANCE OF FEELING RELATED

"We're a business that stresses the value of each person in our firm," said Robert Ready of Hewitt Associates, a consulting firm which specializes in the design of compensation and benefit programs for other companies. "We care about each other."

That was evident in the way staff members spoke to one another and to the visitor. Looking back into the elegant yet homey foyer, I could see the receptionist's small child busily playing at mother's feet while callers were dealt with pleasantly and efficiently. No big deal. Nothing surprising. "She's there every day," I was told. "Nursery school closes before our quitting time."

Mr. Ready pointed with pride to a newly published book, *The 100 Best Companies to Work For in America*. "We're among those companies," he said, "because one of our secretaries wrote the authors. Everyone says coming to work here is like coming home. We have no 'employees'; we have only 'associates.' We have no job descriptions. Everyone just pitches in and does what has to be done. We don't hire egocentrics. The big go-getters are not for us. They will go to our competitors, and we wish them well. We want people who can get along in our environment." The sense of similarity and solidarity suggested Family quite strongly.[53]

Interestingly, employees from more than a fifth of the *100 Best* specifically invoked family images. "Many of the best companies really do view themselves as an extended family," say Thomas Peters and Robert Waterman, authors of *In Search of Excellence*. They then quote Lew Lehr, chairman of 3M on the subject of "family":

> . . . the community in which people live has become so mobile it is no longer an outlet for the individual. The schools are no longer a social center for the family. The churches have lost their drawing power as social-family centers. With the breakdown of these traditional structures, certain companies have filled the void. They have become sort of mother institutions, but have maintained their spirit of entrepreneurship at the same time.[54]

But benevolence may carry hidden penalties. Excessive paternalism, as Peter Drucker warns, in business as in any other area of life eventually destroys itself. "It sets up expectations which, finally, no business enterprise can ever meet." And there is more. Overgenerous benefits are "golden fetters" which bind a man or woman to the job, hampering movement to companies that may offer greater challenge.[55]

Like the enclosed kibbutz, the "extended family" corporation, with its pervasive values, exerts strong pressures
to conform so that the perfectly adjusted individual within
it might be rendered helpless in the face of change. Peters
and Waterman speak to this point:

> "Another worrisome aspect of the strong corporate culture is
> how well those who have spent most of their lives in it will
> fare on the outside should they ever leave, which some do.
> Our observation . . . is that they do less well than might be
> expected. . . . These people often are totally unaware of the
> enormous support system they had going for them in the ex-
> cellent company, and are at the very least initially lost and
> bewildered without it."[56]

In *100 Best,* the authors quote an IBM executive who left
to form his own company. "The hardest part about being
gone was the first few times I tried to make a decision on
my own about anything, like what hotel to stay in, or who
I wanted to hire."[57]

How does a business community, an extended business
"family," accomplish what the old bourgeois family did so
well? How give security while at the same time fostering
individuality, creativity, drive? Perhaps that is something
no "extended family" can do, in or out of business. Perhaps it is enough, for now, simply to achieve a sense of
family order and permanence in a disorderly world.

Some years ago the economist, Karl Polanyi, in his article, "Our Obsolete Market Mentality," observed:

> ". . . instead of the economic system being embedded in so-
> cial relationships, these relationships were now embedded in
> the economic system."[58]

By that he meant that all other aspects of life—education,
government, the arts, marriage and the family—had to
"comply with the utilitarian pattern, or at least, not inter-
fere with the working of the market mechanism."

Today, something quite different seems to be happening. And corporate leaders like Lew Lehr are aware of the change. Business is assuming functions, colorations, motivations long thought peculiar to the *master institution*. This is not to say that all business organizations have reorganized in the family image or will ever do so. It is not to say that economic considerations are absent. Nor is it to deny the effect of public clamor for social remedies government has proved unable to supply. The fact that businesses recognize the family image as an *ideal*, however, says much about shifts in institutional priorities and functions.

When all else fails, work remains. It is the final verity. Business seems willing to make it a "family" verity as well. After all, as S.I. Newhouse put it, "The ties that bind are the ties to each other." [59]

RELIGION AND BUSINESS

THE EYE OF WHOSE NEEDLE?

> *Home mercator vix aut nunquam
> potest Deo placere.*
> *(The man of business is but
> seldom acceptable to God.)*
>
> ST. JEROME [1]

There are other ties that bind. We are visiting an executive meeting of a major corporate subsidiary:

> The chief executive officer rises and hands each section chief seated around the conference table a large mirror. "Look in it," he instructs. They all look. "Do you see there someone who has gone that extra mile for the company today?" Nobody laughs. The leader's manner is too solemn, too riveting to permit levity. Besides, the company is in some disarray. Everyone wants to help put it back on top. It is not just jobs that are at stake. It is something to do with pride, with loyalty, even with emotion. And if playing "Mirror, Mirror on the wall" will help the company, why then, they will play.

We witness, through the eyes of Terrence Deal and Allan Kennedy, a Recognition Event in a company they know well.

> With the ringing of a special bell, employees march down to the executive suite. In solemn tones the manager presents another Attaboy for service above and beyond the call of duty. By using that silly term, the company means to poke mild fun at itself. Funny or not, the Attaboy carries deep meaning for workers. It is an honor each one strives to achieve.[2]

In 1969, anthropologist Thomas Rohlen participated in the training program for 120 new employees of a large Japanese bank:

> During the three-month period, the candidates have lived together in the bank's training center. They have worked at their lessons for ten to sixteen hours a day, six days a week. But the training is not all practicality. Much is devoted to spiritual exercises.
>
> They spend time in a Zen Buddhist temple where they learn to concentrate their spiritual forces, to surmount hunger, thirst, and physical pain. They are exhorted by the priests to avoid worldly temptations, to cooperate unselfishly, to

support the rules of the bank as they do those of the temple.

They visit military installations where they run obstacle courses, learn close order drill, and hear more inspirational lectures about courage and self-sacrifice. They play games together, always in teams. They row boats together, climb mountains together, solicit menial and unpleasant work in farm villages. Finally they take a twenty-five mile walk around a park, first in groups, then singly. They are required to refuse all refreshments even when temptation is deliberately put in their way.

And what is the training meant to achieve? Spiritual strength. Staying power for life's tests. Concentration and patience for the often monotonous tasks that are a part of banking. Resistance to temptation. It is meant to kill the self and build commitment to the group and to the bank. Spiritual commitment. Spiritual assent.[3]

During the 1984 Summer Olympics Games at Los Angeles, the coach of an Indian soccer team was interviewed on television:

"You appear to have Sikhs on your team" observes the questioner.

"And Hindus as well," the coach responds, "and Moslems, too."

"How do you keep religion from being a problem?"

"We have only one religion here," says the coach. "Soccer is our religion."

Interview after interview sounds the same theme with gymnasts, Graeco-Roman wrestlers, volleyball players, and biking sprinters. It is the *sport* that counts. Each has acquired a halo and become a calling holy enough to elicit patient self-sacrifice on the part of its devotees.

The producer of a television "pilot," a drama he hopes to persuade network executives to present as a series, takes issue with his writer:

"What's the matter with you?" he fumes. "You didn't say

anything about protecting THE ENVIRONMENT! You know that means everything to me!"

Never mind that the play is a swords-and-sorcery epic, set in a mythical realm. It must carry the blessing of the holy name.

Confronted by the "new morality," the mother of teenage offspring cries in exasperation, "Anything goes today! Everything goes today! Is nothing sacred?"

All these scenes and examples relate to the institution of religion, though not many churchgoers would be likely to approve. The widest definition of religion used in many textbooks was proposed by the French sociologist Emile Durkheim:

> "A unified system of beliefs and practices, relative to sacred things, binding together those who adhere to these beliefs and practices in a single community."[4]

What is sacred? It involves, among other things, a special commitment to beings or causes larger, more important than oneself. The close observer might be able to locate something at least akin to the sacred in circumstances other than traditionally religious ones, in places a cleric would consider odd, unusual, unexpected.

Shared commitment, shared dedication serves to tie people more closely together. ("Religion," after all, derives from the Latin *religare*—to bind back, to bind firmly.) And when shared dedication, a shared sense of what is truly important is publicly celebrated in ritual, the bonds are made stronger still.

That which is of ultimate importance, that which is sacred supports collective beliefs about what is *right* in the world and what is *real;* what is moral and what is natural. Believing makes it so. That is true whether the "it" refers to one's ability to walk on glowing coals and not be burned or to sell refrigerators to Eskimos. And believing has been big business since human time began.

PROFITABLE CURING RITES

Among people whose lifeways are simple and close to the soil, the religious specialist is part priest, part doctor, equipped with his very own, very direct connection to the Powers. When the healer is summoned, relatives of the sick person had better be prepared to pay up promptly. Special offerings will be required for the Powers and special gifts for the healer himself. And they should all be prominently displayed or the cure might not be effective.

Anthropologist Morris Opler, who lived among the Mescalero Apaches when old beliefs were still cherished, quotes a healer of his acquaintance instructing prospective clients.

> "You must give me what you are going to give me. It must be in sight. I don't do this work on credit. What I mean to do is to give life. . . There must be four gifts. If you would rather give more, it's all right." [5]

In this particular case, the patient's husband gave more. Dr. Opler· was moved to add that, although the Navaho and Apaches did not participate traditionally in a market economy, they nevertheless knew very well where their economic interests lay and were perfectly capable of pressing those interests even "at the points at which they intersect ceremonialism." [6]

So was Sigmund Freud, who shocked members of the Vienna medical profession in the late 1800s by refusing to treat anyone, no matter how impoverished, without demanding a stiff fee. It was part of the treatment, he declared. One believes more strongly, after all, in what one has to pay for. Vienna doctors (as Peter Drucker tells us) came to suspect that Freud might be right. At least in terms of emotional disorders. [7]

Believers have always been willing to put their money where their hearts were. And where else in the world can there be found more troubled hearts and bigger purses than in America? That recognition has drawn to these shores any number of charismatic teachers and healers and encouraged not a few native cult figures to lay up treasures on earth as well as in heaven.

PROFITING FROM BURIAL

A canny combination of faith and business acumen proved the making of that line of rulers who transformed predynastic Egypt into a great nation-state. This finding of archaeologist Michael Hoffman will doubtless occasion some dismay in historical circles long accustomed to viewing Egypt as the most noncommercial (though not nonprofit) of all the ancient civilizations. It was. But all that came later.[8]

Sometime around 3800 B.C., Dr. Hoffman tells us, the town called Nekhen by the Egyptians, Hierokonpolis by the Greeks who came long afterward, began to grow in size and importance. Growth owed to the pottery industry established, apparently, by men important enough to carry the ceremonial mace, which would mark early pharaohs for what they were. Nekhen supported some fifteen kilns, the largest of them built to industrial scale. Some were cleverly situated between desert cliffs where trapped winds could fan the very hot fires needed for the manufacture of quality ceramics. This was always the black-topped red-ware used exclusively for the graves of great personages who believed they *could* take wealth into the afterlife.

The size and extent of Nekhen's industrial development convinces Dr. Hoffman that its tycoons traded up and down the Nile, supplying luxury grave goods to meet the demand. Allowing business to follow belief brought the Nekhen tycoons such wealth and power that their descendants managed, not only to survive droughts and local wars, but eventually to preside over the joined lands of Upper and Lower Egypt. In the years just prior to that great event, rulers came home to be buried among their pottery baron ancestors in Nekhen's ancient cemetery. There they estab-

lished the pharaonic cult of the dead, which was to char-
acterize Egyptian civilization through the millennia. There
they created the images of duality which, repeated everywhere, would serve to unify the nation in much the same
way that thirteen of everything once expressed a hopeful
unity of the first American states.

By 3100 B.C., when Nekhen ceased to be a royal necro-
polis, its beginnings in trade and enterprise had long since
been forgotten. Wealth now came to the state—and would
come ever afterward—by way of tribute or through govern-
ment-owned-and-operated mines and quarries. What long-
distance trade there was occurred at the behest of the monarch and under royal monopoly. Leftovers were handled by
foreign merchants who came and went. And since they were
not Egyptian, after all, who cared whether they benefited
from their mercantile transactions and by how much.

Now, the possession of wealth has always been a matter of concern to all peoples of the world and often in terms
of morality, of religious sanction. It is often not so much a
matter of *how much* as of *who has it*. Who is entitled to
enjoy wealth? Who is allowed to benefit disproportionately
when others do without? Who is allowed to be different?

In Egypt, wealth in this life or the next was perceived as
a glorification of the god-king. From the god-king all blessings flowed. Nobles and gentry, basking in reflected splendor, had the right to land and honors which were Phar-
aoh's to give, the right to wealth drawn from the land by
their tenants, serfs, and slaves. It is a pattern often repeated
in the world. But not in early Mesopotamia, Egypt's contemporary.

PROFIT WITH HONOR

Western scholars have been wont to cast early Mesopotamian commerce in an Egyptian mold; have imagined it
monopolized by temple or palace. Entrepreneurial "capitalism" was presumed to have developed only in the second

millennium with the arrival of another Semitic people. Concerns of the experts about beginnings may reflect a certain aesthetic distaste shared by Friedrich Engels, who noted:

> "Civilization creates a class which no longer concerns itself with production, but only with the exchange of the products—*the merchants*. . . . Under the pretext that they save the producers the trouble and risk of exchange . . . a class of parasites comes into being, 'genuine social ichneumons,' who, as a reward for their actually very insignificant services, skim all the cream off production at home and abroad, rapidly amass enormous wealth . . ."[9]

When a few years ago Melvin Powell wrote an article titled "Sumerian Merchants and the Problem of Profit,"[10] he did not refer to the tender Sumerian conscience troubled about "skimming off cream." He had in mind the modern scholarly conscience and its preference for an economy centrally powered and redistributive. For truth to tell, more and more evidence points to a market economy flourishing from the very beginning of the third millennium—if not earlier. Sumerian proverbs extol the value of competition. Business documents refer freely to borrowing capital at interest. And, with the recently discovered business archives from north Mesopotamian Ebla, with the recognition of an ancient accounting system of tokens, the enterprising, entrepreneurial, mercantile ethos of the area becomes all the more certain. Profits earned in trade were so often dedicated to the greater glory of the local god or goddess as to make their temples thriving business concerns in their own right. Temple endowments seem to represent fulfillment of civic duty as much as attempts to curry divine favor in business. And since the gods maintained their own celestial trading connections, a merchant's money was not only as good as a landowner's purse, but maybe a little better. The inevitable must be faced: profit in Mesopotamia carried honor and a certain whiff of sanctity as well.

PROFIT WITHOUT HONOR

Contrary to Engel's view, production itself can sometimes do with a bit of sanctity. Nowhere is the need more clearly on view than in Africa and among its blacksmiths. Archaeology reveals that knowledge of iron smelting south of the Sahara Desert was beginning to be diffused widely by the fifth century B.C. Exactly what happened to men who learned the new skill, who elected to be different from their peers, archaeology cannot say. A study of living people in the area offers a fascinating glimpse, however. The price of difference in cities all along the Sudan has been enclosure in hereditary and despised castes.

Even among the herding Masai—East African warrior people whose men hunt lions as a test of courage—blacksmiths are different. Though their Masai pedigree is as valid as any other man's, blacksmiths may not be warriors or wear the insignia of courage. They may not herd and wander as do others, for their craft supports them. They may not marry into the clans of other Masai. Why? "Because they make the weapons that draw blood." Perfectly acceptable to wield the weapons. Not to make them. Exclusion: the price of profiting through difference.[11]

Visit Southwest Africa in the forest zone, however, and another story emerges. Smiths, often part-time workers, are highly respected, even revered. Indeed, the forge itself is considered a sanctuary. There are rumors (such things are never directly stated) that smiths hold high office in the powerful male secret societies which dominate certain tribal groups. To kill a smith was, at least in other days, a very serious crime, punishable by death. Iron itself carries such a charge of sanctity that scepters made of it are carried by priests and god-kings in the cities of West Africa. There is even a god of iron among the Yoruba, and very powerful he is, too.[12]

The moral of the stories is simply this: Get a god on your side, get the church on your side and you are on the way to wealth with honor. Difference approved. Profit sanctified.

HONOR WITH PROFIT

Aristotle tells the story of Thales of Miletos and how he acquired wealth:

> Frequently twitted about his poverty as a professional philosopher, Thales resolved to prove the value of his studies. Being something of a meteorologist, he was able to forecast in midwinter a bumper crop of olives come harvest time. He rented forthwith—and at low, out-of-season cost—all the olive presses in Chios and Miletus. The crop of olives was indeed as large as predicted, and presses were in great demand. Thales could then sublet his at whatever rate he chose. He made a tidy fortune.

Not even Aristotle, with his intellectual's scorn of moneylending and moneymaking, bothers to reproach Thales. "He showed the world," crows Aristotle, "that philosophers can easily be rich if they like, but their ambition is of another sort." Indeed, he appears tickled by his colleague's cleverness, his use of monopoly as a ploy and recommends it to statesmen and to public figures who "devote themselves entirely to finance." It is not what is done but who does it. For philosophers and politicians, full steam ahead.[13]

In Rome, as we have seen earlier, a gentleman did not engage in trade. That is to say, he could not be *seen* earning profits. He could, however, sign on as silent partner in business deals. Once out of Rome, once in the provinces (preferably newly conquered territory), there were no holds barred. Conquered states were frequently unable to produce the tribute demanded of them, and rich Romans were glad to float loans at very high interest. When and if a borrower defaulted, a legion or two could always be sent to collect.

One of those patrician money lenders was Brutus, the

assassin of Julius Caesar. Hailed everywhere as a paragon of virtue, this noble soul had no scruples in lending money to Cyprus at 48 percent interest. So we learn from the tattletale letters of Cicero. There were, of course, Roman laws regarding usury. These could always be circumvented by persons with connections and gentility. *What* mattered less than *who*.[14]

POOR IS BETTER

Converts to early Christianity may well have been as much in flight *from* the corrupt and hedonistic worldliness of their time as in flight *to* the all-loving and transcendent Jesus. Renunciation was a dominant theme of Church Fathers, separation from the world and its wicked ways. Their favored heroes and heroines were those who marooned themselves atop pillars or in caves, there to free the spirit through mortification of the flesh.

Later on these saints gathered in celibate monastic communities, for such was thought to be the Master's plan. That not everyone could live so was accepted by the Church Fathers as a concession to human frailty and the necessity of maintaining life on earth. The monastic mode, however, remained an ideal toward which all should aim. A simple life close to the land was the next best thing; and the poorer, the better. Any surplus should be reserved for the destitute who, all through early Christian times, were considered holy beings, necessary to prompt the exercise of charity.

Anyone not working the land fell into the moral danger zone. Some occupations were prohibited outright: actor, prostitute, gladiator, eunuch (surely not something one would choose). Traders and merchants were included in this category. Father Ambrose of Milan (a fourth century divine) thundered against merchants who "farmed the farmer" and who created scarcity. "Your gain is their loss" was his pronouncement. The peasant's image of limited good, sanctified.[15]

It was the role of middleman that churchmen found hard to fathom. The woman who wove a length of wool on her own loom and sold it for profit was clearly without sin. Her skill and labor should be so compensated. But the man who bought her cloth cheaply, sold it dearly elsewhere, and profited from the transaction deserved damnation. He was guilty of usury. Or of avarice. Or of fraud. His profit was *turpe lucrum,* "shameful gain" (which survives in popular parlance as "filthy lucre").

By the eleventh century there were merchants everywhere making *turpe lucrum,* and never mind the danger to their souls. One of these was Godrick, born of poor peasants in Lincolnshire, England:

> His official biography does not relate what happened to his family or how he came to be set adrift. We do know he became a peddler and eventually joined a band of piepowder men traveling from fair to fair. He accumulated enough capital to invest in a piepowder association which hired a ship for trade. He and his fellows specialized in goods known to be scarce—grain, perhaps—and took them where demand and prices were highest. He became a very rich man.
>
> We should not know of him at all were it not for the final events of his life. These made him noteworthy to the only people who could write. He became a saint. Overwhelmed by guilt, he one day gave all his possessions to the poor and turned hermit. Alone in his cell he performed any number of miracles. It was those that served to make him a saint. Voluntary self-impoverishment was not sufficient demonstration of grace. Only a necessary prelude.[16]

Several repentant (though not saintly) merchants turn up in the clerical literature. They are, in fact, the only ones who do. There are the usurers who, on their deathbeds, are persuaded to sign away everything, not to their debtors but to the Church. Others are logged in with endowments of churches, priories, chapels, hospices. All acts of contrition. All atonement for past sins. Never quite enough.

RELIGION AND BUSINESS

About this time, Godrick's time, Church Fathers attempted to align what *should* be done in the now-thriving world of business with what was *being* done. The profits of trade were shorn of their previous connection with usury. But usury itself proved difficult indeed. For long it had been limited to Jews. Christians then found ways to circumvent the prohibition. Venetians and Florentines made no bones about it. And the small town of Cahors in southern France was popularly referred to as "a nest of usurers," so much a civic specialty had the practice become. And then there were the Knights Templar, an order of warrior monks formed during the Crusades. Thanks to generous donations and astute business dealings, they became, in effect, very powerful bankers. So powerful that the king of France suppressed the order in 1312.

"Labor is best. It is honorable and necessary," Church Fathers continued to insist, meanwhile relenting slightly in terms of business. "Trade is dangerous to the soul but, alas, also necessary. Finance we don't know what to do about. If not downright immoral, it is sordid at the very best." Necessary evils.

It was now reckoned lawful to seek the amount of wealth necessary to maintain one's station in life. For kings there was never a limit. Nor for nobles. They were free to wring whatever they could from serfs or tenants. No profit, that. Merely a right. Not what, but who.

The matter of station for the man of business was something else again. What should it be? And what profit was lawful profit? Proper determination required that motivation be carefully weighed. Trading ventures undertaken, not for the merchant's selfish interest but for the benefit of society, were pronounced lawful.

And then there was the dilemma of the "just price," a figure which should take into account the exact cost of one's labor and time. But how to calculate that? And what if the object on sale were rare and precious? How to assess its worth? No wonder Church Fathers preferred that the ruler set the just price for every object and transaction—with their concurrence, of course. To argue every jot and tittle of moral law was growing more complex all the time.

Any number of scholars have voiced objections to this view of the medieval Church. It was not antibusiness, they hold. After all, merchants were among the few people who could be exempted from fasting while going about their affairs. They were as well protected as pilgrims on the road and received equal hospitality. As for the "just price," that was actually determined by market principles for the most part. Never mind what was *said* about merchants; they were *needed* when all is said and done. So were moneylenders. For the monastery, though certainly a retreat from the world, was often a center of wordly business as well; and the papacy itself was very big business indeed. The succor of the poor, the sick, the chronically diseased was a religious responsibility. So was education. And there were the manifold secular obligations attendant upon being a superstate. The papacy could not, therefore, practice what it preached. Increasingly it had to rely on a policy of do-what-I-say-not-what-I-do. A dawning realization of this paradox stimulated the movement for religious reform.

PROFIT REHABILITATED

It is not surprising that the Protestant Reformation took its strongest hold among the northern European cities dominated by men of business. Not surprising that the movement, once underway, fractured into many sects. Not surprising that the more radical ones—those that preached a utopian gospel of common wives, property, and habitation—should have been suppressed by a fast-developing Protestant Establishment.

There were, however, several common themes: the importance of the individual's relationship with his all-powerful God; the importance of following biblical precepts (with strong Old Testament infusions); the importance of reading those precepts oneself; the importance of preparing in this life to gain admittance to the next. How best to prepare? There lay the rub. By baptism, some held. By good deeds, said others. By the communal life. By faith alone.

John Calvin of Geneva told his followers that God had long since chosen His "elect," and there was not much that could be done about it. But who was chosen? How could one know? This question caused so much anxiety among the congregation that eventually Calvinist ministers advised congregants to behave "as if" they had been chosen. They were to show confidence by working hard at a freely chosen "calling" for the greater glory of God. Indeed, Calvinists attached to hard work the same sort of sanctity St. Benedict had preached in the sixth century. In their book, sloth was a sin more deadly by far than envy. Calvin had already told his ministers they might rightfully prosper and display prosperity, for this gained them respect. Eventually, congregants came to believe that their own worldly success was indeed a sign of "election." And prosper they did.[17]

There was just one hitch. Prosperity was *not* to be enjoyed. One was merely steward to one's wealth and must give a good account of it one day to the Great Bookkeeper. Otherwise, clean living and self-denial were the watchwords. One was not to sleep too much, not eat more than was necessary for strength, and certainly not dally with the opposite sex. Study, scientific pursuits, rational thought—these were permitted. Frivolity, play, sports were not. Self-adornment was unworthy of the "elect." Hard, regular labor of the body or mind in the service of one's calling, this was the ideal of living. It was monasticism in the middle of a bustling world. One's duty to that world was to make it as like unto Heaven as humanly possible. (A legacy of reform that resonates in our own time.) Without the comfort of sacraments and a mediating priesthood, one had to plan very carefully for one's salvation—not on a day-to-day basis but in a lifetime strategy.

What was the result of such beliefs? The formation of capital, to begin with. For what could one do with wealth if it could not be enjoyed? Why, plow it back into the business and keep on working. Wealth never excused idleness. As for the experiences in mounting strategy, in dealing with a celestial sense of risk, these—so says Max Weber—helped to create the spirit of capitalism which is the rational, systematically organized, ascetic pursuit of profit. By rational, Weber meant emancipation of business decisions from the bonds of tradition or superstition. By organization, he referred to the division of labor, a specialization into constituent parts. The pursuit of profit was originally devoted to the greater glory of God. (In later years it would be justified by appeals to Community, Humankind, or Society.) The ascetic part, the deliberate renunciation of pleasure, set a seal of sanctity on the endeavor.

Who could be rich? *Anybody* could be rich. And it was *everybody's* positive duty to try. Hear Richard Baxter, a Puritan divine, on the subject:

> "If God show you a way in which you may lawfully get more than in another way (without wrong to your soul or to any other), if you refuse this, and choose the less gainful way, you cross one of the ends of your calling, and you refuse to be God's steward, and to accept His gifts and use them for Him when He requireth it: you may labor to be rich for God, though not for the flesh and sin."[18]

THE PROTESTANT ETHIC IN AMERICA

The Pilgrim Fathers who came to America with dreams of founding the New Jerusalem brought a Calvinist faith still in its nascent state, still so fearful of temptation as to suspect the trader and the merchant exposed to sin. They, too, had a concept of the "just price." Said the Reverend John Cotton,

"A man may not sell above the current price, i.e., such price
as is usual in the time and place, and as another (who knows
the worth of the commodity) would give for it, if he had
occasion to use it . . . but where there is a scarcity of the
commodity, there men may raise their price; for now it is a
hand of God upon the commodity and not the person."[19]

The Reverend John Higginson was moved to add,

"My fathers and brethren, this is never to be forgotten, that
New England is originally a plantation of Religion, not a
plantation of Trade!"[20]

But the merchants, with their energy and international outlook, could not be contained within the bounds of rigid
Puritanism, especially when commerce became the economic saving grace of New England. The Reverend John
Wesley captures the sense of worry and regret:

". . . Religion must necessarily produce both industry and
frugality, and these cannot but produce riches. As riches increase . . . the spirit is swiftly vanishing away. . . . [Yet] we
ought not to prevent people from being diligent and frugal;
we must exhort all Christians to gain all they can, and to save
all they can, that is, in effect, to grow rich."[21]

By the early 1700s rigid Puritanism had faded, had spun
off its own dissident sects, and was challenged by immigrants professing older, more traditional faiths. Nevertheless, the Protestant Ethic made an indelible imprint on the
composite American consciousness traceable in countless
proverbs of daily use:

The devil has work for idle hands.

A penny saved is a penny earned.

Never put off until tomorrow what you can do today.

What is worth doing is worth doing well.

God helps those who help themselves.

It is the thesis of Max Weber that modern capitalism began with the Reformation, specifically with the Calvinist branch. Other scholars dispute this, noting the rational and highly organized pursuit of profit among medieval merchants. And this was as true, they hold, for the merchants of southern Europe (who never turned Protestant) as for those of the North. Perhaps it is not entirely beside the point, however, to note that the Industrial Revolution, the triumph of the machine—beginning, by some estimates, after 1750—made its earliest appearance and essential transformations where Calvinist theology exerted an influence: England first, then northern France, Scotland, America. Holland, that other Protestant haven for commerce, became a great financial clearinghouse.

PROFIT RENOUNCED AND DENOUNCED

As in any revolution, the harmful effects were most visible and most widely publicized. Workers, who had once been known to their employers as individuals, now blended into a faceless commodity called "labor." Living conditions in factory towns became intolerable as displaced rural folk crowded into them. (We tend to forget that life in the country was worse.) Factory owners, members of the now-dominant middle class, appeared heartless, remote, avaricious. As discontent swelled among working people, their self-appointed spokesmen, philosophers and visionaries, moved to repeal the Industrial Revolution, or at least to effect reform.

Ultimately the most charismatic of all the social prophets—and there were many angry voices to be heard at the time—was Karl Marx. He did not seek to wreck the machines, but to install new management and a new order of society. Only when the means of production are owned by the workers themselves he said, can profit be condoned.

For it will accrue, not to individual persons, but to the *people*. (He preferred "proletariat," but as a halo word it never quite cut the mustard.) Truth to tell, a sense of holiness was never far from early communist rhetoric, although Marx himself condemned traditional religion out of hand.

But Friedrich Engels was quick to note the religious character of the movement and even its resemblances to early Christianity. Like Christianity, he said, communism is a movement of oppressed people. Christ preached salvation from bondage and misery. So do we, though our Heaven is to be in a transformed society on earth. Christians were persecuted; so are we. And yet Christianity triumphed. So will communism.[22] He did not mention the similar interest in communal living, the similar dread of the merchant— that snake in a communal Eden. And it was for Lenin, his Russian disciple, to introduce the call to asceticism—"Dissoluteness in sexual life is bourgeois!"[23]

It was early Christianity without Christ, without a shred of forebearance, and certainly without love. The animating principle, indeed, was hatred—which, it must be admitted, does lend its own powerful energy to struggle.

PROFIT AND THE AMERICAN CLERGY

Clerical conscience of the 1880s was frightened by the apparition of socialism/communism. "They mean murder and arson; they mean the distruction of the present social order," fretted the Reverend Dr. Washington Gladden, a religious leader of the time. Yet while clearly unready to topple enterprise from its state of grace, he did entertain worries about corruption of its soul. Was the American economic system too successful for its own good? Was it too profitable?

"The wealth of this country is increasing at a prodigious rate. . . . What has the Christian moralist to say about it? Should he teach that it is a good thing or an evil thing? A blessing to be rejoiced in or a misery to be deplored?"

". . . Something is plainly out of joint in the distribution system. . . . [The moralist] will not deny that the capitalist should have a fair reward for his prudence and his abstinence; he will not refuse to . . . the entrepreneur . . . that large reward to which his intelligence and experience entitle him; but he will still insist that the workman ought to have a larger share than he is getting now."[24]

Most men of the cloth during Reverend Gladden's years and for some time to come were not only willing to give the devil his due; they could, at appropriate moments, wax lyrical in praise of Business and its achievement of prosperity. Through frequent references to "Christian capitalism," ministers sought as well to stir the conscience of the businessman. Far from the baleful threats levied by early Church Fathers, the message delivered from American pulpits was consonant with Old Testament verses which favored Business and saved blame for erring businessmen. The carrot-and-stick approach.

There was as yet no move among churchmen to revamp the economic system itself, though the Reverend Gladden listed ever so gently into the socialist camp:

"The time may come when the nation will be compelled to take under its control, if not into its ownership, the railroads and the telegraphs and administer them for the common good."[25]

THE FALL FROM GRACE

The Great Depression brought profit into near-total disrepute—at least, when associated with Big Business. In his 1933 inaugural address, Franklin Delano Roosevelt consigned it to outer darkness:

"The measure of the restoration lies in the extent to which we apply social values more noble than mere monetary profit."

During this time of moral realignment, political philosophers, social reformers, and politicians themselves outpaced churchmen in defining sin. And it seemed sinful for some to prosper when others were tightening their belts. Sinful enough for Congress to conduct inquisitions of the sort once reserved to Mother Church. Targeted were those individuals and companies which, in one way or another, did business with the government.

Professor Ronald Fernandez of Central Connecticut State University has described one of those hearings in 1934. It was conducted by Senator Hugo Black who was "outraged that aviation companies had earned extraordinary amounts of public tax money flying the nation's mail."[26] Worse still, in his book, were the shockingly high salaries paid to company executives. He branded these men "profiteers" and told them they were gouging the American people.

Penalties and punishments were sought. None could be made to stick. There was no law against an individual's prospering while others were down on their luck. Particularly when all taxes had been duly paid.

President Roosevelt moved to administer chastisement. He canceled all domestic airmail contracts and ordered U.S. Army flyers to do the job. Within a week close to a dozen pilots were dead or injured. Roosevelt then reinstated the private carriers under a new law which limited all executives in companies with airmail contracts to annual salaries of $17,500.

Most of the men grilled by Black's committee were embittered by their treatment. Some left the aviation industry for good. They could not understand what they had done wrong. Their enterprises were earning, they felt, reasonable profits. Those that had won government contracts had offered bids which the losers had labeled ridiculously low. They had done well in a venture at which others were failing. They didn't set market prices, after all. Was it a sin to profit—though in a partially subsidized business—when demand was high? Yes. Was it a sin to make great fortunes on small investments? Yes. Particularly when the great fortune was won, not by hard work, but by "clever maneuvering."

Senator Black spoke of "proper profit." What *is* "proper," after all? What is the "just price?"

NOT WHAT BUT WHO

"Profit," says Peter Drucker, "is the risk premium and the yardstick without which economic life cannot go on."[27] Profitability is rather like popularity. One tells you how much you are liked for your own sweet self. The other tells a company how much its product is liked, how well it is fulfilling a consumer need. But needs change, and products must keep pace. Profit keeps a company competitive in terms of replaced equipment and new research. It is a hedge against technological innovation, the rising cost of capital, social upheaval, governmental requirements, and lawsuits.

Profit pays for risk and pays for growth. It is a gamble on the future. And there had better be a proper care for the future. For not many companies are privately owned and run. Professional managers are in charge and answerable to boards of directors and stockholders—a large proportion of whom are union members through their pension funds.[28] All expect to benefit from their investment; if not, they will take their capital elsewhere. Profit, then, is the cost of staying in business. Electro Scientific Industries, Inc., (a manufacturer of testing equipment for electronics concerns) says just that in its statement of principles:

> "Profit . . . is not the proper *end* of business; it is merely the *means* that makes the achievement of the proper ends possible."[29]

It is, after all, something like seed corn. If you eat it, you won't have a crop next year. Forget the notion of "capitalist rake-off," says Dr. Drucker. Profit after taxes rarely exceeds 5 or 6 percent. Even the Soviets must recognize the importance of profit. Nevertheless, the "rake-off" impression remains.

"When I ask my students what they think is the average profit earned in any business, they give answers ranging from 50 percent to 75 percent." Kevin Gilmartin of the Norwalk (Connecticut) Savings Society was referring to the Project Business classes he conducts in local junior high schools for Junior Achievement. "But that's only at the beginning of the course," he told me.[30] Studies undertaken in 1980 for Junior Achievement, a business-oriented youth organization, uncovered similar notions at the high-school level. So did a poll taken some years ago for the Boy Scouts of America.[31] The aim was to test attitudes among these students and among young workers new to business. Results indicated that, of those polled:

61 percent did not believe in the need for profit;

50 percent believed owners receive an unfair part of net profit;

53 percent believed government ownership of business to be good.

One doubts that high-school students would (then or now) deny profits to Michael Jackson and his brothers. In order to see their heroes up close and in person, young fans are very willing to pay whatever price is asked, "just" or not. The notion of "shameful gain" is irrelevant in this context. Not what, but who?

Parents of the young fans do not begrudge—at least, they do not actively protest—the million-dollar-plus salaries paid to baseball and football stars, to television anchormen and women. The earnings of popular movie actors go unremarked. These individuals pay high taxes, to be sure, and that is all the absolution required. Nor are labor unions, striking for ever-higher pay in industries on the skids, universally condemned. Leaders of cults and sects are expected to do themselves very well indeed. The high fees of attorneys and physicians are paid resentfully, but there is no public outcry for a limitation of income by government decree. Heaven forfend! They might depart these shores. Doctors in India, with profits frozen to a figure generous for that country but puny in comparison with those elsewhere in the world, are doing just that. Leaving.[32]

Again, not what, but who?

The nature of taxation says much about a nation's values, about what is moral and what is in moral limbo. The politician's promise to "soak the rich," to "make business pay its fair share" is always well received. And these promises are sometimes kept. There have been in recent years taxes levied on "excess profits" and on "windfall profits." Unearned income, that which represents profit from investments and savings accounts, has always apealed to the tax man. This is probably a reflection of the Protestant Work Ethic and moral disapproval of money not won by the sweat of labor. ("Dumb," say the Japanese. "Saving is the hardest work there is!") Congress has developed a class of earnings called "extraordinary income"—one that is taxed at higher rates than ordinary income. Graef S. Crystal (vice president of Towers, Perrin, Forster and Crosby, a New York-based consulting firm) explains that into this category fall the astronomical salaries paid to corporation executives. Never mind if these represent the price of keeping an outstandingly talented person in his job. Never mind if, against all reason, these salaries just happen to be the going rate in comparable positions in corporations everywhere. They represent *turpe lucrum*. Particularly suspect are the sudden increases when one company is taken over by another, and the loss of rank and face must be sweetened for the outgoing chief.[33]

Unlike Congress, holds Mr. Crystal, the public does not really object to high salaries if the executive is known to be hardworking and productive. Chrysler CEO Lee Iacocca is his case in point. What Crystal did not note, however, is that Mr. Iacocca is also a performing artist whose pitch for Chrysler automobiles can be seen nightly on home TV screens; he is, therefore, exempt from condemnation. For television carries its own moral sanctions, its own overtones of the sacred. The element of familiarity may also be at work. Can one really object when good old Uncle George wins the lottery? Ditto for good old Uncle Lee.

As for the rest, *turpe lucrum.*

PROFIT IN CHINA, AMBIVALENCE AND CHANGE

In 1981, the central government of the People's Republic urged unemployed citizens to follow the path of free enterprise since employment by the state could no longer be guaranteed. Between then and 1983, according to *New York Times* correspondent Christopher Wren, the numbers of the self-employed increased by over seven million. "Profit is good!" That is the theme sounded by the central government in an effort to convince Communist Believers that there is no moral contradiction involved. But hard-shelled devotees, accustomed to consulting Mao's sacred "Little Red Book" for answers to life's every problem, remain unpersuaded. And since guardians of the Old Morality continue to serve as officials, police chiefs, and magistrates, provincial entrepreneurs are finding themselves in difficulty. Resentful of what seems *turpe lucrum,* local leaders have found in extraordinary taxation an effective means of containing capitalism at the source and of guaranteeing equality.

Both *China Daily* and *Workers Daily* report (with government sanction, of course) individual instances of harassment. In Sichuan and Shandong provinces, businessmen have been charged "a guidance fee for scientific research and technology, a market and managing fee, and a joint security guard fee." Elsewhere, "drunkard's taxes" have been imposed on many restaurants while retail establishments have been penalized for using colored lanterns or other means of sprucing up their shops. In one province, businessmen have been charged loss fees for "having taken customers away from local production brigades' own side-line enterprise." Forty-two separate nuisance fees and taxes have been levied in the Manchurian city of Harbin, twenty-two in Guandong Province. Needless to say, there have been many failures of private business—a consequence not at all pleasing to promoters of the new moral order.[34]

The nature of that new order, with its startling about-face in concepts of sin and salvation, was suggested in an article appearing June 9, 1984 in the Beijing journal, *Renmin Ribao*. (It was translated in *Worldview*, a publication of the Council on Religion and International Affairs.) Here are excerpts:

"The slogan 'rob the rich to help the poor' used by peasant uprising armies in history played a progressive role at the time. In the socialist era this idea of peasant egalitarianism can only have a negative influence by hampering the development of productive force. This idea was very fashionable in rural areas a few years ago. . . . The practice of making various impositions on specialized households under the pretext of 'showing a fine style' is a phenomenon that merits attention. . . . If you do not pay up, you are under suspicion as 'one of the heartless rich.' . . . It is perhaps not going too far to describe this as the past practice of 'robbing the rich to help the poor.'

". . . In advocating that specialized households show fine style, we mainly mean that they should pass on to the peasant households around them their good experiences in management, good methods in applying science and technology, and good ways of developing commodity production, hand over to still more people the 'golden key' to riches, and lead everyone forward to get rich together. In the spiritual field, teaching people to get rich is much better and more realistic than 'taking pleasure in charitable acts.' The latter existed in ancient times, whereas the former is something that only the new-style peasants of the 1980s can do. We must seriously break away from the past practice of 'robbing the rich to help the poor' and vigorously show the fine style of the specialized households in 'teaching people to get rich.' "[35]

The Protestant Ethic alive and well and living in—China?

SIN AND SALVATION, MODERN AMERICAN STYLE

The 1984 electioneering ads for the American Communist party and its presidential and vice-presidential candidates invoked a more conventional Marxist morality. Under the general heading, PEOPLE BEFORE PROFITS, the ads pointed with dismay to various groups of sinners, among them "reactionary sections of Big Business." Although certainly wishing to achieve distance from the Communist party, many American theologians would, nevertheless, find themselves in substantial agreement regarding the nature of sin and the identity of sinners.

In 1981–1982, a poll by the Roper Center queried the nation's teachers of theology about their attitudes regarding America, its economic ethos and value orientation.[36] Findings revealed that

> Theologians thought Americans, as a people, less compassionate than a decade ago. (And this in spite of the fact that, in 1981, individual Americans gave a total of $53.6 billion to charity—up 23.3 percent over 1980 and outpacing the rate of inflation, then at a high level.)[37]

> Eighty-four percent of those polled favored tax exemption for religious purposes.

> Fifty-nine percent were strongly critical in terms of income distribution in American society. A move toward socialism was favored by 37 percent. Theologians of evangelical and fundamentalist denominations were economically more conservative than their fellows.

One in three thought a person could be a Marxist and be, at the same time, a good member of the respondent's congregation.

Seventy percent thought the United States treated the Third World unfairly. The highest number of yes responses on this question came from Episcopalians and Catholics. Respondents holding the Ph.D. as well as the degree in divinity were the most consistent in their critical views.

In this area the Catholic response was by far the most condemnatory. Eighty-one percent thought the United States was unfair. Such a statistic illuminates the rise of liberation theology—a heady mix of Catholicism and Marxism—and its outspoken denunciation by Pope John Paul II.

The British scholar, R.H. Tawney, once analyzed the possible relationships between Business and Religion. Churchmen, he said, may condemn Business and tell congregants they must escape its clutches. Churchmen may label it a necessary evil and ignore it as much as they can. They may try the carrot-and-stick approach and hope to muddle through. They may agitate for revolution and complete change of the social system.[38]

All during 1983–1984 Catholic businessmen and women waited anxiously to discover which position American bishops would take in their promised pastoral letter on the economy. There had been all kinds of trial balloons. In an August, 1984, discussion with Archbishop Rembert G. Weakland, chairman of the drafting committee, Professor Eugene Kennedy elicited the following preview:

The letter will urge that job creation be designated the number one national goal.

It will insist on the national provision of sufficient income for the poor. "A more equitable division of wealth," is how Archbishop Weakland put it.

In trade with Third World countries, it will require Americans to think first of the good of others.

It will recommend the institution of economic planning and policy (presumably centralized).

It will probably reflect the Holy Father's view that workers should share both the profits of business and the means of production.[39]

Businessmen are not sure what that means since many corporations have enacted profit-sharing programs for their workers and encouraged them to buy stock in the company. It is worth noting that factories taken over and managed by workers have not, in the opinion of workers themselves, fared outstandingly well. Such operations are particularly vulnerable when profits diminish. Businessmen have been additionally puzzled by the lack of reference to the many jobs created during the economic recovery—more than in any time period since the 1950s, more than had been created in any other technologically advanced nation in a comparable time period. In other words, they are disturbed by the continued application of the stick without the carrot. Said Walter E. Auch, chairman and CEO of the Chicago Board Options Exchange:

"What I've learned is that the bishop's style is to look for me when they want donations, but not to seek my counsel. . . . I don't want them to put me in a position where I feel driven away from a faith I've worked harder at than my business."[40]

As for the response to Professor Kennedy's article, comments published later in the *New York Times Magazine* on Sunday, September 23, 1984, were four to one in favor of the pastoral letter and its anticipated tone. One reader noted that

"Our economic system has always troubled my conscience because so much of it does seem to rely on greed and exploitation. Its murky workings can only benefit from whatever Christian light can be shed on them by the bishops."[41]

Mounting concern about what were perceived to be real misunderstandings about the nature of business and business enterprise impelled a number of prominent Catholics to form the Lay Commission on Catholic Social Teaching and the U.S. Economy. Its members include such luminaries as Michael Novak, William E. Simon, Alexander M. Haig, Jr., Clare Boothe Luce, J. Peter Grace. Together they produced a statement in praise of the American economic system, the free market, and the individual entrepreneur. They spoke of "the immense creativity of our free economy" and of its "ability to meet a vast array of social needs that lie outside the marketplace." The prosperity generated by such an economy, they held, is the true benefactor of the poor.[42] All in all, a carrot of their own to precede the expected stick.

And stick there was. The bishop's letter, when it came, did not disappoint capitalism's many critics. In spite of a few modest disclaimers—"Religious and moral conviction cannot simply by itself produce solutions to economic dilemmas"—the letter was not miserly with solutions, most of them fairly sweeping in nature. The other shoe had dropped. The position taken was polite revolution: Tawney's mode #4.[43]

Worker participation in industry ownership was advocated, as expected. So was worker participation in management. A "consumerist mentality" was deplored. Means of limiting consumption and the accumulation of wealth should be found, for these constitute avarice. (Limit how? Taxation? Confiscation? Sumptuary Laws? And doesn't consuming make more jobs? Never mind *that*.) Indeed, the bishops were not entirely sanguine about the future of private property. They spoke of a "social mortgage" which very much calls this right into question.[44] Productivity and economic efficiency might be necessary goals (necessary evils?) but not to the detriment of the poor. Presumably some additional leveling mechanisms are desirable, for the bishops held,

". . . the distribution of income and wealth in the United States is so inequitable that it violates this minimum standard of distributive justice."[45]

And not only in America. The world-wide level of inequality was deemed "morally unacceptable." Throughout rang the clarion call for nation and individuals to disgorge as believers once did in the good old days.

"Similarly, the earliest Christians sought to alleviate poverty and called upon the wealthy in their community to relinquish their goods in the service of their brothers and sisters."[46]

Where are you, St. Godrick? Your office is calling.

THE "PROTESTANT ETHIC," REPEALED OR REVEALED?

During a visit to Canada in 1984, the Holy Father himself seemed to reinforce the bishops' concerns. He strongly criticized economic systems that respond "only to the forces of the marketplace" and are governed "by the profit motive of the few rather than the needs of the many." As reported by correspondent E.J. Dionne, the pope advanced the demand by Third World countries for a redistribution of the world's wealth. "In the light of Christ's words," the pope declared, "this poor south will judge the rich north."[47] Again, more stick than carrot.

All the foregoing would seem to guarantee continued moral schizophrenia. The nation's theological leaders (at least, those in the upper set of Christian Establishment) appear to want prosperity for the nation's people. The means by which prosperity may be achieved are morally suspect, nonetheless. As in the late Middle Ages, business is once more a necessary evil. Profit is *turpe lucrum*.

Has the Protestant Ethic been repealed? By some, yes.

BUSINESS AND SOCIETY

Can Business and the Voice of Moral Rectitude find common ground? In the context of Western Civilization, probably not. Except for a brief halcyon period, businessmen and any activity involving money have been conspicuously lacking in the odor of sanctity.

Maybe that's not a bad thing. To be hopelessly unregenerate, that is. For if Business were to follow the dictates of Religion (both of the traditional and secular sorts), it might face a repetition of St. Godrick's performance, thereby rendering itself incapable of creating prosperity. For itself or for society at large. In this regard Adam Smith was moved to write:

> "I have never known much good done by those who affected to trade for the public good. It is an affectation, indeed, not very common among merchants, and very few words need be employed in dissuading them from it. . . . By pursuing his own interest [the merchant] frequently promotes that of society more effectually than when he really intends to promote it."[48]

It must be admitted that the stigma of moral turpitude does not trouble every man and woman of business. Queried about negative image, members of middle management often respond with such disclaimers as, "The CEO has made some speeches about that." Or, "Ask the board chairman. He's out there in the world. I'm just doing my job."

But the problem of profit and its morality is not merely a problem of Big Business and its leading lights. It must also be resolved by proprietors of small businesses and emergent entrepreneurs who have created most of those eight million new jobs supporting the U.S. recovery. Many of them are young, members of the famous Baby Boom generation, whose huge numbers will doubtless dominate the culture for decades to come. This, remember, was the generation whose mothers' oft-repeated decree, "You are special!" gave its members the confidence to turn most of the institutional "how-to's" inside out. These were the reformers who demanded (and got) folk masses and rock masses and religious dance; who demanded (and got) loosened-up and laid-back styles in Establishment religion. Will they, as businessmen and women, be willing to live with moral ambivalence in their work? Will they be willing to accept guilt for "excess profits" or even consider the "just price"?

No pollster has yet taken the generational pulse in this regard. But there are some interesting straws in the wind. Case in point: a story drawn from Earl C. Gottschalk's report in the *Wall Street Journal.*

> "You can have it all *now!*" cries the Reverend (and beautiful) Terry Cole-Whittaker in her San Diego church. "Being rich and happy doesn't carry with it a burden of guilt. If you are poor, you are responsible."
>
> Her parishioners carry her message on the bumpers of their Mercedes Benzes and Datsun 280Zs: "Prosperity is your divine right." It is her right as well. Her salary is $180,000 a year (a far cry from the $14,000 or so which constitutes the ministry average). That figure, of course, does not count royalties from her latest book *How To Have More in a Have Not World,* or from the classes and seminars in how to attain business success.
>
> She calls her teachings the New Christianity. It is a religion without sin, without hell, without guilt. There is no call to give anything up, give anything away, or to be anything more than what money can buy.
>
> Reverend Terry is called a "rising star of the 18-45-year-olds." And there are a lot of them. Two thousand and more regularly show up for Sunday services, and her congregation has an annual budget of $10 million, much of it spent on TV ministry, which brings in its own revenue.
>
> Church services are relentlessly upbeat. Lots of singing, embracing, holding hands; lots of moving around and sharing happiness; lots of cheers and whoops of joy. "You're wonderful!" she exults. That is just what they want to hear.[49]

Not much traditional ritual here on view. Not many of the old Judeo-Christian themes. But the Reverend Terry has a good word for Business. It has become a unifying concept, a tie that binds. That may be enough to make her sect—or those like it—viable options for the future.

9

POLITICS AND BUSINESS

UNEASY PARTNERS

Works of universal and lasting value have often emerged from efforts aimed at the satisfaction of crude material urges.

RENÉ DUBOS[1]

Power and authority. That's what politics is all about." Standard response from the freshman student in a social sciences class. Pressed for distinctions between the two concepts, he might add, "Power is the ability to make people do what you want them to do, whether they like it or not." Bravo. And authority?

"That's the ability to make people *want* to do what you want them to do—at least, to make them think they ought to want to." Bravo again. And if he then adds, "The first goes down better if it's accompanied by the second." Double bravo.

Viewed from this perspective, power plays and ploys turn up everywhere. The mugger with a gun has power (but not authority). And you hope the law will use *its* authorized power to punish *his* power over your wallet. Mother (authority figure) has the power of love withdrawn. The priest has the power, and authority, to trouble a believer's conscience. An employer has the power of the pink slip. His position provides the authority.

Authority and power—formal, informal, legal and otherwise—can be found in all institutional settings. For if there are rules describing how to accomplish a given task, there are prohibitions and often penalties for breaking the rules.

Beyond, above, and in-between institutional forms there is the ancient power of the small group which can effectively implement or circumvent both rules and prohibitions. Consider this 1939 picture of men at work, drawn from life at the Hawthorne Plant of Western Electric by Professors Roethlisberger and Dickson:

> Of all the wiremen and solderers on the factory floor, two cliques stood out. Clique A, which included the most skilled workers on the floor, looked down on Clique B, which included the slowest workers. Did that mean a consistently high output for A? It did for some members of the clique who nevertheless took care to hide their lights under a bushel. The others failed to meet the official "bogey," or standard set by

the industrial engineers. Why? Because the group maintained informally a level of performance which seemed fair to them. Only one member of the "over achievers" regularly reported his output; it was his way of expressing contempt for his colleagues. He was not only excluded for his pains, but given the silent treatment to boot. He had broken the first tenet of the behavioral code: "Thou shalt not turn out too much work—that is "rate busting."

Members of Clique B, on the other hand, regularly broke the second commandment: "Thou shalt not do too *little* work— that's chiseling." Because of their inferiority feelings, commandments three and four were of special importance to Clique B. "Thou shalt not squeal to any supervisor," and "Thou shalt not act uppity and officious, especially if thou art an inspector."[2]

Punishments for infractions of the rules varied in this situation from sarcasm and ridicule to outright isolation. These are the penalties universally available to small groups and universally applied. It is the oldest power ploy known to man, and it is coupled to the authority of "everybody's doing it." Especially when the "everybody" includes all the people an individual cannot do without or escape. Harnessing the power of the group has been the goal of business management in recent years.

Martin E. Fanning, vice president for industrial relations at the Japanese-owned Auburn Steel Company, Inc., near Syracuse, New York, spoke to reporter Audrey Freedman about the importance of the work team. She incorporated his comments in an article she did for *The Conference Board:*

"Individuals become part of a team right from the beginning, since the company normally hires in groups of ten or fifteen. . . . When a team achieves a record, there's a reward. . . . The first element of reward is personal pride. Then there's the esteem of the other teams. And the team that set the record knows full well that the others are coming up right behind it. . ."[3]

What about absenteeism? That, too, is controlled by team pressure, Ms. Freedman was told. Since team members automatically fill in for absent colleagues there is considerable anxiety about letting the others down.

HARNESSING THE POWER OF THE GROUP

The name of the game today is productivity and workers themselves are being asked to call the shots—with or without union involvement. One hears of retail chains in which workers study the entire operation and make recommendations for improved efficiency and productivity. Quite a few companies have adopted the Scanlon Plan, or variations thereof, which not only gives workers a voice in company ways and means, but also a stake in the ends. Under the plan, committees of workers and supervisors meet regularly to discuss plant and product improvement. If proposals are adopted, if costs are lowered and output increased, 75 percent of the savings achieved are passed on to all workers.

The practice of regular meetings between employees and the highest executive officers is by no means a rare occurrence or exclusive to Japanese management. And the consultations appear not to be merely cosmetic. Corporation plans and even financial decisions are aired and discussed. Electro Sci's chief executive officer asks small groups of twelve to fifteen employees, "What can we do better?" Pitney Bowes management opts for "jobholder's meetings" held just before the annual stockholder's meeting, and officers gird for rough questions on a par (in terms of bite and irreverence) with those asked in presidential news conferences.[4]

Corporate executives are not yet being chosen on the basis of "search committee" recommendations. That may happen eventually. It is already the norm in academic settings where search committees study résumés and conduct interviews for every vacant position from that of library technician to college president. Faculty and staff promotions, tenure, and sabbatical leaves also receive at least initial consideration in appropriate committees. Using the authority of the group spreads the responsibility—and spreads the blame.

A large business organization may employ enough people to fill a small town, making the operation of such a working community as much a matter of governance as of management. The trend in governance is increasingly toward participatory democracy. David W. Ewing, writing in 1982 for the *Harvard Business Review,* referred to a growing psychology of entitlement among employees. "Instead of saying they want more influence on how things are run, if possible, employees tend to insist they have a *right* to take part in decisions affecting their jobs."[5] In response, many companies are moving to insure due process in the workplace. The Pitney Bowes pattern is among the most impressive:

> One of the world's largest manufacturers of postage meters (over 20,000 employees in various locations, 6,000 in Stamford, Connecticut), Pitney Bowes has fostered a complex, ambitious deliberative organization. The Council of Personnel Relations (CPR) in every plant is really several councils, each of which meets monthly or bi-monthly. All section employees meet with their elected representative and an appointed management representative. These two attend department meetings with their peers. Elected representatives from this group sit on the Division Council which then sends its own representatives to the Main Council Meeting attended by company officers. Each meeting has co-chairmen, one from the employee group, one from management.
>
> Section representatives, elected for two-year terms, can function as ombudsmen, referral experts, and guides for employees with problems and complaints. Released time is provided for these functions. According to the Office of Employee Relations, CPR is not an arbitration procedure. It is a means of communication and general problem solving. About the CPR, Fred T. Allen, Chairman and President, wrote, "Treat employees like partners and they act like partners."[6]

The Pitney Bowes CPR grew out of experimental councils created when the company made bombsights during World War II. Elsewhere, changes in company governance may owe, in large part, to the influx of highly educated Baby Boomers into the work force. The new modes may simply reflect a continuing shift in basic values as well as in psychology. Increasingly, says Peter Drucker, the job is everywhere "being treated as a species of property" rather more like land or personal possessions than a contractual claim. The job, once allocated, is becoming a right which must not be denied without due process, without appeal, or without redress.

True, this right can jeopardize business flexibility and capacity for quick adaptation to changing economic conditions. Firms in other Western countries have already reported some difficulties in this regard. Fears of a top-heavy staff have prevented many employers from hiring, thus fostering unemployment. Nevertheless, the new mores are here to stay, and American companies are trying to plan creatively for redundancy and for the retraining and reassignment of workers.

The Marxist plaint about the means of production and the workers' separation therefrom is being answered in free societies through recognition of the job as property right. Union pressure did not bring about this change in values. It was not imposed by the political institution. It is simply the end result of a long evolution of beliefs about the nature of land and its proper ownership. For it was, says Drucker, "land which gave access to economic effectiveness and with it to social standing and political power." No wonder *that* property is "real." Ours is now an employee society. The "means of production" is therefore the job which (it is increasingly felt) should not be expropriated without compensation. Like land.[7]

Adam Smith once pointed out to a world wherein slavery was commonplace, the high cost in productivity of forcing men to work against their will. "The work performed by free men," he said, "comes cheaper in the end."[8] That the new perceptions are finding speedy implementation in the business world is owed to a very simple reason: individual freedom *and* security in the workplace make for success in the marketplace. Unintended consequences. Benefits all around.

WHERE BUSINESS RULED
THE ANCIENT ROOST

Temple and palace in varying combinations, with varying degrees of priority: This has long been the model of rule espoused by students of early Mesopotamian civilization. Archaeology may now have found another model, one in which there was a strict separation of church and state, and in which rule was the province of businessmen.

In Syria some 42 miles from Aleppo is the very large "tell" of Mardikh. Excavations by the Italian archaeologist Paolo Matthiae have uncovered the city of Ebla, a once-famous center for the manufacture and export of textiles, metals, wooden objects, and beer.[9] Occupation of the mound began, it is thought, around 3500 B.C., but its time of splendor on the world scene occurred around 2550, give or take a decade or so. It is during this period that Eblaite librarians amassed one of the largest collections of clay documents in the Middle East. Its survival is the unintended consequence of tragedy. A conqueror put the city to the torch, and in the ensuing conflagration the sun-dried tablets were baked so hard as to be well-nigh indestructible.

Predictably, most of this huge trove is devoted to business matters. But even among the ledgers and inventories, some curious facts stand out: the king of Ebla paid city taxes; so did the queen and the queen mother. (Clearly, the treasury was not a royal preserve.) The king, moreover, reigned not by religious favor or through royal blood. He seems to have been "elected," perhaps from among the most important merchant families, and for a stated term of office—seven years, so epigrapher Giovanni Pettinato believes.[10]

The tablets refer to rations of barley for "the king, the queen, and the kings," thereby suggesting an advisory body composed of former kings and perhaps their sons. There are also references to a council of "fathers," representing "axes" or portions of the city. There is also a sort of (elected?) "prime minister" unrelated to the king's family, together with appointed administrators for the city proper and out-lying districts (Greater Ebla included at least 260,000 souls). The documents contain no references to temple or clergy in connection with Ebla's government.

There was, however, no lack of piety. Proper names of most citizens ("sons of Ebla") are deity composites. (Example: *Mi-ca-il, Mi-ca-ya*—"who is like god?" two gods, one form). Indeed, the record of offerings is all-inclusive. Not only are the gods of Ebla and environs represented, but also those from Sumer (Father Enlil is a favorite) and from cities with unfamiliar religious traditions. Even the gods of the Hurrians—an Indo-European-speaking people of Anatolia—figure in the offering lists. The documents refer additionally to free-lance "prophets," or preachers, trudging from town to town, perhaps to organize "revivals." So tolerant was Ebla, so catholic its religious tastes and observances, that every visiting cleric, every visiting scholar (several are mentioned by name and home town), every entertainer on tour, every traveling salesman could find a church home away from home. Why not? If partisan politics are bad for business so is religious intolerance.

The business of Ebla was clearly business. Some of it was apparently state controlled. The queen (or queen mother) managed a large spinning mill employing many women of the city. There was also the "private sector" of merchants in business for themselves (*lu-gar* as opposed to *lu-kas*, the messengers or agents of the state.) Ebla's commercial travelers are sometimes mentioned in the records together with the cities in which they did business.

It was to protect these merchants, to secure the trade routes and the timberlands controlled by Ebla that treaties were sought with Ashur and with other commercial municipalities. Petty kings who raided merchants on caravans or attempted to steal trade were swiftly punished. At one time Ebla controlled a huge part of northern Mesopotamia and parts of Anatolia (including the trade center of Kanesh, whence merchants a century later would send home to Ashur some of the correspondence quoted earlier). All these lands were conquered by mercenary soldiers hired in the main from an allied city in faraway Iran. The Eblaites were not themselves military men. They were too busy with commerce.

However controversial Dr. Pettinato's interpretation may appear to some scholars of the ancient Middle East, it does serve to shed light on other city-states of the mercantile persuasion. Ebla's documents were written with Sumerian figures, but their language was Semitic—specifically an ancient form of the Canaanite later common to the Hebrews and to those peerless traders, the Phoenicians. Phoenician cities can still be seen along the coast of modern Lebanon. With the exception of very ancient Byblos, they flourished no earlier than 1500 B.C. or so.

One of these Phoenician cities was Tyre whose ruler befriended the Hebrew kings, David and Solomon. Of the government of Tyre, biblical sages had little to report; of the friendship, much. ("They two made a league together," is the biblical phrase.) Religious tolerance must (as in Ebla) have prevailed in Tyre, for King Hiram helped build Solomon's great temple. And for years after there were exchanges of princesses as royal wives. We do not hear how the Hebrew girls fared, but Jezebel, Princess of Phoenician Zidon, was certainly not well tolerated in Israel.

Later in time the Prophet Isaiah called Tyre "the crowning city, whose traffickers are the honorable of the earth." Later still Ezekiel said,

> "O thou that are situate at the entry of the sea, which art a merchant of the people for many isles, thus saith the Lord

God; O Tyre, thou has said, I am of perfect beauty . . . thy borders are in the midst of the seas, thy builders have perfected thy beauty . . . the inhabitants of Zidon and Arvad were thy mariners . . . the ancients of Gebal and the wise men thereof were in thee thy calkers . . . They of Persia and of Lud and of Phut were in thine army, thy men of war; they hanged the shield and helmet in thee; they set forth thy comeliness. . . . Syria was thy merchant by reason of the multitude of the wares of thy making . . ."[11]

Throughout Chapter 27 of the book, there are the same references to trade alliances and also to mercenary soldiers that we find in the Eblaite documents, the same relation of business and politics.

A clearer description is available for Carthage (founded 800 B.C.) which was the daughter of Tyre. It comes from the Greek philosopher, Aristotle. In spite of long-standing antipathy to Business and businessmen, he found himself unable to condemn Carthage. Indeed, quite the reverse. And the reason for praise, one suspects, was the stability of the Carthaginian state—so unlike the volatile urban politics which characterized Hellenic cities. Aristotle wrote:

"The superiority of their institutions is proved by the fact that the common people remain loyal to the constitution; the Carthaginians have never had any rebellion worth speaking of, and have never been under the rule of a tyrant.

"Their magistrates . . . are elected according to merit. They have their kings and council of elders. They are not always of the same family nor that of an ordinary one, but if there is some distinguished family, they are selected out of it. . . . Whatever the kings and the elders bring before the people is not only heard but also determined by them, and anyone who likes may oppose it. . .

"Carthage inclines to oligarchy . . . for men in general think that magistrates should be chosen, not only for their merit but for their wealth; a man, they say, who is poor cannot rule well . . . he has not the leisure. . . . They escape the evils of oligarchy by enriching one portion of the people after another by sending them to the colonies . . . This is their panacea and the means by which they give stability to the state."[12]

After Aristotle, the references to Carthage are uniformly unflattering because they are Roman. Typical is that of Polybius: "At Carthage nothing that results in profit is regarded as disgraceful."[13]

One is reminded immediately of that queen city of commerce, the Republic of Venice. Like Carthage, she has been described mainly by her detractors who thought her sinister and evil, called her government the most repressive in the world, and considered her people tarnished by heresy. (Alone among European cities, Venice burned not one heretic.) It is true that she did not scruple to traffick with Moslems, a thing forbidden to Christendom. It is true also that Jews were well treated, that a Greek Orthodox congregation was protected, and, from the early 1500s, so was one of Lutheran faith. Religious intolerance is, after all, bad for trade.

Like Carthage, Venice was an oligarchy, but one very broadly based; the Great Council had a membership of 2,100. Power was exercised through countless committees with an ever-changing membership. If Venice was a dictatorship, it was certainly well concealed. And when Venice finally fell, not a single political prisoner could be found in her prisons.[14]

That event happened in 1798 at the hand of Napoleon. Venice had been free since A.D. 410, the year of her founding.

MERCHANT PRINCES AND LORDS OF THE LAND

Other commercial cities were not so long-lived. Ebla was first swallowed up by Sargon and his Empire of Akkad and then passed onto a succession of imperial landlords. With Carthage, it was not so much a swallowing up by mighty Rome as a grinding down. The scene of her deserted precincts plowed with salt springs to mind.

But the Romans were not interested in Carthaginian trade. They had been sturdy peasants, thrown onto the world scene by way of military prowess. Farming, war, and rule: these were Roman skills. Commerce was an alien activity—something for lesser folk to do. Even after amassing an empire, their views had not changed. Various mercantile cities were "freed" to carry on business as usual. Most of them were Greek. Delos was freed, so was Marsala (modern Marseilles) and Rhodes. Roman tribute was not demanded of them, no provincial governor was quartered on them. They were merely expected to be orderly and profitable. Other cities were freed by virtue of their illustrious pasts—Sparta, Platea, Athens—and they promptly lost their freedom in a futile and ruinous rebellion against Rome. Free or not, the Syrians continued to thrive. "Tyre seethes with every kind of business," was a comment of the time.[15]

The notion of freeing a conquered city to do its own thing was not new with Rome. In Mesopotamia some years after Sargon's empire had fallen, the city of Nippur was freed by the dynasts of Ur from tribute and taxes and its men exempted from the military draft. In the Babylonian Empire, Nippur, Babylon, Sippar, Ashur, and later Haran were freed to trade and to generate imperial wealth. Indeed, the city of Babylon was permitted to indulge in a yearly humiliation of the king. In the temple of Marduk he solemnly swore that he had not offended the city all that year nor had he slapped the face of a *kidinnu* person (any native-born resident of a free city, apparently).[16]

Even cities in Israel and Judah saw fit to be cheeky with their kings, as we learn in Ezra 4:13:

> "Be it known now unto the king, that, if this city be builded, and the walls set up *again*, then will they not pay toll, tribute, and custom, and so thou shalt endamage the revenue of the kings."

Neither cheekiness nor the promise of prosperity availed in the European Dark Ages. Freedom was not a gift. It had to be won.

THE FIRST FIGHT FOR FREEDOM

The settled piepowder of men of medieval cities did not, in the beginning, have freedom in mind. What they wanted were more concessions from the rulers of land and Church. They wanted an abatement of the tolls and taxes that crippled their businesses. The abstract concept of liberty was something quite unimaginable to them. In illustration, Pirenne describes the merchants of Arras who, early in the eleventh century, asked to be named serfs of a local monastery in order to avoid market tolls.[17]

Other schemes had political consequences. When the governor of a town happened to be a great lord's steward he could sometimes be bribed to lighten the tax load and permit a measure of self-government and self-regulation besides. When more directly under a baron's eye, city merchants banded together and offered tribute in a lump sum to replace the string of petty taxes levied on them individually. Barons were often very glad to accommodate. Cash was particularly useful when military ventures were afoot, and if, in order to acquire cash, they had to enfranchise a city or two, why, so be it.

Breaking free of feudal burdens was more difficult when the liege was a prince of the Church. Excommunication, that most feared of all threats, was readily available to the episcopate through Rome. Burghers persisted nonetheless. "My city means more to me than my soul!" was the brave cry often hurled at an oppressive bishop with an army at his back. The burghers had to fight and learned how to do it successfully (which may explain the Church's continuing hostility to the middle class). By the end of the twelfth century, most cities in Italy, Germany and the Low Countries, England, and northern France were free. Free to elect their own magistrates, regulate their own commerce, organize for the common welfare and common defense. They had not set out to achieve democracy. But they did all the same.

Neither did they intend to gain freedom for anyone other than themselves. Yet they accomplished that, too. Free cities needed free labor. Serfs were therefore invited to city sanctuaries. Sometimes city merchants even reimbursed the local barons for their loss. Something ranging from a slow trickle to a mass migration ensued. Those serfs who remained on the land caught the contagion of the cities and tried to organize their own brotherhoods of resistance. They refused this demand and that and became, at length, so obstreperous that lords of the land were forced to give ground. Not everywhere, not all at once, but they conceded because it paid them to do so. The commodities manufactured on their manors by serfs were made better—and sometimes more cheaply—in the towns. Why not, then, buy in town with money charged to the serfs for rent? And why not free the serf to make his rent money by selling produce in town where money was available?

This upheaval in the hallowed order of things was helped along, not only by a general desire for money, but because certain nobles cherished their own grudges against the Church and its restrictions. The burgher revolution was also abetted by medieval kings who favored the growing mercantile class in order to keep their barons at bay. Cities responded with exaggerated loyalty—and money. For cities were the natural home of moneymen.

THE PERILS OF PROMINENCE

Among these, none were more visible than the Jews. In spite of every sort of handicap—legal and otherwise—they managed to thrive sufficiently to attract the royal eye. In England especially and in other medieval polities as well, Jews became wards of the king, to do with as he would. Directly into his treasury went their head taxes, property taxes, commodity taxes—altogether, according to one estimate, some 8 percent of twelfth-century England's total tax bill was paid by Jews who constituted one-quarter of one percent of the total population.[18] And this was just the beginning. At the death of one king and the accession of another, Jewish communities were assessed one-third of their total holdings. In addition to taxing the Jews, kings borrowed from them as well. So did everybody else. From time to time, the king might absolve all debtors (including himself) of their obligations to repay. This certainly occurred during the Crusades, which the Jews very largely financed.

By the thirteenth century, however, Christian financiers were everywhere, with the astute Italians at the head of the list. There was also the Order of the Templars which, by way of lavish gifts (among them the city of Gaza and the island of Cyprus), clerical exemptions from feudal and royal taxes, dues, tolls, and customs, amassed a huge fortune and entered banking. The Templars were known to do business with Moslems but not with the Papacy (which preferred secular bankers) even though the knights' sole allegiance was to the pope himself. After the last Crusader strongholds had fallen in the Middle East, the Templars retreated to their castles in Cyprus and in Europe. Their banking center was in the Paris ruled by Philip the Fair who, envious of Templar wealth and resentful of Templar arrogance, plotted the order's downfall. And succeeded. Some thirteen thousand knights were arrested in one day and turned over to the Church for trial. All were accused of heresy and abominable practices such as worshipping the devil in the form of a cat. Many were tortured for confessions. Some fifty-four (including the grand master) were burned at the stake. Philip managed to appropriate most of the Templar property. He also canceled his debt.[19]

Perilous prominence. Even more perilous pride. Which explains why most affluent men of low degree have favored a profile similarly lacking in elevation. One who did not was the famous—or infamous—Jacques Coeur, money man to King Charles VII of France during the Hundred Years War. Beginning as an assistant in the Bourges mint, he apparently connived with the king to counterfeit the means by which Jeanne d'Arc's army was equipped. His fortunes rose with the king's favor, and for twenty years he was the most famous merchant and financier at home or abroad— even in Moslem lands. His wealth seemed limitless, and he flaunted it outrageously, with a palatial residence, horses shod with silver, a fleet of ships. Though the financier's purse was ever open to the king, with or without a promise to repay, Charles must have been all too mindful of the popular saying, "The king does what he can, Jacques Coeur does what he pleases." [20]

The outcome was inevitable: imprisonment on trumped-up charges (Coeur was said to have poisoned the king's mistress) and confiscation of his wealth. There was yet more. Ceremonial abasement was required. Threatened with torture, the one-time tycoon knelt before the king and his court, confessed, and begged for mercy. All debts canceled at last.

Congresses may be less vindictive than kings but are no more disposed to honor their moneymen. Especially not when they are "proud and passionate" in nature as well as ostentatious. Such a one was Robert Morris, signer of the Declaration of Independence, founder of the First Bank of North America, and merchant prince, self-made. During the darkest days of the Revolution, he labored to keep the new ship of state financially afloat, doubtless with much of his own funds. In 1778 he was accused of fraud by the redoubtable Thomas Paine who was able to whip up a considerable public outcry. The Morris reputation slipped in spite of his clearance on all charges. He was again appointed superintendent of finance and again concluded his task, as Dumas Malone tells us "in a spirit of despair." Later on would come unfortunate speculations and a prison term for debt. He died impoverished and in obscurity. [21]

SPIRITS MARTIAL AND MERCANTILE

Had the government of Great Britain heeded Adam Smith the American Revolution might never have happened. "The empire," Smith declared, "[is] a project which has cost, which continued to cost, and which, if pursued in the same way as it has been hitherto, is likely to cost immense expense, without being likely to bring any profit."[22]

Give it up: that was his recommendation. Give it up, and our trade would recover, our prosperity would increase and,

". . . by thus parting good friends, the natural affection of the colonies to the mother country which perhaps our late dissensions have well nigh extinguished, would quickly revive."[23]

But empires are not made or maintained on the basis of cost effectiveness. Neither is revolution.

If the merchants of America had carried the day, conflict might have been avoided. True, there had been in 1677 an abortive rebellion led and supported by merchants incensed by the mother country's restrictions on American trade.[24] A century later there was less unanimity in mercantile ranks. Law and order were preferred to the threat of violence. And though many American merchants risked lives and fortunes for the cause of independence, others did not.

Commerce does not, in most cases, thrive amid conflict, and merchants hunger neither for conquest nor for glory and would far rather trade than fight any day. This preference among Americans in general was noted in 1831 by Alexis de Tocqueville, a young French visitor whose observations were later published as *Democracy in America,* still considered a political masterpiece and something of an ethnographic marvel as well.

"I know of nothing," he said, "more opposite to revolutionary manners than commercial manners. Commerce is naturally averse to all the violent passions; it loves to temporize, takes delight in compromise, studiously avoids irritation . . . Commerce renders men independent of one another, gives them a lofty notion of their personal importance, leads them to seek to conduct their own affairs, and teaches them how to conduct them well; it therefore prepares men for freedom but preserves them from revolution."[25]

Though not from war which must be prosecuted by the military arm of the government with funds—and perhaps other services as well—supplied by businessmen. For rulers large or small have seen in trade another kind of diplomacy, a tool for every purpose from the sealing of alliances to a bloodless war waged with tariffs, boycotts, and industrial espionage.

JOINT VENTURES

To observe this symbiosis in its simplest form, we shall need to revisit the Yąnomamö, that Venezuelan tribe in whose autonomous, mutually hostile villages, the great warriors still posture and preen.

> A reputation for ferocity may give a village some security against attack. Dependable allies are better. How to win them? By giving feasts during which hosts and guests make sure to demonstrate what awesome prowess they could bring to bear if they really wanted to. When everyone has been suitably impressed, they all sit down to eat and drink in a spirit of détente. They also trade. For trade is the glue of alliance.
>
> All without stated plan or purpose, each village undertakes to supply a need expressed by its partner. It becomes specialized for cotton yarn, dogs, baskets, or some other commodity which the partner village is perfectly able to produce for itself but tactfully suspends for the time being. Dr. Chagnon describes a village which "forgot" how to make clay pots because its partner village kept them in good supply. Later when hostilities recommenced, the villagers suddenly "remembered" the potter's art in order to forge trade bonds with their newest allies.[26]

Here is a scenario which prefigures political usages of contemporary trade as surely as it does the concept of power balance as guarantor of national security.

Then there is the matter of exploration in the quest for markets. The flag, it has been said, follows trade. That was certainly true in ancient Mesoamerica. The *pochteca*, mentioned earlier, not only worked assiduously to expand their commercial boundaries, but those of the Aztec Empire as well. During their forays into the hinterland they are said to have practiced adept espionage, sniffing out cities ripe for the plucking. They even appear to have fomented political quarrels when possible in order that Aztec regiments should be called in to quell the resulting disturbance on behalf of one combatant or another and, in the process, take control.[27]

Although Aztec military heroes despised the trader-spies (perhaps out of pure envy) the sovereign applauded their efforts. He regularly addressed them as "my beloved uncles," using the familial term as a mark of special favor. The additional title "Vanguard Merchants" clearly indicated their position as quasi-military agents of the crown. (No wonder the generals had their noses out of joint.)

Great Britain's mighty empire, on the other hand, was in large part formed as an afterthought, as political ratification of mercantile fact. What trade had joined to Crown, let no man put asunder. During the Age of Discovery, consortia of merchant venturers were busy everywhere. Perhaps the most interesting was the British East India Company. Established by Queen Elizabeth's charter in 1600, the original company of eighty London merchants aimed initially to buy spices in Sumatra. Finding there an eager market for Indian calico, they undertook to supply that demand. Through negotiations with local rajas and the Moghul emperor of India, the merchants acquired land for "factories"—warehouses which, because of the unsettled nature of the time, they fortified strongly. Eventually the company fielded its own private army and practiced diplomacy through its "advisers" placed in as many royal courts as possible.

"The times now require you," said one company director, "to manage your general commerce with your sword in your hands." Another director, Sir Josiah Child, declared in 1687 that the company must

> "establish such a politie of civil and military power and create and secure such a large revenue to maintain both . . . as may be the foundation of a large, well-governed, sure dominion for all time to come."[28]

In spite of financial reverses, it seemed that the company moved from strength to strength. Charles II gave the company many rights and favors (not without return, it must be said) including the city of Bombay which was the dower of his Portuguese wife. But the losses accumulated. The company's financial difficulties had repercussions in America. An effort to maintain their Chinese concessions caused the directors to buy huge amounts of tea. They then ceded to the Crown some powers in order to dump the excess in America—duty free for them, but not tax free for their consumers. A tea party in Boston was the result.

By 1772 the company applied to Parliament for a bailout. Upon their investigation of the company's affairs, Parliament's representatives were sufficiently shocked to appoint a royal governor-general and began to establish national sovereignty. India eventually became part of the empire. Adam Smith had much to say regarding these events:

> "No two characters seem more inconsistent than those of trader and sovereign. If the trading spirit of the English East India Company renders them very bad sovereigns; the spirit of sovereignty seems to have rendered them equally bad traders. While they were traders only, they managed their trade successfully, and were able to pay from their profits a moderate dividend to the proprietors of their stock. Since they became sovereign, with a revenue which, it is said, was originally more than three million pounds sterling, they have been obliged to beg the assistance of government in order to avoid immediate bankruptcy. In their former situation, their ser-

vants in India considered themselves as the clerks of merchants; in the present situation, those servants consider themselves as the ministers of sovereigns."[29]

WARY PARTNERSHIPS

As units of the regular army were sent to India to augment the company's army, aristocratic young officers snooted their self-made colleagues into eclipse. Slowly, social forms resumed their accustomed patterns. Merchants were, through trade, to increase the wealth of the nation and that of aristocratic shareholders. They were to make possible the sovereign's greater glory. But in this joint endeavor they were definitely junior partners. And so it was back home where Parliament was largely populated by the ruling class, and merchants did not aspire above their station—unless, of course, they were rich enough to buy the titles and lands that validated the right to rule.

A similar sense of partnership with much the same allocation of seniority has prevailed from time to time on American shores, with men of business on the junior side of the equation and "old money," intellectuals, and lawyers on the other. (Alexis de Tocqueville held that, in America, the "tastes and habits of the aristocracy may be discovered in the characters of lawyers.")[30] The great economist, John Maynard Keynes, once advised Franklin Roosevelt on his dealings with tycoons:

> "It is a mistake to think that they are more *immoral* than politicians. If you work them into the surly, obstinate, terrified mood, of which domestic animals, wrongly handled, are so capable, the nation's burdens will not get carried to market; and in the end public opinion will veer their way."[31]

Certainly men of business are different from politicians, for they rarely enter elective public office or seek it, though they are willing enough to work in the interest of their cities. The late Joseph Schumpeter, a much admired economist, believed this owed to the fact that city management is rather more businesslike than government on a larger scale. And then there is always the problem of getting elected. Businessmen, he thought, might not be sufficiently glamorous to attract votes or sufficiently habituated to the peculiar demands of political life. A marvel in the business office might be "unable outside of it to say boo to a goose." Aware of his platform deficiencies, said Schumpeter, the businessman, more often than not, wants to avoid and be avoided by politics.[32]

A vain hope, it would seem. For the uneasy partnership of Politics and Business can as easily dissolve into armed truce, and the latter may be the more familiar stance.

Both sorts of relationships—those of uneasy partners and wary adversaries—have surfaced in America. They are often characterized in the political personages of Thomas Jefferson and Alexander Hamilton. As one America-watcher put it, ". . . every American contains within him the seed of Hamiltonian mercantilism and the seed of Jeffersonian agrarianism with its distrust of the merchant. Americans have encouraged unbridled business enterprise as Hamiltonians; they have been suspicious of it as Jeffersonians."[33] Peter Drucker points out that neither model upholds true laissez-faire. The Hamiltonian supports, protects, and encourages business "provided it moves in the direction he deems conducive to national . . . strength."[34] The business-as-adversary model (a uniquely American position) aims at keeping Business pruned, tamed, and at arm's length—"It taints," says Drucker.

Easy enough to identify the Hamiltonian politician. His opposite number is harder to peg. Jeffersonians with a strong populist tilt are apt to cherish a conspiracy interpretation of national woes. ("It's a Jewish cabal at work!" "It's the corporations!" "It's the Trilateral Commission!" "It's the multinationals!")

During the 1984 elections, "the rich, powerful, and greedy" were frequently invoked as agents of evil intrigue. And so they were in 1831 when Alexis de Tocqueville observed, ". . . the more affluent classes of society are so . . . removed from the direction of political affairs . . . that wealth, far from conferring a right to the exercise of power, is rather an obstacle than a means of attaining it."[35] In short, money in America did not then translate into votes and does not now. The business tycoon desirous of buying an election, says Schumpeter, has only a few options at his disposal. He can hire professional thugs to intimidate opponents. He can subvert politicians or journalists.[36] Today, of course, he can dominate the airways. How effectively is another question. Indeed, far from devising government policies, Schumpeter continues, Business must adapt to them. But reality never serves to modify image, particularly when the image is politically useful.

Even those Jeffersonians who reject the "hidden hand"— the ordering of society by conspiracy—are not averse to viewing businessmen as crooks. Woodrow Wilson did. In a *New York Times* interview published November 24, 1907, he asserted that

"The corporation problem resembles a society of burglars legally organized to plunder, against whom criminal proceedings result only in an indictment or a fine, which the plundered themselves must pay."[37]

In order to understand both points of view, Jeffersonian and Hamiltonian, we must consider the basics. What is Politics meant to *do?* What is Business meant to *do?*

TERRITORIAL IMPERATIVES

Adam Smith's assessment of functions peculiar to the Political Institution has never been bettered. He said:

"According to the system of natural liberty, the sovereign has only three duties to attend to; three duties of great importance, indeed, but plain and intelligible to common understandings: first, the duty of protecting the society from the

violence and invasion of other independent societies; secondly, the duty of protecting, as far as possible, every member of the society from the injustice or oppression of every
other member of it, or the duty of establishing an exact administration of justice; and, thirdly, the duty of erecting and
maintaining certain public works and certain public institutions, which it can never be for the interest of any individual,
or small number of individuals, to erect and maintain; because the profit could never repay the expense to any individual or small number of individuals, though it may frequently do much more than repay it to a great society."[38]

Already in his day the British government had usurped a
function previously assigned to the religious institution. Increasingly, government bureaus made provision for the poor
and those who could not care for themselves. And that
function has continued to be recognized in all modern states.
Three functions plus one. Clear enough.

Elsewhere in *The Wealth of Nations* Smith found common institutional ground in what he called the Science of
Political Economy which, he said, proposed two distinct
objects:

"First, to provide a plentiful revenue or subsistence for the
people, or more properly to enable them to provide such a
revenue or subsistence for themselves; and secondly, to supply the state or commonwealth with a revenue sufficient for
the public service. It proposes to enrich *both* the people and
the sovereign."[39]

Here's the rub. Here is where questions proliferate and conflicts simmer. Clearly, public wealth is unattainable unless
private wealth can be secured, unless people can be enabled "to provide such a revenue or subsistence for themselves." (Even socialist polities have begun to face that fact.)
But now to achieve prosperity? What *is* the proper balance
between Politics and Business?

Should politicians and statesmen generate prosperity by
freeing Business from legislative constraints? That is to say,

should they content themselves with the achievement of sound currency, efficient transport, the safety of business-men and businesswomen both within and outside the na-tional borders, a system of arbitration and adjudication to curb excesses and protect consumers? Having accomplished all that, should they then leave Business to businessmen? Meanwhile cheering from the sidelines.

Should they, instead, focus on the pitfalls in a policy of permissiveness? Business is a useful source of government revenue, true, but its practitioners are tricky, out to fleece everyone in sight. They require a watchful eye and careful regulation. Even a measure of repression from time to time. Touch of the lash works wonders, don't you know.

Is that the best stance?

Or is Business too important to be left to businessmen? Would government do a better job at planning and coor-dinating? Would *government* better insure the wealth of a nation and the happiness of its citizens?

One thing is certain. There is already so much overlap in function that separation verges on the impossible. In rec-ognition of this given, Yale University some years ago opened a School of Organization and Management devoted to the training of leaders for both public and private sectors.[40] It is hoped that here professionals will learn to mesh the two areas in which management counts and can learn how to deal with functional overlap—a consummation devoutly to be wished.

INSTITUTIONAL GIVE AND TAKE

All too often forgotten is the fact that government *is* Big Business. Not so long ago, one in every six working people was on the public payroll at some level of government. Mostly to fulfill function #3 on Adam Smith's primary list (social projects unprofitable for individuals) and function #4 which appears on all modern lists. No one gainsays the essential nature of these tasks but businessmen and economists have been questioning methods ever since Smith's time. (Recall his comments about the British East India Company.) Mainly because the cost in taxes grows ever higher. "Why can't the business of government be more businesslike?" So goes the common plaint.

It may be impossible. Government may never be able to adopt business techniques, may never be able to control expenditures. These, after all, have as much to do with the perceptions of the electorate as with rational allocation. And perception matters; politicians must take it into account. Government may never be able to put incentive to work among government employees by rewarding productivity, for that means further expenditure of taxpayer funds. Government cannot easily streamline or eliminate mandated programs, however ineffective they prove to be. Nor can it easily terminate those that have accomplished a given task. Once installed, programs can only grow in size and scope. They have, after all, constituencies and bureaucracies armed with votes and capable of exerting pressure. (Business itself has lost flexibility as it moves toward defining the job as property right.)

Beyond the ballot box (which operates infrequently and sometimes in contradictory fashion), government has no tests to determine what works and what does not. Even if available, such tests might be impossible of application. Why? Because Politics and Business have different ends. Though there may be room for give-and-take.

The recognition that government must provide services but cannot be cost-effective in doing so has prompted government at the local level to transform some tasks into business ventures or to invite business concerns to do the job. St. Paul, Minnesota, is one community that is experimenting with government-for-profit. Faced with a budget that exceeded revenue, with taxes already at the limits of tolerance, and with drastic service cutbacks seemingly the only available option, the city fathers sought advice from the Rand Corporation. Its recommendation: let city departments capable of turning a profit do so. Parks and Recreation and Traffic and Lighting were the departments chosen for immediate commercialization, with the city asphalt plant and sign-making center slated for future business venturing. If the operations are profitable, returns will be used not only in improving department service but in providing pay incentives for doing so.[41]

A number of small communities are welcoming hospitals-for-profit and finding the budgetary results therapeutic. Hospital Corporation of America is one of the thriving chains actively seeking run-down local health centers and even teaching hospitals to own or manage. There are complaints by the private, nonprofit hospitals about "cream skimming" and general hard-heartedness. Corporation spokesmen argue, nonetheless, that nationwide their hospitals provide about 4 percent free care each year—a figure, they claim, is equivalent to the nonprofit record.[42]

How about prisons-for-profit? The idea is simply an extension of the private-guard services now being widely used to supplement municipal police departments. Correction Corporation of America believes it can operate cost-effectively by circumventing government bureaucracy. For one thing, corporation plants can be built more cheaply and in less than half the time it takes to get a public facility in the works. There are even courts-for-profit which guarantee that cases will come to trial in six weeks. No power is involved, of course, no coercion is possible. Litigants must agree to abide by the decisions reached. Many do, because they are guaranteed justice on the spot.[43]

Another instance of institutional cooperation can be found in Switzerland where private industry very largely subsidizes the armed forces. Workers are paid by their companies when called up for military service or training. An officer knows he can use company facilities—photocopying equipment, communications facilities, secretarial help—for military purposes and that, if he is abroad when called for service, his company will fly him home. So much do business executives value the management training accorded military personnel that high rank in the army is a virtual guarantee of high rank in civil employment.[44]

I'll scratch your back, you scratch mine. Give-and-take. There is, however, another broad area of overlap that occurs not because of conscious experimentation, but by way of unintended consequences.

BUSINESS MEANS, POLITICAL ENDS

Statesmen devise agreements, negotiate treaties, draw up constitutions, plan programs designed to alleviate social ills. These are, they argue, political functions. Afterward comes the discovery that Business has done the job as a serendipitous by-product of a wholly commercial end. Cases in point:

> *Poverty.* The reason, says economist Thomas Sowell, that the poor of the 19th century were dressed in second-hand garments, ragged and disease-ridden, and those of the 20th century are not owes to technological invention rather than political intervention. The celebrated Mr. Singer developed the sewing machine thereby making cheap, factory-made clothing universally available.[45]

> Statistics indicate that poverty decreased in the 1950s when welfare expenditures were low and prosperity high; it decreased in the 1960s when expenditures were high and prosperity also high; it did not decrease in the 1970s when prosperity declined. The figures appear to be keyed more to the nation's gross national product, its general level of prosperity, than to the level of assistance provided.[46]

> *Apartheid.* So appalled are many Americans by that racial blight that they demand, not only political exclusion of South Africa, but business penalties as well. If American investment companies and individual investors refuse to buy stock in South African concerns, they reason, if branches of American-owned corporations shut down and come home, then the offending government will have to come to terms.

Black political leaders in South Africa tend to agree. Ordinary workers apparently do not. According to a survey of black factory workers published (Fall, 1984) by sociologist Lawrence Schlemmer, 75 percent disagreed with campaigns to terminate Western investment. Racial progress was perceived by them—and indeed by many white antiapartheid reformers as well—to be dependent on economic development.[47]

In large part because of growing black consumer power, white South African businessmen—including its Afrikaner members of Dutch descent—increasingly oppose apartheid. Indeed, a leading communist in the area told reporter Steve Mufson, "It's only a matter of time before apartheid collapses because it's in the interest of the capitalist system."[48]

Of the importance of business to black freedom, Mangosuthu G. Buthelezi, hereditary leader of the Zulu nation, wrote, "It was the large corporations that broke the apartheid barriers that led to real advancements for black workers." As an example, he cited the courage of Ford executives in the South African plant. They broke the law in hiring black apprentices and, in the process, set an industrial precedent. Large corporations, holds Chief Buthelezi, can definitely be seen as agents of change. And Americans who recommend disinvestment in South Africa are not, in his view, striking a blow against apartheid; they are, rather, working against black hopes.[49]

European Unity. Jean Monnet, guiding light of the European Economic Community, believed that an interlocking economic system was the surest means of achieving political unity. He was right, and his economic solution accomplished what centuries of conflict and conquest had not. The free flow of capital, persons, and goods throughout Western Europe have not resulted in a common government, common language, courts, ideologies and aims, but in another kind of unity, one more lasting in the long run.[50]

The Third World. Should statesmen disgorge, diverting American resources—really charity on a grand scale—into the treasuries of unrepresentative Third World rulers who may or may not have very defined ideas of how to stimulate national enterprise? Or should we try a more direct approach—

one that would inject capital directly into the needy economy on a people-to-people basis?

Professor Michael Vlahos of Johns Hopkins University suggests turning the American passion for travel into foreign aid. How? By targeting societies most in need and offering prospective tourists tax incentives for going there. Even better breaks should be offered those who fly domestic on the way. Such a project would erase those ugly images of Yankee Imperialism, for nobody objects to working for the Yankee Dollar, particularly if he can spend it any way he chooses.

Of course, if the country in question is bedeviled by terrorists, all bets are off.[51]

The Third World and Transnationals. An evolutionary outgrowth of the now largely defunct multinational corporation with its emphasis on national branches and subsidiaries, the new transnationals practice "production sharing." Thus, almost anything from electronics products to lingerie might be designed and marketed by the parent company in a developed nation but manufactured totally or in part elsewhere.

As labor in developed nations grows short following the "baby bust" and increasingly averse to hard and monotonous work, the surplus labor supply in developing countries becomes ever more attractive to business concerns. Jobs are what such countries need far more than grants, loans, and the foreign aid governments can supply. And jobs are what Business creates. It also enhances the skills necessary to create more jobs on native turf. Transnational manufacture is typically managed by local entrepreneurs who, on the basis of guaranteed sales, can float the loans necessary to assemble labor and set up the plants.[52]

One World and Transnationals. For all the dreams and hopes powerfully focused on the United Nations, its solid accomplishments in terms of international amity and order have been very slim. The modern transnational corporation, which integrates people of many cultures in the pursuit of a common practical goal, gives hope of doing a better job. While governments fission and fume, international business becomes more tightly interlaced and interdependent. The modern transnational is just that—beyond the scope, beyond the control of the single national government. It operates in a world market which will one day require—and will get—a more effective world government to perform all the functions that only the political institution can be expected to perform.[53]

FOUR-PART HARMONY

"Oh, for the days," sighed a once-famous movie cowboy, "when men were men and women liked 'em that way!" While not many with-it Americans would permit such a sentiment to cross their lips, they are not beyond nostalgic yearnings for yesteryear. Particularly the yesteryear when institutional harmony prevailed—or, at least, seemed to in small town America. One who studied the small town scene of 1963–1964 was the Indian anthropologist, Surajit Sinha, and he lets us see ourselves as we are seen—or were:

> Dr. Sinha settled in "Maplewood," a middle western town of under 5,000 people, about a quarter of them farmers. By rights, Maplewood should be called a village. Not so, says Dr. Sinha. It was affluent, was very much a part of the wider world, had all modern amenities. It also included all ethnic groups and every church or denomination known to city folk.
>
> The twenty-three industries and businesses in Maplewood sponsored a weekly message in the local newspaper that urged all citizens to attend church: "Without a strong church, neither democracy nor civilization can survive." Not all the sponsors or civic leaders attended church, nor were they criticized on that account. Clearly, however, the business world was on record as supporting the churches. All of them.
>
> So did the family. Even the professed atheists in the community were likely to sing in various church choirs and to send their children to Sunday school.
>
> In all the Maplewood churches, the American flag was displayed as prominently as the symbols of the church. Ministers in all services called down the blessings of God on the

president and others in public office. Says Dr. Sinha, "One gains the impression that, not only does the Church bless the American flag, but the autonomous sacredness of the flag also lends sanctity to the church." God was asked to give strength of character to deal with problems and to fortify "the American way of life." Children declared they learned in Sunday school to obey their parents and that lying, cheating, and stealing were bad. Said one little girl, "Jesus is the best American."[54]

But that was then.

It is a truism of the social sciences that institutions must hang together or they will surely hang separately. Ever since the Counterculture years, however, Family, Business, Religion, and Politics have not only lost authority singly but have been singing out of tune.

NECESSARY DISSONANCE?

Indeed, the four major institutions are singing different songs altogether. Perhaps that is only to be expected. For, although means may overlap, each has different ends in view. Each taps different wellsprings of motivation, mounts a different appeal. And the aims, the ethos of each—developed over a long history of increasingly specialized function—put them unavoidably at odds. Let us count the ways:

Family values celebrate the small and the personal. Religion, Politics, and Business have increasingly grown large and impersonal. In order to function at all, they must employ bureaucratic methods of organization.

Politics and Religion are exclusive and must be so—"*Us* against *them.*" "*Our* way." "*Our* God." "*Our* creed." Business is, for the most part, inclusive. Anybody can buy. One needs only the wherewithal.

Politics and Religion set up boundaries and must do so. Business must seek to knock them down.

Religion is answerable to its own view of morality. Politics is answerable to popular pressure. Business is answerable to the market.

For Business profitability is the direct, constant, immediate measure of performance. For Politics there is the ballot box, which may yield one answer on the national level and quite another on the local level. For Religion the test is congregational commitment, and the results are never immediate or without ambiguity.

Politics innovates in the face of threat, external and internal. Religion innovates in the face of abandonment. Business innovates constantly, or it is out of business.

Fanaticism finds sanctuary in Politics and Religion but seldom in Business. Fanaticism does not sell in the marketplace.

Politics and Religion foster martyrs, heroes, and causes. Business is not only unheroic but often finds its own goals and interests difficult to defend.

When strategies and projects fail, Religion and Politics find scapegoats to blame (frequently Business). When Business fails, it can blame only itself.

Religion demands. Politics compromises. Business adapts.

Politics and Religion deal with hopes, fears, promises, dreams. They must cope with abstractions and perceptions—with what people want to be so or think *is* so. Business must deal with what actually *is*. Not with what people say they do but with what, in fact, they *do*.

Religion insists that human interactions should be based on altruism. Politics holds that harmony should prevail, and it functions best when moral consensus supports the law. Business can be transacted without altruism and in the absence of amity, respect, or political agreement.[55]

A better mutual understanding of institutional imperatives might point the way to friendlier collaboration, with a strengthened society as the beneficiary. One thing is hard to miss, however. Business does affect the social climate in which the great events of life transpire. For all its "materialistic" aims, it has today a greater—though unintended—

impact on national confidence than Religion or Politics can muster. Adam Smith noted this in the late 1700s:

> ". . . It is in the progressive state, while the society is advancing to the further acquisition, rather than when it has acquired its full complement of riches, that the condition of the labouring poor, of the great body of the people, seems to be the happiest and the most comfortable. It is hard in the stationary and miserable in the declining state. The progressive state is in reality the cheerful and the hearty state to all the different orders of the society. The stationary is dull; the declining melancholy."[56]

And Alexis de Tocqueville, nearly a hundred years afterward, sounded a similar theme.

> "General prosperity is favorable to the stability of all governments, but more particularly of a democratic constitution which depends on the disposition of the majority and, more particularly, of that portion of the community which is most exposed to feel . . . want . . . the physical causes, independent of the laws, which promote general prosperity are more numerous in America than they have ever been in any country in the world, at any other period of history. In the United States, not only is legislation democratic, but Nature herself favors the cause of the people."[57]

It is the rising tide which lifts all boats, so the old saying goes. If a people's optimism as well as their liberty depend on the opportunity to achieve a better life for themselves and their children, then Business can make its own contribution to the pursuit of happiness.

But as an unintended consequence.

10

CLASSES, MASSES, AND BUSINESS

REDISCOVERING THE RUGGED ME

Look at this place. This is my painting! This is my book! I created it.

GENE SCARANGELLA[1]

Institutions may set the stages of life but people play the parts. Their acting and their dialogue depend a great deal on what they bring to their roles but also on whether they are type cast. There are many social types and scenes. These, for example:

SCENE 1
On a whim, a middle-aged, not very affluent couple stop at an automobile dealer's showroom. They have been gardening and look a little seedy. So does the small foreign car in which they have arrived.

They ask an affable, beaming salesman to see his popular economy model. Then the husband inquires about the jaunty sports number in the corner. After another visual scan, the salesman says, in effect, "You can't afford it."

Shortly after, the couple leave without buying anything, the husband feeling vaguely putdown and wishing that he had shaved beforehand.

SCENE 2
A banker's office in Smalltown, America, sometime around 1925. The banker is chatting with a local businessman. The latter's accent marks him as an immigrant. He has come for a loan with which he will buy the house his wife very much wants. Where is the house? On the edge of the city's poshest residential section.

After some hemming and hawing, the banker suggests that might not be such a good idea. "Why?" asks the businessman. "I've got the downpayment. You know I can keep up the mortgage." The banker agrees this is indeed so and then adds, "I don't think your wife's going to be very happy there. Does she have a maid? All her new neighbors will have maids. Does she lunch at the country club? All those ladies do. Think it over."

The businessman says he understands but worries how he can break the news to his wife.

SCENE 3
A ramshackle cottage on the edge of a contemporary suburban nature preserve. A group of young people are sharing a

joint and a bottle of Ripple. They are dressed in old-fashioned Counterculture garb and hang on the words of their host, older but similarly accoutered. The nature park, his personal fiefdom, is the topic of conversation. Everyone is elated because, thanks to a large corporate grant, the park will survive. Their host recounts his experience in fund raising with mingled triumph and scorn. One devotee expresses some surprise. "If you sniffed at the Widget Company president like that, it's a wonder he didn't throw you out of his office!"

"Au contraire, dear girl," the leader replies, "He was very glad to pay for what I had to offer." The others are clearly puzzled. What could be offered by someone with his hat in his hand—apart from the hat?

"Absolution," the leader says smugly. "Absolution for his black corporate sins. I gave him the chance to pay conscience money for raping the environment."

The amazement grows. "How do widgets rape the environment?"

"Never mind," the host says, loftily, "they're *all* to blame. All those corporations."

All the above are scenarios of class. They represent differences in what people have, what they do for a living, and how they view the world. Not only as individuals and people but as types, as categories into which numbers of people fit.

Business has always recognized class; every automobile manufacturer takes care to present a series of models geared to ascending position and purse. In the new "life-style" markets, taste may demand more in the way of design and marketing than position. Certainly, engineers are outdoing themselves to satisfy the requirements of Yuppies, those affluent members of the Baby Boom generation.[2]

However society's subdivisions shift and change, business must remain alert to the marketing possibilities therein. Attuned as he is to social nuances, the businessman must also wonder from time to time where to locate himself in the social landscape.

WHO'S ON FIRST?

Location is the appropriate word but the appropriate metaphor should suggest the vertical rather than the horizontal. Something rather more like a ladder than a map. For class connotes rank and its focus is the individual climber who can rise to the heights but might also descend even more precipitously. "From shirtsleeves to shirtsleeves in three generations," is the traditional American comment on class mobility. There is an alternative: from peddler to merchant prince to university professor or Anglican bishop, enabled by secure trusts to sneer at Daddy's dirty money or Grandad's lack of couth.

The subdivision of society on the basis of rank is as old as civilization itself—as we have seen—and, as a means of sanctifying *difference,* may have been a necessary precursor to civilization. Rank as social subdivision takes two forms. *Caste* membership, we have observed, is inherited, immutable. Individuals move up or down the scale only if their entire category moves relative to other caste positions. One is also born into the *class* of one's parents but need not be fixed there forever. One can rise through individual luck, marriage, or effort. How much effort depends on one's starting point, the nature of qualification, and the degree of closure exerted by those who have already arrived. Class, like caste, also carries a specific subculture—special language, tastes, outlook—possessors of which are instantly recognizable to others of their ilk. It takes one to know one.

Wealth—or, let us say, privilege—nearly always accompanies membership in one of society's higher classes but is never a sole criterion. Ted Turner, owner of Cable News Network, has observed that in America, people who want to get rich go into business; in Communist countries, they go into government. The Soviet Union certainly provides plenty of "perks" for its elite: cars, country houses, special schools, special health services, special stores with luxury goods, travel abroad. Clearly, the deciding factor in class is

Communist party membership and/or degree of usefulness thereto. Favored artists, musicians, and the like are IN.[3]

The existence of social stratification has been a chief concern of social scientists. And no wonder. The self-conscious concept of "class"—with all its attendant meanings and permutations—came into being at the same time that the disciplines of social science began to develop.

Nobody has done more to pique interest in the subject than Karl Marx for whom class conflict provided the ultimate engine of history and just about every other thought and activity known to man. Of classes over time and space he recognized only two: those of "free man and slave, patrician and plebeian, guild master and journeyman, lord and serf, exploiters and exploited, bourgeoisie and proletariat, those who own the means of production and those who work for wages." Anomalies such as farmers and self-employed artisans hardly mattered. Neither did "social scum, that passively rotting mass thrown off by the lower layers of old society." This "lumpenproletariat" was hardly worth mentioning and certainly played no part in the Marxian drama of class revolution. When workers had thrown off their chains, there would indeed have been achieved the truly classless society in which all would be equal at last.[4]

Sociologist Max Weber pronounced this economic view of the social divisions altogether too narrow, noting that factors other than financial wherewithal were involved. Prestige was certainly a factor: all those traits or qualities or emblems to which a society accords honor. And power was definitely involved. What is more, he thought, the three might assort quite independently.[5] Social scientists Deena and Michael Weinstein illustrate that proposition in the dialogue of an oil millionaire, a Boston blue blood, and a political boss:

Millionaire: Man cannot live by bread alone;
All I want is a little respect.

Blue Blood: Money can't buy you love, but
prestige can buy you anything.

BUSINESS AND SOCIETY

Boss: I can make them or break them, but
I can't get into their country club.[6]

Whatever the components of class, occupation figures importantly in the prestige department. Sociology texts almost invariably include lists of occupations with degree of prestige assigned on the basis of opinion polls. Physicians, judges, lawyers, scientists invariably rank high. The business occupations (such as bank teller, factory owner, salesman) are far down the list, if they achieve mention at all.

SOMETHING OLD, SOMETHING NEW

Nothing surprising about that. In terms of prestige, the man of business has seldom been on first. Not in what we would call The West, certainly. And for as far back as reckoning goes. In classical Greece there was no class to include merchants, traders, and the like, for they were more often than not foreign "guests" in their cities of residence. It was not to them Aristotle referred when he said, "The best political community is formed by citizens of the middle class." He had in mind freeholders of comfortable circumstances who did not actually have to *work* for a living.[7]

The merchant as "guest" (or more likely, "pariah") was certainly the early medieval norm. For the man who did not in some way make his living from the land was an outsider in more ways than one. And if he was also, alas, an outsider in the religious universe—as were the Jews— all the more reason to exclude him.

The foreign merchant is not an unknown character on modern stages. There are the Lebanese and Indian shopkeepers in Africa. Some years ago, Idi Amin expelled the Indians from Uganda under particularly bloody circumstances. And in Southeast Asia there are the Chinese. Thomas Sowell tells their story in his book, *The Economics and Politics of Race:*

Some 600 years ago, Chinese began to leave the impoverished southeastern provinces of their country. They settled, in the main, throughout Southeast Asia from the Philippines to Malaysia—more in some places than in others—accounting in time for about 5 percent of the total area population. In spite of their peasant backgrounds, they tended to settle in cities. Whether through continued exchange with the motherland or because of persistent loyalty to the mother culture, Chinese communities were largely indigestible; separate from the native populations.

There was another reason. Though they began their lives in Southeast Asia as the poorest of the poor, the Chinese managed, through grinding effort and self-denial, to climb to affluence. Everywhere they settled, they became, like the Jews in Europe, financiers, moneylenders, and middlemen. They handled trade, wholesale and retail, and acquired many industries. Avoiding a high political profile, they spent their energies on business. They were, in Sowell's words, "politically weak, foreign, prosperous, visible, and unpopular."

Like the Jews they were confined to ghettos, banned from entering certain occupations, burdened with special taxes. Various petty rulers, thinking to stimulate enterprise, invited them to settle and then, when they became a focus of popular envy and resentment, used them as scapegoats or expelled them outright. Sometimes only to reissue invitations when the economy suffered in their absence. Like the Jews, ethnic Chinese suffered massacres and pogroms at the hands of their hosts.

After World War II, when many Southeast Asian nations won independence, discrimination against the ethnic Chinese increased. Quotas were installed to keep them out of preferred positions and to insure native placement. Their schools were regulated or suppressed. Many Chinese were deported to "homes" in Taiwan or mainland China their families had not seen for generations.

After the Communist takeover in Vietnam, Laos, and Cambodia, conditions worsened again. The world was witness to the tragedy of the "boat people," 70 percent of whom were ethnic Chinese. Between 1975 and 1979 alone a million refugees fled. Pirates indulged their hatred of Chinese by killing as well as robbing passengers on refugee boats. Other Southeast Asian nations often refused them permission to land, fearing—they candidly admitted—upsetting the ethnic balance in their populations.

Those who have survived this ordeal—some 200,000 in America—are lifting themselves again, thriving again, proving that persecution can knock them down but never out.[8]

Why? Thomas Sowell credits their long history of success to "human capital," determination, willingness to sacrifice, entrepreneurial skills honed over many generations. But we must also recognize the creative power of the obstacle. Creative because it can stimulate in some the will to win in spite of—indeed *because* of—being outsiders, being different, even being despised.

THE BOURGEOISIE AND WHAT BECAME OF IT

Being outside was certainly a spur to the merchants of Europe who, safe in their cities, created a class for themselves—the middle class, the bourgeoisie. Once secure, however, the class produced its own subdivisions, its own graded scale of snobbery.

Outside the cities, among the landed aristocracy, the merchant might be held in low esteem. In his own city, however, the merchant was at the top of the heap and, as if to assuage indignities visited upon him by the gentry, employed all the marks of rank available. In London's civic documents of the time, subdivisions are clear. Greatest esteem and heaviest responsibilities were accorded to the *pluis sufficeantz*, men of sufficient respect and wealth. Enfranchised middling folk were *probis homines*, good men. Of the *inferiores* little was expected in terms of taxes or civic duties. The wife of a great merchant was addressed as "lady." Women of lesser standing were "goodwives." Daughters of merchants aspired to marry *up* or at least within their own rank. Ditto the daughters of any other guild member. Sons of merchants might, on the other hand, marry *down* with no stigma attached.

Life in London revolved not only around the rules and rituals of the various guilds, but around the church-centered fraternities as well. In time, even the local gentry petitioned for membership in some of these "clubs"—Edward III himself was admitted to one.

Merchants constituted the upper, the patrician class and sometimes bought themselves into the landed gentry. Painters, poulterers, brewers were upper-middle class, and so the ranks descended, occupation by occupation. The foreign artisan was segregated with his fellows and loaded with disabilities until he could procure guild approval of citizenship and six sureties to guarantee his financial solvency and ability to pay city taxes.[9]

By the 1730s the business classes in London and elsewhere thought pretty well of themselves. If they rose into the gentry, why, well and good; the gentry were lucky to get them. Hear Daniel Defoe deliver himself of several homilies on class:

On social intermingling:

> "The conversation of gentlemen may be used as a diversion or as an excursion; but [the tradesman's] stated society must be with his neighbors and people in trade. Men of business are companions for men of business; with gentlemen he may converse pleasantly, but here he converses profitably."[10]

> "I am not for making a galley-slave of a shopkeeper, and have him chained down to the oar; but if he be a wise, a prudent, and a diligent tradesman, he will allow himself as few excursions as possible."[11]

On class behavior (female):

> "There is nothing more ridiculous than the double pride of the ladies of this age, with respect to marrying what they call below their birth. Some ladies of good families, though but of mean fortune, are so stiff upon the point of honor, that

they refuse to marry tradesmen, nay, even merchants, though vastly above them in wealth and fortune . . ."[12]

"But this stiffness of the ladies in refusing to marry tradesmen . . . is not near so weak as the folly of those who, first stooping to marry thus, yet think to maintain the dignity of their birth . . ."[13]

On class behavior (male):

"The gentlemen of quality, we see, act upon quite another foot than the ladies, and, I may say, with much more judgement. . . . When a noble family is loaded with titles and honor rather than fortune, they come down into the city and choose wives among the merchants and tradesmen's daughters . . ."[14]

"Trade is so far here from being inconsistent with a gentleman, that, in short, trade in England makes gentlemen, and has peopled this nation with gentlemen; for, after a generation or two, the tradesman's children, or at least their grandchildren, come to be as good gentlemen, statesmen, parliamentmen, privy-counsellors, judges, bishops, and noblemen, as those of highest birth . . ."[15]

And do we need them anyway?

"In how superior a port or figure . . . do our tradesmen live, to what the middle gentry either do or can support! An ordinary tradesman . . . shall spend more money by the year than a gentleman of four or five hundred pounds a year can do. . . . I say a shoemaker in London shall keep a better house, spend more money, clothe his family better, and yet grow rich, too."[16]

ARE THERE CLASSES IN AMERICA?

Being a Frenchman and therefore possessing an acute sensitivity to the causes and effects of revolution, Alexis de Tocqueville was alert to the possibilities and pitfalls of social inequality in the United States of 1831. Apart from the oppressive problem of slavery, he noted few root causes of revolution. Yes, there was wealth and poverty, but

> ". . . the poor, instead of forming the immense majority of the nation, as is always the case in aristocratic communities, are comparatively few in number, and the laws do not bind them together by the ties of irremediable and heredity penury . . . The wealthy, on their side, are few and powerless; they have no privileges that attract public observation . . . As there is no longer a race of poor men; so there is no longer a race of rich men; the latter spring up daily from the multitude and relapse into it again."[17]

In terms of inequality of prestige, he noted little at all:

> "In America, where the privileges of birth never existed and where riches confer no peculiar rights on their possessors, men unacquainted with one another are very ready to frequent the same places and find neither peril nor advantage in the free interchange of their thoughts . . . the distinctions of rank in civil society are slight, in political society they are nil . . . Despising no one on account of his station, he does not imagine that anyone can despise him for that cause, and until he has clearly perceived an insult, he does not suppose that an affront was intended."[18]

But de Tocqueville noted "yet another double of the human heart":

> "An American is forever talking of the admirable equality that prevails in the United States; aloud he makes it the boast of his country, but in secret he deplores it for himself, and he aspires to show that, for his part, he is an exception to the general state of being which he vaunts."[19]

There are differences, then, but they are not like the "lofty, stationary barriers" common to aristocracies. In a democracy the divisions are, rather, those of "many small and almost invisible threads which are constantly broken or moved from place to place."[20]

Over the years American sociologists have found this to be true. There are indeed differences in worth, even differences in class, but they are so varied and shifting—from locale to locale and from time to time—that the specialists are hard put to find a common ladder, much less a durable one. In one city as many as six social strata might be identified by local citizenry on the basis of occupation, family longevity, education, residence, income. In another city, the specialist might elicit recognition of only two.

Rethinking class has become, in recent years, something of a favored intellectual pastime. And not only in America. Michael van Notten, director of the Brussels-based European Institute (a "think tank" in the familiar American mode), reports that young Belgian liberals ("liberal" because in opposition to prevailing Marxian orthodoxy) have reoccupied the master's battleground of class, with the same economic rationale but with different antagonists. Yes, say the young turks, there *is* an oppressor class. Yes, there *are* the oppressed. Oppressors, in their view, are "those who consume taxes (the bureaucracy and its clients)"; the oppressed are "those who produce taxes (the workers and savers in the economy)." Wage earners may no longer be viewed as the oppressed class, as a proletariat, because when they purchase food and clothing, wage earners employ the producers of these necessities. When they save or invest, "they are capitalists—and through pension funds, very significant capitalists."[21]

Sociologist William C. Levin also invokes economic categories, though of a more traditional sort, when he identifies American classes as follows: (1) business owners and entrepreneurs—those who invest and gain therefrom; (2) professionals and managers—those high salaried individuals who function at the upper levels of business, government, the military, etc.; (3) skilled, organized labor—blue-collar, unionized; (4) lower level, less secure blue-collar workers; and (5) nonworking, dependent poor. There are, he points out, overlaps in income. Small business owners may earn less than high-powered professionals.[22] There are also gaps in terms of taste and prestige.

Paul Fussell set out to plug these in his book, *Class*, with a complex system of gradations ranging from "top out of sight" to "bottom out of sight." He includes savory comments on what is IN and what is OUT in terms of residence, food, recreation, and idiom among other symbols of social place. He also identifies a Category X—what he calls an "unmonied aristocracy" with lots of taste but largely without the wherewithal.[23]

It is this Category X that has puzzled, outraged, and fascinated some social analysts for years. Joseph Schumpeter spoke in the 1940s of "the intellectuals." Not everyone with a college education could be so labeled, he thought, nor could all professionals be included—doctors were OUT; journalists were IN. A concept rather similar to the Duke of Wellington's "scribbling set" seems to be what he had in mind. Intellectuals, he said,

> "develop group attitudes and group interests sufficiently strong to make large numbers of them behave in the way that is usually associated with the concept of social classes. . . . . . The intellectual group cannot help nibbling [at the foundation of capitalist society] because it lives on criticism, and its whole position depends on criticism that stings. . . . Perhaps the most striking feature . . . is the extent to which the Bourgeoisie . . . absorbs the slogans of current radicalism and seems quite willing to undergo a process of conversion to a creed hostile to its very existence."[24]

Tom Wolfe, who has skewered so many American pretentions, calls this clot of intellectuals, would-be intellectuals, and their devotees "the clerisy," a nonreligious clergy, thereby invoking not so much class as *mission*. The clerisy, though sharing a general worldview, recognizes internal subdivisions. There is, for example, the art clerisy, mediating what Wolfe believes is the only true religion of the educated class. It then follows that, for the lower orders, museum-running is the only true equivalent to social climbing. When city fathers and corporate giants are bullied by the art clerisy into commissioning (at great expense) monumental art devoid of cultural connection—fields of rocks, slabs of rock, perforated rocks and metal twists—it is not surprising that the viewing public, artistically unwashed, responds with the cry "Emperor's clothes!" No matter, says Wolfe, "public bafflement or opposition is taken as evidence of an object's spiritual worthiness."[25]

In line with this reasoning, one might invoke a political clerisy. That academic credentials (even when coupled with membership in a favored gender) do not suffice to guarantee clerisy membership was demonstrated in 1983 in three academic settings where Dr. Jeane Kirkpatrick, ambassador to the United Nations, was twice hooted from the podium by local clerisies and once disinvited from making a commencement address.[26] Dr. Kirkpatrick lacks the requisite "radical chic" (another Wolfe phrase) for membership.

Would you believe a criminology clerisy ("Every crime has two victims; only Society is the perpetrator.")? How about an economic clerisy ("The recovery is unreal; a *managed* economy is best.")? Or a morality clerisy ("Only two sins exist: making a profit and getting fat.")? All clerisies, according to Wolfe, maintain their hallowed purity by studious avoidance of common sense and the common touch.[27]

Sociologists Peter and Birgitte Berger and Irving Kristol, professor of social thought at New York University's Graduate School of Business, see in the "scribbling set" not a secular clergy, not something "like" a class, but a *true* class. It is a true class, say the Bergers, because "it has a particular relation to the economic system" (many of its members are "on the public payroll or are publicly subsidized"). It has, moreover, particular collective interests (the extension of the welfare state and, it might be added, an antipathy to Business). It also has a distinctive and special subculture.[28]

Subculture includes, among other things, a class-approved vocabulary shorn of any word which could be considered (even innocently) racist or sexist ("person" is idiomatically very big) and which self-consciously and conscientiously substitutes a four-letter obscenity for bourgeois "nice-talk." (No more "goshes," "darns," or "fudges," for those who are really IN.) If there is to be class struggle in the Marxian sense, it is likely to ally the Business Class and the Working Class in resentful antagonism to intellectuals.

Yet it is not precisely accurate, say the Bergers, to label the entire category. Intellectuals may be seen as an upper crust on this stratum "whose members include all those who derive their livelihood from the production, distribution, and administration of symbolic knowledge"—the educators, the therapeutic "helping" complex, most of the government bureaucracy, the media and publishing industries.[29] For the Bergers, these comprise "the Knowledge Class."

In 1958 John Kenneth Galbraith identified a "New Class" of the educated whose sense of superiority derived from work undertaken for fulfillment rather than mere remuneration.[30] Dr. Kristol's "New Class"—composed of professionals such as scientists, lawyers, city planners, social workers, educators, criminologists, sociologists, public-health doctors, and so on—is constellated around a sense of mission. "The New Class," says Kristol, "feels itself supremely qualified . . . to shape the peoples' wishes and character according to some version of the public good."[31]

Seen in that light, members of the Clerisy, the New, the Knowledge Class might better be thought of as self-appointed "Guardians" after the communistic aristocracy of Plato's perfect state. It was, you'll remember, the responsibility of the Guardians to guarantee an even distribution of wealth and to ensure that vulgar acquisitiveness did not get out of hand among the lower orders. Indeed, the Guardians were to endeavor always to elevate the morals, tastes, opinions, and sensibilities of those lesser beings. This was their great mission in life—apart from the contemplation of pure philosophy.[32]

GUARDIANS IN ACTION

The usual college text in sociology will dutifully present the theories regarding class and consider whether class causes social conflict, alleviates conflict, or does a little of both at different times. It will not include references to New Class, Knowledge Class, Clerisy, and certainly not to the Guardians. Class itself is often labeled Social Inequality with an emphasis on differences in financial position and life chances. The "American Dream" will be contrasted with rude reality. The professed national belief in equality will be weighed against the continued existence of great differences in wealth. Millionaires will be numbered. So will those living below the poverty line. A slight modification may be added to include the fact that percentages of the poor have steadily diminished since 1949. There may also be some reference to relative deprivation—which means that the definition of "poor" in America is not quite what it might be, say, in India; perhaps also some indication of whether the calculation of "poverty line" takes into consideration government assistance in the form of health care, child care, food stamps, and rent subsidies. In any case, America's efforts in class leveling are nearly always found wanting, especially when compared with those of other welfare states. Notably Sweden.

In Federico and Schwartz, *Sociology*, Dr. Joseph Schwartz of Columbia University points out that, in Sweden, there are far fewer differences to single out the haves from the have-nots. Indeed, there are no have-nots. The fact that the haves are taxed at a far higher rate than in the United States ensures equal distribution. In striking the contrasts, he notes,

> ". . . one of the major differences between the ideology of entitlement in Sweden and the United States is that the Swedes, contrary to Americans, view the various social programs as a right of the citizen and an obligation of society to ensure the well-being of all."[33]

There are indeed classes in Sweden, says Dr. Schwartz. Not

everyone may be university-educated, for example; that depends on merit. Of those who are so educated, however, most appear to go into government service, into the powerful bureaucracy.

Roland Huntford, who was in 1971 Scandinavian Correspondent for the *Observer* (London), noted that bureaucrats are far more respected, trusted, even revered than are politicians or judges. The former are Guardians, the latter are not. Businessmen are, of course, at the very bottom of the respect ladder. ("Half-criminals," is the way Swedish economist Sven Rydenfelt describes society's attitude.)[34] Businessmen are acquiescent nonetheless. "There are no conflicts of loyalty," the managing director of a bank told Roland Huntford. "Between the State and the customer, the State always wins."[35]

But is there a tiny snake in this socialist Eden? It all depends on how much a group person you happen to be. For group is everything in Sweden. "How can you have an opinion on your own?" a Swedish intellectual queried Roland Huntford. "It doesn't make sense. You've got to get your ideas from a group."[36]

What if you happen to be that Swedish anomaly, an individualist? What if you are a Catholic? What if you are politically conservative? Why then, you are OUT. You are not listened to, not read, and (with difficulty) published. The inner strains of achieving conformity, says Roland Huntford, may in part explain Sweden's high suicide rate—much higher than that of the United States. For those who kill themselves are nearly always the gifted and talented. The society has many ways to punish the nonconformist. Case in point: Ingmar Bergman, the internationally admired film director.

> On January 30, 1976, while rehearsing his actors in a Strindberg play, Mr. Bergman was arrested by two policemen, carted off to police headquarters where he was grilled for three hours about tax evasion. Passport confiscated, he was escorted to his home which was searched. The whole event was highly publicized (because of police leaks to the press, it was said).

Like all Swedes Bergman paid taxes at a hefty rate, about 80 percent of income for him. If found guilty he would be fined and sentenced to several years in prison. Deep humiliation triggered a nervous breakdown and hospitalization.

A public outcry followed together with accusations that the bureaucracy was hounding Sweden's foremost artists. (Bibi Anderson, the actress, underwent a similar experience.) One senior civil servant commented, "Bergman is . . . a symbol of something that threatens people."

Harry Schein, chairman of the Swedish Film Institute, said, ". . . we call it 'the royal Swedish envy,' . . . [it is] an active dislike of people who are supposed to be better. . . . Everyone must be equal."

Another friend told Bernard Weinraub, correspondent for the *New York Times*, "There's a Swedish saying, 'No one's allowed to grow too tall.' "

In March 1976, the tax fraud charges against Bergman were dropped. No crime could be found. Bergman prepared to move to Italy.[37]

In that same year the Social Democratic Party, in power since 1932, was voted out of office. No massive changes in policy appear to have followed. This, says Swedish economist Sven Rydenfelt in an article for the *Wall Street Journal*, owes to the fact that all parties—at whatever end of the political spectrum—have come to share a common worldview. Even if they did not, the powerful civil service, a product of Social Democratic choice, would assure continuity, would guarantee consensus.[38]

OF HIVES, HERDS, AND MASSES

Consensus in education, has long been a Swedish goal. Over and over Sweden's Guardians assured Roland Huntford this was so.

"The new school rejects individualism . . . rejects competition and teaches cooperation."[39]

Liberty is not emphasized. Instead, we talk about the freedom to give up freedom."[40]

"We must avoid the encouragement of young people's imaginations."[41]

"We are not interested in inventions. We want applications. The great original inventions are made abroad, and we need to be able to exploit them."[42]

"Technology demands the collective. People feel they lose too much if they develop their own individuality."[43]

Educators are not the only advocates of the Hive. As one old entrepreneur told Roland Huntford, "You can't build up a company as I have done without being an individual. But that's all over and done with now. I don't want my children and grandchildren to be taught to be individuals. They'd only be unhappy."[44]

Children get the message. It is not one we usually associate with a great nation-state but rather with the village universe. The message is this: difference is dangerous. Difference is disruptive. Safety lies in being exactly like everybody else. Safety from what? From *envy*.

Unlike jealousy which stems from the fear of losing what one has, envy is the desire for what one has not. And it is an emotion universally dreaded (most Americans would admit to *anything* but envy) because everywhere, says anthropologist George M. Foster,[45] people understand, consciously or subconsciously, the danger it carries for social harmony and inner peace. Everywhere people fear to feel envy and counter it with familiar plaints: "I'm just no good!" or "Lady Luck wasn't with me!" Worse, we fear being envied for some good fortune others do not possess (their envy might cause us to lose it). We have mechanisms to deal with this, too: "Oh, my salary may be big, but I'm putting my son through college. There's hardly anything left." Or, "Hey, man, I was just lucky; *anybody* could have won the marathon!"

Societies of smaller scale and less sophistication have

more concrete ways of forestalling envy. They simply punish difference. After all, everyone in the village universe is the *same*, must be the same. Since this is so, there can be no individual gain except by way of compensatory loss—to someone else or to the group. How can it be that someone has more beauty, more skill, can be richer in children and goods without his having cheated someone else? Such an average-raiser had better find ways to atone, or at least to divide up the goodies, else people will begin to whisper that he is a witch and deserves death. If he happens to fall ill they will conclude he is himself a victim of witchcraft, that evil, unconscious power summoned always by envy.

If in the village universe social health requires sharing the poverty, how much more reasonable to suppose that, in the affluent society (especially one with an ethos of equality), social health requires shared wealth. Seen in the light of hive mentality, the emergence of classes in the primitive world represents a mandate for difference, a release of individual energy. And since it is a difference that accrues to many and does not set a single individual apart, it is socially tolerable. Because sanctioned by groupness, because there is insulating social distance between categories (and their envy), class stratification has marked every complex society right down to modern times. The society that denies or attempts to obliterate class distinctions risks the tyranny of the hive. This must have concerned Greek philosophers when they spoke slightingly of democracy as "empowered envy."

Alexis de Tocqueville, for all his admiration of the American political achievement, did warn that, when castes or classes are abolished, individualism is not enhanced but tends, rather, to suffer:

> "In the ages of aristocracy [he said] even those who are naturally alike strive to create imaginary differences between themselves; in the ages of democracy even those who are not alike seek nothing more than to become so and to copy each other, so strongly is the mind of every man always carried away by the general impulse of mankind . . . In democratic

countries, the moral power of the majority is immense . . .''[46]

Men of democratic nations must be ever wary, for, he
thought, their rulers are not likely to be tyrants but rather
''guardians'' who will seek to ''keep their subjects in per-
petual childhood,'' who will labor to provide for their security, their necessities, their industry, their happiness and
will endeavor ''to spare them all the care of thinking and
all the trouble of living.''[47]

AMERICAN CONTRADICTIONS

What de Tocqueville saw so plainly in the American soul
was the contest between individuality and equality. The
passion to achieve set against the fear of giving offense by
one's achievement. He spoke of the man who said, ''I am
above the throng,'' but only in his heart, never out loud.

Americans revere the image of the rugged individualist,
playing the game *his* way and winning (or losing) big. The
Horatio Alger hero was a favored prototype of other years.
The picture of the frontier farmer, building his cabin one
day and fighting Indians from it the next, looms large in
American imagery. So does the remembrance of Gary Cooper
in *High Noon*, deserted by cowardly townsfolk, tackling sin-
glehandedly a gang of outlaws. Americans identify with
Marshal Gary, not the local Hive. (This is borne out in the
results of a 1980 questionnaire answered by students taking that year's College Board exams. Asked how they rated
themselves in leadership ability, 70 percent felt themselves
above average and only 2 percent below.)[48] We are, we
like to think, a can-do, make-do, know-how, get-up-and-
go people. To a large extent that is true. More so at some
times than others, however.

Although we stoutly aver that, human beings are created equal only in terms of God, the law, and opportunity,
the truth is that Americans, now as in de Tocqueville's day,

feel the pull of the Hive which really dictates identity—that everyone should be the same, or at least seem so.

> "I know of no country [said de Tocqueville] in which there is so little independence of mind and real freedom of discussion as in America. An author may write what he pleases [but if opposed by the majority] subsides into silence as if he felt remorse for having spoken the truth . . . If great writers have not at present existed in America, the reason is [that] there can be no literary genius without freedom of opinion, and freedom of opinion does not exist in America."[49]

Within de Tocqueville's lifetime and not long afterward, American entrepreneurs and inventors—in a burst of creativity—built railroads spanning the continent, harnessed electricity, invented the telephone. Much later would come radio, motion pictures and television.

How could he have predicted that these very exercises in individuality would tip the balance even further toward Hive? How foresee that inventions in transportation would erase the boundaries of region and also of class? How imagine that inventions in communication would become tools for serving (and homogenizing) mass opinion and mass taste? How understand that business would become Big and that labor, in a combined movement to battle exploitation, would also become Big?

THE HIVE SWARMS

In its organized beginnings, labor confronted management as a Hive, united, determined and with a single aim: to improve its lot. In time the Big Unions in Big Manufacturing—automobiles, steelmaking and related industries—became so successful in collective bargaining that their blue-collar members earned more than many white-collar workers in corporate offices. So successful that by the 1970s their wages began to price the products they manufactured out of the world market. Other countries were able to make steel and automobiles more cheaply. Suddenly, the once-sunny prospect of ever-escalating plenty turned gray with uncertainty.

There were, of course, additional sources of blame, among them technological backwardness and managerial blunders. But the fact remained: what had been the industrial strongholds of Big Labor were fast disappearing. And laid-off union workers, for so long dependent on union leadership for a comfortable, secure, predictable life were being asked to learn new skills, to rethink and largely remake themselves. They were asked to leave the Hive and forage on their own, to negotiate wages and benefits for themselves in nonunion shops whose managers, having profited from past mistakes, have become increasingly eager to deal with the worker as an individual rather than as a member of a Hive.[50]

Just as the numbers of blue-collar union members diminish, those of unionized white-collar workers and professionals are on the increase, with teachers in the van. And this at a time of public dismay about the deficiencies of public education. A spate of remedies has been proposed, among them the testing of teacher competence in subject matter and the provision of money incentives for teacher effectiveness. "No way," say the union leaders, recognizing that difference triggers envy, which threatens the solidarity of the Hive.

Any large and purposeful association can succeed only through a method of organization. The larger the association, the more bureaucratic the method tends to become. This holds true for anything Big whether a religious denomination, a government, or a business corporation. Bureaucracy entails the rigid hierarchy of responsibility, the ubiquitous job description, the specialization of tasks, and paper, paper, paper. In short, "red tape." Tight organization also tends to produce—at least among the middle echelons of corporate employment—a recognizable type. In 1956 William H. Whyte dubbed this type "The Organization

Man,"[51] even tempered, loyal, appropriately gregarious, dependably orthodox, gray-flannel-suited. (In reminiscing about his years at General Motors, John de Lorean spoke of the executive who was sent home because he came to work wearing a brown suit.)[52] For smooth functioning, Whyte observed, the organization required young executives willing to conform, convinced that ideas arrived at collectively were the best ideas. The organization harbored suspicions of the strong personality and so, though there was cutthroat competition to rise through the ranks, one earned points for dissembling, for appearing always to be a team player.

Schools for the children of Organization Men have been described by some observers of the 1950s scene as destructively competitive; by others as warm-ups for the collective. Some college classes, it seemed to Whyte, were more important as vehicles for group discussion than for the explication of their subject matter. Whyte thought Organization Man and his values would set the American temper for the foreseeable future, would dominate the culture. He was wrong. The Counterculture was then in formation.

An Age-Hive, led in tastes and aspirations by its university Guardians, toppled Organization Man from his bureaucratic perch. It disavowed dirty business, scorned rational process, and atoned en masse for its bourgeois upbringing by affecting the clothes and look of the vagabond poor. Hive values mandated the drug-assisted exploration of the inner self while the outer self was expected to locate a vocation— "Do your own thing." Since so many Counterculture members found their own thing was exactly what everyone else was doing, the Hive ethos of Organization Man was not replaced by rugged individualism but simply by another Hive: one part of it passive, the other aggressive; one awash with love, the other with hate. Individual competition was decried (Down with grades! Down with body-contact sports!), but group confrontation with "the Establishment" was definitely à la mode. Older Hive members who did not drop out altogether aimed at careers in the public sector, which seemed somehow nicer, more idealistic, and more loving than Business. And the government bureaucracy soon clogged with personnel and red tape. Some of the Counterculture young found this equally oppressive and fled into the safety of the commune, whatever the religious orientation.[53]

JUST THEN FLEW DOWN A MONSTROUS CROW

> ". . . as big as a tar barrel,
> Which frightened both the heroes so
> They both forgot their quarrel."

That was in *Alice in Wonderland*. The crow that jolted the American Tweedledum and Tweedledee in their march toward a collectivist future was economic. Its "caw" announced that America had fallen behind, had forfeited leadership in technology, was under economic threat. And not only that, "stagflation" jeopardized a comfortable expectation of lifelong prosperity.

Jordan D. Lewis of the Wharton School, surveying the scene in 1982, concluded that we had better get cracking. Cut the social conflicts and—like Tweedledum and Tweedledee—unite to face a foreign foe, face the threat of losing our position of number one. Sure, he said, groupness is important. But we had better find ways of unleashing individual creativity.[54]

Many large companies have, and most are trying. In the 1950s the corporate loner with an idea was thought of as a "captive screwball," useful to have around but, alas, not a "team player." Today the idea-driven nuts, those who can innovate and believe so much in their innovation that they will do anything to push it through are called "champions." And big companies do everything possible to nourish and protect them. Often executives create just enough suggestion of obstacle to stimulate determination. Often companies cultivate a certain messiness of organization in hopes of freeing the entrepreneurial spirit. Support is common for "skunkworks," dingy, off-campus labs and workshops where scrounging champions tinker with dud products developed by the corporate engineering teams. Sometimes unauthorized geniuses work in covert competition with the designated hitters. Indeed, internal competition of all sorts is becoming a corporation way of life as employees chase the spirit of enterprise in a supportive environment. They are encouraged to achieve as individuals while remaining part of the larger whole.[55]

A splendid policy for the highly educated Baby Boomers who bypassed the public sector or who are now deserting it for Business. (The public sector has, after all, long since ceased to expand.) A fine policy for the later Boomers just now moving into professional and managerial positions. But what are they discovering as they take their places in Business? That there is no room at the inn. They cannot hope to advance as rapidly as did their predecessors because those same predecessors are blocking the way, and they are not much older than the Boomers themselves. In short, the pipeline is full, and they can't move.

And that's not the only problem. There are not as many jobs in Big Business and Big Manufacturing as once there were. In the past six years alone, Peter Drucker estimates, about three million jobs have been lost for good. And, in addition to the labor glut of the Baby Boom, there are suddenly older (and younger) women in great numbers seeking work. These are women who, in other years, would have depended on hubby to bring home the bacon. Where are they going, all these talented, young (and not so young) people? They are making their own businesses. They are becoming entrepreneurs, and the risk is all their own.[56]

THE NEW PIONEERS

Ah, you will say, they are taking the plunge into high tech. Not so. That field has only so much absorptive capacity.

The new entrepreneurs are prospecting for *wants* out there in consumer land and capitalizing on their own often unique interests and activities to create new markets. Case in point:

> Three young women, all aerobics instructors, organize a training program to certify more instructors for the rapidly expanding health and fitness market. They dragoon friends, young instructors in medicine and anatomy, to handle the academic department. Then they go to a lawyer to start incorporation proceedings. Nervously, they inquire as to his fee. "Nothing," he tells them, "because you couldn't pay it now. I'll be a corporate officer, and one day I'll be rewarded. I believe in you! You're going to make it!" That is their venture capital.[57]

Most of the new entrepreneurs have defined notions about what constitutes good management:

> "You must talk to my boss," said Nancy Stamas. She is a writer for Technicomp, Inc. a Cleveland, Ohio, company which designs training programs for firms introducing their employees to new technology and equipment, new systems, new organization.
>
> "Boss" is Eric Berg—"a Renaissance man," says Nancy—who is interested in each of his seventeen employees, in their families, their responsibilities, their needs. "He wants us to be healthy," she said, "so he underwrites our memberships in local health clubs and pays for a confidential counseling service. He wants us happy and growing, so our hours are flexible. We have to meet deadlines, but how we do it is pretty much up to us."
>
> She spoke of the company's success. "When we broke $1 million in sales, he gave us a party. There were lots of balloons, seventeen of them bearing our names. On the end of each string was a check for a thousand dollars."[58]

When I spoke with Eric Berg, I asked him how he had come to be in this particular line of work:

> "By accident," he said. "I came out to Cleveland to help in private secondary schools which were developing courses in

values clarification. A friend was already developing pro-grammed instruction for corporations. I loved the work. It gives tremendous exposure to a broad range of issues, ideas, and organizations. I can learn about everything from tacos to computers. I can work with small companies and huge cor-porations. I find the business world fascinating, and I didn't expect that."

How did he learn management techniques?

"By reading *all* the books. By watching others. In this kind of work I'm both insider and outsider, and I've seen good management and bad. I'm lucky to have a small company in which I can test my own personal theories in management. So far everything's been great!"[59]

It is in these small-and-medium-sized businesses, entrepre-neurial businesses, that the nation's new jobs are being cre-ated—enough of them to offset the loss (and the antici-pated continued loss) in the old smokestack industries. Enough to soak up the surge of new bodies into the job market. Enough to outpace by a country mile the job growth in every other Western nation. So important to the econ-omy is this explosion of commercial creativity that the aca-demics (always on the heels of a trend) are trying to teach entrepreneurialism in the classroom. It helps, of course, that venture capital—once thought to be in short supply—is suddenly available, thanks, perhaps, to government tax policies.

But the existence of venture capital is not the whole story and certainly not the spur. The young couple whose high-nutrition cookies, baked lovingly at home and ped-dled door to door, can easily pioneer a going concern with-out an initial capital investment. Belief gets them started—belief in their product and also in themselves. A recent Ca-nadian study of small business ventures suggests something similar—particularly among women entrepreneurs who are there taking the plunge more frequently than men. The study found that women are likely to use their own savings as start-up money and to meet costs out of income. Why had they chosen the capitalist road? Among the 275 women proprietors polled, "challenge" was the number one reason, with "to be my own boss" a close second. "Monetary reward" was far down the list. Even so, most of the new entrepreneurs are not ashamed to say they want pleasures and comforts and the good things in life.[60]

STRIKING THE BALANCE

Who would have believed it twenty years ago? Who could have imagined the Youth of Aquarius joining what John Kenneth Galbraith calls the "heartless society," too affluent to be compassionate?[61] Who could have foreseen that those who once disdained the business world would find in it a joyous challenge? Stung by their very numbers, the youthful mass, which once shared something very like a Jungian "unconscious," has atomized into its self-conscious individual parts, each one seeking to strive, thrive, and beat out the all-too-threatening competition. The nation's balance swings away from the mass—again.

And yet, the questions raised during the Counterculture years (as they have been again and again in recent centuries) echo still:

What is the proper balance between big and small, between the will of the individual and the needs of the mass?

How to remedy deprivation without destroying incentive?

How to foster individual creativity without submerging the uncreative?

How use the spur of competition without maiming those unable to compete?

How help those who lag behind without hobbling those who can forge ahead?

How prevent the leaden weight of the many from stifling the able few?

How use the power of the group without choking individual initiative?

How, in an ethos of equality, permit necessary inequity without unleashing destructive envy?

In other societies this last question has been answered by the creation of class structure. It is true, of course, that undue closure can exert another kind of inhibition. An open system, however, would seem to offer scope to individual merit, whatever the inequities involved. And since we do not fully understand the role of the obstacle in stimulating achievement, it might be shortsighted to condemn social stratification out of hand.

Perhaps the society as pendulum, continually swinging between the ideal of the individual and the ideal of the mass is the best we can achieve—together with an ever-shifting construction of class and class values. For classes, like individuals, can fall as they can rise. Aristocracy fell. The bourgeois middle class rose in Europe and fell in the Soviet Union, where its members were purged. It does not require extraordinary prescience to envision the reemergence of the old Business Class with its own crust of intellectuals—academics, artists, scientists sympathetic to business concerns because they are themselves entrepreneurs in a new social terrain. Until the pendulum swings back again.

BACK TO BASICS

None of these queries troubles (or troubled) the New American, the immigrant to these shores. In the early 1820s Godfried Duden, a German traveler in the western frontier, wrote as follows:

"The poverty, the administrative coercion, the oppressive financial systems, the tolls and excises, form with us invisibly, and therefore the more dangerously, a kind of serfdom for the common people which in some instances is worse than legally recognized slavery. . . . The puerile idea that one could fill his pockets with gold on the very shores of America has ceased; but one thing is unquestionably guaranteed to the immigrant: a high degree of personal liberty and assurance of comfortable living to an extent that we cannot think of in Europe. Millions can find room on the magnificent prairies and valleys of the Mississippi and Missouri and a nature that has long been waiting for the settler and farmer."[62]

His work was too subversive to be published in the German states of his time but was printed in Switzerland. It was read by Germans, nonetheless.

In 1848, one Anton Riesner, cooper, set sail for the Texas coast, hoping to settle in Houston. Years later his son, Benjamin August, became a magnate in structural steel and a City Father of Houston. He began his working life, aged twelve, as a blacksmith's apprentice. At nineteen, with $500 capital borrowed from Father Anton, he went into business for himself. ("B.A. Riesner, Schmiedemeister and Wagenmacher," the firm was called. Texas then had a large German speaking population.) Two years later he repaid the debt and in 1930 still had the cancelled check. "My father's confidence in me was strengthened," he said, "because he knew I was a worker." That is what he told me, his granddaughter.[63]

Word of opportunities in America came back to Greece by way of letters from those who had gone before.

In 1900 Louis Vlahos, aged twelve, traveled steerage to New York. With his brothers he sold chestnuts on the street and, at night, slept on newspapers in any vacant room they could find. A tip that there were jobs to be had in Springfield, Massachusetts, sent them scrounging for railway tickets, only to wind up in Springfield, Ohio, thanks to a ticket-seller's mistake. Even there they found another Greek, someone willing to teach them the candymaker's art. This Louis parlayed into a leading restaurant and himself into a thriving businessman. His grandchildren—my children—know his story.

I asked Henry Klein (founder of Klein's of Westport) what had prompted him, aged eighteen, to leave Hungary in 1919 and travel alone to the New World. Had there been letters? Invitations? Glowing reports? No, he said, "Everyone wanted to come to America. This was the place. This was freedom. This was where the opportunities were. And opportunity was important. Though Hungarian Jews were not in such bad shape as in Russia, they were limited in terms of occupation."

So he came to America and, after working at dozens of jobs, formed in marriage what was to be a lifelong business partnership. The young couple saved for a year in order to open a stationery store on Long Island.

Later they set up shop in Westport, Connecticut, then a haven for writers and artists. But nobody bought the books they had to sell. " 'I have a charge account at Brentano's,' they would tell me, and I had to persuade them we could offer as many services. We worked seven days a week, sixteen hours a day and raised two children into the bargain. We not only tried to sell books, we ran a lending library. We offered books newer than those in the public library, so we did well. You know, the big market for books began only thirty-four or so years ago."

Klein's grew with the market. By 1965 it had quadrupled in size and today has seventy employees, all enrolled in a profit-sharing plan. At some point, toys were added, then music, photographic equipment, television sets, office equipment, high-tech equipment. Old lines went out when they ceased to be cost effective; new ones came in. "Today you have to know where opportunities are," said Henry Klein. "You have to seek them out. A person needs to be educated to stay in business. But you know," he added, "I'm not afraid of competition because we offer service. Besides, if your business neighbor does well, you do, too."[64]

Adam Smith had much the same thing to say about the nations of the world prospering individually if they prospered collectively.

Then there is the story of "BoBo" Woo who came to Houston in 1949 to start a Chinese restaurant.

> He soon discovered [reports Kevin Helliker] that Texans preferred to "eat Mexican." So BoBo gave the customers what they wanted and called his restaurant El Sombrero instead of The Golden Palace or something equally exotic. In short order, he became a millionaire, owner of shopping centers, a director of the First Bank of Houston. And he is at last to have his Chinese restaurant. In fact, he is going to have his very own Chinatown, complete with theaters, a bank, shops, and nightclubs. He'll be competing with two other glossy new Chinatowns. The Orientals in Texas don't do things by halves. "Nothing is impossible!" says Mr. Woo.[65]

It is the philosophy of every man or woman who ever risked life savings on a hardware store, a hot-dog stand, a cleaning establishment, a variety store. They scrape by on profits of a few cents per item and survive by luck, pluck and sweat. They can be badly hurt by big stores and chains that can buy in huge quantities and charge less in consequence. And if the landlord raises the rent, they can be put out of business altogether.

Asked why he and other small businessmen did not band together to find answers to common problems, Gene Scarangella, owner of Gene's Variety Store, had this to say:

> "Small business people won't do that. Even if it would help. They'd have to give out information about what they are doing and how. Small business people are independent and (I know you'll think this funny) kind of introverted, even kind of paranoid. They want to do their thing their way—even if they make mistakes. It's *their* mistake. They're tired of being told what to do. I understand that.
>
> "Look at this place. It's mine. The greeting cards here—the stationery there. The gifts, the magazines, the school supplies. I can't expand the floor space, so I move up the walls. I decide to take a chance with a new item. I give it a good display, I push it. And if it goes—say, what a *high!*"

"Look at this place. This is my painting! This is my book! I created it."[66]

Yes, Virginia, the rugged individualist is alive and well and living in Gene's Variety Store. And a lot of other places in America.

PART THREE

DOING BAD,
DOING GOOD,
DOING WELL

THE CASE AGAINST BUSINESS

TERRIBLE TYCOONS AND ALL THAT

*Do you really care about anything
besides profit and loss?*

REPORTER TO WARREN M. ANDERSON,
CHAIRMAN, UNION CARBIDE[1]

$\mathcal{S}$aint Augustine, that greatest of the early Christian Fathers, quoted in his book a conversation (probably imaginary) with a man of business, a merchant. Upbraided by the saint for following such a sinful profession, the merchant protested that he was performing a beneficial public service. Was not a laborer worthy of his hire? Were not shoemakers and farmers capable of lies, blasphemies, and perjury? Why then did the saint not condemn their occupations? Should he not separate the trader from his trade? Should he not condemn the man rather than his work? Saint Augustine had to agree.[2]

Not many of his colleagues did, however. They had their eyes fixed on temptation. And it is certainly true that, in the acts of getting and spending, there are plenty of occasions for sin. Depending, of course, on the definition of sin, which may or may not coincide with the legal definitions. For the three concepts—morality, legality, and sin—not only assort independently through time and place, but change their shape as well. The line between sinner and hero is narrow and easily breached.

Let us revisit with Leo Pospisil the New Guinea Kapauku before the Western intrusion into their domain. Let us meet a successful man of business (really a composite of Dr. Pospisil's friends). He is called *tonowi,* a term we might translate as "tycoon":

> We hear his howls and cries as we enter the village. There he squats in his house, cringing from the blows of his ten-year-old son. He had just refused to repay two shells he had borrowed from the boy, and the young creditor has lost his temper. By doing so, he has forfeited his right to collect. Furious and frustrated, he storms out of the house. The father smiles broadly, "Ah," he says with pride, "my boy will be quite a business man, but he must learn not to trust anybody." Had the boy kept his cool and assembled sufficient muscle, he might have seized his father's property as punishment for defaulting on the loan. Even the golden rule—*do not unto others what you would not have done unto you*—is here subject to interpretation.

Our tonowi then rises and goes into his garden where his "apprentices" work diligently. They have come to live with him so as to learn "business administration." Meanwhile, they serve as farm hands and body guards. Later, each will receive a generous loan (the Kapauku have no concept of the gift) in order to procure a wife. For a career begins with a wife. She tends the sweet potatoes which will feed the pigs which will make the budding tycoon's fortune.

Our master tycoon has himself done everything "right" from the Kapauku point of view. He has manipulated gardens, pigs, and wives to best advantage. He has loaned shell money (at interest when possible). He has traded profitably with neighboring tribes. He has hoarded his assets—the precious bailer shells—until their value rose sufficiently to net him a killing on the market.

And what does our tycoon do with his fortune? He gives vast pig feasts or sponsors markets. At each the meat is "sold." He gives and he gets. But the more spectacular the show, the more he puts his rivals in the shade. And the more his counsel will be sought in time of war or peace. Of course he must be self-confident, even eloquent. The diffident rich man gets no respect.

He does not, nevertheless, trumpet his financial success and goes about the village plainly attired. The costly ornaments he is able to afford are loaned to others to wear. He does not indulge in conspicuous show and tells no one the extent of his fortune. Otherwise he might be hounded for loans.

Of course, he must not appear unwilling to lend. A reputation for stinginess could render him very dead one day. Even his relatives would combine against him. But if he atones for wealth by sufficient generosity, he is something of a hero.

"They can have their praise and respect," was the cynical comment of one tonowi to Dr. Pospisil. "I do not care for them. I prefer to collect and lend the money. This way one becomes rich and the debtors are dependent anyway. I am a headman not because the people like me, but because they owe me money and are afraid."[3]

Is that bad? "Bad for whom?" the tonowi (or any fellow tribesman, for that matter) would ask. The Kapauku calmly accept the reality of good and bad and practice what might be called situational morality.

THE TONOWI, AMERICAN STYLE

So did American tycoons of an earlier era. And not without exciting admiration, it must be said. The *London Daily News* in 1853 trumpeted the arrival of Cornelius Vanderbilt in his private yacht. "It took Florence nearly fifteen centuries to produce one Cosimo [de Medici], and she never brought forth another. America was not known four centuries ago; yet she turns out her Vanderbilts, small and large, every year."[4] The *New York Times* (considerably less impressed) likened the same gentlemen to "those old German barons who, from their eyries along the Rhine, swooped down upon the commerce of the noble river and wrung tribute from every passenger that floated by."[5]

Much the same ambivalence was earlier attendant upon the career of John Jacob Astor, son of a German butcher, a one-time flute player and seller of musical instruments. On his death in 1848 James Gorden Bennett of the *New York Herald* called him "a self-invented money machine."[6] The pastor of a New York church was, however, moved to observe that the tycoon's word was as good as gold; no one would refuse a promissory note signed by him, so great was the public faith in his word.

John Jacob Astor arrived in New York in 1784. By 1800 he had made a quarter of a million dollars. He amassed his fortune in the fur trade (as was noted earlier), working first as a fur cleaner and then as trader with the Indians. In this dangerous and dirty business (literally dirty; there is nothing dainty about unprocessed furs), he did so well that he soon hired a staff of traders whose activities he supervised closely. John Jacob Astor displayed an interesting combination of uncouth manners and infectious charm. The latter must have outweighed the former for he was able to retain the lifelong friendship of influential men. He was also able to persuade the British East India Company to permit his entry into the China trade (no easy task).

Coup followed coup. Just before the War of 1812, American ships were locked up in American harbors because of the government-imposed embargo. Undaunted, Astor sent a supposed Chinese mandarin to New York's senior senator requesting passage home to attend a dying father. The senator received permission from President Jefferson, and off went the mandarin—in an Astor ship laden with furs. In due time the ship returned—the first in a year—bearing tea and spices which Astor sold at a net profit of $200,000.

His agents scouted the Northwest Territory and set up trading stations. He courted the Russians in order to beat out British competition, and it was largely because of his commercial presence that the United States laid claim to Oregon. Astor agents are said to have practiced every nasty trick in the book and been treated themselves to even nastier tricks by their employer. (The reality probably lies somewhere between good and bad; see Chapter 4.)

When profits dwindled, John Jacob Astor gave up the fur business and turned his hand to New York real estate. His guiding precepts in this new calling were two: "Buy and hold; let others improve" and "Buy the acre; sell the lot." He is said to have advised his son and successor as follows: "The man who makes it the habit of his life to go to bed at nine o'clock usually gets rich . . . it's a matter of habit, and good habits in America make any man rich."[7]

Although not known for enthusiastic good works (he is said to have known to the penny and to the day who owed him what in rent and when it was due), he was persuaded to endow a sanctuary for the poor in his German home town of Walldorf. He was also responsible for endowing the Astor Library, eventually to become the New York Public Library. Even this was wheedled out of him. "The disposition to do good does not always increase with the means,"[8] he once informed a suppliant. It was left to his descendants to atone in good works for the founder's good fortune.

HOW FAR IS TOO FAR?

When do sharp business practices become criminal? When they don't work, one is tempted to note. When they outrage general sensibilities. When unpleasant consequences multiply. Case in point: Dengu of the East African Barabaig, as described by anthropologist George Klima, whose work we have noted earlier. Among the Barabaig, honor and prestige turn on the ownership of cattle:

> When his wife gave birth, Dengu needed an ox to slaughter for her special food. He went to Gilagwend, member of a different clan, a rainmaking clan, and offered to exchange one of his pregnant cows for an ox. This is a standard transaction by which the ox lender gets to keep the anticipated calf in payment while the cow is returned to its original owner.
>
> Later, when Dengu retrieved his cow, Gilagwend was not at home, nor was he informed of Dengu's visit. Later still, learning that his cow's offspring had proved to be a prolific breeder, Dengu schemed to turn negligence to his own account.
>
> To one and all he complained that his cow had never been returned to him and, hailing Gilagwend before the elders, demanded *all* the calf's progeny in reparation. All parties took an oath by licking the iron blade of a spear. "If it is in my hand [if I have lied]," said Gilagwend, old and forgetful though he was, "may my home be destroyed."
>
> Two things happened. The rains failed (Gilagwend's fault, claimed the elders); then followed the deaths of Gilagwend's aged wife and Gilagwend himself. Dengu was thus upheld in his claim. But not for long.
>
> Gilagwend's younger second wife countersued, claiming that Dengu was responsible for the drought, not her deceased husband. New oaths were necessary, much more binding and solemn ones. Plaintiff and defendant would have to lick blood

from the cut ears of the cattle in question. Frightened by the oath, Dengu bribed the chief to find in his favor without the oath.

Again he had his way—until he reneged on the bribe. Hell hath no fury like a bribee denied. The elders promptly found Dengu responsible for the drought and imposed a death curse. Dengu did not oblige by dying. He lived on, says Dr. Klima, "a man without a home, lonely and shunned, isolated by his avarice."[9]

How far is too far? When you overreach and all the options run out.

A would-be tycoon not too dissimilar from Dengu is Robert Vesco, late of the United States, now a man without a country. Having skipped nimbly from Costa Rica to the Bahamas to Nicaragua, he is now in Cuba and presumably out of reach. But, unlike Dengu, he is not shunned. Any number of people—lawyers, accountants, bankruptcy trustees—search the newspapers for clues to his whereabouts. They want to give him a new residence in a selected United States prison.

Even though liquidators have managed to recover about $500 million of the money allegedly stolen from investors in Vesco's dummy corporations, they are determined to collect every last dollar he has. "It's a moral commitment," attorney Raoul Gersten told *Wall Street Journal* reporter David Y. Yermack.[10]

By all accounts, Robert Vesco is a charming man. So charming that his pursuers fear he will somehow wriggle out of criminal charges and then accuse them of libel. And what has this charming man done, apart from manipulating and looting mutual funds to his benefit? He is *suspected*, says Yermack of running guns and drugs and of bribing public officials, among them (according to one accuser) fund-raisers for Richard Nixon's reelection campaign. The objective of the bribes: to forestall a pending Securities and Exchange Commission investigation. "The moral restraints on him, to the extent that there were ever any, have gone over the years,"[11] says John Lewis, a Philadelphia attorney, who adds to Vesco's list of iniquities the supplying of black market U.S. currency to Cuba.

There are laws to reinforce "moral restraints," and Vesco has fallen afoul several of them. The affront to the golden rule is unambiguously plain.

TESTING THE LIMITS

Applying the golden rule is to some extent easier when claims of kin or kind can be invoked. Books of the Old Testament, for example, prescribe lower rates of interest when the borrower is a relative. When familiarity figures in a transaction, when repeat business is anticipated, the golden rule is more easily followed. "How long," asked Edward Page in a 1980 business symposium, "would producers stay in business if people felt deceived?"[12] It is certainly true that the Kapauku who welshed on a debt or who failed to pay a promised interest on a debt might never be able to borrow again.

It is when the personal connection or personal interest is removed that the golden rule becomes an abstraction. It is the seller of houses, the dealer in used cars, those who may never see the purchaser again, who tend to worry less about repeat business and more about present gain. Certainly this applies to the faceless, nameless owners of stock in a mutual fund. Thus Mr. Vesco's temptation.

Here is where legitimate business most nearly intersects with law and has since Sumerian statutes (as in the recodification of Ur-Nammu) insured that weights and measures should be exact and carried penalties against "grabbers" (presumably grafters and chiselers). Moral codes echoed similar sentiments. A hymn to the goddess Nanshe of Lagash mentions sinners who incur her displeasure. Among them are those

"Who substituted a small weight for a large weight, Who substituted a small measure for a large measure . . . Who

having eaten [something not belonging to him] did not say
'I have eaten it.' Who having drunk, did not say 'I have drunk
it,' " . . .[13]

Whatever the sanctions of religion, law operates where the
incentives for honesty and honor are weak and the temptations to mulct the stranger strong.

When neither the laws of the market nor the laws of
the court operate, consumers will suffer. So will workers
hired to make or distribute a given product. Case in point:
the magazine sales crew.

> The young man appeared at our door, nattily dressed, jaunty,
> full of personality and jive. Would we buy a subscription to
> this magazine or that? Ah, surely *House and Garden* was just
> our style! He could satisfy any reading taste, and his list of
> clients was all-inclusive.
>
> No, we said. We had all the publications we needed or
> wanted or could find room for. Well, then, could he do an
> imitation of Frank Sinatra for us? Would that persuade us to
> buy? He was sure he was headed for the big time. He would
> be a star one day. If only we would help. Oh, please, please.
> He had come from a welfare home with ten fatherless broth-
> ers and sisters. By now tears were running down his face. "If
> I don't sell you a subscription, I won't make my quota. I *have*
> to make my quota!"
>
> We couldn't understand his desperation. Later on we did.

Anne Mackay-Smith described such selling operations in
the *Wall Street Journal*. Privately owned sales agencies around
the country contract with magazine publishers to sell subscriptions. The agencies, in turn, contract with independent
crew chiefs who will supervise the door-to-door solicita-
tions. Of the subscription money, one-quarter goes to the
magazine, one-quarter to the agency, one-half to the crew
chief. He recruits a sales force—usually young people just
out of high-school—and hires a bus to cart them from town
to town. The youngsters are promised good hotels, fine
meals, and the chance to earn big bucks. None of these

promises are kept, according to some crew members whose parents have attempted to bring suit against the publishers. Indeed, the young people often seem to be fed only when sales quotas are met. Meanwhile they must deal with irate or abusive homeowners (one young woman was raped by a prospective subscriber), police patrols, and angry crew chiefs. Oklahoma City police recently identified the body of a strangled girl as a member of a magazine crew passing through. They suspect she was murdered by the crew chief. Why don't the young people just go home? Extremely difficult to leave in mid-tour, they say.[14]

Can the law protect the young sales representatives? A federal judge in New York, writes Ms. Mackey-Smith, dismissed a suit brought against publishers by a group of former sales-crew members. "It's not our fault," say the publishers. "They are outside contractors." "It's not our fault," say the sales agencies, *"we* signed a contract." Crew chiefs on the road cannot be located for comment.

The circulation director of *Mother Earth News* said his firm would not do business with the agencies because so many were reputed to entice young workers with big but empty promises. "I didn't want our publication to have any rub-off from that," he said. The head of a subscription agency, however, denied that young people were being misled by recruiters. "People just don't listen too well when they are interviewed," he said.[15]

It is a good thing they don't—from the crew leader's point of view. Else, he'd never be able to put together that fresh, appealing, bright-eyed sales force he needs to wheedle subscriptions from Mr. and Mrs. Suburban America. An uncomfortable conscience can always be soothed with thoughts about tomorrow. What an invaluable sales experience he is providing for his young charges! How poised they have become. How self-confident. How quick and clever and customer-wise. And they *have* escaped Mom and Dad. Isn't that what they really wanted? So what if he can't afford to pay them what has been promised? They'll go on to better things. And he will never see them again.

Nearly a hundred years ago owners of garment district sweatshops were saying much the same things. The workers they sought were not gullible, restless high-school students, but new immigrants without the language skills to tackle any other work. Conditions were poor. Pay was low. Profits were narrow. "If I change," the sweatshop owner was apt to say, "I'll be out of business."

Workers may have complained to relatives back home. Their stories, however, were not sufficiently horrifying to prevent more and more Europeans from taking ship to America and, once here, from entering sweatshops in great numbers.[16] In time, the sweatshop as a legal enterprise *was* put out of business. The International Ladies Garment Workers Union was responsible for that. The sweatshop as an *illegal* entity staffed by illegal aliens continues, while products from the legal sweatshops of the Orient compete successfully with the higher-priced garments made legally by unionized labor.

Morality, legality, and sin. Definitions are slippery and subject to change. And, as industrialist George N. Alger said in 1908, "[Business] suicide answers few problems."[17]

That comment was offered to the senior class of the Sheffield Scientific School, Yale University. With Mr. Alger on the lecture podium were five prominent men of business who attempted to address ethical problems peculiar to production (Alger himself), competition (Henry Holt), credit and banking (A. Barton Hepburn), public service (Edward W. Bemis), corporations and other trusts (James McKeen). Edward W. Page, who had endowed the ongoing lecture series, spoke of the morals of trade in the making. "We have grown rich and powerful," said Alger in reference to attitudes common in the business community, "and we are proud of our development and the prospects for the future. But with it, thank Heaven, we have greatly developed the capacity for self criticism."[18]

Nevertheless, the group was distressed by the "muckrakers" who "have said in their haste that all men are liars." Edward W. Page expressed dismay about an attorney's

comment that he had overheard. "Businessmen are corrupt," the attorney had said. "They want me to tell them
how crooked they can get without going to jail."[19] Mr. Page
objected to the stereotype. There might be, he admitted,
corrupt railroad men guilty of favoring certain customers
with rebates; guilty of poor customer service and avoiding
responsibility; guilty of bribery. Don't tar us all with the
same brush, he begged.

HARDY PERENNIALS, NEW BLOOMS

Iniquities peculiar to transport have been with us since the
invention of sail and wheel. The seller of spavined horses,
the piratical boat captain are staples of business rapacity.
Yesterday's villains ran the railroads—at least, according to
Edward Page. Today's villains are said to make automobiles—an impression doubly enhanced by exposés ghost-
written for former automotive executives nursing a grudge.
The Ford Pinto and its exploding rear end has been cited as
the prime example of a corporation's placing "cost benefit
analysis" over the value of human life. And not only that.
Ford has been accused of willful failure to use safer gas
tanks for which it owned the patent.[20]

Few have noted the changes in highway construction
occurring at the time of the Pinto tragedies. Old style undivided highways gave rise to head-on collisions, to which
engineers gave thought in designing the front end of cars.
Divided superhighways, on the other hand, gave rise to rear-
end collisions. The problems with the Pinto and other small
cars of the time, says Holmes Brown, might be seen in that
context.[21]

General Motors, that automotive monolith, has been
accused of single-handedly encompassing the demise of the
railroads, the streetcars, the trolley cars, and interurban lines.
Other analysts have wondered whether bad management
of the railroads was as much to blame.[22]

All these events represent battles of titans which attract

headlines, stir righteous indignation, and yield inconclusive outcomes. There are less spectacular, more common instances of business corruption. In 1980, a prominent corporate defense attorney had this to say about crookedness:

> "These business crimes are perceived by individual actors as victimless. We all grew up in an environment in which we learned that thou shalt not murder, rape, rob, probably not pay off a public official . . . but not that it was a crime to fix prices."[23]

He was speaking to Irwin Ross, then preparing for *Fortune* magazine a study of lawlessness in big companies. In a survey of 1,043 major corporations, Ross found that 117, or 11 percent, had been involved in one or more "major delinquencies" between 1970 and 1979. What were they? A few citations for short-weighting and defrauding; a lot for price fixing and kickbacks, illegal contributions, and bribery. Why so much bribing among major corporations? Perhaps high visibility enhances that impression. Mr. Ross notes that such activities among businesses of smaller size were fairly commonplace, involving usually the bribery of purchasing agents. Why? Because of competitive pressures as well as industry customs and structure. The time element is particularly crucial in building, shipping, and trucking. The delay of materials needed for construction or of perishables due to be shipped can result in enormous financial losses. "Where bribes are not freely offered, they are often extorted," he says. He also notes that stringent government regulations might give rise to bribery. In certain situations (the liquor business, for example) normal selling incentives, such as discounts and rebates, are forbidden. Illegal gifts are offered to encourage retailers to promote the product. ("Suicide answers few problems.")

If bribery is illegal in the United States, how does the businessman deal ethically with the greasing of foreign palms? That question appears to be standard in the many courses in ethics now mushrooming in business curricula across the country. Standard but moot. Laws were passed in the 1970s forbidding American corporations abroad to observe local customs even though the bribery of foreign officials and businessmen is not only a permanent feature of the cultural landscape but a condition of doing business. Other industrialized countries have ignored the ethics and freed their businessmen to make the bucks. Can shareholders eat righteousness?

In the winter of 1984, there occurred the terrible Bhopal tragedy in which two thousand people were killed by gas leaking from a Union Carbide plant. Whose fault was it? The finger of blame pointed immediately to Warren Anderson and his corporation. Shouldn't Union Carbide have exercised the same safety precautions customary in its other plants? Yes.

But wait. The plant's operations were controlled by the Indian corporation in partnership with Union Carbide. It was staffed by locals most of whom cannot read and are without "industrial culture," to use the words of Rashmi Mayur, a founder of the Bombay Urban Development Institute. "The Indian government should have protected its citizens," he said. In reference to a similiar situation in which the Pennwalt Corporation of Philadelphia and its foreign partner, Nicaragua, did not see eye to eye, a public-relations executive told *New York Times* reporter Stuart Diamond, "If we had insisted that the Nicaraguans make the changes (a $650,000 pollution control system), we would have been accused of being ugly Americans, the gringo who knows best. Instead, we were criticized in America for not doing enough."[24]

Legality, morality, and sin. Here complicated by cultural misunderstandings, national aspirations and necessities, lack of international referees.

There is never a dearth of ethical quandaries. Some vary with fashions and changing perspectives. Thomas Donaldson, a philosophy professor at Chicago's Loyola University, mused about this with Tamar Lewin of the *New York Times.*

When the business ethics movement began, he told her, the primary question was "whether the ultimate function of the corporation was just maximizing profits. Now almost everybody believes that corporations should be concerned about something more than making money."[25] In the 1970s, he noted, the major concerns focused on "foreign bribes, employment discrimination, false advertising, and pollution." Concerns of the 1980s have shifted to the "invisible issues"—to corporate governance.

Some sins are hardy perennials. In the Middle Ages, certain business practices were forbidden by common law. *Forestalling, engrossing,* and *regrating* constituted ways of cornering a market, of controlling the commodities therein and of charging whatever one pleased. Those practices were still so labeled in 1730 when Daniel Defoe declared,

> "All regrating and forestalling of markets, is accounted so pernicious in trade, that there are laws against it, as there are against combinations and engrossing also. In short, a man thus overgrown in trade and wealth, is an engrosser and forestaller of course; he is also a combination in himself. How often have we seen one over-rich tradesman attempt, at an India sale, to buy all the coffee, another all the pepper, and so of other goods, and then put their own price upon those goods for awhile, and so impose upon the whole nation!"[26]

Price fixing is a term in use today, and, of all the "delinquencies" noted in Irwin Ross' study, that one appeared most frequently. According to Mr. Ross, some executives have preferred to maintain price levels. Advantages have been seen in "sharing the market and keeping marginal firms alive." Indeed, he points out, some companies would have done better for themselves had they competed actively, expanded their share of the market and driven out weaker competitors. That is legal.[27]

Cut-throat competition offends the tender-hearted but benefits the consumer through lowered prices and improved product quality. Are we to view price-fixing as income insurance or survival insurance? Either or both, it would seem, depending on circumstance and personal conviction.

Income insurance is the more familiar rationale for price fixing. And Adam Smith knew it well. Though a friend of Business so long as trade was free, he was not a friend of the businessman tempted beyond his strength. In *Wealth of Nations* there is a comment that might well surprise those who consider the treatise a license for greed:

> ". . . the mean rapacity, the monopolizing spirit of merchants and manufacturers, who neither are nor ought to be, the rulers of mankind . . . In every country it always is and must be the interest of the great body of the people to buy whatever they want of those who sell it cheapest." [28]

THE SPIRIT OF MONOPOLY

But what is monopoly but the desire to protect, defend, and prosper number one? Whether number one be self, family, tribe, nation, belief—the sense of propriety excites bias. Religion has always favored monopoly of belief and achieved it (ruthlessly and sometimes bloodily) everywhere but in the United States. Politics is virtually synonymous with monopoly. For what is the one-party state—the totalitarian regime—but a monopoly? What else but monopoly is the ideology that forestalls dissent? Our Founding Fathers labored to prevent an engrossing of power through ideology, but nobody can stem the tides of fashion. For there are fashions in ideas as in all else, and sometimes these can favor limitation of choice as ultimate chic. Given the nature of the American ethos, however, and the strenuous efforts of the Founding Fathers, it is not surprising that the spirit of monopoly has found uneasy residence on these shores. "The United States is one of the few modern democracies that has made anti-trust legislation a fundamental policy of government toward business."[29] Those words were written by George Benson who knows whereof he speaks. Like the group of businessmen who strove in 1908 to chart the moral high ground, Dr. Benson has labored in the field of applied ethics, not only in terms of Business but for Americans in general. Formerly president of Claremont—McKenna College in California, he now heads the Henri Salvatori Center for the Study of Individual Freedom in the Modern World.

Monopoly in business has a long history. The first monopolies appeared with the first guilds, which—as far as we can tell—appeared with the first Mesopotamian cities. And we have had occasion to observe the guild as restraint to trade in a number of settings, both traditional and modern. We have seen how merchant guilds in Yoruba cities effectively choked off foreign competition. Ditto guilds in Rome. Ditto the guilds of China and of the European Middle Ages.

> "All industrial groups [says Henri Pirenne] were united in their determination to enforce to the utmost the monopoly which each enjoyed and to crush all scope for individual initiative and all possibility of competition . . . never has the conception that each profession is the exclusive possession of a privileged body been pressed to such extremes . . . for each group the notion of the common good gave way before that of its own interests."[30]

But someone has to see to the common good, and that someone was usually the mayor of the city. Insuring the food supply was a problem, and every possible contrivance was employed to keep the prices down. The result was often a maze of regulations and inspections. In London the brewers and caterers were particularly suspect when it came to pushing up the tab. In 1478 the brewers combined to raise the price of ale. Declining to use the threat of jail or pillory, the mayor simply invited country brewers to sell their wares in town, and at a lower figure. The same technique failed to bring the powerful fishmonger's guild to heel. Their leaders appealed to the king for a charter which would enable them to prevent nonresident fishermen from selling in town. Quite soon thereafter, Londoners were paying twice as much for fish as were consumers in the countryside. Eventually the mayor was able to persuade Parliament to annul the charter.[31]

THE CLOTHING BUSINESS: ITS ETHICAL UPS AND DOWNS

The great industry of the Middle Ages was that of weaving. The wealth of some cities, particularly those of the Lowlands, was based on it. Municipal governments took care to keep the goodies all to themselves by means of laws, regulations, and royal decrees. At Ghent in 1297 it was ordained that all cloth woven in the surrounding countryside had to be fulled in the city before it could be sold. (Fulling was a process designed to shrink and thicken woolens.) Other municipalities followed suit. Market privileges were then denied to all country weavers, wherever their cloth had been fulled. Next came a law prohibiting all weaving within a three-mile radius of the city, and armed men were sent to destroy illegal looms and fulling vats. Finally, Ypres, Ghent, and Bruges brought the industries of all surrounding towns under their control.

There were protests, but they began inside the cities and were directed at the merchants who sold cloth. These merchants had begun to buy raw wool for parceling out to various weaving establishments. They stipulated pattern and weight, and when the cloth was finished, sent it elsewhere for dying and fulling. The weavers not only protested, they rose in revolt.

The merchants detested the violence and civil unrest stirred by the weavers and chafers under town rulers which obliged them to enroll in the Weavers' Guild in order to do business. The conflicts developed into municipal revolution and something of a class war as well. Yet the war solved nothing. Even when, after several bloodier engagements, the weavers took control of the cities, their economic conditions did not improve. The impasse was resolved by economic suicide. The constant strife, the wage demands of weavers, antiquated methods of production retained by guild regulations resulted in the flight of both parties to the fray. Some merchants and weavers went to Italy. Most settled in England which now became the center of the textile industry.[32]

An interesting switch can be found in the modern story of homebound knitters who make ski caps for a Vermont corporation. They were found in violation of a 1942 regulation prohibiting cottage industries of this sort. When the Labor Department moved to prosecute, the knitters (backed by the National Alliance of Home-Based Business Women) rose in protest. Why, asked one woman, did she have to put her children in a day-care center ("much like mothers do in the Soviet Union") in order to help make a living for her family?[33]

The Labor Department then moved to lift the ban on homework only to be confronted by the International Ladies Garment Workers Union whose attorneys pointed out that most home workers were not suburban New England knitters, but illegal immigrants being victimized by contractors in league with organized crime. The union could not protect workers dispersed through the countryside, they said. Worse, wages would be in jeopardy.

Xerox Corporation's vice president Paul Strassman, who spoke to *New York Times* reporter Bill Keller, countered that unions should not buck the trend to labor decentralization but rather train members to negotiate high wages in the new free market.[34]

As of December 5, 1984, the ban was lifted, but companies planning to hire home workers will have to register with the government.

As Thomas Sowell has pointed out, monopolies—especially those involving labor—are rarely effective over the long haul. That goes for movements organized to hold wages down as well as those aiming for the opposite. After the

Black Death in fourteenth-century England, labor was in short supply and employers combined to keep wages at preplague levels. The wages rose nevertheless, amid cries of "traitor!" aimed at employers who paid more to attract good help. The same thing occurred when slaves were freed after the Civil War.[35] The same applies to producer monopolies and to the great international cartels. Chief among these is the mighty OPEC which can no longer enforce its protective prices in the face of shrinking international demand for oil.

HOW BAD IS BIG?

It all depends on the time. During periods of populist fervor, corporations are seen as "organizations for the plunder of the community." In the 1908 symposium at Yale University James McKeen was moved to assure Yale students that

> "Corporations, instead of being the natural agents of predatory wealth, are the natural instruments whereby a multitude of people of moderate means are enabled to combine and thus to compete with men of great individual wealth, whose selfish inclinations sometimes make them predatory."[36]

After World War II and the general rise in prosperity (as George Benson tells us) Americans were disposed to make do with Big Business. During the Counterculture years, however, its image took another nosedive. Corporations were held responsible for shoddy products and for criminal irresponsibility toward consumers. Inceasingly, manufacturers were expected not only to test for product safety under ordinary use, but to anticipate all possible misuses to which a product could be put. Corporations were held responsible for polluting the environment (whether deliberately or through negligence) and for foot-dragging on the cleanup. (Very true, says Peter Drucker, but cleanup will require the generation of additional electricity, thereby creating additional pollution. Unless nuclear generators are used. A trade-off.) [37]

Of greatest concern, however, was the matter of power. And corporations were perceived to exercise a monopoly in that department. In 1973, Daniel R. Fusfeld, Professor of Economics, University of Michigan, warned that the United States was fast becoming a corporate state. For a few super corporations dominated the domestic economic scene and would soon impose their will upon the world. What could be done about it?

> "We need," he said, "more than prosperity, economic growth, and stable prices . . . We need a redistribution of wealth. . . We must move to nothing less than a revolutionary transformation of our economic and political institutions." [38]

Professor James C. Knowles of the University of Southern California confined his studies to the Rockefeller Financial Group and noted,

> "The likely directions in which Rockefeller Group political power will be exercised in future may both threaten world peace and impose economic burdens on the domestic front." [39]

A dozen years have now gone by, and, in the view of some Business watchers, the frightful corporate ogre has begun to seem more like a timid giant, eager to "get along by going along" with government decrees (whether kind to Business or not). Protests about excessive regulations have come, rather, from small- and medium-sized businesses. Not from the biggies. Indeed, the corporate structure often seems pitifully vulnerable to threats of adverse publicity or boycott. [40]

The authors of *The 100 Best Companies to Work For in America* describe how Anheuser-Busch in 1982 was pressured by the Reverend Jesse Jackson, the civil-rights leader (later a presidential nomination contender), to sign a pact with Operation PUSH. The company was to promise a number of affirmative actions and benefits, among them the selection of black distributors. Anheuser-Busch pointed out its record of 18 percent black employee representation and refused to sign. Jackson then traveled to several black communities encouraging a boycott of Anheuser-Busch brands. He was followed everywhere by Wayman Smith, a black vice president of the company, and the boycott was concluded with a face-saving treaty.[41] Several other corporations, facing the same boycott threat, signed the original agreement, among them Coca-Cola, Seven-Up, Heublein, and Miller Brewing Company. In 1984 PUSH and the N.A.A.C.P. achieved a similar accord with Adolph Coors Company amounting to $325 million. Terms included a promise by Coors to invest 8 percent of its ready cash in black-owned banks. La Raza, the Hispanic organization, persuaded Coors to agree to a similar affirmative action-investment deal worth $300 million. "The amounts of the packages," says *New York Times* reporter, Iver Peterson, "were tied to the minority groups' buying power."[42]

Then there is the story of Procter & Gamble, their rumored pact with the devil, and the consumer punishment that followed:

> In one month of 1982 the company received 15,000 calls on its toll-free lines. Over and over operators were asked, "Why do you have a Satanist symbol on all your products?" (That is the familiar logo, the bearded man-in-the-moon contemplating thirteen stars.) "Do your executives tithe to the Church of Satan?"
>
> What? Satan in the 20th century? Indeed, yes, it would appear, and living in the P&G logo. Nobody thought the sign evil in the 1850s when illiterate dock workers used it to identify boxes of William Procter's candles. The firm's founder deemed the thirteen stars wonderfully patriotic. And P&G through the years has enjoyed a reputation as squeaky-clean as its products. How did it become associated with the Prince of Darkness? Nobody knows for sure.

Procter & Gamble sought help from the ministry. And, after leaders of Southern Baptist churches offered reassurance, the rumor-mongering came to an end. Or so it seemed.

The rumors resurfaced in the fall of 1984, this time with the support of Catholic nuns and priests in rural Pennsylvania. Grimly P&G struggled to restore the company's reputation. They knew they must succeed before the few customers then returning their cans of P&G Folger's coffee ("We won't drink the devil's brew!") turned into an avalanche.

As Father Weber, pastor of a Pennsylvania church, told reporter Jolie B. Solomon, "So many people have lost their jobs . . . So many are upset by [the idea of] nuclear war . . . they think they are being punished. It's easier to blame it on the devil."[43]

And the devil has not yet been laid to rest. In April 1985, unsigned memos were being circulated by members of small church groups in Fairfield County, Connecticut. One of the memos arrived on my desk. It describes a "recent appearance" by the president of Procter & Gamble on "the Phil Donohue T.V. Interview Program."

According to the announcement, "the President stated that a LARGE portion of Procter & Gamble's profit goes to the church of satan, also known as the devil's church." When Donohue inquired whether this revelation would tend to hurt P&G's business, "the President replied, 'THERE IS [sic] NOT ENOUGH CHRISTIANS IN THE UNITED STATES TO MAKE A DIFFERENCE.' "

A complete list of P&G products follows. All concerned citizens are advised to "beware of his [the devil's] symbol." That being, of course, the familiar starry logo. Now defunct as of April 1985. Unconditional surrender by P&G.

If the devil can be connected to a large corporation there is a way to strike back at all those "slings and arrows of outrageous fortune." There is *someone* to blame. For a corporation is a kind of person (can a corporation have a soul?) If a faceless public can be cheated with less qualm than can a familiar customer, it follows that a faceless seller—monolithic and distant—is equally susceptible to maltreatment. Indeed, the faceless corporation virtually invites attack.

Alexis de Tocqueville perceived the importance of the personal touch:

> "In democratic times, you attach a poor man to you more by your manner than by benefits conferred. . . . [The rich] are very ready to do good to the people, but they still choose to keep them at arm's length; they think that is sufficient, but they are mistaken. They might spend fortunes thus without warming the hearts of the population around them; that population does not ask them for the sacrifice of their money, but of their pride."[44]

RAIDERS OF THE LOST CORP

"It was a period of cutthroat competition," writes Samuel Eliot Morison of the panics of 1873 and 1893. "The big fish swallowed the littles and then tried to eat each other."[45] Railroad tycoons cut prices on freight until stockholders' dividends ceased. Competitors were driven out of business right and left, with stockholders' money used as ammunition. It was warfare waged with property.

The big men of business were, all in all, not unlike the tribal Kwakiutl of the Northwest Coast of North America, as described by Franz Boas, Helen Codere, Irving Goldman and any number of talented anthropologists. We have been introduced in Chapter 6. Let us return to Vancouver Island and see Kwakiutl tycoons locked in combat, using the capital of *their* stockholders:

> The hundred or so members of a *numema*, a long house, worked all summer to acquire the goods which would permit their chief to feast other chiefs and their households during the sacred winter season and to give away the riches they had produced. They expected him to uphold their collective reputation. If he failed they might call him "rottenface" and move to other numema where relatives could be found. "Now,

you great one," they exhorted, "busy yourself. You give presents to them. You give again double amount."

There were also tribal giveaways, and "trusts" were formed to put rivals out of business. "Let both our tribes strive against the Kwakiutl," said a Nakwaxdax chief to a Koskimo, "so that we can take off two finger widths of their highness." And the Kwakiutl, alarmed, told each other, "If we do not open our eyes and awake, we shall lose our high rank."

It was indeed true, says Irving Goldman, that large tribes could assemble more property and so best the smaller ones—drowning them, so to speak, in a sea of property. They could cover the face of every chief with goods equal and more than equal to his rank.[46]

Whether or not such displays took place in a ritual context, whether or not the statistics of conquest were preserved, the clash of rivalry phrased in economic terms sounds a familiar note in American ears. Instead of sea-otter furs, blankets, and copper shields, we deal in other emblems of conspicuous display: "greenmail" and "golden parachutes." Herewith some contemporary battles with property drawn from Ann Crittenden's descriptions in the *New York Times:*[47]

She tells how, in 1982, a pinnacle of excess was reached when two titan corporations, Bendix and Martin Marietta, tried to swallow up each other. After a lengthy standoff, a third company, Allied Corporation, acquired Bendix. Martin Marietta was now burdened with a huge debt for Bendix stock though still afloat. William M. Agee of Bendix was gifted with a golden parachute of $4 million to cushion his fall.

"It's a raid, it's a raid!" cried employees of Walt Disney Productions as they heard of a hostile takeover bid by Saul Steenberg's Reliance Group Holdings, Inc. No "white knights" were in the offing. All stock maneuvers failed. Disney paid the would-be raider $325.5 million in greenmail to lay off the company.

Raiders who talked with Ann Crittenden refused to shoulder any blame. Management was at fault, they said, for it was nepotistic and sloppy. Assets were underutilized. If only the raider were allowed to occupy a seat on the board of directors, things could be turned around. But, no. Management chose to pay greenmail instead.

"People are tossing around companies like they were sardines," one anonymous critic told Ann Crittenden, "but we're talking about dislocation of employees, communities, production, and hundreds of thousands of jobs."[48]

A secretary who lost a job when her company was swallowed up told me, "It's true. Management was pretty poor. But what happened was worse. The president got a golden parachute. The big executives got the equivalent of a year's salary and the rest of us a lump sum for every year we had worked. But some of the women executives had been around fifteen years or more. They had climbed to high positions without college degrees. Now they can't find comparable work. They are out."

Are mergers inherently bad? No, says George Benson, our professor of ethics. Often merger is a better choice for a company than starting a totally new business. And besides, he adds, some believe mergers are likely to increase competition.

Maybe yes and maybe no. The indigestibility of some companies is already being demonstrated in a wave of divestitures. Kendall Wills describes the gasket company of Joseph Hrudka, taken over by W.R. Grace and Company for $12 million. But the little company stagnated under Grace management and some years later, when offered the opportunity to buy it back, Mr. Hrudka did, thereafter building up revenues sufficiently to make his action "worth the gamble."[49]

Why the sudden popularity of "fighting with property?" Leonard Rapping of the University of Massachusetts, Amherst, speaks of a situational shift that encourages gambling. "Now if that gambling spirit is dominating the markets," he says, "that would explain some of the unpredictability we see. . . . Whatever is driving people, it's not rational calculation, it's passion."[50]

Others call it managerial greed or a swing to national greed or even the death of institutional loyalty. Still others blame boards of directors. They should hire their own auditors. No, says Irving Kristol, that would be rather as if "the owner of a baseball team hired a group of minor-league managers to judge the performance of a major-league manager." There is no need for radical overhaul.[51]

"It's the fault of the investment bankers," one executive told me. "They want to finagle. They initiate any number of takeovers. If you are working in acquisitions, you'd better have a strong stomach. The other side will try to discredit you. The bankers just sit back and see what happens. They'll come out on top either way."

Whatever the explanation, there are some painful, demoralizing results—among them the loss of America's competitive edge in the world economy. Executives are forced to focus on immediate threats instead of planning long-range market strategy. And the hostile takeover is rarely in the best interests of the company or the stockholders. And yet, says Peter Drucker, most stock is held by "trustees" of pension funds and, to a lesser extent, mutual funds, and they are bound to accept whatever gives their beneficiaries the highest immediate return. If they refuse a raider's bid that turns out to have been higher than the subsequent stock-market quotation, they are culpable. They cannot rightfully consider the interests of the enterprise. Their beneficiaries must come first. "The wave of unfriendly takeovers is thus the price we pay for that great achievement, the pension fund,"[52] says Drucker.

Can we see an end to all this storm and struggle? Is there a way to "tame the corporate takeover?" A number of suggestions are now being debated, most of them requiring governmental intervention. Some focus on the importance of personal interest and involvement. If owners of stock managed it themselves—so this line of reasoning goes—if they had a personal stake in an enterprise, they might be more committed to its long-term growth and well-being.

Better still, make sure the chairman or CEO enjoys some ownership rights and is therefore interested in more than his salary.[53]

In other words, personalize investment. Bring back the tycoons.

TV OR NOT TV, THAT IS THE QUESTION

But they are already back and television has got them. Every night the fictional images of business movers and shakers appear on the home screen. And what do audiences think of these tycoons? What attitudes toward Business do they elicit?

Benjamin Stein, a free-lance writer living in Los Angeles, asked groups of students from four area high schools about the matter. Free associate, he asked them. What comes into your mind when the word "business" is mentioned? Common answers were: "shaky," "cutthroat," "dishonest," "very intelligent but only looking out for themselves."

Did they know any big businessmen? No. Their impressions were all derived from "Dallas," "Dynasty," "Falconcrest," or "Bare Essence." Probably those were exaggerations, they thought. Nevertheless, all but one student believed that businessmen would be willing to kill primitive tribesmen to get at oil reserves or would knowingly manufacture defective automobiles. "I used to think that individual endeavor, like with Rockefeller or Carnegie, was something to be admired," said one student. "When I watch TV, it looks corrupt and scheming and terrible . . . there must be some good about it. . . . But I sure wouldn't want to be part of it anymore."[54]

In an eight-week survey of cops-and-robbers drama on three networks during 1981, Linda and Robert Lichter (social scientists at Columbia University) found that criminals on TV shows are usually upper-class white males, rich and greedy. "Typical of these is the businessman whose selfish pursuit of profit leads him into illegal activity," they found.[55]

Asked about this trend, about the persistent "bad guy" image, many of the businessmen with whom I spoke felt a certain sad resignation but guessed that *somebody* had to be cast as a villain and maybe writers felt more comfortable attacking businessmen. After all, businessmen were unlikely to fight back.

It is not only in the dramatic scenario that Business plays the villain—at least in the view of some media watchers who were dismayed by the television coverage accorded the economic recovery. Holmes M. Brown, president of the Institute for Applied Economics, holds that all three networks managed to turn good news into bad. The institute helped conduct a six-month, seven-nights-a-week survey of news coverage in 1983. During the entire period, says Brown, there were four to fifteen reports a month of a factual, economic-statistical nature. Of these, 95 percent announced good news. (Inflation was coming down. Employment was going up. Factory output increased. The rate of growth of the gross national product rose.) Analysis and in-depth coverage of the statistics, however, was overwhelmingly negative. Of 104 stories of this nature, 89 percent focused on pockets of poverty, talk of suicide, and people left behind in the wake of recovery. Even the lowering of inflation was given an ominous cast. "The economic news was good in the second half of 1983," says Brown. "The coverage on network television was still in recession."[56]

Nonsense, Dan Rather told Marie Torre for a 1984 article in *Television Quarterly*. "They complain that we're too pro-labor, too anti-business, anti-entrepreneurship, anti-capitalist. All of which I categorically reject. . . . We made a commitment not to cover the recession by Washington handouts. . . . We in journalism have been slow to address the whole question of what is to be this country's economic base in the post-technological age."[57] Is a leadership role envisioned?

The same sense of adversarial media—in this case the press—concerned businessmen in 1908. Edward Page complained:

"Modern journalism in its efforts to expand circulation concerns itself mostly with the exploitation of the exceptional,
publishes by preference all deviations from accepted moral
code, and relegates to the obscurity of the uninteresting the
humdrum occurrences which, as actual experience most definitely shows, constitute nineteen-twentieths or more of
life . . . Too often the reader forgets that, in the race for
circulation, the press has in large measure degenerated into a
purveyor of fiction . . ."[58]

In 1830, Alexis de Tocqueville had arrived at somewhat
similiar conclusions. Of the press he said:

"I approve of it from a recollection of the evils it prevents
than from a consideration of the advantages it ensures . . .
America is perhaps, at this moment, the country of the whole
world that contains the fewest germs of revolution; but the
press is not less destructive in its principles there than in France,
and it displays the same violence without the same reasons
for indignation. In America as in France it constitutes a singular power, so strangely composed of mingled good and evil
that it is at the same time indispensable to the existence of
freedom and nearly incompatible with the maintenance of
public order."[59]

Of the individual laborers in media vineyards his opinion
was scarcely warmer:

"The characteristics of the American journalist consist in an
open and coarse appeal to the passions of the populace; and
he habitually abandons the principles of political science to
assail the characters of individuals, to track them into private
life and disclose all their weaknesses and errors. Nothing can
be more deplorable than this abuse of the powers of
thought."[60]

WHAT'S MY LINE?

The real question hinges on the nature of identity. Do the
media—press, radio, television—comprise a special and sa-

cred tool of democracy, or are they Big Business? Should they be regarded as education or as recreation? Are they to function as Guardians of the Hive or as reflections of fashion in tastes and ideas? Are they leaders or followers?

Either or both, it would seem, depending on situational necessity. First Amendment protections are invoked when public figures threaten libel suits; the laws of the marketplace when regulation or boycotts are afoot. "We cannot force anyone to watch a program he deems unsuitable for himself or his children," is the prim disclaimer heard most frequently when parents protest the increasing display of pornography and violence on the home screen. When critics invoke possible social consequences and cite social science surveys to support their claims, network representatives produce surveys bearing opposite conclusions. "Don't blame us," they say, "for the rise in crime, violence, and the general level of kinkiness. Television drama merely reflects the real world." And, it could be added but never is, "what the market will bear."

What the market will bear is usually tested at the time of the "sweeps"—the quarterly measurements of audience interest which are used to set advertising rates. In order to lure viewers, networks broadcast their most provocative dramas at these times, and the limits of the forbidden are tested right along with the ratings.

In a 1984 *Television Quarterly* article, Arthur Unger, TV critic for the *Christian Science Monitor*, wondered how far television could go, how far it *should* go in tackling hitherto tabooed subjects, such as incest. Can we one day expect to see bestiality on the home screen? The barriers are falling so rapidly as to suggest as much. "Are we," he asked, "approaching a new era when hypocritical rationales must be set aside for the good of our society?"[61]

In other words, is profit more important than the public good?

This is precisely the question network news commentators and dramatists pose to other corporations, to the rest of Big Business. Who is holier than whom?

Those other corporations are not only being held accountable for unanticipated errors in manufacturing, for unforeseen product failure, for negligence. They are increasingly being asked—and by way of the courts—to anticipate the kinds of misuses to which their products could be put. If television is Big Business, should it not be equally responsible for its impacts, for the unanticipated consequences of its dramatic portrayals?

There is little question that television has great impact on the young. A study of the teen environment prepared in 1979–1980 by The Robert Johnston Company found that, in terms of influence over the young, the media (TV, radio, records, cinema) rank third. Parents, who used to wield the greatest influence, have slipped to second place. They now rank behind peers.[62]

The big surprise in the study is the rapid growth in importance of the media. (In 1960 the media ranked eighth as an agent of teen influence.) Its message is, moreover, doubly reinforced. For the friends and peers, who are the teenager's first line of influence, are also media consumers (with or without parental consent).

(Since Roman times, George Benson reminds us, the first rule of business—large or small—has been *salus populi supreme lex est*, "public health and safety is the supreme law." The second is *sic utere tuo uo alienium non laedas*, "so use your property that it does not damage others.")[63]

Should the viewing public cry foul and call in the regulators? Should it threaten boycotts of firms that advertise on television, network or cable? Should prospective advertisers exert censorship on their own account? Or should disaffected viewers simply wait for public ire to crescendo (if it ever does)? It should be remembered that smoking diminished when hazards to health were widely and effectively publicized. It has now become something of a sin to smoke in public (and the nicotine addict stands in imminent danger of chastisement by some perfect stranger if he does). Alcoholic beverages are on a similar slide, and brewers and distillers are scrambling to produce "lighter" beers and liquors.[64] (Alcohol makes one *fat,* after all.) The current fascination for violence and pornography may not abate until some health hazard can be successfully attached. Or until the law of the market comes into play.

Years ago Robert Redfield, the great anthropologist, considered the problem of the observer in the field. Should he strive in his ethnography to eliminate a personal point of view and personal values? Should he seek to produce a balanced portrayal of a people's way of life? No, said Redfield, referring to a suggestion published in the *New Yorker,* "we do not want balanced textbooks; we want balanced libraries."[65] In other words, present many perspectives. Offer choice. Widen the market.

In terms of the media market, the trick is to make old-fashioned family virtues—along with all the other standard good behavior practiced by nineteen-twentieths of the population—gripping, vital drama. The trick is to bring to such drama the technical expertise lavished on subjects formerly tabooed and now prime grist for the media mill. It is a challenge for some bold entrepreneur to discover whether as much money *can* be made in sweetness-and-light as in wild-and-woolly. And the producer who finds a way to make the honest businessman exciting will surely find gold behind the silver screen.

PERSONALIZING THE TOUCH

If television has been used to magnify corporate failings and tarnish the spirit of enterprise, it nevertheless offers a powerful tool for creating good will. No profession lacks its sinners. The woods are full of crooked lawyers, lying politicians, plagiarizing academics, and doctors who play fast and loose with Medicare. Their sins are their own; their callings remain untouched. That Business itself carries a negative stereotype may owe something to the fact that it is Big. And because big, faceless.

Chrysler is not faceless. It is Lee Iacocca. Consumers

appreciate Perdue chickens as much for Frank as for the taste of the product. Victor Kiam is Mr. Remington Shaver, and his employees are thrilled that he is out there in great big television land, being the chief of their *numema,* giving them much "face." These gentlemen do not appear on talk shows or venture to cross swords with media inquisitors. They do not take lessons in avoiding media traps and emerging from television interviews with all systems still on "go." They stick to the television commercial. Despised and snooted, the commercial can powerfully showcase the individual able to make use of its special possibilities. For it has a kind of immediacy, a concentrated appeal uniquely its own. It offers a way of making BIG seem SMALL, of making the impersonal personal, of giving the faceless giant a face—and even a soul to boot.

When men and women of business finally conclude that the social and cultural climate in which business is done has a bearing on the success of the enterprise, they may also begin to choose and train executives for newer skills and purposes. The capacity for effective, personal communication may one day be a condition to advancement in business. And possession of a strong media personality essential for any chief.

Bring back the tycoons!

12

ON THE OTHER HAND

BUSINESS AND THE COMMON GOOD

*I did not find the world desolate
when I entered it, and as my
fathers planted for me so do I
plant for my children.*

TALMUDIC PARABLE QUOTED
BY DR. BERN DIBNER, FOUNDER,
BURNDY CORPORATION[1]

In describing the traditional business man of eastern New Guinea, Australian anthropologist Andrew Strathern has emphasized continuity in the midst of change. Although the entrepreneur is hospitable to Western values, says Strathern, he is nevertheless mindful of his fellows and takes care to keep them happy and content. His truck must be used, not just for business errands, but to transport people to feasts. He sponsors dances. He buys pigs. He lends money.

> "If a capitalist [says Dr. Strathern], he at least plows more of his profit into his immediate community than does the capitalist in an industrial society."[2]

One might, with justice, point out that communal goodwill does constitute a necessary condition of business life in New Guinea. Doing well and doing good needs must go hand in hand. Even so, a question properly remains. How fair is Strathern's cross-cultural comparison? Is the Western industrialist truly a hard-hearted Scrooge from whose overloaded pockets beneficence must be forcibly pried? Certainly that is an image with which many Americans would tend to agree. ("You're studying businessmen?" a data processor queried. "What a bunch of skinflints!") There are, it is true, some who would comfortably fit the mold. But all?

Americans cherish at the same time a truly touching faith in the ability of Business—particularly of the great corporations—to remedy social ills. Whether this reflects growing skepticism about Government's ability to do the job or whether it simply represents long-standing ambivalence about Business, the expectations are clear. A 1973 Harris Poll revealed that, of those questioned: 83 percent believed that Business could wipe out poverty; 84 percent that it could rebuild cities; 84 percent that it could eliminate racial discrimination; 92 percent that it could control environmental pollution; and 72 percent that it could reduce death on the highways.[3] That such sentiments were being expressed at a time when condemnation of "corporate tyranny" was all the rage only serves to heighten the paradox.

The general public has little or no realization, notes ethicist George Benson, of the nature of the corporation as a public enterprise or of the nature of its ownership. There is little understanding that people buy shares in a company with the expectation of personal profit and security. The corporation that diverts a disproportionate share of its resources toward public betterment risks lawsuits by angry stockholders. It risks bankruptcy. It risks the fury of those it sets out to help, for it cannot hope ever to do enough with the funds available after all costs—including taxes— are met. In order to offer any help at all, it must first follow the prime directive: stay profitable.

There also remains the matter of legality. Peter Drucker describes a conversation between Alfred Sloan, president of General Motors in the 1940s, and his opposite number in another corporation. "We have a responsibility toward higher education," said the latter. "Do we in business have any *authority* over higher education?" asked Sloan. "Should we have any?" "Of course not," was the reply. "Then let's not talk about responsibility. You are a senior executive of a big company, and you should know the first rule: authority and responsibility must be congruent and commensurate to each other. If you don't want responsibility and shouldn't have it, don't talk about authority."[4]

DOING GOOD TO DO WELL

Eighty years ago public anxiety focused not so much on corporate benefactions at the shareholders' expense, as on corporate shenanigans at the shareholders' expense and corporate hard-heartedness at the workers' expense. In the early 1900s journalists were becoming famous for investigative reporting, mainly of abuses by Business—the vast monopolies, the trusts, big companies which gobbled up little operators to form giant concerns. President Theodore

Roosevelt, though heartily in favor of curbing the abuses of "trusts," was nevertheless apprehensive that the spate of negative stories might cause the public to hate Business and, in his view, that would not be at all in the interests of society. "Muckrakers," he called the journalist-sleuths.[5]

One of the biggest muckrakers of them all was Ida Minerva Tarbell, a self-made female superstar in a man's world, who investigated the operations of the Standard Oil Corporation for *McClure's Magazine.* Standard Oil was the creation of John D. Rockefeller, cordially detested among the independent oilmen in Titusville, Pennsylvania (where Ida Tarbell grew up); monopolist par excellence (according to Tarbell's research); insatiable devourer of small competitors (Tarbell called this "cutting to kill"—pricing competitors out of the market).

Of the series, publisher Sam McClure maintained (according to Tarbell), "We were after interesting reader material, and if it contributed to the general good, so much the better."[6] Of the investigation, Tarbell herself said, "As I saw it, it was not capitalism but an open disregard of decent ethical business practices by capitalists which lay at the bottom of the story."[7]

Some years later she set out to uncover the "decent" and the "ethical" wherever these could be found. The results of her search appeared initially in *American Magazine* as the series, "The Golden Rule in Business." Later the articles were published as a book, *New Ideals in Business.*

As Kathleen Brady (Tarbell's biographer) reports, the journalist was not popular in the role of praise singer. The reading public wanted muckraking. Indeed, many companies themselves begged to be "exposed" since such had become distinctly à la mode. She was accused of being in the pay of the corporations. Union adherents pronounced her antiunion. Even the female suffragists of the day considered her insufficiently devoted to the cause. All because of a few kind words, to wit:

"The wider my observation of our working life extended, the

more I was impressed that there were forces at work which, properly developed, were bound to overcome many, if not all, of the industrial evils with which we have become so familiar."[8]

She was impressed with the management techniques prescribed by Frederick Taylor, who was the first man to study how work is done and how it can be made more productive. The scope of the changes described by Tarbell—management's efforts to provide more personal satisfaction for workers and the fervor with which these efforts were undertaken—presents an interesting parallel to contemporary enthusiasms and applications. She went on to say that,

> "The new management employs not only science but humanity, and by humanity I do not mean merely or chiefly sympathy, but rather a larger thing, the recognition that all men, regardless of race, origin, or experience, have powers for greater things than has been believed . . ."[9]
>
> Nothing is introduced which I have not seen in operation; nothing which has not seemed to me to be good for the worker, skilled and unskilled, nothing which has not been carried to the point of profit, nothing which an active intelligence and a just spirit cannot realize."[10]

Tarbell spoke of the new dedication to safety in the factories she visited and of the good working conditions she found at surprisingly many plants. International Harvester was among the first, she reported, to realize the importance of bright, airy shops, cleanliness, availability of tools. She marveled at the machines designed for human comfort during operation. She spoke of mills at which workers were encouraged to garden during rest periods and of the factories designed for beauty and built from scratch. She described the Eastman Company's beautiful Kodak Park with its "tennis courts and ball fields."[11]

She spoke of experiments in profit-sharing. She spoke of worker pride in product ("This cloth we are weaving for the sails of a cup defender!").[12] She spoke of efforts to root out alcohol addiction among workers and attention given to health and fitness. She spoke of company dining rooms offering good meals at cost. She spoke of the Pilgrim Laundry of Brooklyn whose manager said, "No girl can do 2000 collars a day if she doesn't have something interesting to think about,"[13] and so planned activities for her charges— plays, dances, excursions. "They sing over the machines,"[14] said Tarbell.

She quoted a young lady in a white goods factory who told her, "You don't know how changed life has been for me since Miss A— came here and showed us how to organize clubs and things."[15] The speaker was editor of the factory newspaper. (Shades of the *Lowell Offering,* circa 1830!) In plant after plant, workers told Ida Tarbell, "My, but this is a fine place to work!"[16] The book reads for all the world like an anticipation of *The 100 Best Companies to Work For.*

Over and over managers assured Tarbell that "working smart" and keeping workers happy paid off in productivity. Since Americans seem to reinvent the wheel every twenty-five years, it comes as something of a shock to realize that today's "frontiers" have sustained earlier travel. Then as now there were roses amid the thorns and probably more of the former than the latter. Then as now, doing good was found to result in doing well. Attention to the quality of worklife paid off handsomely. Never mind the motivation behind improvement.

THE CLIMATE FOR BUSINESS

The relationship of Business and the other institutions of society is not without stress and strain. In order to promote some degree of understanding among leaders in business, government, and education, Paul Hoffman, first administrator of the Marshall Plan, helped to create the Committee for Economic Development (CED). This is a research and education panel composed, in the main, of presidents and board chairmen of corporations and presidents of universities. The two hundred members are committed to searching out "through objective research and informed discussion, findings and recommendations for private and public policy which will contribute to preserving and strengthening our free society . . . to unite business judgment and experience with scholarship."[17]

Studies undertaken over the years have included such topics as providing jobs for the hard-to-employ, the public work force and its management, energy policy, and fighting inflation. One of the recent publications dealt with problems of organizing and administering the transnational corporations, including the matter of cross-cultural business ethics. In the long run, however, the committee's efforts in bridge building may be more important than the outcome of any specific report. For the ultimate rationale hinges on the climate in which business is done:

> "CED believes that by enabling businessmen to demonstrate constructively their concern for the general welfare, it is helping business to earn and maintain the national and community respect essential to the successful functioning of the free-enterprise capitalist system."[18]

In another organization, the Business Roundtable, corporate leaders endeavor not only to study public-policy issues, but to communicate business positions to the government. Like the CED, the Business Roundtable is composed of two hundred executives of major corporations (there is some overlap in membership). Members are assigned to task forces dealing with specific issues. The principle of consensus is observed both in the study groups themselves and when their findings are presented to the full membership for discussion. The requirement of consensus ensures considerable difficulty but also intensive study.[19]

Support for these and other study groups comes from voluntary contributions of individuals and of corporations. Effective relations with the outside world, some concern for the climate in which business is done, are necessary costs of staying in Business. The greater general understanding, the increased institutional harmony stimulated by such groups really represent extra added attractions. They are nonetheless important for all that.

AS THE TWIG IS BENT

Two years after Ida Tarbell's probusiness book was published, Horace Moses president of the Swarthmore Paper Company of Springfield, Illinois, founded Junior Achievement with Thomas Vail, chairman of American Telephone and Telegraph. He wanted to promote better understanding of Business—especially of corporate organization—among students at the secondary-school level. The program aimed at teaching by doing (it still does). Boys who joined a JA "club" would actually produce a product, sell shares in the company, market the product, keep track of profits, and learn how they are used. Advisers to these clubs would be local businessmen, released by their companies for this special task.

By the early 1970s the program had languished everywhere except, unaccountably, in Ohio. Polls taken for the staff indicated that a revamping was necessary in order to appeal to the new teenage culture. Girls were then admitted to Junior Achievement, and special programs were developed for junior high-and elementary-school levels. This last is now taught by high-school Junior Achievers.

> "I really loved teaching the little kids about business," said Eleanor Rudolph, an achiever to warm the heart of Horace Moses. "They're always so surprised to discover how little profit is involved in making and selling something." How was she prepared for the task? "Of course I didn't have to go in cold," she said. "We were given lots of training sessions."
>
> How did she hear about the program? "The chairman of a local corporation came to our school to tell us about it. I just thought it was something I'd like, so I joined. Our group formed a company to make 'Trouble Light,' a flashlight that

plugs into a car's cigarette lighter." That year she won the Salesperson of the Year Award, the Top Dollar Sales Award and later on the Ann Hasting Richards Spirit of Achievement Award for Future Businesswomen.

"There are all kinds of competitions, regional and national, among the individual companies and among individuals," she told me. "There are awards for President of the Year, Vice President of the Year, and Outstanding Young Businessman or Businesswoman. And you really have to work hard for those awards, take all kinds of written and oral tests. You have to know things like the difference between net profit and pure profit. You have to read a break-even chart. You have to know what should be done in all kinds of difficult situations."

"Of course," she admitted, "there are problems. Not every group elects just the right officers. Sometimes these guys get in by way of family connections—they've got a business mother or father rooting for them. One of our officers embezzled funds. He STOLE money from the corporation! Just like in the real world!"[20]

Eleanor Rudolph is now in college, studying for a career in business and running her own small typing service on the side. "I'm going to be president of a great corporation one day," she declared. It is easy to believe she will.

In addition to Junior Achievement, schools in twenty-five cities are offering a credit course in applied economics developed jointly by the national Junior Achievement staff and the Institute for Applied Economics. Holmes Brown explains the course: "It is really a basic offering in economic education with practical training in how to use this system and its economic institutions wisely and effectively."

Underlying all these efforts is Holmes Brown's battle cry, "Business is *not* crooked, and businessmen are *not* crooks! Only know us a little better and you'll see."[21] In other words, let's keep the nation safe for free enterprise. Let's exercise climate control at the source.

But there is yet another result. By performing these educational functions, businessmen are helping children (whatever occupational field they plan to enter) to become capable of generating wealth and security for themselves and their future families. They are training for independence.

OTHER KINDS OF EDUCATION

The business community has come to accept the large stake it has in general education as well as education in the fundamentals of business. For one thing, employees poorly trained in the basics of literacy tend to make costly mistakes, as corporation executives have discovered. One answer: on-site teachers of reading, writing, and arithmetic. The Planter's Peanuts factory, just to mention one example, offers employees four hours a week of elementary-school course work on company time. What to do about workers of the future? Or, for that matter, what to do about future consumers who may or may not be able to read warning labels on a company's products? Another answer: get involved in education. How? (Particularly if one has Alfred Sloan's strictures in mind.) Some say the answer is adoption. Local companies should adopt local schools. And do what? Some companies donate cash needed for special projects. Many more release talented, enthusiastic employees to visit classes, tutor students, offer career counseling.[22]

In October 1984 the *New York Times* described several such working partnerships. One involved the Chicago advertising firm of Ogilvy and Mather whose employees work with English classes in Roberto Clemente High School. The students are predominantly Hispanic, and the dropout rate is over 60 percent. The volunteer teachers build language skills by concentrating on what they know best—their own business. Students are asked each year to produce an advertisement about a social issue. The first to be addressed was the dropout issue.

The *Times* article described just one of the many happy outcomes resulting from the school partnership. A seventeen-year-old student came to work on a part-time basis in

Ogilvy and Mather's graphics department. "If I could get a contract to work here forever, I would sign it," he said, "because they've given me direction, an income, and an education I never would have received."[23]

Not all partnerships are built around remedial education. Some are directed to students with special interests and talents. Whatever the end in view, the partnership concept is expanding rapidly. In Dallas, Texas, where the program has been in place since 1965, 174 out of 179 public schools have been adopted by local companies. St. Louis, Pittsburgh, and Los Angeles are some of the other cities with business-partnered schools. Educators told the *New York Times* that partnerships "lent relevance to textbook lessons and motivated the students to master the school work."[24] Company representatives pronounced the school partnerships a terrific boost to their own employees' morale.

"Some of our people work with science teachers," said Julianne Grace, assistant to the president of Perkin-Elmer Corporation. A pioneer in the fields of precision optics and electro-optical systems, the Norwalk, Connecticut, multinational firm is best known as the builder of the space telescope to be orbited by NASA in 1986. "Often we bring teachers to see what we are doing and the ways in which science and business interrelate." Then she added, "I worry a lot about education. We all do. Our efforts to help sometimes just seem like a drop in the bucket. We have to remember that lots of drops fill the bucket."[25]

LEARNING TO LOVE COMMERCIALS

Gather any fair-sized family group around a television set, and you might hear the following comments:

"Do we have to watch these commercials?" That from the young art historian about to earn her master's degree. "*Please* let's turn to Public Broadcasting."

"Wait a minute," the visiting uncle objects. "If people

don't watch commercials, how to you think I'm going to sell
TIDYBROOM?"

"That's a beer-break for me," says Dad.

"My sociology prof claims that commercials have real re-
deeming social value." That from the college freshman. "If
you want to read the current state of the culture, he tells us,
watch commercials. They tell you all about the changing roles
of men and women. Values. Goals. All that. In fact, I have to
write a paper about it. Leave the commercials on." Sister sniffs.

"I just like the stories." Grandma offers a minority opinion in favor of content itself. "Nice things happen in commercials. Not like those regular shows."

Nuisance, necessity, or a nation's vision of itself, the commercial message is here to stay. One of its major—though
often unrecognized—roles in the economy is that of employer. The entertainment industry never has jobs enough
for all the aspiring actors, dancers, singers, and theatrical
production people available. Their numbers have grown over
the years. Why? Because of changes in social values.

In the eighteenth century, so Adam Smith tells us, "opera singers and dancers" earned high pay—not because their
talent was rare but because there were so few of them willing to suffer social censure. Professional singers, actors,
dancers were at the very bottom of the prestige scale, thought
to be courtesans on the side—or worse.[26] A gentleman might
drink champagne from a soprano's slipper; he certainly was
not going to take her home to Mother.

Now that all fences are down, now that anything goes,
we should not be surprised that talent gluts the market.
Film, television drama, the theatre, even repertory companies cannot take up the slack. But television commercials
can. And do. The necessities of the business world have
provided a whole new and thriving market for artistic talent.

Athletes, too, have reason to be grateful to advertising
and to the need of businesses to sell their products and bol-
ster their corporate images. The 1984 Olympic Games were
almost totally financed by corporate sponsors who used the

opportunity to give their products enhanced visibility through commercial messages tastefully keyed to the occasion. Unlike such events in the past, the Twenty-third Olympiad left no debts in its wake. And Business did more than support the presentation. Many of the athletes were themselves sponsored by business concerns, given jobs in business concerns while they pursued their training regimens. The entire American women's volleyball team was so sponsored. The First Interstate Bank of California employed sixteen Olympic hopefuls. Such sponsorships mean that older athletes and poorer athletes—those not matriculated at a college or university—are enabled to compete, thus strengthening the entire American team.[27] In the past, support of their athletes by Soviet-bloc governments has produced virtually unbeatable competitors. A highly necessary outcome, by their lights, for the games are something more than glory; they constitute what Muskogee Indians used to call "the little brother of war." American Business, not American Government, has taken up the Soviet challenge—justifiable because of advertising.

The same rationale applies to museum exhibits, ballet, opera, and theatrical presentations on television. Even though the hard sell may be reduced to a small announcement of presence—"this program is made possible by a grant from Widgets International"—corporate concern for the arts has been expressed. A bonus in goodwill can be expected.

Not always, however. Many a young cynic has been heard to comment, "Widgets International already has all the money in the world; now they want to tell you how goody-two-shoes they are." Absolutely true. And there may be other practical outcomes in view as well. Citibank's manager of corporate contributions told Lynn Asinof of the *Wall Street Journal* that the bank sought art programs that provided visibility, "the opportunity to entertain clients, and a chance for employees to get involved in the community."[28] Equitable Life Assurance Society's new building in New York City will be part museum, sheltering the largest branch of the Whitney Museum of American Art, together with a specially commissioned selection of art. (Corporate interest has opened up a lively new market for university-trained art historians and curators.) Such largesse is not entirely for the sake of art, of course. Considerable real estate near Equitable Center is owned by the company. And, since the neighborhood is going somewhat to seed at a number of points, the museumlike center is considered part of a campaign to restore property values. Do such practical considerations tarnish the result? Only if you are a purist.[29]

Texaco has been an active corporate supporter of the Metropolitan Opera since 1941 through its sponsorship of live performance broadcasts. It continues to spearhead a drive to create an endowment fund for that venerable musical treasure. Texaco's chairman, John McKinley, in a magazine interview with Martin Mayer, claimed this was not a matter of charity. "You reach through to ten million listeners, and there are all these letters, old people, young people, who tell you their first appreciation of music was these broadcasts. You get loyal customers and loyal stockholders."[30]

"In the long run," Technicomp's Eric Berg told me, "the bottom line is what counts. You may have the missionary spirit, but the only criterion is profit. The real challenge, the exciting challenge to all of us is to find ways to do right from the human point of view AND from the business point of view."

Doing good depends on doing well.

KEEPING THE CITY SOLVENT

So bound together were the fortunes of the medieval businessman and his city that one could hardly separate the two. Merchant guilds often undertook management of civic finances or, at the very least, supplemented the city treasury. In times of stress, guild members were called on to make provision for civic safety, civic sustenance, and the greater glory of the civic enterprise. It is no surprise to discover, here and there, modern business groups resuming these ancient burdens.

In 1981 Kathleen Teltsch of the *New York Times* reported on the cooperation between Business and Government in Minneapolis. Forty-five companies there belong to the Five Percent Club—the amount of their taxable income given annually to charitable or civic causes. Another twenty-five companies are members of the Two Percent Club. The federal government encourages these donations as an allowable tax deduction. Still and all, that hardly accounts for the booster spirit animating members. And there are tangible results: a revitalized and thriving urban center and restored residential neighborhoods.

"Out of pocket philanthropy" is opposed by a number of economists such as Milton Friedman, who believes that the business of Business is the supplying of wants and needs and the earning of profit for investors. Charity, they hold, should be the responsibility of the individual. Many industrialists agree, asserting that more good can be done by creating jobs than by moralizing. It is an argument hard to counter. The publicly owned company, caught between community expectations, on the one hand, and those of stockholders on the other, must indeed show just cause and successful outcome for corporate philanthropy.[31]

The privately owned company can do what it pleases with profits. Hallmark Cards earmarks at least 2 percent of its pretax profits to charity and undertook (in 1967) the urban renewal of an 85-acre section of Kansas City, Missouri.[32] DeWitt and Lila Wallace, sole owners of *Reader's Digest* (he died in 1981, she in 1984) encouraged all employees to enjoy the spring season and gave them Friday holidays in which to do so. Lila Wallace devoted her time and wealth to projects as diverse as the town of Mt. Kisco, New York; the New York Metropolitan Museum of Art; the Juilliard School; the New York Zoological Society; and historic restorations such as the Egyptian temple of Abu Simbel, Boscobel on the Hudson, and the home of French Impressionist Claude Monet.[33]

Dr. An Wang is the Shanghai-born, Harvard-educated founder of Wang Laboratories, Inc., one of the fastest-growing high-tech firms in the country. Together with his family, he owns anywhere from 40 percent to 55 percent of the company's stock (depending on the source consulted). His philanthropic heart belongs to Massachusetts, specifically Lowell (once home to the textile industry, whose employees authored *The Lowell Offering*). Thanks in great part to Dr. Wang, Lowell is reborn—complete with employee country clubs and day-care centers. But Boston, too, enjoys Wang beneficence. He and his wife not only saved that city's main performing arts center, but later dispatched a corporate vice president to help sharpen its management. He is constructing a new $15 million plant in Boston's Chinatown so as to create jobs for inner-city residents.

Harvard University, his alma mater, is a favored recipient. "I was fortunate," he says, "that as soon as I got to the United States in 1945, I was admitted to Harvard [where I was] introduced to computers . . . in the very early stage of their development. I am honored that Harvard lets me show my appreciation."[34] In addition to the academic programs he supports at Harvard, Dr. Wang has created the Wang Institute of Graduate Studies for software engineers and China scholars. In 1983 the institute offered a fellowship program which supported a number of scholars engaged in full-time research relating to any period or area of Chinese studies.[35]

PLANTING FOR THE CHILDREN

It could be reasonably argued that America's intellectual life and development derives as much from businessmen riding their hobbyhorses as from the directives of church or state. Only count the colleges endowed by philanthropic businessmen, the libraries established, the research funded, the academic chairs created, the art collections and sculpture gardens assembled. Not to mention the foundations to assure perpetuation. It makes an impressive list.

One of the first of the great philanthropists was Andrew Carnegie, the erstwhile bobbin boy and telegraph messenger who practically created Big Steel. His burning interest in life was learning, and he determined to make it possible for others to learn. The development and growth of the American public-library system owes largely to his efforts. "No millionaire will go far wrong in his search for one of the best forms for the use of his surplus who chooses to establish a free library in any community that is willing to maintain and develop it."[36] Many philanthropists have followed his example.

In Norwalk, Connecticut, there is a small, exquisite structure built to house the Burndy Library of the History of Science and Technology. Inside are treasures to tempt the bibliophile and scholar: three pocket notebooks of Louis Pasteur, rare volumes printed in Europe before 1500, a Chinese volume printed in 1085, a 631-year-old Florentine monastery bell designed by Leonardo da Vinci. The library has hosted meetings of the prestigious History of Science Society. Annually it publishes a monograph on a theme relating to science or technology. The most recent is a translation and facsimile edition of *Kodu Zuroku,* a Japanese treatise on the smelting of copper, originally published circa 1801. Some eleven thousand of its volumes have been given to the Smithsonian Institution for a spin-off collection. The library is located across the street from the offices and factory of the Burndy Corporation, a manufacturer of electrical devices, now operating thirty plants around the world. Both the library and the corporation were founded by Dr. Bern Dibner.

"It was in 1904," he told me, "that my father brought his wife and eight children to this country from Czarist Russia. Sixteen of his descendants—sons, grandsons, great grandsons—fought for their adopted land, some in two wars." And he showed me a 1946 photograph of the smiling, uniformed Dibner men. "We wanted to repay our debt to a nation that had accepted a family of immigrants and given us a chance to grow and flourish."

Flourish they did. Dr. Bern managed to become an electrical engineer instead of the electrician he had set out to be. Somewhere during the course of developing his own inventions and creating a company to manufacture them, he discovered Leonardo da Vinci, Leonardo the inventor rather than the artist. The life and works of the Florentine genius became his own animating spirit. Already in command of four languages, Dr. Bern mastered Italian in order to read Leonardo's books. And, in 1936 while seeking treatment in Switzerland for his ailing wife, he entered into the serious studies and began the collections that would, in 1938, become the Burndy Library. "Of course, we at Burndy have always tried to fulfill our duties to the community," he said, "but the library is special—something in which I gloried because it expanded my spirits."

The library has been chartered in New York and Connecticut as a public educational institution, and Bern Dibner, now 87 and Chairman Emeritus of Burndy, is its director. He authors many of its monographs and is considered a leading Leonardo scholar. The city of Milan feted him during its 1982 celebration of Leonardo's move there from Florence hundreds of years earlier. He has served as one of three consultants for the CBS television presentation, "I, Leonardo," and was a contributor to the McGraw-Hill book, *The Unknown Leonardo.* [37]

However passionate their devotion to learning, neither Andrew Carnegie nor Bern Dibner ignored (while active men of business) the prime directive: DO WELL! And they gave to the effort their single-minded concentration.

But how many successful tycoons, eager to apply their surplus to the common good, know how it should be done or, indeed, where the area of greatest need lies? In order to ensure the most intelligent application of their philanthropic dollars (as well as philanthropic perpetuation), many wealthy donors and many corporations have established foundations for giving. Foundations also serve another function: They separate the donor from his gift. He need not be personally involved.

Andrew Carnegie heartily disapproved of this sort of separation, believing that the man of wealth should invest himself as well as his money in the act of charity. (Carnegie had the time, of course. Philanthropy was the sole occupation of his later years.) Yet, in spite of skepticism about foundations, he did establish several which continue today to make the charitable most of the $311 million he gave away in his lifetime.[38]

As private charitable foundations multiplied (there are twenty-two thousand at last count), a clearinghouse for information became necessary. In 1956 The Foundation Center was created with funds from—where else?—foundations. Today it operates four regional libraries for the use of potential grant seekers and 145 cooperating collections. These house and keep up to date the center's array of indices, guide books, and catalogues. The 1983 Foundation Directory, which describes only the 4,000-plus largest foundations, is a hefty tome running to 750 pages in very small print. The Ford family alone accounts for six foundations, all based in Detroit. Not to mention the Ford Motor Company Fund. Not to mention the huge (over $2 billion) Ford Foundation in New York, whose recipients run the gamut from aspiring playwrights to inner-city projects.[39]

GRACE IN GIVING

The granddaddy of all philanthropists was Cosimo de Medici, founder of "that family who for so many generations took a chief part in all that interests us in Florence; whose care for learning and art produced such wide effects." So wrote G.F. Young who chronicled the Florentine magnates in 1933. Venice is dismissed for its "inordinate love of money." He concedes that Florence "also loved money, but it was not her chief interest." (Aristocratic Rome, of course, scorned the Florentines as shopkeepers.)[40]

Money was certainly necessary when Florence played host to Greek prelates and scholars who met with their opposite numbers in 1439 to discuss the reunification of the churches. Cosimo, the banker and trader, supplied cash, palaces, hospitality. Fifteen years later, when the Turks overran Byzantium, those same scholars returned to friendly Florence as refugees. Their presence stimulated that resurgence of classical learning we call the Renaissance.

More impressive still was Cosimo's grandson, Lorenzo the Magnificent, who not only gave, but gave in style. He supported innumerable artists, poets, scholars, musicians; founded museums and a great library; contributed lavishly to civic works and causes. What is more, Lorenzo could discuss music with musicians, art with artists, and wrote fair poetry when the mood struck. Indeed, he was such a thoroughgoing devotee of the arts that he nearly went broke and had to request a bailout by the city treasury. No wonder. He had long been too preoccupied with munificence to give proper thought to business affairs, leaving them in the hands of appointees. Adam Smith had this to say about Lorenzo:

> "The agents of a prince regard the wealth of their master as inexhaustible; are careless at which price they buy; are careless at what price they sell; are careless at what expense they transport his goods from one place to another. Those agents frequently live with the profusion of princes, and sometimes . . . acquire the fortunes of princes. . . . It was thus . . . that the agents of Lorenzo of Medicis, not a prince of mean abilities, carried on his trade."[41]

Eventually, says Smith, Lorenzo had to give up trade and fall back on real estate—as did John Jacob Astor in New York, though not owing to the same unbridled philanthropy.

It is the quality of philanthropy more than its quantity

that often seems crucial in a tycoon's social redemption and place in history. Style counts, it would seem. One must be worthy of giving. Writing in 1958, Lucius Beebe wondered, "What has become of the American generation of rich men worthy of the name or the possession of wealth?" Those old tycoons, he mused fondly, had risen "above Cadillacs, drum majorettes, and a taste for cola drinks instead of champagne. They didn't affect being plain as an old shoe."[42]

Where were the elegant big spenders in 1960? Busy making money, wrote John Kenneth Galbraith in an article published that year. They were "identified in spirit with the hard-bitten entrepreneurship but not with the other interests of Henry Clay Frick, Andrew Mellon, and J. Pierpont Morgan." He spoke approvingly of Charles Lang Freer, the builder of railroad cars, who, seemingly, made money only to serve his interest in Whistler and oriental art. These were the times, said Galbraith, when the great tycoons proved by their art collections (amassed with the assistance of the connoisseur and instructor of the wealthy, Lord Duveen) "that they were not mere money-grubbers."[43]

In 1984 the distinguished economist replayed the same theme in an article for the *New York Times Magazine*. Ignoring today's philanthropic descendants of tycoons, he chose to focus on the affluent working stiff. Though diligent and broad-minded, "a far more agreeable figure than his predecessor, the great captain of industry, the prototypical entrepreneur," Corporate Man remains, in Dr. Galbraith's view, a strait-jacketed creature of the organization who would never "make any personal contribution in music, painting, the theatre, film, writing, serious learning, or the lower art of politics." Corporate Man can be expected only to "write a check in support of those achievements."[44]

Not surprisingly, the professional humanist considers his own line of work superior to all others and expects general agreement to the proposition that Business is a sort of necessary evil: at worst, greedy and dehumanizing; at best, grubby and gray. Redemption for the business man or woman is to be found only in a suitable avocation. That

Business can offer its own creative challenges and rewards is—for many academics—an unimaginable possibility. Daniel Defoe didn't think so. He said:

> "Trade must not be entered into as a thing of light concern. It is called Business very properly, for it is a business for life. . . . He that trades in jest, will certainly break in earnest."[45]

Ask the professional writer or artist whether he prefers the businessman as a writer of checks or as dabbler in the arts. Odds are he'll prefer the former to the latter.

ASSESSING THE QUALITY OF MERCY

Society's response to the rich man and his generosity has always teetered precariously between gratitude and scorn, admiration and condemnation. In 1889 Andrew Carnegie considered that ambivalence in an essay titled "The Gospel of Wealth":

> "Time was when the words concerning the rich man entering the kingdom of heaven were regarded as a hard saying. . . . But is it so very improbable that the next stage of thought is to restore the doctrine in all its pristine purity and force . . . ? In Christ's day, it is evident, reformers were against the wealthy. It is none the less evident that we are fast recurring to that position to-day; and there will be nothing to surprise the student of sociological development if society would soon approve the test which has caused so much anxiety: 'It is easier for a camel to enter the eye of a needle than for a rich man to enter the kingdom of heaven.' . . . It will be but a step for the theologian from the doctrine that he who dies rich dies disgraced, to that which brings upon the man punishment or deprivation hereafter."[46]

That time seemed to have arrived when Ida Tarbell and other investigative reporters were raking muck and sounding alarms in corporate offices. Kathleen Brady reports that, within a year of Ida Tarbell's first articles on Standard Oil, the Rockefeller Institute for Medical Research made unexpectedly large gifts to charitable organizations. Did benevolence represent a cynical effort to maintain image?

Rockefeller's descendants have a different perspective. In 1974, following the Watergate debacle, the newly named vice president, Gerald Ford, succeeded to office and chose Nelson Rockefeller his vice president. In a lengthy statement to the Senate Rules Committee, Rockefeller described the family history and values. The family of the founder, he said, had been dirt poor, yet John D.'s father

> "[D]emanded self-reliance, thrift, and industry . . . and insisted on precision, promptness, and responsibility in everything the young man did. . . . Thus the roots of our family ethic were deeply implanted . . .
>
> My grandfather's early training in giving to help those in need became an increasingly absorbing part of his life. With the growth of his earnings, his giving increased. In the later years, with the phenomenal growth in the oil industry, he devoutly believed that Providence had made him a trustee of his fortune for the benefit of man, and was not to be kept but to be wisely distributed." [47]

Atonement, altruism, self-protection? Perhaps all three. The fact remains: he made the money, and he gave much of it away. Do motivations really matter? "Yes," say the purists. "Motivation counts." That is why the socialist concept of the benevolent state as ultimate (and often only) source of charity carries such appeal. (Like the foundation, the benevolent state makes charity impersonal and abstract; it takes the giver out of giving.) "Don't implore the rich man for funds to feed the poor," urges the motivational purist. "Just tax him. And tax him *good!*" And so it is that the word "compassion" gets a workout only as an attribute of Government in its function of tax redistribution. Neither Business nor business people are ever described as "caring" no matter how large their gifts.

American administrations have vacillated in their policies regarding charity and how it should be provided. It was in 1913 that the income tax was established by the Sixteenth Amendment to the Constitution. Since then tax rates on income in excess of $200,000 have varied from low (1 percent to 7 percent) to high (91 percent) to medium (50 percent). Very high income taxes have seemed not only to discourage charity but incentive to produce as well. (Roland Huntford reported in 1972 that Sweden's citizens, burdened by the world's highest taxes, had long since ceased to find it better to give than to receive.) Allowable deductions for charitable gifts have served to create incentives for generosity if not for economic growth. "But," the purists will insist, "that still leaves something to be desired in the motivation department." [48]

What about that? How does a society encourage altruism—particularly among those best able to be generous?

OTHER INCENTIVES

In Greek city states of classical times, rich men were moved to undertake "liturgies," acts of public service to God. Such service could extend to the outfitting of warships, to the construction of walls or temples—any civic enterprise for which funds were not available in the treasury. (Certainly a canny means of skirting deficits.) That the word "liturgy" continues in religious usage testifies to the solemnity and sacred connections of the original obligation. To accept a liturgy was to earn the respect and honor of one's fellow citizens and an odor of sanctity as well.

In the beginning, we are told, such burdens were voluntarily and cheerfully assumed; indeed, men vied for liturgies. One could be proud of being rich. But all honors tarnish in time and especially with indiscriminate use. By the fourth century B.C. liturgies came to represent intolerable impositions. City Fathers had to agree that a "liturgist" could be absolved if he could find someone richer than he. And the well-to-do strove to disguise affluence. "When I was a boy," mourned the sophist Isocrates, "wealth was regarded as a thing so secure as well as admirable that almost everyone affected to own more than they possessed." [49] But "almost everyone" could also tell the difference between obligation and depredation. Goodbye, liturgy.

The fact remains. Honor is an incentive to service. And human beings will compete for honor as surely as for gain. Anthropologist Charles Erasmus reports that Santiago, Chile, is the world's largest city having a fire department completely staffed by volunteers. Fire fighters in each center constitute a brotherhood with unique traditions and rituals. Gaining acceptance into a brotherhood is no easy matter. There is always a long waiting list and considerable vying for position. Many are called; few are chosen. Since membership in a group is held in such high esteem, expulsion carries shattering disgrace. [50]

Then there is the cargo system (sometimes called *cofradia*) of Maya Indians in Mexico and Guatemala. A Spanish word, *cargo,* is used by them to represent ceremonial and charitable responsibilities perceived as a sacred burden borne on the back. Ancient Maya gods were thought to take turns carrying the "year" in such a manner, and it may be that wealthy men in the once-glorious old temple centers served the public good in divine imitation.

Today their village descendants imitate *them* in an act of cultural remembrance.

> Make no mistake about it. Assuming a cargo is no light task. So anthropologist Evon Vogt tells us in describing the modern Maya village of Zinacantan.
>
> There are long waiting lists for the available positions, and men must work very hard to amass the wealth necessary to live for a year in the ceremonial center, contributing to the costs of feasts and ritual paraphernalia. An equivalent American experience, said Dr. Vogt's colleague, would require him to take an unpaid leave of absence from his post at Harvard and spend some $18,000 in fulfilling religious obligations. (That was in 1970; the cost would be much higher today.)
>
> No sooner does the cargo-bearer doff his burden, finan-

cially cleaned out and in heavy debt, than he starts the process all over again. He signs up for the next higher ceremonial office. Only the truly enterprising can accumulate the necessary wherewithal and may do so by planting maize for the market instead of merely for family subsistence. This requires borrowing from the Mexican government and hiring extra farm hands. The aspiring cargo-bearer has to hustle and plan.

And what does he get for his pains? Prestige and lots of it. Fame is the spur. Honor is the spur. Together with a glowing sense of pride in having lived up to the best values of one's society.

There are some negative incentives as well. The rich man disinclined to pick up the ceremonial burden, the energetic man who excites the envy of his peers is a potential target for witches. And if he refuses to spend freely for the common good, he is certain to be a victim.[51]

Honor and shame. Carrot and stick. But more of one than the other

Just before Thanksgiving 1984, the Knight-Ridder News Service released the story of China's first millionaire—in Chinese money, of course. A peasant from one of China's central provinces, the new tycoon had made his fortune in a prefabricated cement factory, in the sale of electrical appliances, and in acres of fruit trees. Not so long ago such achievements would have merited arraignment as a "capitalist running dog" and a lengthy stay in jail. Today a grateful government presents a plaque bearing these words: "Wealthy man one hundred times ten thousand."[52] The message to the populace is loud and clear. It is "Go ye and do likewise." The budding Chinese entrepreneur is not burdened (at least not yet) with liturgies, cargos, or immoderate taxes. He is not (at least not yet) labeled by a hostile media as "greedy and uncaring." The media are, in fact, little moved by philanthropy. "Teaching people to get rich," holds *Renmin Ribao*, "is much better and more realistic than taking pleasure in charitable acts."[53] First do *well*. That is all the government asks. First raise the general level of prosperity. *Then* do good.

Alexis de Tocqueville in the 1830s expressed similar sentiments about America:

> "Commercial business is there like a vast lottery by which a small number of men continually lose, but the State is always a gainer. Such a people ought therefore to encourage and do honor to boldness in commercial speculations."[54]

In spite of the Horatio Alger myth, America has only rarely seen fit to bestow such honor and never unalloyed with suspicion. Yet American men of business have done exceedingly well, and the nation has done well because of them. They have also made enormous contributions toward ensuring the common good. Without much hoopla, it must be said. Indeed, their gifts have often been overlooked or discounted, probed for motivation, graded on style, belittled in terms of content. In spite of it, American Business continues to do well *and* to do good.

Perhaps the time has come for an award. It could be called "The Philly" and given every year to an outstanding philanthropist. Actually, the idea has already surfaced in Washington circles. And why not? Everything else is honored. There is a Teacher of the Year and a Mother of the Year. Miss World and Miss Universe each has a year of glory. Ditto Miss, Mrs., and Miss-Teenage America. There is not a sport without its annual trophy holder. Every year the Academy Award honors the best film, and there is an Emmy for the best TV program.

The time has come for philanthropy. If the Chinese can honor the man who makes a million, America can honor him who gives it away.

EPILOGUE

THE BUSINESS OF AMERICA

"Trade must not be entered into as a thing of light concern; it is called Business very properly, for it is a business for life."[1]

DANIEL DEFOE

It's certainly much easier to be IN than OUT," said Julianne Grace of Perkin-Elmer. We were discussing the ways in which cultural climate affects the way business is done:

> "During the 60's we were OUT. The environment was terribly hostile. Top level business leaders were being attacked whenever they made public statements. Companies simply could not recruit on college campuses—particularly if they were in any way defense-related. Students wouldn't talk to us. And they certainly weren't taking business courses. All the best and brightest were going into other fields. Even the lower levels of employment were affected. It was just plain difficult to hire."

What about those who were in business at the time? How did they react to the hostility?

> "They found pride in their jobs and tried not to pay attention to what people outside were saying. They managed. We managed. But there were so many obstacles to overcome."

Have things changed today?

> "It's better for us. Business may not be IN but we're not altogether OUT, either. Business is still labelled 'bad' (particularly if it is also big), but more selectively."[2]

She is right. Approval ratings have climbed and the level of interest as well. Business magazines and journals have increased in readership, in scope, and in general glossiness. Programs of business news and features are now regularly carried on radio and television. Books about business management constitute a thriving genre.

Only when the busy executive strays into the "other" world does he catch a strong whiff of disfavor. Network news and television drama dependably accentuate the negative. The Broadway play he attends is likely to be entirely configured around his sins and shortcomings (*Glengarry Glen*

Ross heads the current list). Even the reviewers of such plays follow suit. (Herbert Mitgang on the play, *Tender Offer:* "What's missing is the very stuff appearing daily on the business pages—satire and menace.")[3] Unless our man of business worships in a church of the evangelical-fundamentalist persuasion, he cannot expect aid and comfort from the pulpit. And religious publications ranging from the Unitarian-Universalist Newsletter to the Catholic bishops' pastoral letter regularly consign his life and works to outer darkness. Nor will the traditional academic excuse his faults (unless, of course, he offers to write a check). A visit to his college student's class in philosophy or sociology will introduce him to unfamiliar terrain largely populated by sinister figures tagged "capitalist." He may later protest to son or daughter, "*I'm* not like that. My company's not like that. Maybe the others are. I don't know." Like most businessmen, he is apt to wax defensive when exposed to Guardians.

"There *is* one thing that bothers me," he may at some point confide to the interviewer disposed to be sympathetic. "Why do clerics, professors, reporters, and every garden-variety politico assume they know more about business than do we who work at it? We don't tell clerics what to preach or professors what to teach. We don't even fuss about reporters unless they wiggle the truth. Sometimes not even then. We don't stick our noses into their business; we mind our own. Why do they think they can do a better job of it than we can?"

The anthropologist, that traveler in time and space, recognizes an old question when he hears one. That particular plaint must have been voiced when the first trader brought home a skin bag of weapon-stone and, instead of thanks, received only criticism for having failed to placate the water goddess on his way into town. In those ancient times when there were but three truly legitimate professions (ruling, preaching, and curing) and everyone else was tied to the soil, the man of business must have seemed a bit of an upstart. Imagine the nerve! Trying to live without any visible means of support. How dared he get rich doing what doesn't come naturally? How dared he get rich when men commanding bodies of respected lore—acquired after long years of study—remained poor? For what lore was required in order to do business? Nobody then equated forethought with lore. Nobody factored daring into the trader's professional capital. Nobody took into account the trader's knowledge of people, languages, mediums of exchange, nature of risk. Above all, nobody much considered and valued not at all his ability to make lightning assessments of changing conditions and possible advantage. "Opportunism," said geographer James Vance, "is the rule of trade. . . . The opportunism of the ancient trader was his living but also his stigma."[4] Society did not then and does not now much appreciate the capacity to jump whichever way the wind blows.

There is something else to consider. Those other ancient professionals had attained positions created by society to meet defined needs. Those positions would not be abandoned. Never mind how cruel the leader or corrupt the priest, no one would cry, "Throw the rascals out!" They would simply look for replacements. Men of enterprise, however, and indeed enterprise itself can be and have been thrown out of many societies over time and place. Why? Because the trader, the merchant venturer is *self* created. Society in its beginnings did not ordain his position or push him into being. He pushed himself. He emerged as a filler of social gaps, a shaker of social sameness. He was the bringer of new ideas and so inevitably disturbed (and disturbs) the status quo—whatever it happens to be. No wonder rulers distrust the man of business. So do priests. And sometimes even establishment figures in Business itself. Anyone with a proprietary interest in the-way-things-are-and-should-be. Never mind that the venturer brings prosperity to the group while prospering himself. It is the *way* things are done that counts.

Never has *way* been more in the ascendant than during the past twenty years. Never was a generation, together with its Guardians, more opposed to the business institutions than that of the Boomers. And yet, with the senior members of that generation now pushing forty, a strange new thing has happened, unpredicted in anybody's crystal ball. "It was," puzzles John Kenneth Galbraith, "the unarticulated assumption of American liberals, as of Social Democrats in other countries, that the newly affluent would in gratitude have political attitudes different from those of the older rich. And so, presumably, would their more fortunate offspring. The liberals were wrong."[5]

Not only have the Boomers failed to follow expected political pathways, they are not going into Government, the clergy, the "helping professions" which once claimed all their hopes. They are going into Business. Why?

Eric Berg of Technicomp, Inc., has some answers. A product of the late 1960s, he was graduated from Earlham, a Quaker college in Indiana.

> "I was a classic New Jersey liberal of the Vietnam Era," he told me. "My college had no business major and was generally hostile to the idea. My degree was in political science, and later I worked in the Kennedy campaigns and in social service. Everything in my background made me hostile to business. That was the last sort of career I could have imagined. But here I am. Sometimes I am shocked to hear myself being a proponent of business. But I'm that now."

From the Counterculture to Business? Surely that is a journey to be reckoned in light-years. How, I asked him, did his fellows come to embrace the enemy so fervently? Was it because of the recession?

> "Emphatically no," he said. "The motivation was not primarily economic. We found things in the business world we hadn't expected. We found the same levels of freedom in business and the ability to control our own lives that we yearned for in the 60s. It's not so much that values have changed. Institutions have changed. New management is largely entrepreneurial. Young people see business firms as

places where they can do exciting things, different things, good things. It grips the imagination.

"All the real innovations in life are coming from business. They're not being funded by the government. They're funded by venture capital. And people are risking their own money. The rewards can be big. No wonder the real heroes today are the high-tech entrepreneurs. They've got the same glamour as rock stars."

The humanist and deep thinker may have as much difficulty associating glamour with the young tycoon in high-tech as he does with the rock star. The reading public has had less difficulty in that regard. Nor do its members deny the visionary spirit to at least some men of business. Witness the runaway popularity of four recent books about business executives and business management (*The Art of Japanese Management* by Richard Pascale and Anthony Athos; *Theory Z* by William Ouchi; *Corporate Cultures* by Terrence Deal and Allan Kennedy; *In Search of Excellence* by Thomas Peters and Robert Waterman.)[6] Opinion makers and academics have not yet seen fit to wonder why these books are—according to bookstore owners—being read by a large nonbusiness audience. They should.

All four describe visionary executives and well-managed corporations in America and abroad. All contain prescriptions for excellence. But there have been many such prescriptions before. The success of these books lies elsewhere, lies in what is implied but not said, lies in a curious transference from the arena of business to the larger society.

All four speak of culture and culture consensus, of identity and belonging, of belief and mission and corporate patriotism, of ritual and heroes and values, of community and extended family, of the creative individual in a nurturing environment, of achievement and excellence, of devotion to human potential. It is, the authors hold, commitment to these intangibles that makes for successful business enterprise. But wait. This same commitment makes for a successful society and contented citizens. By locating these intangibles in a business context where the accent is on the practical and the possible, the authors strike deep chords of yearning in a readership more than a little daunted by the current state of society with its bitter divisions and its seemingly insoluble problems, daunted by the steady erosion of old verities. "All the new innovations are coming from business," said Eric Berg. The reading public seems to agree. This is where things are happening. This is the locus of optimism.

How startled and pleased Joseph Schumpeter would have been to witness this turn of events. He had always believed that the linchpin of capitalism was the entrepreneurial role which

> "though less glamourous than that of the medieval warlord, great or small, also is . . . another form of individual leadership acting by virtue of personal force and personal responsibility for success. His position, like that of the warrior classes, is threatened as soon as this function in the social process loses its importance."[7]

The entrepreneur, the creation of new consumer goods, the development of new forms of organization and new methods of production—all of these, he said, mold capitalism, which is a powerful engine for prosperity but also an engine for change for it can never stand still.

And yet, this believer in the system was pessimistic about its future. For the spirit of enterprise, he thought, had been so successful as to encompass its own demise. It had, by its very triumph, created and educated the enemies who wished to see it destroyed:

> "The socialist order," he wrote, "presumably will command that moral allegiance which is increasingly refused to capitalism. . . . Faced by the increasing hostility of the [intellectual] environment and by the legislative, administrative, and judicial practice born of that hostility, entrepreneurs and capitalists—in fact the whole stratum that accepts the Bourgeois way of life—will eventually cease to function."[8]

In such an environment, would not venture capital simply dry up and go away? And besides, how many new areas of need remained unexploited?

But the new young entrepreneurs are finding them with a zest and imagination Joseph Schumpeter had sadly concluded were in irreversible decline. How not? Throughout all the years since World War II individual creativity in business was distinctly out of focus. Here and just about everywhere else.

In China the years of the Cultural Revolution coincided with America's Counterculture phenomenon. Both movements upheld the sanctity of the Group. Both flouted the traditional and the "obsolete." The result of those years now when enterprise and the market have been restored in China is, says Rusen Ko of Occidental Oil, "A lost generation. Many are too old to learn the new technology."[9] Amanda Bennett adds, "without skills or education, they watch their younger brothers and sisters leapfrog them to the top . . . they are still a constant source of potential disaffection." And they yearn for the old excitement, the time of revolution. "It was like a bird that's been caged up being let loose for the first time," said one former Red Guard, now middle-aged.[10]

Members of America's Counterculture did not become a lost generation. Most appear to have departed the good old days with no regret. New slogans and images are on the scene. Some are halo words. "Entrepreneur," for example. Just to utter the sounds creates potent magic that one hopes will rub off. There are books which tell the reader how to be among the lucky ones. Colleges are suddenly offering courses in entrepreneurship. (Earlham is among them, Eric Berg tells me.) If ever a new dance step is invented it will surely be called the Entrepreneurial Gallop.

Nobody is struggling harder than the large corporations to bring back the spirit of enterprise to the industrial bureaucracy, to make an "intrapreneur" of the Organization Man. (The new term refers to the in-house innovator, driven to succeed.) Rosabeth Moss Kanter, sociologist and management consultant, calls this transformation "the new corporate Renaissance." And she goes on to say, "Individuals make a difference":

> "That's the positive side of 'American individualism'—entrepreneurs not afraid to break the mould in seeking to break a record or competing to win a game. . . . Strong individuals, along with a tradition of teamwork, bring productive accomplishments into being. . . . 'American-style' participation does not and should not mean the dominance of committees over individuals, the submergence of the individual in the group, or the swallowing of the person by the team, but rather the mechanism for giving more people at more levels a piece of the entrepreneurial action. . . . In an American corporate Renaissance, we could see the reawakening of a dormant spirit of enterprise at all levels of organization, among all kinds of workers."[11]

Not everyone is charmed. "What do you mean—'spirit of enterprise?' " they object. "Call it, rather, the spirit of greed."

Greedy for what? one well might ask. Is it not possible to be as greedy for achievement, recognition, fulfillment as for money? Is it not possible to yearn as passionately for the discovery of something absolutely new as for the Gucci bag? Is it not as possible to express creativity in a business venture as in a work of art? ("This store is my painting," said Gene Scarangella. "It is my book!")

But, come to think of it, what's so bad about the almighty dollar? More dollars make more spenders, and more spenders make more jobs. The poor man hires no help. Besides, there's no great trick to being greedy. Any number can play. People have been certifiably greedy since human time began. (Else why is greed the primary sin among hunting-and-gathering folk?) The real trick is to acquire, accumulate, or otherwise amass material goods through and because of superior productivity.

Productivity: that is another halo word just now. Why? Because, like "entrepreneur," it represents and encompasses values that have traditionally constituted the

American ethos. Anthropologists who have focused their attention on what it means to be American agree on certain dominant themes common to and expressed by most Americans, though certainly not all. The importance of work is one. Effort and optimism ("Give it your best shot! Never say die!") is another. Material well-being ("I cannot *function* without a word processor!") is yet another. Then there are the potent pairs of opposites. Individuality and equality. Competition but also cooperation. Individual achievement, yet group identification. Being different but also being the same. The use of pragmatic ingenuity to solve problems is a well-known American penchant. ("Can do!") So is the fondness for (though not always the exercise of) common sense and rationalism.[12]

These are all qualities necessary to success in business. Alexis de Tocqueville was one of the first to recognize the connection:

> "The Americans are at the same time a Puritanical people and a commercial nation. Their strictly Puritanical origin, their exclusively commercial habits, even the country they inhabit, which seems to divert their minds from the pursuit of science, literature, and the arts . . . a thousand special causes . . . have singularly concurred to fix the mind of the American upon purely practical objects."[13]

Americans, he said, were not rooted to old ways and habits and could thus embrace the new. And yet, "the idea of novelty is there indissolubly connected with the idea of amelioration."

> "It would seem as if every imagination in the United States were upon the stretch to invent means of increasing the wealth and satisfying the wants of the public."[14]

That the American ethos was also a business ethos dismayed de Tocqueville not one whit. Indeed, he found in the pursuit of commerce a special kind of valor, particularly when seaborne.

"The Americans show a sort of heroism in their manner of trading. The European merchant will always find it difficult to imitate his American competitor, who, in adopting the system that I have just described, follows not only a calculation of his gain but an impulse of his nature."[15]

"Americans are often shipwrecked, but no trader crosses the seas so rapidly. And as they perform the same distance in a shorter time, they can perform it at a cheaper rate."[16]

"I accost an American sailor and inquire why the ships of his country are built so as to last for only a short time; he answers without hesitation that the art of navigation is every day making such rapid progress that the finest vessel would become almost useless if it lasted beyond a few years. In these words, which fell accidentally, and on a particular subject, from a man of rude attainments, I recognize the general and systematic idea upon which a great people direct all its concerns."[17]

"They are born to rule the sea, as the Romans were to conquer the world."[18]

The entrepreneurial Yuppies of the Boomer generation seem born to conquer the world of business, not by their numbers, not by changing traditional American values, but by rediscovering them—perhaps even by reinventing them. They have turned away from this or that call to perfection, from this or that formula for utopia and placed their faith in themselves. Says reporter Brett Duval Fromson (himself a generational emissary), "Yuppies, if we do anything at all, respect those who deliver the goods."[19] Effort. Practicality. Common sense. The bottom line.

In their reaffirmation of the individual, they are also reaffirming cultural diversity. Just when some social scientists, such as the distinguished archaeologist Grahame Clark, were expressing worry about the increasing *sameness* the world over ("impoverishment by homogenization," he called it)[20] and others, such as anthropologist Marvin Harris, were decrying the trend to oligopoly—the facelessness of the huge—along comes the entrepreneur.[21] "There may be very large corporations in the future," said Eric Berg, "but maybe fewer than we've known and those not the same ones that dominate the scene today. One thing is sure: there are going to be lots of little companies, more all the time. Each one will be different in terms of its internal atmosphere. Every working person can now find just the right place to be, the right 'culture' for him."

So things are looking up. Business has attracted the young who see in it the challenge of the new as well as a way to get-rich-quick (or poor, as the case may be). It has seized their imaginations. This is not to say that a state of grace has been achieved. That day will not have arrived until more novels like Sinclair Lewis's *Dodsworth* are written. Not until dramatists choose their "heavies" from occupations other than Business. Not until writers of social-science texts stop gushing about European welfare states long enough to note that they are doing the Entrepreneurial Gallop all the way to the free market. Sweden, too. Swedish economist Sven Rydenfelt made that clear in a recent article for the *Wall Street Journal:*

> "Businessmen used to be looked upon as half-criminals with dirty jobs and dirty profits; today, however, successful businessmen are hailed as providers of wealth and much needed jobs. One might almost say they are now regarded as national heroes."[22]

They are not yet so regarded in America. Certainly not by everyone. Total rehabilitation may be on the way, however. Business will soon be IN for fair. Home free.

For how long? Until Business becomes fat, complacent, and bureaucratic, unmindful of its workers and their quality of life. Until it stifles enterprise in organization. Until it ignores the cultural climate in which business must be done. Until it becomes too tired to poke and pry, seeking opportunity, advantage, and advance. Until the children of today's entrepreneurs can so take prosperity for granted as to sniff at Daddy's or Mommy's dirty money. Until the nation itself can once again afford to bite the hand that feeds.

EPILOGUE

One superscandal, one desperate depression, and Business will be OUT again. Not physically, not altogether. Certainly not in this country. America has become too accustomed to having needs and wants met more-or-less well. But a change in goals and values can once again consign the practitioner of business to outer darkness, without trust, honor, or recognition.

Maybe that's not such a bad thing after all. The anthropologist, who is a professional outsider, can speak to the virtues and possibilities of that position. The outsider has a view of the world quite different from that of the insider preoccupied with his territorial imperatives. The outsider can see similarities the insider does not. Can see brave Toàn of the Yurok behind every young entrepreneur. Can see a New Guinea *tonowi* comfortably at home among peers of the Business Roundtable. Can see the Yoruba market woman and today's traveling saleswoman as one and the same.

The outsider has the chance to grow, to revise, to change, all unconstrained by the weight of habit and received wisdom. He has incentive to change, for, like anyone else, he wants to be liked, to be valued, to belong. The business outsider has the added incentive of profitability. He wants to be both popular *and* successful. To achieve that, periodic overhaul is in order. As it is for the businessman, so it is for Business. The other institutions of society—slower to change—are not under such painful necessity. And are less successfully inventive in consequence.

As Business has been alternately IN and OUT in the nation's esteem, so Americans have been alternately IN and OUT in the world's esteem. OUT because of their brash, venturesome, commercial bias. IN when that bias works, when it brings prosperity and opportunity. The commercial bias ensures acquaintance with obstacles. But also the strength, inventiveness, practicality, and hope to find a way around them.

Calvin Coolidge had it right: The business of America *is* business. Again. And in the spirit of Silent Cal, one might well add, "And about time, too."

NOTES

PROLOGUE

1. Plato, *The Republic*, book 8.
2. Quoted in Robert McC. Adams, "Anthropological Perspectives on Ancient Trade." *Current Anthropology* (September 1974), 248.
3. Sam Pickering, Jr., "Head and Heart," *National Review*, July 24, 1981, 840.
4. See Herodotus of Halicarnassus, *The Histories*. 2 vols. (Translated by Hany Carter), (New York: Heritage Press, 1958.)
5. Alexander Pope (translator), *The Odyssey of Homer*. (New York: Heritage Press, 1942), p. 111.
6. Aristotle, *Politics*, book 1, chap. 10.
7. *Ibid.*, book 7, chap. 9.
8. Horace, *Epodes*, 2, 1.
9. Quoted in M.I. Finley, *The Ancient Economy* (Berkeley: University of California Press, 1973), p. 41.
10. See Ssu-ma Chi'en, *Records of the Grand Historian of China*, 2 vols. (Translated by Burton Watson), (New York: Columbia University Press, 1961). See also Marcel Granet, *Chinese Civilization* (New York: Meridian Books, 1958).
11. See Donald Richie, "The Japanese Art of Tattooing," *Natural History Magazine* (December 1973).
12. See Bernardo de Sahagun, *The Florentine Codex*. Translated by C.E. Dibble and Arthur J.O. Anderson. Monograph of the School of the Museum of New Mexico, #14, 1961.
13. Cited in Henri Pirenne, Economic and Social History of Medieval Europe, I.E. Clegg, translator (New York: Harcourt, Brace and World, 1937), p. 14. Latin phrase translated by John Vlahos.

14. See Milton and Rose Friedman, *Free to Choose* (New York: Harcourt Brace Jovanovich, 1979).

15. See William L. Shirer, *The Rise and Fall of the Third Reich* (New York: Simon and Schuster, 1960).

16. See Charles J. Erasmus, *In Search of the Common Good.* (New York: Macmillan, 1977).

17. Quoted in Arnold Beichman, "Karl Marx Goes to College." *Wall Street Journal,* May 14, 1982.

18. Peter F. Drucker, *Adventures of a Bystander* (New York: Harper & Row, 1979), p. 286.

19. Charles A. Reich, *The Greening of America.* (New York: Random House, 1970), p. 18.

CHAPTER 1. THE ENTREPRENEUR

1. Quoted in Leslie Wayne, "A Pioneer Spirit Sweeps Business." *New York Times,* March 25, 1984.

2. Drawn from Horatio Alger, Jr., *Ragged Dick, or Street Life in New York With the Bootblacks.* (Boston: Loring, Publisher, 1868).

3. Budd Schulberg, *What Makes Sammy Run?* (New York, Random House, 1941); Shepherd Mead, *How to Succeed in Business Without Really Trying* (New York: Simon and Schuster, 1952).

4. Drawn from Theodora Kroeber, *The Inland Whale.* (Berkeley: The University of California Press, 1971). See also Alfred Kroeber, *Law of the Yurok Indians.* Proceedings, International Congress of Americanists, #22, vol. 2, 1926. See also R.F. Heizer and M.A. Whipple, editors, *The California Indians.* (Berkeley: University of California Press, 1970).

5. Drawn from Ben R. Finney, "Bigfellow Man Belong Business in New Guinea," *Ethnology* (October 1968). See also Robert J. Gordon, "Nation in the Making," *National Geographic* ((August 1982) and Robert E. Read, *The High Valley* (New York: Scribner, 1965).

6. Drawn from A. Leo Oppenheim, "Seafaring Merchants of Ur," *Journal of the American Oriental Society* (1954), 74: 6–17.

7. Samuel Noah Kramer, *History Begins at Sumer* (Garden City, N.Y.: Doubleday, 1959) pp. 14–15.

8. See Marvin A. Powell, "Sumerian Merchants and the Problem of Profit." *Iraq* (1977), 39: 23–29.

9. Adams, *op. cit.*

10. Drawn from Demosthenes, *On the Crown,* etc., Loeb Library, and J.B. Bury, *et al., The Cambridge Ancient History.* (New York: Macmillan, 1927).

11. Drawn from Virginia Cowles, *The Rothschilds: A Family of Fortune,*

(New York: Knopf, 1973) and Frederic Morton, *The Rothschilds: A Family Portrait*. (New York: Atheneum, 1962).

12. See Yuri Brokhin, *Hustling on Gorky Street* (Translated by E.B. Kane and Yuri Brokhin. Foreword by Professor Andrew R. MacAndrew) (New York: Dial Press, 1975).

13. Drawn from an article in *Time Magazine*, June, 1980, "Living Conveniently on the Left," p. 50. See also *U.S. News and World Report*, "Capitalism in Soviet Georgia," February 27, 1978.

14. Brokhin, *op. cit.*

15. *Ibid.*

16. Joseph Campbell, *Hero With a Thousand Faces*, (Cleveland and New York: World Publishing Co., 1970), p. 3.

17. Quoted in Marshall Fishwick, "The Rise and Fall of Horatio Alger," *Saturday Review*, November 17, 1956, p. 15.

CHAPTER 2. TRADE

1. Adam Smith, *An Inquiry into the Nature and Causes of the Wealth of Nations* (London: W. Strahan and T. Cadell in the Strand, 1776), book 3, chap. 4.

2. *Ibid* vol. 2, book 4, Introduction.

3. From "I dream'd in a dream . . ." Walt Whitman, *Leaves of Grass* (Avon, Conn.: Heritage Press, 1937), p. 118.

4. Plato, *The Republic*, book 6.

5. John and Barbara Hammond, *The Age of the Chartists, 1832–54* (New York: A.M. Kelley, 1967), p. 365.

6. Karl Marx and Frederick Engels, *The Communist Manifesto* (New York: Vanguard Press, 1926), p. 53.

7. Lewis Mumford, *The City in History: Its Origins, Transformations, and Its Prospects*. (New York: Harcourt, Brace & World, Inc., 1961), p. 573.

8. See Paolo Soleri, *Arcology: the City in the Image of Man*. (Cambridge, Mass.: M.I.T. Press, 1969).

9. Paul Goldberger, "Union Carbide's New Corporate Home," *New York Times*, February 20, 1984, pp. B1–2.

10. See Vere Gordon Childe, *Man Makes Himself* (New York: New American Library, 1951).

11. Descriptions of Tell Leilan appear in Harvey Weiss, "The Capital City of a Lost Empire," *Yale Alumni Magazine and Journal* (October 1981) and "History from Bits of Clay," *Journal* (February 1984).

12. Arguments about the origins of civilization are reviewed and pro-

pounded in recent works such as Robert McC. Adams, "The Origin of Cities," *Scientific American* (September 1960), and "Anthropological Perspectives on Ancient Trade," *Current Anthropology* (September 1974); Jeremy A. Sabloff and C.C. Lamberg-Karlovsky, editors, *Ancient Civilization and Trade* (Albuquerque: University of New Mexico Press, 1974) and *The Rise and Fall of Civilizations* (Menlo Park: Cummings Publishing Co., 1974); Ronald Cohen and Elman R. Service, *Origins of the State* (Philadelphia, Publication of the Institute for the Study of Human Issues, 1978); T. Earle and J.E. Ericson, editors, *Exchange Systems in Prehistory* (New York: Academic Press, 1977); Philip L. Kohl, "The Balance of Trade in Southwestern Asia in the Mid-Third Millenium, B.C." *Current Anthropology* (September 1978); Henry T. Wright, "Recent Research on the Origin of the State," *Annual Reviews of Anthropology* (Palo Alto: Annual Reviews, Inc., 1977); Norman Yoffee, "The Decline and Rise of Mesopotamian Civilization: An Ethnoarchaeological Perspective on the Evolution of Social Complexity," *American Antiquity* (January 1979); Karl Polanyi, *et al.*, *Trade and Market in Early Empires* (Glencoe, Illinois: Free Press, 1957).

13. There are many references to salt pilgrimages in the Southwest. See Micha Titiev, *Old Oraibi*, Papers of the Peabody Museum of American Archaeology and Ethnology, vol. 22, #1, 1944.

14. See Bronislaw Malinowski, *Argonauts of the Western Pacific* (New York: E.P. Dutton, 1961).

15. Down-the-Line Trade has been described by Colin Renfrew in "Alternative Models for Exchange and Spacial Distribution," Earle and Erickson, *op. cit.*

16. Leopold Pospisil, *The Kapauku Papuans of West New Guinea*, 2nd ed. (New York: Holt, Rinehart & Winston, 1978), p. 19.

17. *Ibid*, p. 89.

18. Descriptions of Jericho drawn from Kathleen Kenyon, "Excavations at Jericho," *Palestine Exploration Quarterly* (July–December 1960), and "The Neolithic of Western Asia: 1945 to 1975, a Retrospect," *Ancient Europe and the Mediterranean*, Vladimir Markotic, editor, (London: Aries & Phillips, Ltd, 1977); John R. Bartlett, *Jericho* (Guildford, Great Britain: Lutterworth Press, 1982).

19. Quoted in Robert H. Colbean, Michael D. Coe, *et al.*, "Obsidian Trade at San Lorenzo Tenochtitlan, Mexico," *Science*, vol. 74, pp. 666–71.

20. See J.E. Dixon, J.R. Cann, Colin Renfrew, "Obsidian and the Origins of Trade," *Scientific American* (March 1968).

21. See Harriet Crawford, "The Mechanics of the Obsidian Trade: A Suggestion," *Antiquity* (July 1978).

22. Dr. Hole's comment appeared in the discussion portion of Robert McC. Adams, "Anthropological Perspectives on Ancient Trade," *Current Anthropology* (September 1974).

23. See Andrew M.T. Moore, "A Pre-Neolithic Farmer's Village on the Euphrates," *Scientific American* (August 1979).

24. See James Mellaart, *Çatal Hüyük* (New York: McGraw-Hill, 1967).

25. See Pirenne, *op. cit.* and *Medieval Cities,* F.D. Halsey, translator, (Garden City, N.Y.: Doubleday, 1956). See also Richard Hodges, *Dark Age Economics,* (New York: St. Martin's Press, 1982). Hodge refers to numbers of slaves sold on p. 128.

26. Quoted in Fritz Rorig, *The Medieval Town* (Berkeley: University of California Press, 1967) p. 27.

27. Quoted in Oppenheim, *Ancient Mesopotamia,* (Chicago: University of Chicago Press, 1964) p. 121.

28. Samuel Eliot Morison, *The Maritime History of Massachusetts, 1783–1860* (Boston: Houghton Miflin, 1961), p. 18.

29. James E. Vance, Jr., *The Merchant's World: the Geography of Wholesaling* (Englewood Cliffs, N.J.: Prentice-Hall, 1970), p. 10.

30. Bernard Bailyn, *The New England Merchants in the 17th Century* (New York: Harper & Row, 1964), p. 95.

31. Mayor Martinez was interviewed on television on March 29, 1984. The author's thanks to Mr. Gary Braddock of the Mayor's Office for help in recalling dates.

32. See William Robbins, "Cities Going Where the Business Is," *New York Times,* June 24, 1984. Business section.

33. See Maxine Pollack, "Industry Stakes a Claim in Space," *New York Times,* June 24, 1984. Business section.

CHAPTER 3. RECORDS

1. D.H. Trump, *The Prehistory of the Mediterranean* (New Haven: Yale University Press, 1980), p. 63.

2. Daniel Defoe, *The Complete English Tradesman* (London: J. Rivington, 1745), p. 13. vol. 1.

3. *Ibid.,* p. 12

4. *Ibid.,* p. 12

5. A. Leo Oppenheim, *Letters from Mesopotamia* (Chicago: University of Chicago Press, 1967), pp. 74–77.

6. Benjamin R. Foster, "Commercial Activity in Sargonic Mesopotamia," *Iraq* 39, (Spring 1977), p. 41.

7. *Ibid.,* p.42

8. See note 1 above.

9. See John Chadwick, "Life in Mycenaean Greece," *Scientific American* (October 1972). See also M.I. Finley, "The Mycenaean Tablets and Economic History," *Economic History Review,* vol. 10, pp. 128–41, 1957; *The World of Odysseus* (New York: Meridian Books, 1963).

10. See Marcia Ascher and Robert Ascher, *Code of the Quipu* (Ann Arbor: University of Michigan Press, 1981).

11. See Melville Herskovits, *Dahomey: An Ancient West African Kingdom* (Evanston: Northwestern University Press, 1967).

12. Defoe, *op cit,* p. 311, vol. 1.

13. See Denise Schmandt-Besserat, "Earliest Uses of Clay in Syria," *Expedition* (Spring 1977); "The Earliest Precursor of Writing," *Scientific American* (June 1978); "The Envelopes That Bear the First Writing," *Technology and Culture,* 21 (111) 347–85, 1980; "Decipherment of the Earliest Tablets," *Science,* January 16, 1981. See also Joran Friberg, "Numbers and Measures in the Earliest Written Records," *Scientific American* (February 1984).

14. For more on the Indus script, see Walter Fairservis, Jr., "The Script of the Indus Civilization," *Scientific American* (March 1983).

15. For more about early Chinese writing and Shang traders, see K.C. Chang, "Ancient Trade as Economics or as Ecology" in Sabloff and Lamberg-Karlovsky, *op. cit.; Shang Civilization* (New Haven: Yale University Press, 1980); "In Search of China's Beginnings: New Light on an Old Civilization," *American Scientist* (March–April 1981).

16. Hung-Hsiang Chou, "Chinese Oracle Bones," *Scientific American* (April 1979), p. 141.

17. See Marco Polo, *The Adventures of Marco Polo,* edited by Richard J. Walsh (New York: John Day Co., 1948).

18. See Thomas Sowell, *The Economics and Politics of Race* (New York: Morrow, 1983).

19. Pospisil, *op. cit.,* p. 94.

20. Quoted in Vance, *op. cit.,* p. 166

21. Patricia Cline Cohen, *A Calculating People: The Spread of Numeracy in Early America.* (Chicago: University of Chicago Press, 1982), p. 117.

22. Edward Meadows, "Peter Grace Knows 2,478 Ways to Cut the Deficit," *National Review,* March 9, 1984, p. 26.

23. Cohen, *op. cit.,* p. 4.

24. Cited in Frank T. Cary, "Education Is Everybody's Business," *Enterprise* (April 1984), p. 7.

25. Linda Stevens, "She Didn't Know Nothin' and Made a Million," *New York Post,* May 3, 1984.

CHAPTER 4. THE CUSTOMER

1. In a letter to the editor of the *New York Times,* July 22, 1984.

2. Jody Peters, in an interview on "Fast Track for Women," a program aired on CNN Business News, April 16, 1984.

3. Charles Newman Crewdson, *Tales of the Road* (Chicago: Curtis Publishing Co., 1905), p. 15.

4. William H. Baldwin, *Traveling Salesmen: Their Opportunities and Their Dangers,* an Address to the Young Men's Christian Union, November 22, 1874. (Boston: Nathan Sawyer and Son, 1874), p. 10.

5. *Ibid.*, p. 9.

6. *Ibid.*, p. 18.

7. See J.R. Dolan, *The Yankee Peddlers of Early America* (New York: Clarkson N. Potter, Inc., 1964). See also Penrose Scull, "Pack Roads to Yesterday," *American Heritage* (April 1956).

8. Theo W. Landphair, "Today's 'Drummer' Finds It's Drive, Drive, Drive," *National Observer*, Monday, September 2, 1968, p. 18.

9. See Pirenne, *op. cit.*, p. 86.

10. Polo, *op. cit.*, pp. 35, 114, 115, 118.

11. *Ibid.*, 189–90.

12. Ihmed Ibn Fadlan, "Scandinavians on the Volga in 922" reprinted in Alan Dundes, ed., *Every Man His Way* (Englewood Cliffs, N.J.: Prentice-Hall, 1968), p. 17. See Also Eric Oxenstierna, "The Vikings," *Scientific American* (May 1967).

13. *Ibid.*, p. 18.

14. Lewis O. Saum, *The Fur Trader and the Indian* (Seattle: The University of Washington Press, 1965). See also Hiram Martin Chittenden, *The American Fur Trade of the Far West* (New York: F.P. Harper, 1902).

15. George D. Spindler and Louise S. Spindler, "American Indian Personality Types and Their Socio-Cultural Roots," *American Academy of Political and Social Sciences* (May 1957).

16. Saum, *op. cit.*, p. 60

17. *Ibid.*, p. 59.

18. *Ibid.*, p. 171.

19. *Ibid.*, p. 140.

20. *Ibid.*, p. 166.

21. See Calvin Martin, *Keepers of the Game: Indian-Animal Relationship and the Fur Trade* (Berkeley: University of California Press, 1978) and "The War Between Indians and Animals," *Natural History Magazine* (June–July 1978).

22. See Harold E. Driver, *Indians of North America* (Chicago: University of Chicago Press, 1972).

23. Oscar Lewis, *The Effects of White Contact Upon Blackfoot Culture, With Special Reference to the Role of the Fur Trade.* (Seattle: University of Washington Press, 1942).

24. See Kent Flannery, "The Olmec and the Valley of Oaxaca, a Model for Inter-regional Interaction in Formative Times," *Dumbarton Oaks Conference on the Olmec*, Elizabeth P. Benson, ed. (Washington: Dumbarton Oaks Research Library and Collection).

25. *Ibid.*

26. Dr. Coe's comment appeared in the discussion period following Kent Flannery's presentation. Dumbarton Oaks Conference, *op. cit.*, p. 112.

27. See Charles C. DiPeso, "Macaws, Crotals, and Trumpetshells," *Early Man* (Autumn 1980).

28. See Jeremy A. Sabloff and William J. Rathje, "The Rise of a Maya Merchant Class," *Scientific American* (October 1975).

29. *Ibid.*, p. 81.

30. Crewdson, *op. cit.*, p. 35.

31. Drawn from Edward T. Hall and William Foote Whyte, "Intercultural Communications: A Guide to Men of Action," *Human Organization* (Spring 1960).

32. Drawn from David A. Ricks, *Big Business Blunders* (Homewood, Illinois: Dow Jones–Irwin, 1980).

33. See Edward T. Hall and Mildred Reed Hall, 'The Sounds of Silence," reprinted in James P. Spradley and David W. McCurdy, eds., *Conformity and Conflict*, 5th ed. (Boston: Little Brown and Co., 1984).

34. Drawn from Carrie Dolan, "Bytes in the Boonies: Door-to-Door Appeal Sells Apples in Idaho," *Wall Street Journal*, June 14, 1984.

35. Arthur Miller, *Death of a Salesman*, text and criticism. Edited by Gerald Weales (New York: Viking-Penguin, 1977), p. 138.

36. Personal communication from Kirby Lumber Corporation.

37. Landphair, *op. cit.*, p. 18.

CHAPTER 5. THE MARKET

1. Peter F. Drucker, *The Age of Discontinuity* (New York: Harper & Row, 1969), p. 165.

2. Pirenne, *Economic and Social History, op. cit.*, p. 11. See also *Cities, op. cit.* for the revival of trade, fairs, markets.

3. Paul Bohannon, "The Tiv of Nigeria," *Peoples of Africa*, James L. Gibbs, Jr., ed. (New York: Holt, Rinehart & Winston, 1966). See also Paul Bohannon and George Dalton, *Markets in Africa* (Garden City, N.Y.: Doubleday, 1965) and Paul Bohannon, "Place for All Things," *Natural History Magazine* (October 1964).

4. Quoted in William Bascom, *The Yoruba of Southwestern Nigeria* (New York: Holt, Rinehart & Winston, 1969), p. 25.

5. See Bascom, *op. cit.* Also Janheinz Jahn, *Through African Doors*, Oliver Coburn, translator (London: Faber and Faber, Ltd., 1968) and P. C. Lloyd, "The Yoruba of Nigeria" in Gibs, *op. cit.*

6. Defoe, *op. cit*, p. 245.

7. See S.F. Nadel, "Witchcraft in Four African Societies: An Essay in Comparison," *American Anthropologist* (January/March 1952).

8. See Robert LeVine, "Sex Roles and Economic Change in Africa," *Ethnology* (April 1966).

9. See Enid Schildkrout, "Young Traders of Northern Nigeria, *Natural History Magazine* (June 1981).

10. See Susan Keech and Roderick M. McIntosh, "West African Prehis-

tory," *American Scientist* (November/December 1981); "Finding West Africa's Oldest City," *National Geographic* (September 1982); "Forgotten Tells of Mali," *Expedition* (Winter 1983); "Current Directions in West African Prehistory," *Annual Reviews of Anthropology,* vol. 12, 1983.

11. Quoted in E.W. Bovill, *The Golden Trade of the Moors* (London: Oxford University Press, 1968), p. 135.

12. *Ibid.,* p. 149.

13. *Ibid.,* p. 148.

14. Bascom, *op. cit.*

15. See Smith, *op. cit.,* vol. 2, book 4, chap. 8

16. See Robert Nisbet, *Prejudices: A Philosophical Dictionary,* (Cambridge, Harvard University Press, 1982). See also Kevin Phillips, "Old Political Labels No Longer Fit," *Wall Street Journal,* November 27, 1984.

17. Smith, *op. cit.,* vol. 2, book 4, chap. 5

18. *Ibid.*

19. *Ibid.,* vol. 2, book 5, chap. 2.

20. See Philip A.M. Taylor, *The Industrial Revolution in Britain: Triumph or Disaster?* (Boston: D.C. Heath & Co., 1958).

21. Defoe, *op. cit.,* vol. 1, p. 252

22. Marx and Engels, *op. cit.,* p. 38

23. Ibid., p. 65

24. *Ibid.,* p. 47

25. Smith, *op. cit.,* vol. 1, book 1, chap. 2.

26. Karl Marx and Frederick Engels, *Letters to Americans: 1848–1895,* translated by Leonard E. Mins (New York: International Publishers, 1953) Letter to Joseph Weydemeyer, March 5, 1852.

27. Lewis S. Feuer, ed., *Marx and Engels: Basic Writings* (Garden City N.Y.: Doubleday, 1959), Introduction, p. XX.

28. Marx and Engels, *Manifesto, op. cit.,* pp. 35–36.

29. Quoted in Art Pine, "Africa's Poorest: Sub-Saharan Countries Take First Steps to End Economic Nightmare," *Wall Street Journal,* September 16, 1982.

30. James P. Sterba, "Sales Pitch Resounds Again in Shanghai," *New York Times,* August 2, 1981.

31. Victor Fung, "Chinese Snap Up Corporate Shares," *Wall Street Journal,* July 19, 1984. See also Amanda Bennett, "China's Cash Hoard Symbolizes Its Problems," *Wall Street Journal,* July 12, 1984.

32. John F. Burns, "Soviet Study Urges Relaxing of Controls to Revive Economy," *New York Times,* August 5, 1983. Also "Excerpts from Soviet Study on the Need for an Overhaul of the Economy." Same source and date, p. A4.

33. *Ibid.,* p. A4.

34. David Brand, "Free Enterprise Helps to Keep Russians Red But Creates Problems," *Wall Street Journal,* May 2, 1983.

35. John F. Burns, "Marxist Puritans Scowl at Lonely Hearts," *New York Times,* September 2, 1982.

36. This ad appeared in the *New York Times,* July 23, 1984, p. B2.

37. Christopher S. Wren, "Make Us a Match, Chinese Lonely Hearts Ask," *New York Times,* July 30, 1984.

38. See Ernest Dichter, *Handbook of Consumer Motivations* (New York: McGraw-Hill, 1964). See also Chester R. Wasson, *Marketing Management: The Strategy, Tactics, and Art of Competition* (Charlotte, N.C.: ECR Associates, 1983).

39. Discussion with Holmes Brown, July 19, 1984.

40. See Peter F. Drucker, *Managing in Turbulent Times* (New York: Harper & Row, 1980).

41. Marcel Mauss, *The Gift,* Ian Cunnison, translator (Glencoe, Ill.: Free Press, 1954), p.74.

42. John Maynard Keynes, *The General Theory of Employment, Interest, and Money* (London: Macmillan & Co., 1936), p. 155.

43. Blustein, Paul, "Is the Stock Market Really Efficient? Go Ask a Bubba," *Wall Street Journal,* March 15, 1982.

44. See Manning Nash, *Primitive and Peasant Economic Systems* (San Francisco: Chandler Publishing Co., 1966).

45. Karl Polanyi has written most eloquently of the concept of embeddedness. See his *Primitive, Archaic and Modern Economies,* edited by George Dalton (Garden City, N.Y.: Doubleday, 1968) and *Trade and Market in the Early Empires, op. cit.* See also Scott Cook, "The Obsolete Anti-Market Mentality: A Critique of the Substantive Approach to Economic Anthropology," *American Anthropologist,* vol. 66, #2.

CHAPTER 6. MONEY

1. James Boswell, *The Life of Samuel Johnson* (New York: Heritage Press, 1963), vol. 2, p. 141.

2. Herskovits, *op. cit.* and Melville J. and Frances S. Herskovits, *Dahomean Narratives* (Evanston: Northwestern University Press, 1958).

3. See Harold W. Scheffler, "Big Men and Disks of Shell," *Natural History Magazine* (December 1965).

4. Alfred Kroeber, in Heizer and Whipple, *op. cit.,* p. 345.

5. See Heizer and Whipple, *op. cit;* R. F. Heizer, ed., *Handbook of North American Indians,* vol. 8, California (Washington, D.C.: Smithsonian Institution, 1978); Kroeber, *op. cit;* Erik H. Erikson, *Observations on the Yurok* (Berkeley: University of California Press, 1938); Walter Goldschmidt, "The Ethical Prescriptions of Yurok Society," *American Anthropologist,* vol. 53, #4, 1951.

6. See Bruce G. Trigger, ed., *Handbook of North American Indians,* vol.

15, Northeast (Washington D.C.: Smithsonian Institution, 1978) and George R. Hamell, "The Magic of Glass Beads," paper given at a meeting of the Northeastern Anthropological Assn., March 1981.

7. See George Dalton, "Primitive Money," *American Anthropologist*, vol. 67, pp. 44–65; Paul Einzig, *Primitive Money* (Oxford, England: Pergamon Press, 1966); Victor E. Morgan, *A History of Money* (Middlesex, England: Penguin, 1965); Polanyi, *op. cit.;* Friedman, *op. cit.*

8. See Trigger, *op. cit.;* Hamell, *op. cit.*

9. See Heizer, Heizer and Whipple, Kroeber, *op. cit.*

10. See Lorna Marshall, "The !Kung Bushmen of the Kalahari Desert," *Peoples of Africa*, edited by James L. Gibbs (New York: Holt, Rinehart, & Winston, 1966)

11. See Leonard Woolley, *The Beginnings of Civilization*, part 2, vol. 1 of *History of Mankind* (New York: Harper & Row, 1963). See also John A. Wilson, *The Culture of Ancient Egypt* (Chicago: University of Chicago Press, 1951).

12. See E. Adamson Hoebel, *The Cheyennes* (New York: Holt, Rinehart & Winston, 1978). See also G.B. Grinnell, *The Cheyenne Indians: Their History and Ways of Life* (New Haven: Yale University Press, 1923).

13. See Franz Boas, *Ethnology of the Kwakiutl*, Bureau of American Ethnology, 35th Annual Report, 1913. See also Ruth Benedict, *Patterns of Culture* (New York: Houghton Mifflin, 1934); Helen Codere, *Fighting with Property*, Monograph of the American Ethnological Society, Vol. 28, 1950; Irving Goldman, *The Mouth of Heaven* (New York: John Wiley & Sons, 1975).

14. See C.W.M. Hart and Arnold R. Pilling, *The Tiwi of North Australia* (New York: Holt, Rinehart & Winston, 1979). See also A.P. Elkin, *The Australian Aborigines* (Garden City, N.Y.: Doubleday, 1964).

15. See James L. Gibbs, "The Kpelle of Liberia," *Peoples of Africa, op. cit.*

16. Napoleon Chagnon, *Yanomamo: The Fierce People* (New York: Holt, Rinehart & Winston, 1977).

17. Livy, *The History of Early Rome*, translated by Aubrey de Selincourt (New York: Heritage Press, 1960).

18. Woolley, *op. cit.*

19. Einzig, *op. cit.*

20. Herodotus, *op. cit.*

21. See Finley, *The Ancient Economy, op. cit.* and Jean-Phillippe Levy, *The Economic Life of the Ancient World* (Chicago: University of Chicago Press, 1964).

22. Mary Douglas, *Purity and Danger* (New York: Praeger, 1966), p. 69 Polanyi, *op. cit.*, has applied to money the language metaphor.

23. See William Henry Furness, *The Island of Stone Money* (Philadelphia: Lippincott, 1910); Von P. Salesius, *A Contribution to the Knowledge of the Land and Peoples in Our German South Sea Colonies* (Berlin: W. Susserott, 1907); H.G. Barnett, *Being a Palauan* (New York: Holt, Rinehart & Winston, 1979).

24. See Wyman W. Parker, *Connecticut's Colonial and Continental Money,* The American Revolution Bicentennial Commission, Hartford, 1977.

CHAPTER 7. FAMILY AND BUSINESS

1. Quoted in Dan Rottenberg, "All in the Family: The Top Privately Held Companies in America," *Town and Country* (August 1984), p. 124.
2. *Ibid.*, p. 121.
3. Discussion with Gene Scarangella, August 5, 1984.
4. See, for example, George J. Klima, *The Barabaig* (New York: Holt, Rinehart, & Winston, 1970).
5. See Francis L.K. Hsu, *Clan, Caste, and Club* (New York: D. Van Nostrand and Co., 1963). See also Martin C. Yang, *A Chinese Village* (New York: Columbia University Press, 1945).
6. Matsuyu Takizawa, "The Disintegration of the Old Family System," reprinted in *Tribal and Peasant Economies,* edited by George Dalton (Garden City, N.Y.: Doubleday, Natural History Press, 1972), p. 359.
7. Rorig, *op. cit.*, p. 114.
8. See Hosea Ballou Morse, *The Guilds of China* (London: Longmans, Green and Co., 1932).
9. Drawn from Victor Fung, "China Allows the Rebirth of Some Private Corporations," *Wall Street Journal,* August 10, 1984.
10. Oppenheim, *Letters, op. cit.*, p. 74.
11. *Ibid.*, p. 77. See also K. R. Veenhof, *Aspects of Old Assyrian Trade and its Terminology* (Leiden, Holland: E.J. Brill, 1972).
12. William W. Pilcher, *The Portland Longshoremen* (New York: Holt, Rinehart & Winston, 1972), p. 66.
13. Will Durant, *The Age of Faith* (New York: Simon and Schuster, 1950), p. 619. For more about the *Hanse* see Pirenne, *op. cit.* and Rorig, *op. cit.*
14. See George M. Foster, "Peasant Society and the Image of Limited Good," *American Anthropologist,* vol. 67, #2, 1965. See also Jerome Blum, *Our Forgotten Past: Seven Centuries on the Land* (London: Thames and Hudson, 1982). Quote on p. 65.
15. See Brigitte Berger and Peter L. Berger, *The War Over the Family* (New York: Anchor Press–Doubleday, 1983).
16. Defoe, *op. cit.*, p. 84.
17. Peter F. Drucker, "Working Women: Unmaking the 19th Century," *Wall Street Journal,* July 6, 1981.
18. Marx and Engels, *op. cit.*, pp. 48–49.
19. Adolphus J.F. Behrends, *Socialism and Christianity* (New York: Baker and Taylor, 1886), p. 286.

20. See Lewis Henry Morgan, *Ancient Society* (New York: Holt, Rinehart, & Winston, 1877).

21. Frederick Engels, *The Origin of the Family, Private Property, and the State* (New York: International Publishers, 1942), p. 58.

22. William M. Kephart, *Extraordinary Groups* (New York: St. Martin's Press, 1982), p. 102.

23. *Ibid.*, p. 131.

24. Kate Wenner, "How They Keep Them Down on the Farm," *New York Times Magazine*, May 8, 1977, p. 83.

25. Melford E. Spiro, *Kibbutz: Venture in Utopia* (New York: Schocken Books, 1970), p. 60.

26. *Ibid.*, pp. 222–23.

27. Melford E. Spiro, "Is the Family Universal?" *American Anthropologist* (October 1954). *Addendum, 1958* published with original article in the Bobbs-Merrill Series in the Social Sciences, S–276.

28. Spiro, *Kibbutz*, p. 172.

29. Melford E. Spiro, *Children of the Kibbutz* (New York: Schocken Books, 1965), p. 448.

30. Spiro, *op. cit.*, p. 182.

31. In a letter addressed to critics of her earlier article. *The Nation*, April 5, 1980, p. 392.

32. Jean Bethke Elshtain, "Feminists Against the Family," *The Nation*, November 17, 1979, p. 498.

33. Sheila Rowbotham, a British Marxist feminist, quoted by Elshtain in article above, p. 500.

34. See Robert Levering, Milton Moskowitz and Michael Katz, *The 100 Best Companies to Work for in America* (Reading, Mass: Addison Wesley Publishing Company, 1984).

35. See Urie Bronfenbrenner, "The Origins of Alienation," *Scientific American* (August 1974).

36. Defoe, *op. cit.*, vol. 1, p. 116.

37. *Ibid.*, vol. 1, p. 107.

38. Claude Brown, "Manchild in Harlem," *New York Times Magazine*, September 16, 1984, p. 37.

39. See Levering, Moscowitz, and Katz, *op. cit.*

40. Drawn from descriptions in Paul Johnson, *Modern Times* (New York: Harper & Row, 1983) and Peter F. Drucker, *Management* (New York: Harper & Row, 1974).

41. Steve Lohr, "The Japanese Challenge," *New York Times Magazine*, July 8, 1984, p. 23.

42. Benita Eisler, *The Lowell Offering: Writings by New England Mill Women, 1840–1845* (Philadelphia and New York: Lippincott, 1977), p. 15.

43. *Ibid.*, p. 56.

44. *Ibid.*, p. 57.

45. *Ibid.*, p. 57.

46. *Ibid.*, p. 64.

47. *Ibid.*, p. 65.

48. See Robert C. Alberts, "Good Provider," *American Heritage* (February 1972). The story of H. J. Heinz.

49. See Rosabeth Moss Kanter, *Work and Family in the United States* (New York: Russell Sage Foundation, 1977).

50. See Levering, Moskowitz, and Katz, *op. cit.* and Thomas J. Peters and Robert H. Waterman, Jr., *In Search of Excellence* (New York: Harper & Row).

51. Peter F. Drucker, *Concept of the Corporation* (New York: John Day Co., 1946) and *Adventures of a Bystander, op. cit.*

52. See Gene I. Maeroff, "Aid for the Employed," *New York Times,* December 30, 1983 and Robert A. Hamilton, "Businesses Seeking Social Workers," *New York Times,* August 12, 1984.

53. Discussion with Robert Ready, Hewitt Associates, May 21, 1984.

54. Peters and Waterman, *op. cit.*, p. 261.

55. Peter Drucker speaks of "golden fetters" in *Management, op. cit.* and in *Discontinuity, op. cit.* Quote, *Management*, p. 295.

56. Peters and Waterman, *op. cit.*; note, p. 79.

57. Levering, Moskowitz and Katz, *op. cit.*, p. 158.

58. Polanyi, *Economies,* op. cit., p. 70.

59. See note 1 above.

CHAPTER 8. RELIGION AND BUSINESS

1. Pirenne, *Economic and Social History, op. cit.*, p. 14.

2. See Terrence E. Deal and Allan A. Kennedy, *Corporate Cultures* (Reading, Mass.: Addison Wesley, 1982).

3. Drawn from Thomas P. Rohlen, "Spiritual Education in a Japanese Bank," *American Anthropologist* (October 1973).

4. Emile Durkheim, *The Elementary Forms of the Religious Life,* translated by Joseph Ward Swain (New York: Collier Books, 1961), p. 62.

5. Morris E. Opler, "Remuneration to Supernaturals and Man in Apachean Ceremonialism," *Ethnology* (January 1969), p. 371.

6. *Ibid.*, p. 390.

7. See Drucker, *Bystander, op. cit.*

8. See Michael A. Hoffman, *Egypt Before the Pharaohs* (New York: Knopf, 1979) and "Where Nations Began," *Science 83* (October 1983).

9. Engels, *op. cit.*, p. 151.

10. See Powell, *op. cit.*

11. See C. Daryll Forde, chap. 14, *Habitat, Economy and Society* (New York: E.P. Dutton & Co., 1963).

12. See Gibbs, *op. cit.* and Sandra J. Barnes and Paula Ben-Amos, "Benin, Oyo, and Dahomey: Warfare, State Building, and the Sacralization of Iron in West African History," *Expedition* (Winter 1983).

13. See Aristotle, Book 1, chap. 11, *Politics, op. cit.*

14. Smith, *op. cit.*, book 1, chap. 9.

15. John W. Baldwin, "The Medieval Theories of the Just Price," *Transactions of the American Philosophical Society*, vol. 40, pt. 4, pp. 14 and 15. See also J. Gilchrist, *The Church and Economic Activity in the Middle Ages* (London: Macmillan, 1969).

16. Drawn from Pirenne, *City* and *Economic and Social, op. cit.*

17. See Max Weber, *The Protestant Ethic and the Spirit of Capitalism*, translated by Talcott Parsons (London: George Allen & Unwin, 1930). See also S.N. Eisenstadt, ed., *The Protestant Ethic and Modernization: A Comparative View* (New York: Basic Books, 1968); James L. Peacock and A. Thomas Kirsch, *The Human Direction* (New York: Appleton-Century Crofts, 1970); Lewis W. Spitz, *The Reformation: Material or Spiritual* (Boston: D.C. Heath & Co, 1962); R.H. Tawney, *Religion and the Rise of Capitalism* (New York: Harcourt Brace & Co., 1937).

18. Quoted in Weber, *op. cit.*, p. 162.

19. Quoted in Bailyn, *op. cit.*, p. 21.

20. *Ibid.*, p. 140.

21. Quoted in Weber, *op. cit.*, p. 175.

22. Friedrich Engels, "On the History of Early Christianity," *Marx and Engels: Basic Writings*, edited by Lewis S. Feuer (Garden City, N.Y.: Doubleday Anchor, 1959).

23. Michael Walzer, "Puritanism as a Revolutionary Ideology," in S.N. Eisenstadt, ed., *The Protestant Ethic and Modernization* (New York: Basic Books, 1968) p. 127.

24. Washington Gladden, *Applied Christianity: Moral Aspects of Social Questions* (Boston and New York: Houghton, Mifflin Co., 1886), p. 14.

25. *Ibid.*, p. 101.

26. See Ronald Fernandez, *Excess Profits* (Reading, Mass.: Addison-Wesley, 1983), p. 1.

27. Drucker, *Concept, op. cit.*, p. 231.

28. Although much has been written about pension funds, Peter Drucker was probably the first to examine the economic, social, and political impacts of pension funds in *The Unseen Revolution: How Pension Fund Socialism Came to America* (New York: Harper & Row, 1976). See also *Managing in Turbulent Times* (New York: Harper & Row, 1980) in which he says "These employee pension funds are the only large owners, the only ones that fit the traditional definition of 'capitalist'." (p. 182).

29. Levering, Moskowitz and Katz, *op. cit.*, p. 103.

30. Discussion with Kevin Gilmartin, September 11, 1984.

31. Poll taken for Junior Achievement by the Robert Johnston Company, New York. Also synthesis of 18 studies for youth and value oriented clients 1954–1980. Also poll undertaken for Boy Scouts of America by Opinion Research Corporation, Princeton, N.J., excerpted and released by Exploring of BSA, 1977.

32. Drucker, *Turbulent, op. cit.*, p. 136.

33. Graef S. Crystal, "Congress Thinks It Knows Best About Executive Compensation," *Wall Street Journal*, July 30, 1984.

34. See Christopher Wren, "Free Enterprise in China: The Unbroken Shackles," *New York Times*, September 15, 1984.

35. Excerpts were culled from daily reports of the U.S. government's Foreign Broadcast Information Service and appeared in "Listening In," a regular feature of the journal *Worldview* (August 1984).

36. See Everett Carll Ladd and G. Donald Ferree, Jr., "The Politics of American Theology Faculty," *This World* (Summer 1982).

37. "Charity Gains Even As Times Get Tough," *U.S. News and World Report*, April 19, 1982. Includes figures released for 1981 by American Association of Fund-Raising Counsel, Inc. in New York.

38. See Tawney, *op. cit.*

39. See Eugene Kennedy, "America's Activist Bishops: Examining Capitalism," *New York Times Magazine*, August 12, 1984.

40. *Ibid.*, pp. 25–26.

41. Letters in response to Professor Kennedy's article published in the *New York Times Magazine*, September 23, 1984.

42. Lay Commission on Catholic Social Teaching and the U.S. Economy, *Toward the Future: A Lay Letter*, 1984, p. 19.

43. See Tawney, *op. cit.*

44. Bishops' Pastoral, *Catholic Social Teaching and the U.S. Economy*, NC Documentary Service, November 15, 1984, p. 354.

45. *Ibid.*, p. 364.

46. *Ibid.*, p. 356.

47. See E.J. Dionne, Jr., "Pope Calls for Governments to Finance Church Schools," and "The Pope Condemns Imperialist Monopoly," *New York Times*, September 13 and 18, 1984.

48. Smith, *op. cit.*, book 4, chap. 2.

49. Drawn from Earl C. Gottschalk, Jr., "The Reverend Terry Has a Gospel to Cheer the Me Generation," *Wall Street Journal*, August 23, 1984.

CHAPTER 9. BUSINESS AND POLITICS

1. Rene Dubos, *Celebrations of Life* (New York: McGraw-Hill, 1981), p. 113.

NOTES

2. Drawn from Fritz Jules Roethlisberger and William John Dickson, *Management and the Worker* (Cambridge: Harvard University Press, 1939).

3. Audrey Freedman, "Japanese Management of U.S. Work Forces," *Conference Board, Inc.*, New York, 1982.

4. See Levering, Moskowitz, and Katz, *op. cit.* See also David W. Ewing, "Due Process: Will Business Default?" *Harvard Business Review* (November/December 1982).

5. Ewing, *ibid.*, p. 118.

6. Quoted in the Pitney Bowes packet "The Council of Personnel Relations." See also Ewing, *op. cit.*, and Levering, Moskowitz, and Katz, *op. cit.*

7. Peter F. Drucker, "The Job as Property Right," *Wall Street Journal*, March 4, 1980.

8. Smith, *op. cit.*, book 1, chap. 8.

9. See Paolo Matthiae, *Ebla*, translated by Christopher Holme (New York: Doubleday, 1980).

10. See Giovanni Pettinato, *The Archives of Ebla* (New York: Doubleday, 1981).

11. Ezekiel 27:1–16.

12. Aristotle, *Politics*, book 2, chap. 11.

13. Quoted in Will Durant, *Caesar and Christ* (New York: Simon and Schuster, 1944), p. 41.

14. See John Julius Norwich, *A History of Venice* (New York: Knopf, 1982).

15. M. P. Charlesworth, *Trade Routes and Commerce of the Roman Empire*, 2nd ed. (London: Cambridge University Press, 1926), p. 98.

16. Oppenheim, *Mesopotamia, op. cit.*, p. 122.

17. Pirenne, *Cities, op. cit.*, p. 123.

18. Will Durant, *The Age of Faith* (New York: Simon and Schuster, 1950), p. 374.

19. Morris Bishop, "The Knights Templar," *Horizon* (Autumn 1973).

20. Marshall Davidson, "How Jacques Coeur Made His Fortune," *Horizon* (Winter 1976), p. 83.

21. Dumas Malone, *The Declaration of Independence* (London: Oxford University Press, 1954).

22. Smith, *op. cit.*, book 5, chap. 3.

23. *Ibid.*, book 4, chap. 8, pt. 3, p. 582.

24. See Bailyn, *op. cit.*

25. Alexis de Tocqueville, *Democracy in America*, translated by Henry Reeve (New York: Colonial Press, 1900), vol. 2, book 3, chap. 21.

26. Drawn from Chagnon, *op. cit.*

27. See Bernardino de Sahagun, *op. cit.*

28. Sir Percival Griffiths, *The British Impact on India* (New York: Archon Books, 1965), p. 57. See also Michael Edwardes, *British India* (New York: Taplinger Publishing Co., 1967).

29. Smith, *op. cit.*, book 5, chap. 2, pt. 1.

30. De Tocqueville, *op. cit.*, vol. 1, chap. 16.

31. John Maynard Keynes, Letter to President Roosevelt. F.D.R. Library, Hyde Park, New York.

32. Joseph Schumpeter, *Capitalism, Socialism, and Democracy* (New York: Harper & Row, 1950), p.138.

33. Lewis Galantiere quoted in Max Lerner, *America as a Civilization* (New York: Simon and Schuster, 1957), p. 348.

34. See Drucker, *Management, op. cit.*, p. 355. It is important to note that a number of scholars take a somewhat different view. Milton and Rose Friedman, *op. cit.*, p. XVIII, emphasize Jefferson's vision of government-as-umpire and Hamilton's tariff protectionism.

35. De Tocqueville, *op. cit.*, vol. 1, chap. 10.

36. See Schumpeter, *op. cit.*

37. Quoted in Ripley Hitchcock, editor, *Morals in Modern Business*. Lectures in the Page Lecture Series at Yale University. Published by Yale University Press, New Haven, 1909.

38. Smith, *op. cit.*, vol. 2, book 4, chap. 8.

39. *Ibid.*, vol. 2, book 4, Introduction.

40. See Jeffrey Schmalz, "On the Management Frontier at Yale," *New York Times*, March 18, 1984.

41. Gale Tollin, "St. Paul Tests 'Profit Centers'," *Sunday Post*, Bridgeport, Connecticut, September 30, 1984 (AP release).

42. Daniel Q. Haney, "Chains Make a Profit, Change Ways Hospitals Operate," *Sunday Post*, Bridgeport, May 13, 1984 (AP release). See also D'Vera Cohn, " 'Circus' Enlarges Medibucks Debate," *New Haven Register*, Sunday, December 16, 1984 (UP release); Lawrence K. Altman, "Health Care as Business," *New York Times*, November 27, 1984.

43. See Philip E. Fixler, Jr., "Behind Bars We Find an Enterprise Zone," *Wall Street Journal*, November 29, 1984. Descriptions of prisons and courts for profit was aired during the spring of 1984 on Public Broadcasting Service program, "Enterprise."

44. See John McPhee, *La Place de la Concorde Suisse* (New York: Farrar, Straus & Giroux, 1984).

45. Thomas Sowell, "Non-causes, Non-cures," *Policy Review* (Summer 1981).

46. See Charles A. Murray, "The Poverty War: Great Society vs. Trickle-Down," *Wall Street Journal*, March 25, 1982.

47. Cited in *"South African Embarrassment,"* *Review and Outlook*, *Wall Street Journal*, September 28, 1984.

48. Steve Mufson, "Why South Africa's White Businessmen Oppose Apartheid: It's Good for Business," *Wall Street Journal*, January 18, 1985.

49. Mangosuthu G. Buthelezi, "Disinvestment is Anti-Black," *Wall Street Journal*, February 20, 1985.

50. See Johnson, *op. cit.*, and Drucker, *Turbulent, op. cit.*
51. Personal communication from Dr. Vlahos.
52. See Drucker, *Turbulent, op. cit.* See also Ralph E. Winter, "Making Machine Tools Increasingly Requires Ties to Foreign Firms," *Wall Street Journal,* September 4, 1984; Clyde Farnsworth, "Haiti's Allure for U.S. Business," *New York Times,* June 17, 1984.
53. See Drucker, *Turbulent, op. cit.*
54. Drawn from Surajit Sinha, "Religion in an Affluent Society," *Current Anthropology,* vol. 7, #2, 1966.
55. Many specialists have sounded themes which suggested this treatment. Among them are Thomas Sowell, Robert Nisbet, Peter F. Drucker, Irving Kristol, George Gilder, Joseph Schumpeter, Adam Smith, and Milton Friedman.
56. Smith, *op. cit.*, book 1, chap. 8.
57. De Tocqueville, *Democracy,* vol. 1, chap. 17.

CHAPTER 10. CLASSES, MASSES, AND BUSINESS

1. Discussion August 5, 1985.
2. See Donald Woutat, "Detroit Auto Makers Try to Increase Sales to Young Professionals," *Wall Street Journal,* September 27, 1984.
3. See Mervyn Matthews, *Privilege in the Soviet Union* (London: George Allen and Unwin, 1978).
4. Marx and Engels, *op. cit.*, pp. 31 and 42.
5. Max Weber, *Economy and Society,* G. Ross and C. Willich, eds. (Berkeley: University of California Press, 1978).
6. Deena and Michael Weinstein, *Roles of Man* (Hinsdale, Ill.: Dryden Press, 1972), p. 70.
7. Aristotle, *Politics,* book 4, chap. 11.
8. Drawn from Thomas Sowell, *The Economics and Politics of Race* (New York: Morrow, 1983). Quote p. 29.
9. See Sylvia L. Thrupp, *The Merchant Class of Medieval London: 1300–1500* (Ann Arbor: University of Michigan Press, 1962).
10. Defoe, *op. cit.*, vol. 1, p. 30.
11. *Ibid.*, p. 67.
12. *Ibid.*, p. 225.
13. *Ibid.*, p. 225.
14. *Ibid.*, p. 226.
15. *Ibid.*, p. 246.
16. *Ibid.*, p. 241.
17. De Tocqueville, *op. cit.*, vol. 2, book 3, chap. 20.
18. *Ibid.*, vol. 2, book 3, chap. 2.
19. *Ibid.*, vol. 2, book 3, chap. 3.

20. *Ibid.*, vol. 2, book 3, chap. 13.

21. Michael Van Notten, "Free Market Ideas Sprout in Brussels," *Wall Street Journal,* February 29, 1984.

22. William C. Levin, *Sociological Ideas* (Belmont, California: Wadsworth Publishing Co., 1984).

23. Paul Fussell, *Class: A Guide Through the American Status System* (New York: Summit Books, 1983).

24. Schumpeter, *op. cit.*, p. 146. Also *Social Classes*, Heinz Norden, translator (New York: Augustus M. Kelley, Inc., 1951).

25. Tom Wolfe, interviewed by Ron Reagan in *Geo* (October 1983), pp. 14–26; and "The Worship of Art," *Harper's* (October 1984).

26. See Diane Ravitch, "The Shameful Treatment of Mrs. Kirkpatrick," *Wall Street Journal,* March 10, 1983.

27. These have been alluded to by Robert Nisbet, *op. cit.*; Irving Kristol, "Whatever Happened to Common Sense?" *Wall Street Journal,* January 17, 1984, and "Most Economists Ignore Reality," *Wall Street Journal,* July 16, 1984; Jan van Houten, "Why Intellectuals Abroad Love to Hate America," *Wall Street Journal,* August 3, 1983. See also P.T. Bauer, "Why Conservatives Govern in Name Only," *Wall Street Journal,* March 29, 1983. Also Tom Wolfe.

28. Berger, *op. cit.* and Irving Kristol, *Reflections of a Neoconservative* (New York: Basic Books, 1983).

29. Berger, *op. cit.*, p. 38.

30. See John Kenneth Galbraith, *The Affluent Society* (New York: Houghton Mifflin Co., 1958).

31. Kristol, *op. cit.*, p. 216.

32. Plato, *The Republic.*

33. Quoted in Ronald C. Federico and Janet S. Schwartz, *Sociology,* 3rd ed. (Reading, Mass.: Addison-Wesley Publishing Co., 1983), pp. 359–60.

34. Sven Rydenfelt, "Today's Sweden Looks to the Entrepreneurs," *Wall Street Journal,* December 5, 1984.

35. Roland P. Huntford, *The New Totalitarians* (Briarcliff Manor, New York: Stein and Day, 1980), p. 81.

36. *Ibid.*, p. 92.

37. Drawn from Bernard Weinraub, "Ingmar Bergman's Taxes: Swedes Brood Over the Case," *New York Times,* March 16, 1976, and "Bergman Tax Case Dropped in Sweden," *New York Times,* March 25, 1976.

38. Rydenfelt, *op. cit.*

39. Huntford, *op. cit.*, p. 210.

40. *Ibid.*, p. 215.

41. *Ibid.*, p. 233.

42. *Ibid.*, p. 234.

43. *Ibid.*, p. 249.

44. *Ibid.*, p. 224.

45. George M. Foster, "The Anatomy of Envy: A Study in Symbolic Behavior," *Current Anthropology* (April 1972).

46. De Tocqueville, *op. cit.*, footnote, vol. 3, book 3, chap. 26.

47. *Ibid.*, vol. 2, book 4, chap. 6, p. 318.

48. "Results of College Board Poll" as reported by psychologist David G. Meyers in *Psychology Today* (May 1980).

49. De Tocqueville, *op. cit.*, vol. 1, book 1, chap. 15.

50. See "Adam Smith," "If 'Smokestack America' Shrinks, Can Psychology Cure the Depression?" *Esquire* (April 1984). See also Thomas J. Raleigh, "Adapting to a Union-Free Environment," *Wall Street Journal*, October 22, 1984.

51. William H. Whyte, Jr., *The Organization Man* (New York: Simon and Shuster, 1956).

52. See J. Patrick Wright, *On a Clear Day You Can See General Motors* (Grosse Pointe, Michigan: Wright Enterprises, 1979).

53. See Landon Y. Jones, *Great Expectations* (New York: Random House, 1980); Jerome Lettvin, "You Can't Even Step In the Same River Once," *Natural History Magazine* (October 1967); Theodore Roszak, *The Making of a Counter Culture* (New York: Doubleday & Co., 1969); Charles Frankel, "The Nature and Sources of Irrationalism," *Science*, June 1, 1973; Paul Johnson, "The Lost Ideals of Youth," *New York Times Magazine*, March 25, 1984.

54. See Jordan D. Lewis, "Technology, Enterprise, and American Economic Growth," *Science*, March 5, 1982.

55. See Peters and Waterman, *op. cit.*

56. Peter F. Drucker, "Why America's Got So Many Jobs," *Wall Street Journal*, January 24, 1984, and "Executives are 'Aging' at 42," *Wall Street Journal*, March 7, 1984.

57. Personal communication, Melissa Vlahos, vice president, The Physical Image, Inc.

58. Discussion with Nancy Stamas, November 23, 1984.

59. Discussion with Eric Berg, November 28, 1984.

60. "Canada's New Capitalists" in *World Press Review* (July 1982). See also Leslie Wayne, "A Pioneer Spirit Sweeps Business," *New York Times*, March 25, 1984.

61. John Kenneth Galbraith, "The Heartless Society," *New York Times Magazine*, September 2, 1984.

62. Quoted in Moritz Tiling, *The German Element in Texas from 1820–1850* (Houston, Texas: Moritz Tiling, 1913), p. 14.

63. Personal recollections and *Houston (Texas) Chronicle*, May 26, 1926.

64. Interview with Henry Klein, March 8, 1985.

65. Drawn from Kevin P. Helliker, "Chinatowns Sprout In and Near Houston With a Texas Flavor," *Wall Street Journal*, February 18, 1983.

66. Discussion with Gene Scarangella, August, 1984.

CHAPTER 11. THE CASE AGAINST BUSINESS

1. Cited in Thomas J. Lueck, "Crisis Management at Carbide," *New York Times,* December 14, 1984.

2. Baldwin, *op. cit.,* p. 15.

3. Drawn from Pospisil, *op. cit.* Quotation on p. 63.

4. Wayne Andrews, *The Vanderbilt Legend* (New York: Harcourt Brace & Co., 1941), pp. 45–46.

5. *Ibid.,* p. 63.

6. Lucy Kavaler, *The Astors* (New York: Dodd Mead & Co., 1966), p. 37.

7. *Ibid.,* pp. 25, 27, 31.

8. *Ibid.,* p. 35.

9. Drawn from George J. Klima, *The Barabaig* (New York: Holt, Rinehart & Winston, 1970).

10. See David L. Yermack, "After Years on Case, Those Pursuing Vesco Still Make a Career of It," *Wall Street Journal,* September 13, 1984.

11. *Ibid.,* p. 1.

12. Edward W. Page, "Morals of Trade in the Making," Hitchcock, ed., *Morals in Modern Business, op. cit.,* p. 4.

13. Samuel Noah Kramer, *History Begins at Sumer* (New York: Doubleday & Co., 1959), p. 106.

14. See Ann Mackay-Smith, "Some Youths Who Hit Road to Sell Magazines Come Back Embittered," *Wall Street Journal,* September 17, 1984.

15. *Ibid.,* pp. 1 and 13.

16. Milton and Rose Friedman speak of this in chap. 1 of *Free to Choose, op. cit.*

17. George N. Alger, "Production" in Hitchcock, *op. cit.,* p. 28.

18. *Ibid.,* p. 23.

19. Page, *op. cit.,* p. 3.

20. See Mark Dowie, "Pinto Madness," *Mother Jones* (September/October 1977).

21. Holmes Brown, personal communication.

22. See Bradford Snell, "American Ground Transport," Jerome H. Skolnick and Elliott Currie, *Crisis in American Institutions* (Boston: Little Brown, 1985). See also Drucker, *Management, op. cit.*

23. Irwin Ross, "How Lawless Are Big Companies?" *Fortune,* December 1, 1980, p. 58.

24. Stuart Diamond, "Corporations Forced to Reassess Risks and Review Safety Rules," *New York Times,* December 16, 1984, p. 18. See also Philip M. Boffey, "Modern Pesticides Aid in Insuring More Food for Poorest Countries," *New York Times,* December 16, 1984; Francine Schwadel, "Bhopal Disaster Fails to Unnerve Workers Making

Deadly Gases," *Wall Street Journal,* January 28, 1985; Robert Reinhold, "Disaster in Bhopal: Where Does Blame Lie?" *New York Times,* January 31, 1985.

25. Tamar Lewin, "Business Ethics New Appeal," *New York Times,* December 11, 1983, p. 4F.

26. Defoe, *op. cit.,* vol. 2, p. 111.

27. Ross, *op. cit.,* p. 62.

28. Smith, *op. cit.,* vol. 2, book 4, chap. 3.

29. George C.S. Benson, *Business Ethics in America* (Lexington, Mass.: Lexington Books, 1982), p. 154.

30. Pirenne, *Economic and Social History, op. cit.,* p. 206.

31. See Thrupp, *op. cit.*

32. See Pirenne, *op. cit.*

33. Bill Keller, "Unions Battle Against Jobs in the Home," *New York Times,* May 20, 1984. Quote on p. 32. See also his article, "Of Hearth and Home and the Right to Work," *New York Times,* November 11, 1984.

34. *Ibid.* See also Marilyn Webb, "The Rise in Industrial Homework," *The Village Voice,* February 10–16, 1982.

35. See Sowell, *op. cit.*

36. James McKeen, "Corporations and Other Trusts," in Hitchcock, *op. cit.,* p. 148.

37. Peter F. Drucker, "Saving the Crusade," *Toward the Next Economics and Other Essays* (New York: Harper & Row, 1981).

38. Daniel R. Fusfeld, "The Rise of the Corporate State in America," *Journal of Economic Issues* (March 1972). Reprinted as Warner Modular Publication #102, pp. 1 and 19.

39. James C. Knowles, "The Rockefeller Financial Group," a Warner Modular Publication, #343, 1973, p. 53.

40. See "Big Is Powerless" in Review and Outlook, *Wall Street Journal,* November 18, 1981.

41. See Levering, Moskowitz, and Katz, *op. cit.*

42. See Iver Peterson, "Making Big Business a Threat It Can't Refuse," *New York Times,* December 2, 1984.

43. Drawn from Martin E. Marty, "Satanism: No Soap," *Across the Board,* December, 1982, and Jolie B. Solomon, "Procter & Gamble Fights New Rumors of Link to Satanism," *Wall Street Journal,* November 8, 1984.

44. De Tocqueville, *op. cit.,* vol. 2, book 2, chap. 4.

45. Samuel Eliot Morison, *The Oxford History of the American People* (New York: Oxford University Press, 1965), p. 762.

46. Drawn from Irving Goldman, *The Mouth of Heaven: An Introduction to Kwakiutl Thought* (New York: John Wiley & Sons, 1975). Quotes p. 172. See also Codere, *op. cit.,* who originated the phrase, "fighting with property." See Boas, *op. cit.*

47. Drawn from Ann Crittenden, "The Age of 'Me-First' Management," *New York Times,* August 19, 1984.

48. *Ibid.,* p. F13.

49. Kendall J. Wills, "A Twist in the Merger," *New York Times,* June 17, 1984.

50. Quoted in Crittenden, *op. cit.,* p. F13.

51. Irving Kristol, "Dilemma of the Outside Director," *Wall Street Journal,* September 11, 1984.

52. Peter F. Drucker, "Taming the Corporate Takeover," *Wall Street Journal,* October 30, 1984.

53. Michael Blumstein, "Executives Being Challenged on Salaries and Self-Interest," *New York Times,* May 8, 1984.

54. Benjamin Stein, "The Video Generation Gives Business Low Ratings," *Wall Street Journal,* April 1, 1983.

55. Linda and Robert Lichter, "Prime Time Crime: Who and Why?" *Wall Street Journal,* January 6, 1984.

56. Holmes M. Brown, "How TV Reported the Recovery," *Wall Street Journal,* March 6, 1984.

57. Marie Torre, "Labor Looks at Television—and Vice Versa," *Television Quarterly,* vol. 12, #11, p. 31.

58. Page in Hitchcock, *op. cit.,* pp. 5–6.

59. De Tocqueville, *op. cit.,* vol. 1, chap. 11.

60. *Ibid.,* vol. 1, chap. 11.

61. Arthur Unger, "Television's Search for the Last Taboo," *Television Quarterly,* vol. 12, #11, p. 11.

62. The Robert Johnson Co., Inc., "Growth Strategies for Junior Achievement, Based on a Study of the Teen Environment, 1979–1980" (New York), p. 15.

63. Benson, *op. cit.*

64. See Trish Hall, "Americans Drink Less, and Makers of Alcohol Feel a Little Woozy," *Wall Street Journal,* March 14, 1984.

65. Robert Redfield, *The Primitive World and Its Transformations* (Ithaca: Cornell University Press, 1953), p. 157.

CHAPTER 12. ON THE OTHER HAND

1. Discussion with Dr. Dibner, December 2, 1984.

2. Andrew Strathern, "The Entrepreneurial Model of Social Change: From Norway to New Guinea," *Ethnology* (October 1972), p. 378.

3. Benson, *op. cit.,* p. 90.

4. Drucker, *Bystander, op. cit.,* pp. 292–93.

5. Kathleen Brady, *Ida Tarbell: Portrait of a Muckraker* (New York: Seaview/Putnam, 1984), p. 140.

6. *Ibid.*, p. 139.

7. *Ibid.*, p. 123.

8. Ida Minerva Tarbell, *New Ideals in Business* (New York: Macmillan Co., 1917), p. 1.

9. *Ibid.*, pp. 2–3.

10. *Ibid.*, p. 3.

11. *Ibid.*, p. 47.

12. *Ibid.*, p. 300.

13. *Ibid.*, p. 45.

14. *Ibid.*, p. 49.

15. *Ibid.*, p. 45.

16. *Ibid.*, p. 40.

17. Research and Policy Committee, *Transnational Corporations and Developing Countries: New Policies for a Changing World Economy* (New York: Committee for Economic Development, 1981), p. 88.

18. *Ibid.*, p. 88.

19. See Lindley H. Clark, Jr., "How to Get the Message to People in Washington," *Wall Street Journal*, April 3, 1984.

20. Discussion with Eleanor Rudolph, December 1984. See also "Changing the Way America Thinks About Business." Annual Report, 1982–1983, Junior Achievement, Inc.

21. Discussion with Holmes Brown, November 1984. See also Janet E. Wright and John A. Seeley, "A Comparison of Applied Economics With Regular Economics," Formative Evaluation Research Associates (September 1984).

22. See "How Business is Joining the Fight Against Functional Illiteracy," *Business Week*, April 16, 1984, p. 94.

23. "Growing Ties to Schools Seen as Aid to Business and Youth," *New York Times*, October 28, 1984, p. 34.

24. *Ibid.*, p. 34.

25. Discussion with Julianne Grace, December 17, 1984.

26. Smith, *op. cit.*, vol. 1, book 1, chap. 10, pt. 1.

27. "Corporate Sponsors Gird for the Social Whirl," *New York Times*, July 15, 1984. See also H. Joachim Maitre, "The Olympics Along U.N. Lines?" *Wall Street Journal*, August 10, 1984. See full page ad, *The Journal*, July 30, 1984, in which the Los Angeles Organizing Committee thanks its business partners.

28. See Lynn Asinof, "Big Companies Affect the Arts," *Wall Street Journal*, April 24, 1984, p. B1.

29. Martin Gottlieb, "Equitable Life Will Mix Art and Commerce," *New York Times*, September 21, 1984.

30. Martin Mayer, "The Big Business of Grand Opera," *Fortune*, October 17, 1983, p. 160.

31. Kathleen Teltsch, "Corporate Aid Helping Twin Cities to Thrive," *New York Times*, July 27, 1981.

32. Rottenberg, *op. cit.*

33. "Lila Wallace, a Philanthropist with Magazine Fortune, Dies," *New York Times*, May 9, 1984.

34. Fox Butterfield, "Chinese Immigrant Emerges as Boston's Top Benefactor," *New York Times*, April 5, 1984. See also David Wessel, "In a Volatile Industry, Wang Laboratories is Consistent but Flexible," *Wall Street Journal*, November 6, 1984. And Geraldine Brooks, "Old New England City Heals Itself; Can One in Midwest Do So Too?" *Wall Street Journal*, February 1, 1985.

35. An announcement appearing in *Academe* (November-December 1983).

36. Andrew Carnegie, *The Gospel of Wealth and Other Timely Essays*, (Cambridge: Belknap Press of Harvard University Press, 1962), p. 39.

37. Discussion with Dr. Bern Dibner, December 2, 1984.

38. Carnegie, *op. cit.*

39. Publications of The Foundation Center, 79 Fifth Ave., New York, N.Y. 10003.

40. G.F. Young, *The Medici* (New York: Modern Library, 1933), pp. 5 and 8.

41. Smith, *op. cit.*, vol. 2, book 5, chap. 2, pt. 1.

42. Lucius Beebe, "Richesse Oblige," *Horizon* (November 1958), p. 148.

43. John Kenneth Galbraith, "The Muse and the Economy," *Horizon* (September 1960), p. 37.

44. John Kenneth Galbraith, "Corporate Man," *New York Times Magazine*, January 22, 1984 ("About Men" section).

45. Defoe, *op. cit.*, vol. 1, p. 33.

46. Carnegie, *op. cit.*, pp. 48–49.

47. Excerpts from the text of a statement submitted to the Senate Rules Committee by Vice-President Designate Nelson A. Rockefeller, September 24, 1974, *New York Times*.

48. See Jerome S. Rubin, "Art and Taxes," *Horizon* (Winter, 1966).

49. Durant, *Greece, op. cit.*, p. 466. See also Finley, *Ancient Economy, op. cit.*

50. Erasmus, *op. cit.*, p. 71.

51. Drawn from Evon Z. Vogt, *The Zinacantecos of Mexico* (New York: Holt, Rinehart & Winston, 1970).

52. "Fortune cookie: China has its first millionaire," Knight-Ridder News Service. Appeared in the Springfield (Ohio) *News and Sun*, November 21, 1984.

53. See Note 34, chap. 8.

54. De Tocqueville, *op. cit.*, vol. 2, book 3, chap. 18.

EPILOGUE. THE BUSINESS OF AMERICA

1. Defoe, *op. cit.*, vol. 1, p. 33.
2. Discussion with Julianne Grace, December 17, 1984.
3. Herbert Mitgang, "Stage: 'Tender Offer,' a Corporate Comedy." A review in *New York Times*, September 16, 1984.
4. Vance, *op. cit.*, p. 62.
5. John Kenneth Galbraith, "The Heartless Society," *New York Times Magazine*, September 2, 1984, p. 44.
6. Terrence E. Deal and Allan A. Kennedy, *Corporate Cultures* (Reading, Mass.: Addison Wesley, 1982); William Ouchi, *Theory Z* (Reading, Mass.: Addison Wesley, 1981); Richard Tanner Pascale and Anthony G. Athos, *The Art of Japanese Management* (New York: Simon and Schuster, 1981); Thomas J. Peters and Robert H. Waterman, Jr., *In Search of Excellence* (New York: Harper & Row, 1982).
7. Schumpeter, *op. cit.*, p. 133.
8. *Ibid.*, pp. 211 and 156.
9. John Roderick, "China Revisited," *Sunday Post* (Bridgeport, Conn.), November 25, 1984 (AP release). See also Amanda Bennett and James P. Sterba, "Peking Turns Sharply Down Capitalist Road," *Wall Street Journal*, October 25, 1985. See also Christopher S. Wren, "Improving Quality of Life is First Priority in Peking," *New York Times*, December 16, 1984.
10. Amanda Bennett, "In Today's New China Red Guards of the 60's Are a Lost Generation," *Wall Street Journal*, January 4, 1985, pp. 1 and 6.
11. Rosabeth Moss Kanter, *The Change Masters* (New York: Simon and Schuster, 1983), pp. 364–365.
12. See Conrad M. Arensberg and Arthur H. Niehoff, *Introducing Social Change* (2nd ed.) (Chicago: Aldine-Atherton, 1971); Cora Du Bois, "The Dominant Value Profile of American Culture," M. Lantis, ed., *The U.S.A. As Anthropologists See It, American Anthropologist*, 57: 1232–39; Lucy R. Garretson, *American Culture: An Anthropological Perspective* (Dubuque, Iowa: William C. Brown Co., 1976); John P. Gillin, "National and Regional Cultural Values in the United States," *Social Forces* 34: 107–13; Francis L.K. Hsu, *Americans and Chinese* (New York: Henry Schuman, Inc., 1953); George D. Spindler and Louise S. Spindler, "Anthropologists View American Culture," *Annual Review of Anthropology*, vol. 12 (Palo Alto, Cal.: Annual Reviews, Inc., 1983).
13. De Tocqueville, *op. cit.*, vol. 2, book 1, chap. 9.
14. *Ibid.*, vol. 2, book 2, chap. 4.
15. *Ibid.*, vol. 1, chap. 18 ("Some Considerations on the Causes of the Commercial Prosperity of the United States").
16. *Ibid.*

17. *Ibid.*, vol. 2, book 1, chap. 8.

18. *Ibid.*, vol. 1, chap. 18.

19. Brett Duval Fromson, "Reaganomics Lure for the Yuppies," *New York Times,* October 2, 1984. See also Herb Gold, "Zen and the Art of Counter Cultural Business," *Wall Street Journal,* February 25, 1983.

20. Grahame Clark, "Archaeology and Human Diversity," *Annual Review of Anthropology,* vol. 8 (Palo Alto, Cal.: Annual Reviews, Inc., 1983), p. 15.

21. Marvin Harris, "Why It's Not the Same Old America," *Psychology Today* (August 1981).

22. Rydenfelt, *op. cit.*

SELECTED BIBLIOGRAPHY

Adams, Robert McC. "Anthropological Perspectives on Ancient Trade." *Current Anthropology*, Vol. 15, #3, September, 1974.

Arensberg, Conrad M. and Arthur H. Niehoff. *Introducing Social Change*, Second edition. Chicago: Aldine-Atherton, 1971.

Bailyn, Bernard. *The New England Merchants in the Seventeenth Century*. New York: Harper & Row, 1964.

Baldwin, John W. "The Medieval Theories of the Just Price." *Transactions of the American Philosophical Society*, Vol. 40, Part 4, 1959.

Bascom, William. *The Yoruba of Southwestern Nigeria*. New York: Holt, Rinehart & Winston, 1969.

Beard, Miriam. *A History of the Businessman*. New York: Macmillan, 1938.

Belshaw, Cyril S. *Traditional Exchange and Modern Markets*. Englewood Cliffs, NJ: Prentice Hall, 1965.

Benson Elizabeth, ed. *Dumbarton Oaks Conference on the Olmec*. Washington: Dumbarton Oaks Research Library and Collection, 1968.

Benson, George C. S. *Business Ethics in America*. Lexington, MA: Lexington Books, 1982.

Berger, Brigitte and Peter L. Berger. *The War Over the Family*. New York: Doubleday/Anchor, 1983.

Berger, Peter L. *Invitation to Sociology: A Humanistic Perspective*. New York: Doubleday/Anchor, 1963.

Boas, Franz. *Ethnology of the Kwakiutl*. Bureau of American Ethnology, 35th Annual Report, 1913.

Bohannon, Paul and George Dalton. *Markets in Africa*. Garden City, N.Y.: Doubleday/Anchor, 1965.

Bovill, E. W. *The Golden Trade of the Moors*. London: Oxford University Press, 1968.

Bury, J.B. et al. *The Cambridge Ancient History.* New York: Macmillan, 1927.

Carnegie, Andrew. *The Gospel of Wealth and Other Timely Essays.* Cambridge: The Belknap Press of Harvard University Press, 1960. Originally published 1900.

Chagnon, Napoleon A. *Yanomamo: the Fierce People,* Second edition. New York: Holt, Rinehart & Winston, 1977.

Chang, K. C. *Shang Civilization.* New Haven: Yale University Press, 1980.

Charlesworth, M. P. *Trade Routes and Commerce of the Roman Empire,* Second edition. London: Cambridge University Press, 1926.

Coe, Michael D. *Mexico,* Third edition. New York: Thames & Hudson, 1984.

Cohen, Ronald and Elman R. Service. *Origins of the State.* Philadelphia: Publication of the Institute for the Study of Human Issues, 1978.

Dalton, George, ed. *Tribal and Peasant Economies.* Garden City, N.Y.: Natural History Press/Doubleday, 1967.

Deal, Terrence E. and Allan A. Kennedy. *Corporate Cultures.* Reading, MA: Addison-Wesley, 1982.

Defoe, Daniel. *The Complete English Tradesman* in two volumes. London: J. Rivington, 1745.

De La Vega, Garcilaso, El Inca. *Royal Commentaries of the Incas and General History of Peru.* Austin: University of Texas Press, 1966.

De Sahagun, Bernardino. *Florentine Codex: General History of the Things of New Spain.* Translated from the Aztec by C. E. Dibble and Arthur J. O. Anderson. Monograph of the School of American Research and the Museum of New Mexico, #14, Part II, 1961.

De Tocqueville, Alexis. *Democracy in America.* Translated by Henry Reeve. New York: The Colonial Press, 1900. Originally published 1835.

Dichter, Ernest. *Handbook of Consumer Motivations.* New York: McGraw-Hill, 1964.

Dolan, J. R. *The Yankee Peddlers of Early America.* New York: Clarkson N. Potter, 1964.

Driver, Harold E. *Indians of North America.* Chicago: The University of Chicago Press, 1972.

Drucker, Peter F. *Concept of the Corporation.* New York: John Day, 1946.

———. *The New Society.* New York: Harper & Row, 1950.

———. *The Landmarks for Tomorrow.* New York: Harper & Row, 1957.

———. *The Age of Discontinuity.* New York: Harper & Row, 1968.

———. *Management: Tasks, Practices, Responsibilities.* New York: Harper & Row, 1974.

———. *Adventures of a Bystander.* New York: Harper & Row, 1979.

———. *Managing in Turbulent Times.* New York: Harper & Row, 1980.

———. *Toward the Next Economics and Other Essays.* New York: Harper & Row, 1981.

SELECTED BIBLIOGRAPHY

Drucker, Philip. *Indians of the North Pacific Coast.* New York: McGraw-Hill, 1955.

Durant, Will. *The Life of Greece.* New York: Simon & Schuster, 1939.

―――. *The Age of Faith.* New York: Simon & Schuster, 1950.

Earle, T. and J. E. Ericson, eds. *Exchange Systems in Prehistory.* New York: Academic Press, 1979.

Eells, Richard. *The Government of Corporations.* Glencoe, N.Y.: Free Press of Glencoe, 1962.

Eisenstadt, S. N., ed. *The Protestant Ethic and Modernization: A Comparative View.* New York: Basic Books, 1968.

Engels, Frederick, *The Origin of the Family, Private Property, and the State.* New York: International Publishers, 1942.

Erasmus, Charles J. *In Search of the Common Good: Utopian Experiments Past and Future.* New York: Macmillan, 1977.

Finley, M. I. *The World of Odysseus.* New York: World Publishing, 1953.

―――. *The Ancient Greeks.* New York: Viking Press, 1964.

―――. *The Ancient Economy.* Berkeley: University of California Press, 1973.

Finney, Ben R. "Bigfellow Man Belong Business in New Guinea." *Ethnology* 7:394–410, 1968.

Foster, Benjamin R. "Commercial Activity in Sargonic Mesopotamia." *Iraq* 39: 31–44, 1977.

Foster, George M. "Peasant Society and the Image of Limited Good." *American Anthropologist,* Vol. 67, #2, 1965.

―――. "The Anatomy of Envy: A Study in Symbolic Behavior." *Current Anthropology,* April, 1972.

Friedman, Milton and Rose Friedman. *Free To Choose.* New York: Harcourt Brace Jovanovich, 1979.

Galbraith, John Kenneth. *The Affluent Society.* Boston, MA: Houghton Mifflin, 1958.

Gibbs, James L., Jr., ed. *Peoples of Africa.* New York: Holt, Rinehart & Winston, 1966.

Gilder, George. *Wealth and Poverty.* New York: Basic Books, 1981.

Gladden, Washington. *Applied Christianity: Moral Aspects of Social Questions.* Boston, MA: Houghton Mifflin, 1886.

Glazer, Nathan. *Ethnic Dilemmas 1964–1982.* Cambridge: Harvard University Press, 1983.

Glover, John D. *The Revolutionary Corporations.* Homewood, IL.: Dow-Jones-Irwin, 1980.

Goldman, Irving. *The Mouth of Heaven: An Introduction to Kwakiutl Religious Thought.* New York: John Wiley & Sons, 1975.

Granet, Marcel. *Chinese Civilization.* New York: Meridian Books, 1958.

Hall, Edward T. and William Foote Whyte. "Intercultural Communications: A Guide to Men of Action." *Human Organization,* Spring, 1960.

Heizer, Robert R., ed. *The Handbook of North American Indians*, Vol. 8, "California." Washington, DC: The Smithsonian Institution, 1978.

Heizer, R. F. and M. A. Whipple, eds. *The California Indians*. Berkeley: The University of California Press, 1970.

Herodotus of Halicarnassus. *The Histories*. Translation by Harry Carter. New York: Heritage, 1958.

Herskovits, Melville. *Dahomey: An Ancient West African Kingdom*. Evanston, IL: Northwestern University Press, 1967.

Himmelfarb, Gertrude. *The Idea of Poverty: England in the Early Industrial Age*. New York: Knopf, 1983.

Hitchcock, Ripley, ed. *Morals in Modern Business*. Lectures in the Page Lecture Series at Yale, 1908. New Haven: Yale University Press, 1909.

Hodges, Richard. *Dark Age Economics: The Origins of Towns and Trade A.D. 600–1000*. New York: St. Martin's Press, 1982.

Hsu, Francis L. K. *Americans and Chinese*. New York: Henry Schuman, 1953.

Huntford, Roland. *The New Totalitarians*. New York: Stein & Day, 1972.

Johnson, Paul. *Modern Times*. New York: Harper & Row, 1983.

Jones, Landon Y. *Great Expectations*. New York: Random House, 1980.

Kanter, Rosabeth Moss. *The Change Masters*. New York: Simon & Schuster, 1983.

Keynes, John Maynard. *The General Theory of Employment, Interest, and Money*. London: Macmillan, 1936.

Klima, George J. *The Barabaig: East African Cattle Herders*. New York: Holt, Rinehart & Winston, 1970.

Kraeling, E. and R. M. Adams. *City Invincible*. Chicago: University of Chicago Press, 1960.

Kramer, Samuel Noah. *History Begins at Sumer*. New York: Doubleday, 1959.

———. *The Sumerians*. Chicago: University of Chicago Press, 1963.

Kristol, Irving. *Reflections of a Neoconservative*. New York: Basic Books, 1983.

Kroeber, Alfred. *Law of the Yurok Indians*. Proceedings, International Congress of Americanists, #22, Vol. 2, 1926.

Lerner, Max. *America as a Civilization*. New York: Simon & Schuster, 1957.

Levering, Robert, Milton Moskowitz, and Michael Katz. *The 100 Best Companies to Work For*. Reading, MA: Addison Wesley, 1984.

Levi, Maurice. *Economics Deciphered*. New York: Basic Books, 1981.

Levy, Jean-Phillippe. *The Economic Life of the Ancient World*. Translated by John G. Biram. Chicago: University of Chicago Press, 1964.

Lewis, Jordan D. "Technology, Enterprise, and American Economic Growth." *Science*, March 5, 1982.

Malinowsky, Bronislaw. *Argonauts of the Western Pacific*. New York; E. P. Dutton, 1961.

SELECTED BIBLIOGRAPHY

Martin, Calvin. *Keepers of the Game: Indian–Animal Relationships and the Fur Trade*. Berkeley: University of California Press, 1978.

Marx, Karl and Friedrich Engels. *The Communist Manifesto*. New York: Vanguard Press, 1926.

Matthews, Mervyn. *Privilege in the Soviet Union*. London: George Allen & Unwin, 1978.

Mauss, Marcel. *The Gift*. Translated by Ian Cunnison. Glencoe, IL: The Free Press, 1954.

Morison, Samuel Eliot. *The Maritime History of Massachusetts, 1783–1860*. Cambridge: The Riverside Press, 1961.

———. *The Oxford History of the American People*. New York: Oxford University Press, 1965.

Mundell, Robert A. *Man and Economics*. New York: McGraw-Hill, 1968.

Nash, Manning. *Primitive and Peasant Economic Systems*. San Francisco: Chandler, 1966.

Nisbet, Robert. *Prejudices: A Philosophical Dictionary*. Cambridge: Harvard University Press, 1982.

———. *The Social Bond*. New York: Knopf, 1970.

Oppenheim, A. Leo. "Sea-Faring Merchants of Ur." *Journal of the American Oriental Society*, 74:6–17, 1954.

———. *Ancient Mesopotamia: Portrait of a Dead Civilization*. Chicago: University of Chicago Press, 1964.

———. *Letters from Mesopotamia*. Chicago: University of Chicago Press, 1967.

———. *Ancient Mesopotamia* (Erica Reiner, ed.) Chicago: University of Chicago Press, 1970.

Ouchi, William. *Theory Z*. Reading, MA: Addison Wesley, 1981.

Parker, John, ed. *Merchants and Scholars: Essays in the History of Trade and Exploration*. Minneapolis: University of Michigan Press and the James Ford Bell Collection, 1965.

Pascale, Richard Tanner and Anthony G. Athos. *The Art of Japanese Management*. New York: Simon & Schuster, 1981.

Peacock, James L. and A. Thomas Kirsch. *The Human Direction*. New York: Appleton Century Crofts, 1970.

Peters, Thomas J. and Robert H. Waterman, Jr. *In Search of Excellence*. New York: Harper & Row, 1982.

Pirenne, Henri. *Medieval Cities*. Translated by Frank D. Halsey. Garden City, N.Y.: Doubleday, 1956. First published 1925.

———. *The Economic and Social History of Medieval Europe*. Translated by I. E. Clegg. New York: Harcourt Brace & World, 1937.

Polanyi, Karl. *Trade and Markets in the Early Empires*. (Conrad M. Arensberg and Harry W. Pearson, eds.) New York: The Free Press, 1957.

———. *Primitive, Archaic, and Modern Economies: Essays of Karl Polanyi*. (George Dalton, ed.) New York: Doubleday, 1968.

Polo, Marco. *The Adventures of Marco Polo.* (Richard J. Walsh, ed.) New York: John Day, 1948.

Pospisil, Leopold. *The Kapauku Papuans of West New Guinea,* Second edition. New York: Holt, Rinehart & Winston, 1978.

Powell, Marvin A. "Sumerian Merchants and the Problem of Profit." *Iraq,* Spring, 1977.

Renfrew, Colin. *Before Civilization.* New York: Knopf, 1975.

Ricks, David A. *Big Business Blunders.* Homewood, IL: Dow-Jones-Irwin, 1980.

Rorig, Fritz. *The Medieval Town.* Berkeley: University of California Press, 1967.

Sabloff, Jeremy and C. C. Lamberg-Karlovsky, eds. *Ancient Civilization and Trade.* Albuquerque: University of New Mexico Press, 1974.

———. *The Rise and Fall of Civilizations.* Menlo Park, CA: Cummings, 1974.

Sabloff, Jeremy and William J. Rathje. "The Rise of a Maya Merchant Class." *Scientific American,* October, 1975.

Saum, Lewis O. *The Fur Trade and the Indian.* Seattle: University of Washington Press, 1965.

Scammell, G. V. *The World Encompassed: The First European Maritime Empires c. 800–1650.* Berkeley: University of California Press, 1981.

Schlesinger, Arthur M. *The Colonial Merchants and the American Revolution, 1763–1776.* New York: Frederick Ungar, 1966.

Schmandt-Besserat, Denise. "Decipherment of the Earliest Tablets." *Science,* January 16, 1981.

———. "The Envelopes that Bear the First Writing," *Technology and Culture,* 21 (111), 347–385, 1980.

———. "The Earliest Precursor of Writing." *Scientific American,* June, 1978.

Schumpeter, Joseph A. *Capitalism, Socialism, and Democracy,* Third edition. New York: Harper & Row, 1950.

———. *Social Classes.* Translated by Heinz Norden. New York: Augustus M. Kelley, 1951.

Skolnick, Jerome H. and Elliott Currie. *Crisis in American Institutions.* Boston: Little, Brown, 1985.

Smith, Adam. *The Theory of Moral Sentiments.* Originally published in 1759. Reprinted in New York: Augustus M. Kelley, 1966.

———. *An Inquiry into the Nature and Causes of the Wealth of Nations.* London: W. Strahan and T. Cadell in the Strand, 1776.

Sowell, Thomas. *The Economics and Politics of Race.* New York: Morrow, 1983.

Spitz, Lewis W. *The Reformation: Material or Spiritual?* Boston: D.C. Heath & Co., 1962.

Ssu-ma Chi'en. *Records of the Grand Historian of China.* Translated by Burton Watson. New York: Columbia University Press, 1961.

SELECTED BIBLIOGRAPHY

Strathern, Andrew, "The Entrepreneurial Model of Social Change: From Norway to New Guinea." *Ethnology,* October, 1972.

Tarbell, Ida Minerva. *New Ideals in Business.* New York: Macmillan, 1917.

Taylor, Philip A. M., ed. *The Industrial Revolution in Britain.* Boston: D.C. Heath Co., 1958.

Tawney, R. H. *Religion and the Rise of Capitalism.* New York: Harcourt Brace, 1937.

Thrupp, Sylvia L. *The Merchant Class of Medieval London: 1300–1500.* Ann Arbor: University of Michigan Press, 1962.

Trigger, Bruce G. *Handbook of North American Indians.* Vol. 15, "The Northeast." Washington, D.C.: The Smithsonian Institution, 1978.

Vance, James E., Jr. *The Merchant's World: the Geography of Wholesaling.* Englewood Cliffs, N.J.: Prentice-Hall, 1970.

Veenhof, K. R. *Aspects of Old Assyrian Trade and its Terminology.* Leiden: E. J. Brill, 1972.

Wasson, Chester R. *Marketing Management: The Strategy, Tactics, and Art of Competition.* Charlotte, NC: ECR Associates, 1983.

Weber, Max. *General Economic History.* New York: The Free Press, 1927.

————. *The Protestant Ethic and the Spirit of Capitalism.* Translated by Talcott Parsons. London: George Allen & Unwin, 1930.

————. *Economy and Society.* Edited by G. Ross and C. Willich. Berkeley: University of California, 1978.

Whyte, William H., Jr. *The Organization Man.* New York: Simon & Schuster, 1956.

Wilson Edmund. *To the Finland Station.* Garden City, N.Y.: Doubleday, 1940.

Wright, Henry T. "Recent Research on the 'Origin of the State.' " *Annual Reviews of Anthropology.* Palo Alto, CA: Annual Reviews, Inc., 1977.

INDEX